Fundamentals of Spanish Grammar

FUNDAMENTALS OF SPANISH GRAMMAR

RICHARD ARMITAGE

WALTER MEIDEN

RICHARD NEFF

The Ohio State University

HOUGHTON MIFFLIN COMPANY · BOSTON

Atlanta Dallas Geneva, Illinois Hopewell, New Jersey Palo Alto London

PREFACE

Fundamentals of Spanish Grammar presents in topical form the main points of Spanish grammar in such a way that they can be easily understood by a learner who has had little previous contact with the language. It is suitable for use in conjunction with almost any other Spanish grammar as an additional language learning aid.

Users at all levels of instruction -- secondary school, college, adult education classes, etc. -- can benefit from the clear, uncomplicated grammatical explanations contained in *Fundamentals of Spanish Grammar*.

The topical organization will be especially helpful to learners who have experienced some difficulty in mastering certain concepts in their regularly assigned text and who would benefit from another presentation of specific grammatical topics. For example, if you are having difficulty understanding the relative pronoun *cual*, you can look in the Index under *cual*, "relative pronouns," or "pronouns (relative)" and find that *cual* is discussed in grammar section (§[1]) 37 A and B (page 43). The principles defining the use of the forms of *cual* are stated very simply and examples are provided.

Because the book contains all important aspects of a given grammatical topic in one place, it constitutes, in effect, a summary of Spanish grammar at the elementary level. You have the opportunity of viewing each grammatical topic in its entirety. For example, §§ 30--31 (pages 35--36) cover all aspects of the position and order of object pronouns. In a page and a half, a compact explanation is given of when object pronouns precede and when they follow the verb, in what order two object pronouns come, and a simple discussion of the sometimes confusing problem of the use of *se* for *le* and *les*.

Fundamentals of Spanish Grammar is divided into three main sections:

I   Grammar
II Exercises
III Answers

In Section I, each topic is introduced by a simple explanation in English, followed by examples in Spanish with their English equivalents, illustrating the point being explained.

In Section II, there are exercises designed to help achieve mastery of each grammatical topic. Each set of exercises has the same section number as its corresponding explanation in the grammar. Thus, exercises on the position and order of object pronouns will be found in §§ 30--31 of Section II (pages 180--182), and drills on the use of the relative *cual* will be found in § 37 A and B of Section II (pages 187, 188).

There are two types of exercises: all-Spanish, in which you simply fill in blanks or replace one word with another, and English-to-Spanish translations. To save paper, no answer blanks are provided.

---

[1]The symbol § is used throughout the book to designate a specific grammar section.

In Section III, to make the book a more useful self-instructional teaching tool, answers to the exercises are provided.

To maximize the usefulness of this book, we suggest the following study procedures:

1 Carefully study those topics in which difficulty is being experienced. You can locate any grammatical topic quickly through the Table of Contents or the Index.

2 Do the all-Spanish exercises in Section II first, since they concentrate on a single point; then do the English-to-Spanish translations which not only concentrate on the point in question but also require an acquaintance with other phases of Spanish.

3 Resist the temptation to look at the answers before or while doing an exercise, but check your answers after completing a given exercise in order to avoid practicing incorrect responses.

Essentially, then, *Fundamentals of Spanish Grammar* is a compact summary of Spanish grammar which can be kept as a handy reference the entire time you are studying Spanish. We hope that it will make learning Spanish an easier and more rewarding experience.

TABLE OF CONTENTS

THE PRONOUN

THE PREPOSITION

CONJUNCTIONS

MISCELLANY

THE VERB

I Organization of the Spanish Verb

II Formation and Use of Tenses and Other Parts of the Verb

III Uses of Certain Verbs

IV Special Types of Verbs

V The Conjugation of the Verb

SPELLING AND PUNCTUATION

THE PRONUNCIATION OF SPANISH

CONTENTS

GRAMMAR

THE ARTICLE—EL ARTÍCULO

In English the definite article is *the*. The indefinite article is *a* or *an*.

1 / Forms of the Indefinite Article — *Formas del artículo indeterminado*

In English the indefinite article has only the forms *a* and *an*. In Spanish the indefinite article has several forms.

A. The singular forms of the Spanish indefinite article are:

un   used with masculine singular nouns.

     un continente   *un* país   *un* edificio

una   used with feminine singular nouns.[1]

     una nación   *una* parte   *una* cultura

B. The plural forms of the Spanish indefinite article, expressed in English by *some*, *any*, or *a few*, are:

unos   used with masculine plural nouns.

Pasamos por *unos* pueblos pequeños.	We passed through *some* small villages.

unas   used with feminine plural nouns.

Tengo aquí *unas* fotografías.	I have *some* photographs here.

2 / Forms of the Definite Article — *Formas del artículo determinado*

In English the definite article has but one form: *the*. In Spanish the definite article has four forms.

A. The singular forms of the definite article are:

el   used with a masculine singular noun.

    el centro   *el* continente   *el* edificio   *el* país

---

[1] For reasons of pronunciation feminine singular nouns beginning with a stressed *a–* or *ha–* usually take *un* as an indefinite article. EXAMPLES: *un* aula, *un* águila.

la used with a feminine singular noun.[1]

la ciudad   *la* capital   *la* parte   *la* cultura   *la* nación

B. The plural forms of the definite article are:

los used with masculine plural nouns.

los centros   *los* continentes   *los* edificios   *los* países

las used with feminine plural nouns.

las ciudades *las* capitales *las* partes *las* culturas *las* naciones

3 / Contractions of the Definite Article — Contracciones del artículo determinado

A. The definite article *el* contracts[2] with *de* as follows:

$$\text{de} + \text{el} = \textbf{del}$$

el centro *del* gobierno mexicano   the center *of the* Mexican government

B. The definite article *el* contracts[2] with *a* as follows:

$$\text{a} + \text{el} = \textbf{al}$$

La avenida va del parque de Cha-   The avenue goes from Chapultepec
pultepec *al* centro de la capital.   park *to the* center of the capital.

4 / Uses of the Articles [3] — Modos de usar los artículos

In Spanish as in English, the indefinite article indicates one of a class without being specific, and the definite article points out a very definite object.

Norte América es *un* continente.   North America is *a* continent.
México es *una* parte de Norte Amé- Mexico is *a* part of North America.
rica.
La capital es *el* centro *del* gobierno *The* capital is *the* center of *the*
mexicano.   Mexican government.

There are, however, a number of cases in which the definite and indefinite articles are used or omitted in Spanish but not in English.

---

[1] For reasons of pronunciation feminine singular nouns beginning with a stressed *a–* or *ha–* require *el* as a definite article. EXAMPLES: *el* aula, *el* águila, *el* agua. However, if an adjective comes between the article and the noun, *la* is used. EXAMPLES: *la* primera águila, *la* buena agua.
[2] For contractions with *el* used as a demonstrative pronoun, see page 39, note 1.
[3] For the use of the definite article with adjectives to form nouns, see § 5 A, § 13.

A. The article *el* is normally used with names of languages.

La lengua nacional de México es *el español*.	The national language of Mexico **is** *Spanish*.

But when the unmodified[1] name of a language immediately[2] follows verbs such as *hablar*,[3] *entender*, *aprender*, *enseñar*, *escribir*, *estudiar*, *leer*, or *saber*, or the prepositions *en* or *de*, generally no article is used.

¿ Habla usted *inglés*?	Do you speak *English*?
Estudio *inglés*.	I study *English*.
El señor García es un profesor *de español*.	Mr. García is a *Spanish* teacher.
Vimos señales como DESPACIO y CURVA escritas *en español* y *en inglés*.	We saw signs like SLOW and CURVE written *in Spanish* and *in English*.

B. In English a noun unmodified by any article is often used to designate something taken in a general sense. In Spanish nouns used in a general sense must ordinarily be preceded by their definite article.

La instrucción en México es un gran problema.	*Education* in Mexico is a great problem.
Los médicos no ganan mucho dinero en el campo.	*Doctors* do not earn much money in the country.

C. The article is normally used before titles of respect when speaking *of* a person.

La señora García está ahora en casa.	*Mrs. García* is now at home.
El general Porfirio Díaz fué elegido presidente.	*General Porfirio Díaz* was elected president.

But the article is omitted when addressing a person and always before the title *don*.

— *Señora García* ¿ tiene usted un cuarto desocupado ?	"*Mrs. García*, do you have a vacant room?"
Don Porfirio estableció una dictadura.	*Porfirio*[4] established a dictatorship.

---

[1] The article is used when the language is modified. EXAMPLE: Estudio *el inglés de Londres*.

[2] When adverbs come between the verb and the language, the article is generally used. EXAMPLE: Usted habla *muy bien el español*.

[3] Only with *hablar* is it obligatory to omit the article before the name of the language. The article may be used with the other verbs, but the present tendency is to omit it.

[4] The Spanish title *don*, which is used before given (first) names, has no English equivalent.

GRAMMAR § 4

D. The article is omitted in Spanish before unmodified nouns which designate profession, nationality, religion, political beliefs, etc. English uses an indefinite article in such constructions.

Felipe nota que Roberto es *extranjero*.	Philip notices that Robert is *a foreigner*.
Roberto es *norteamericano*.	Robert is *a (North) American*.
Juárez se hizo *abogado*.	Juárez became *a lawyer*.

But when such nouns are modified, the indefinite article is used.

Roberto es *un norteamericano* que estudia en la universidad.	Robert is *a (North) American* who is studying in the university.

E. The article *el* is regularly used with the days of the week except after forms of the verb *ser*.

Salimos de San Luis *el lunes* por la mañana y llegamos a la frontera *el martes* por la tarde.	We left St. Louis on *Monday* morning and arrived at the border on *Tuesday* afternoon.
Hoy es *lunes*.	Today is *Monday*.

The plural article *los* is used before the days of the week to indicate a regular occurrence each day of the week on the day mentioned. In English, –s is often added to the day of the week or the word *every* is placed before the day of the week.

Estos indios van al mercado *los viernes*.	These Indians go to market *Fridays (every Friday)*.

The word *todos* may also be used with *los* before the days of the week to indicate a regular occurrence each week on the day mentioned.

Todos los domingos por la tarde la gente va a la plaza de toros.	*Every Sunday* afternoon the people go to the bull ring.

F. The definite article is generally used instead of the possessive adjective before articles of clothing or parts of the body especially when (1) the identity of the possessor is clearly understood, and (2) the noun in question is the direct object of the verb.

Vemos con *los ojos*.	We see with *our eyes*.
En *la boca* tenemos una lengua y treinta y dos dientes.	In *our mouths* we have a tongue and thirty-two teeth.
Las mujeres llevan sobre *la cabeza* grandes cestos sin utilizar *las manos*.	The women carry large baskets on *their heads* without using *their hands*.
Roberto se pone *el abrigo*.	Robert puts on *his topcoat*.

If the act is performed on some other person, the article which modifies the part of the body is reinforced by an indirect object personal pronoun referring to the person on whom the act is performed.

Spinola *le* pone la mano sobre *el* hombro.	Spinola puts his (own) hand on *his* (the other person's) shoulder.

G. Nouns in apposition, that is, nouns which follow other nouns in order to explain them, are not modified by any article if they help clarify the noun they follow.

Entré por Nuevo Laredo, *ciudad mexicana* enfrente de Laredo.	I entered by Laredo, *a Mexican city* opposite Laredo.
Entraron en el Palacio de Bellas Artes, *enorme edificio* donde está un gran teatro.	They entered the Palacio de Bellas Artes, *an enormous building* where there is a large theater.

Notice that English uses an article with nouns in apposition.

But if the noun in apposition simply states an already well-known fact, the definite article modifies the noun in apposition.

Éstos son los frescos de Diego Rivera, *el pintor* más conocido de México.	These are the murals of Diego Rivera, **the** best-known *painter* in Mexico.

H. As in English, the definite article is ordinarily not used with names of countries and continents.

Bolivia y *Venezuela* son países de *Sud América*, pero *México* no es un país de *Sud América*.	*Bolivia* and *Venezuela* are countries of *South America*, but Mexico is not a country of *South America*.

Contrary to English usage, the article is generally used with the following countries: la Argentina, el Brasil, el Canadá, la China, el Ecuador, la India, el Japón, el Perú. But there is an ever-increasing tendency to omit the article with many of these countries.

México y *el Canadá* tienen civilizaciones muy diferentes.	Mexico and *Canada* have very different civilizations.

When the name of the country is modified, the article must be used.

¿ En dónde se nota la influencia de los aztecas en *el México de hoy* ?	In what respect can one see the influence of the Aztecs on *present-day Mexico*?

I. Contrary to English usage, the indefinite article is never used with *otro* and is often omitted before *cierto*.

Tampico es *otro* puerto del Golfo de México.	Tampico is *another* port on the Gulf of Mexico.
Ustedes tienen que llegar a su trabajo a *cierta* hora de la mañana.	You have to arrive at your work at *a certain* time in the morning.

5 / *The Neuter Article* lo — *El artículo neutro* lo

A. The neuter article *lo* may be placed before the masculine singular[1] form of an adjective or past participle to express an abstract idea which in English translation often requires the word *thing*.

Lo interesante es que antes de 1900 este viejo barrio constituía la ciudad de Barcelona.	*The interesting thing* is that before 1900 this old district constituted the city of Barcelona.
Los cristianos refugiados en el norte comenzaron a reconquistar *lo perdido*.	The Christians who took refuge in the north began to reconquer *what had been lost*.

B. The neuter article *lo* is used with adjectives in certain idiomatic expressions.

A lo largo de la costa el terreno es muy bajo.	*Along* the coast the terrain is very low.
Por lo general, en primavera y en verano hace buen tiempo.	*In general*, in spring and summer the weather is good.

C. The neuter *lo* may be used as a pronoun to refer to a previous idea, state or condition.

Ya en el siglo XI los cristianos eran dueños de todo el norte de España hasta Toledo, y en menos de dos siglos *lo* eran hasta Sevilla.	Already in the eleventh century the Christians were masters of all the northern part of Spain as far as Toledo, and in less than two centuries they were (masters) down to Seville.

D. The neuter *lo* may be used as a pronoun meaning *the affair of*, *that business of*, etc.

Lo de las hamacas me convence.	*That business of* the hammocks convinces me.

---

[1] When the adjective is followed by *que*, however, the article often means *how*, and if the following verb is *ser*, *estar*, or their equivalent, the adjective agrees in gender and number with the word(s) in the following clause to which it refers. EXAMPLES: Desde las ventanillas del tren notamos *lo distinta* que es la arquitectura de las casas españolas. Y sabes *lo buenas* que son la paella y la horchata valencianas. Comprenderás *lo merecidas* que tienen sus vacaciones.

E. The neuter *lo* is used with the relative pronouns *cual* and *que* to refer to a previously mentioned idea or concept, which, of course, has neither gender nor number. We express this same idea in English by *which*.

España tiene algunas ciudades con calles anchas y rectas y un gran número de pueblos pintorescos construidos en la Edad Media, *lo cual* hace de este país uno de los más interesantes para el viajero.	Spain has some cities with wide and straight streets and a great number of picturesque towns constructed in the Middle Ages, *which* makes this country one of the most interesting for the traveler.

F. The neuter *lo* is used with the relative pronoun *que* to refer to an idea. The combination *lo que* is expressed by the English *what*, meaning *that which*.[1]

He visto *lo que* hace la gente en estos paseos.	I have seen *what* the people do on these boulevards.
Sentía curiosidad por saber *lo que* decían.	I was curious to know *what* they were saying.

THE NOUN[2]—EL NOMBRE

A noun is a word that names a person, place, or thing. EXAMPLES: *man, child, Robert, country, city, desk, radio*

6 / Gender of Nouns — Género de los nombres

In English, nouns that refer to males are masculine, nouns that refer to females are feminine, and all other nouns are neuter.

boy *masculine*   lady *feminine*   pencil *neuter*

The gender of English nouns constitutes no difficulty at all.

A. In Spanish all nouns are masculine or feminine, and it is necessary to know the gender of each noun in order to speak and write Spanish correctly.

un continente *masculine*   una parte *feminine*

---

[1] The neuter *lo* is also used in the expression *todo lo que* (*all that*). EXAMPLE: *Comimos todo lo que pudimos.* We ate all we could.

[2] For the use of articles with adjectives to form nouns, see § 5 A, § 13.

B. While there is no way of determining the gender of all Spanish nouns, the endings of the nouns indicate their gender in most cases. This is especially apparent because more than half of the Spanish nouns end in either –*o* or –*a*.

1. Nouns ending in –*o* are masculine. [1]

| el aspecto | el centro | el edificio | el mexicano | el gobierno |

2. Some nouns ending in –*ma*, –*pa*, and –*ta* [2] are masculine.

| el clima | el problema | el mapa | el especialista | el artista |

3. Nouns ending in –*a* are feminine. [3]

| la cultura | la mezcla | Bolivia | Colombia |

4. Nouns ending in –*ión*, [4] –*dad*, [5] –*tad*, and –*umbre* are feminine.

–ión	–dad	–tad	–umbre
nación	ciudad	libertad	costumbre
civilización	universidad	dificultad	legumbre
región	realidad	facultad	lumbre

7 / Plural of Nouns — Plural de los nombres

In English most nouns form their plurals by adding –*s* to the singular, as, for instance, *part* (singular)—*parts* (plural).

A. Spanish nouns ending in a vowel generally [6] form their plurals by adding –*s* to the singular.

SINGULAR	PLURAL
continente	continentes
parte	partes

---

[1] But *mano* (*hand*) is feminine.

[2] Often nouns in –*ta* refer to persons and are masculine or feminine, depending on the person to whom they refer, as *el* or *la artista*.

[3] But *día* (*day*) is masculine.

[4] But *camión* (*truck*) and *avión* (*airplane*) are masculine.

[5] The Spanish nouns in –*dad* and –*tad* correspond to English nouns in –*ty*: *ciudad* — *city*; *universidad* — *university*; *libertad* — *liberty*; *dificultad* — *difficulty*.

[6] A few nouns ending in a stressed vowel add –*es*. EXAMPLE: rubí, rubíes.

B. Nouns ending in a consonant or in –*y* form their plurals by adding –*es* to the singular. [1]

SINGULAR	PLURAL
país	países
ciudad	ciudades
rey	reyes

C. Nouns ending in –*z* change the –*z* to –*c*– before adding –*es*. [2]

SINGULAR	PLURAL
vez	veces
voz	voces

THE ADJECTIVE—EL ADJETIVO

An adjective is a word that modifies the meaning of a noun or pronoun. EXAMPLES: the *big* house; the *good* man; The book is *interesting*. It is also *expensive*.

8 / Agreement of Adjectives — Concordancia de los adjetivos

In English the adjective does not change in form to indicate the gender or number of the noun. EXAMPLE: the *big* house; the *big* houses

A. In Spanish the adjective agrees with its noun in gender and number.

el edificio *público*	the *public* building
los edificios *públicos*	the *public* buildings
la calle *pública*	the *public* street
las calles *públicas*	the *public* streets

B. When an adjective or a past participle modifies a masculine and feminine noun or two or more masculine nouns, it requires the masculine plural form.

Se pierde uno en medio de centenares de *arcos* y *columnas* **maravillosos**.	One gets lost in the midst of hundreds of *marvellous arches* and *columns*.

---

[1] Words such as *nación* and *millón* have a written accent in the singular but none in the plural (*naciones, millones*) because of the operation of the normal rule for stress. (PRONUNCIATION § 7 B)

[2] The –*z* is changed to –*c*– because in Spanish –*z*– is not ordinarily followed by –*e*–.

A. Adjectives whose masculine singular form ends in *-o* have a feminine form in *-a*. The plural is formed by adding *-s* to each form.

	MASCULINE	FEMININE	
SINGULAR	bello	bella	*beautiful*
PLURAL	bellos	bellas	
SINGULAR	público	pública	*public*
PLURAL	públicos	públicas	

B. Adjectives whose masculine singular form does not end in *-o* usually have the same form for both genders. The plural is formed just as the plural of nouns. [1]

	MASCULINE	FEMININE	
SINGULAR	diferente	diferente	*different*
PLURAL	diferentes	diferentes	
SINGULAR	natural	natural	*natural*
PLURAL	naturales	naturales	

C. But adjectives of nationality whose masculine singular form ends in a consonant add *-a* to form the feminine. The plural is formed just as the plural of nouns. [2]

	MASCULINE	FEMININE	
SINGULAR	español	española	*Spanish*
PLURAL	españoles	españolas	
SINGULAR	inglés	inglesa	*English*
PLURAL	ingleses	inglesas	

10 / Apocopation of Adjectives — Apócope de los adjetivos

Apocopation is the dropping of certain letters from the end of a word.

A. The following adjectives [3] drop their final *-o* before a masculine singular noun:

---

[1] For the plural of nouns, see § 7. Note that the plural of the adjective *feliz* (*happy*) is *felices*.

[2] This same rule applies to adjectives ending in *-án, -ón, -in* and *-or* (not derived from a Latin comparative). EXAMPLE: *conservador, conservadora*

[3] The adjectives *bueno* and *malo* are not apocopated unless they immediately precede the noun. In case of the others, an adjective may come between them and the noun.

ENTIRE FORM	APOCOPATED FORM	ENTIRE FORM	APOCOPATED FORM	ENTIRE FORM	APOCOPATED FORM
uno	un	bueno	buen	primero	primer
alguno	algún	malo	mal	tercero	tercer
ninguno	ningún			postrero	postrer

Tiene que hablar *algún* dialecto indio.	He has to speak *some* Indian dialect.
A veces no hay *ningún* médico.	Sometimes there is *no* doctor.

The adjective is never apocopated when it *follows* a masculine singular noun.

No soy *buen* poeta.	I am not a *good* poet.
No soy un poeta muy *bueno*.	I am not a very *good* poet.

The adjective is never apocopated in the plural.

En *algunos* países nadie habla español.	In *some* countries no one speaks Spanish.

B. The adjective **grande** normally becomes **gran** before a singular noun of *either* gender.

La instrucción en México es un *gran* problema.	Education in Mexico is a *great* problem.
Aunque una *gran* parte de México está en la zona tórrida, el país tiene muchas montañas.	Although a *great* part of Mexico is in the torrid zone, the country has many mountains.

C. The numeral **ciento** becomes **cien** before a noun of either gender and before a number larger than itself.

En México existen casi *cien* dialectos diferentes.	There are almost a *hundred* different dialects in Mexico.
Muchas ciudades de Alemania tienen más de *cien mil* habitantes.	Many cities of Germany have more than *a hundred thousand* inhabitants.

But the full form **ciento** is used both in multiples of a hundred and when a number smaller than itself follows.

Monterrey tiene más de *trescientos* mil habitantes.	Monterrey has more than *three hundred* thousand inhabitants.
Puebla es una antigua ciudad situada a unos *ciento treinta* kilómetros al sudeste de la capital.	Puebla is an ancient city situated some *one hundred thirty* kilometers to the southeast of the capital.

D. The masculine singular **santo** becomes **san** before masculine singular names of saints except those beginning with *Do–* and *To–*.

San Esteban   San Agustín   San Luis   San Juan   San Francisco

but

Santo Tomás   Santo Domingo

E. The indefinite adjective **cualquiera** ordinarily becomes **cualquier** before a singular noun.

cualquier hombre   cualquier pueblo
cualquier arte   cualquier calle

11 / Position of Adjectives — Colocación de los adjetivos

In English adjectives are placed *before* the nouns they modify.

EXAMPLE: the *big* house; the *green* grass; the *Mexican* customs

A. In Spanish some adjectives habitually precede the noun they modify; many usually follow. A number of adjectives may either precede or follow their noun, often with a slight change of meaning. Sometimes the position of the adjective depends on the relative length of the noun and adjective and upon the rhythm of the sentence.

muchos edificios *públicos*   *many public* buildings

B. Most descriptive adjectives follow their nouns, and especially adjectives of color and nationality. They differentiate the noun they modify from the same noun without the adjective.

una ciudad *bella*   a *beautiful* city
el gobierno *mexicano*   the *Mexican* government
el pico *blanco*   the *white* peak

C. Adjectives which indicate a quality usually attributed to the noun and which therefore tend not to differentiate it from the same noun without the adjective often precede their nouns. Such adjectives are often epithets.

la *magnífica* ciudad   the *magnificent* city
sus *horribles* sacrificios their *horrible* sacrifices
la *peligrosa* marcha   the *dangerous* march
una *feroz* batalla   a *ferocious* battle

D. Demonstrative and interrogative adjectives precede their nouns.

Algunos de *estos* barrios son elegantes.	Some of *these* districts are elegant.
¿*Cuántos* habitantes tiene la capital?	*How many* inhabitants does the capital have?

E. Possessive and indefinite adjectives[1] ordinarily precede their nouns, but when emphasis is desired, such adjectives may follow their nouns.

En *nuestro* patio *mis* hermanas cuidan *sus* pájaros.	In *our* patio *my* sisters take care of *their* birds.
Conozco a tres muchachos mexicanos que son ahora como hermanos *míos*.	I know three Mexican boys who are now like *my* (*very own*) brothers.
Todavía existen regiones donde no hay *ninguna* escuela.	There still are regions where there is *no* school.

F. Numerals, both cardinal and ordinal, usually precede their nouns, but cardinals used instead of ordinals above *ten*[2] follow their nouns.

las *dos* culturas   la *primera* lección   la lección *once*

G. Certain adjectives have *one* meaning when they precede and *another* when they follow the noun they modify. The most common of these are:

ADJECTIVE	MEANING WHEN PRECEDING	MEANING WHEN FOLLOWING
cierto	certain	definite, reliable
diferente	various	different
grande	great	large
mismo	same, very	–self, very
nuevo	different	new (not old)
pobre	unfortunate	poverty-stricken
propio	own	characteristic of, suitable to
puro	sheer	pure
simple	mere	simple-minded
varios	several	miscellaneous

---

[1] The possessive adjectives that follow have different forms from those that precede. See § 14.

[2] For the uses of cardinals and ordinals, see § 18.

There are three degrees of comparison: the *positive*, the *comparative*, and the *superlative*. The English adjective is compared by adding *-er* (comparative) and *-est* (superlative) to the positive form or by placing *more* or *less* (comparative) and *most* or *least* (superlative) before the positive form.

POSITIVE	COMPARATIVE	SUPERLATIVE
high	higher less high	highest least high
beautiful	more beautiful less beautiful	most beautiful least beautiful

A. In Spanish adjectives are compared by placing **más** (*more*) or **menos** (*less*) before the positive form.

POSITIVE	COMPARATIVE	SUPERLATIVE
alto	más alto menos alto	el — más alto el — menos alto

The superlative form of the adjective is the same as the comparative, but its noun is modified by the definite article.

POSITIVE	México es *montañoso*.	Mexico is *mountainous*.
COMPARATIVE	México es *más montañoso* que los Estados Unidos.	Mexico is *more mountainous* than the United States.
SUPERLATIVE	México es *el* país *más montañoso* de Norte América.	Mexico is the *most mountainous* country in North America.

Also note the superlative as a predicate adjective, that is, a superlative without a noun used after a form of the verb *ser*.

SUPERLATIVE	De todos los países del continente, México es *el más montañoso*.	Of all the countries of the continent, Mexico is *the most mountainous*.

B. In Spanish the superlative form of the adjective generally follows the noun.

El pico *más alto* de México es el Orizaba.   The *highest* peak in Mexico is Orizaba.

C. The following four adjectives are compared irregularly:

| bueno | mejor | grande[1] | mayor |
| malo | peor | pequeño[2] | menor |

D. The suffix *-ísimo* is often attached to the stem of an adjective to give it a superlative force. This superlative force may be expressed in English by having the adverbs *very*, *highly*, or *extremely* modify the adjective.

| España es un país de grandes contrastes: edificios *modernísimos* al lado de monumentos muy antiguos; regiones *fertilísimas* al lado de terrenos improductivos. | Spain is a country of great contrasts: *extremely modern* buildings along side of very old monuments; *very fertile* regions along side of unproductive lands. |

E. In English the superlative is usually followed by *in*. In Spanish *de* is regularly used after the superlative.

| El pico más alto *de* México es el Orizaba. | The highest peak *in* Mexico is Orizaba. |

F. The English word *than* is usually expressed in Spanish by *que*.

| El Popocatepetl es menos alto *que* el Orizaba. | Popocatepetl is less high *than* Orizaba. |

But the following exceptions occur:

1. Before numerals, *than* is expressed by *de*.

| Monterrey tiene *más de* trescientos mil habitantes. | Monterrey has *more than* three hundred thousand inhabitants. |

2. But in negative sentences, the usual[3] form is *no más que*, translated *only*.

| Algunos niños *no* van a la escuela *más que* tres o cuatro años. | Some children go to school *only* three or four years. |

G. In English we say: Detroit is *as large as* Cleveland. This construction with **as ... as** is called the comparative of equality. In Spanish the comparative of equality is expressed by **tan ... como**.

---

[1] The adjective *grande* is also compared regularly. The comparative *mayor* means both *greater* and *older*. When *mayor* and *menor* refer to age, they always follow the noun they modify.

[2] The adjective *pequeño* is also compared regularly. The comparative *menor* means *less* and *younger*, whereas *más pequeño* means *smaller*.

[3] The expression *no más de* is occasionally used before numerals to convey a slightly different meaning. EXAMPLE: *No tiene más de dos pesos.* He has *no more than* two (i.e., two at the most) pesos.

| La meseta central no es *tan alta como* las montañas. | The central plateau is not *as high as* the mountains. |
| Las selvas tropicales son *tan impenetrables como* las regiones montañosas. | The tropical forests are *as impenetrable as* the mountainous regions. |

H. When the comparative is followed by a clause with an inflected verb, if the comparison is with a particular noun, *than* is expressed by *del que, de la que, de los que,* and *de las que.*[1]

| Recibimos más cartas *de las que* escribimos. | We received more letters *than* we wrote. |

I. When the comparative is followed by a clause with an inflected verb, if the comparison is with the entire idea of the preceding clause, *than* is expressed by *de lo que.*[1]

| Se nos hace el tiempo más largo *de lo que* es. | It makes the time seem to us longer *than* it is. |

13 / Adjectives Used as Nouns[2] — Adjetivos usados como nombres

In Spanish adjectives are often used as nouns and may take the appropriate form of the article.

| Tienen criadas todos *los ricos*. | All *the rich people* have servants. |
| En México hay muchos *pobres*. | In Mexico there are many *poor people*. |

14 / Possessive Adjectives — Adjetivos posesivos[3]

The English possessive adjectives are *my, his, her, its, our, your,* and *their.* They do not change in form. EXAMPLE: *my* book; *my* books.

A. The Spanish possessive adjectives are **mi, su,** and **nuestro.** The adjective **su** may mean *his, her, its, your,* or *their.* Spanish possessive adjectives have a singular and plural form, and **nuestro** has all four forms.

---

[1] There is a colloquial tendency to use *que* only in some of these constructions.

[2] For the use of the neuter article *lo* with adjectives to form nouns, see § 5 A.

[3] For the use of the definite article in Spanish where English would use a possessive adjective, see § 4 F

In Spanish, the possessive adjectives agree with the noun they modify, that is, with the object possessed. The forms of the possessive adjectives are:

with singular nouns		with plural nouns		
MASCULINE	FEMININE	MASCULINE	FEMININE	
mi	mi	mis	mis	*my*
su	su	sus	sus	*his, her, its, your, their*
nuestro	nuestra	nuestros	nuestras	*our*

B. The familiar forms of the Spanish possessive adjectives are:

with singular nouns		with plural nouns		
MASCULINE	FEMININE	MASCULINE	FEMININE	
tu	tu	tus	tus	*your* (singular)
vuestro	vuestra	vuestros	vuestras	*your* (plural)

C. Since **su** and **sus** mean *his, her, its, your,* and *their*, their meaning may be clarified by using

article + noun + *de* + prepositional form of pronoun[1]

Los padres de él visita a *los padres*   *His parents* visit *her parents.*
de ella.

D. There is a set of stressed possessive adjectives which have the same forms as the possessive pronouns.[2] The common forms of these stressed possessive adjectives are:

with singular nouns		with plural nouns		
MASCULINE	FEMININE	MASCULINE	FEMININE	
mío	mía	míos	mías	*my*
suyo	suya	suyos	suyas	*his, her, its, your, their*
nuestro	nuestra	nuestros	nuestras	*our*

The familiar second person forms are:

with singular nouns		with plural nouns		
MASCULINE	FEMININE	MASCULINE	FEMININE	
tuyo	tuya	tuyos	tuyas	*your* (singular)
vuestro	vuestra	vuestros	vuestras	*your* (plural)

[1] For the prepositional forms of the pronouns, see § 29.
[2] For the possessive pronouns, see § 32 A, B.

E. These adjectives follow their nouns and are used to express the equivalent of the English *of mine, of his*, etc.

Conozco a tres muchachos mexicanos que son ahora como hermanos *míos*.	I know three Mexican boys who are now like brothers *of mine*.

15 / Demonstrative Adjectives — Adjetivos demostrativos

Demonstrative adjectives point out objects more definitely than the definite article *the*. Compare: *The* book is old. *This* book is old. In English the demonstrative adjectives are *this, that, these,* and *those*. In English *this* and *these* refer to objects that are near the speaker, while *that* and *those* refer to objects that are farther away from the speaker.

In Spanish, there are three demonstrative adjectives which express three concepts of distance.

A. The demonstrative adjectives corresponding to the English words *this* and *these* and referring to objects **near the person speaking** or closely associated with the speaker:

	MASCULINE	FEMININE	
SINGULAR	este	esta	*this*
PLURAL	estos	estas	*these*

En *este* parque hay una colina.   There is a hill in *this* park.

B. The demonstrative adjectives corresponding to the English words *that* and *those* and referring to objects **near the person spoken to** or closely associated with the person addressed:

	MASCULINE	FEMININE	
SINGULAR	ese	esa	*that*
PLURAL	esos	esas	*those*

Esa silla que está a tu lado es muy vieja.	*That* chair that's beside you is very old.

C. The demonstrative adjectives corresponding to the English words *that* and *those* and referring to objects **away from both the speaker and the person spoken to** or to indicate remoteness with no reference to real space·

	MASCULINE	FEMININE	
SINGULAR	aquel	aquella	*that*
PLURAL	aquellos	aquellas	*those*

Aquellos misteriosos toltecas eran arquitectos magníficos.	*Those* mysterious Toltecs were magnificent architects.

D. These demonstrative adjectives have no written accent and are thus differentiated from the demonstrative pronouns[1] which bear a written accent.

16 / Interrogative Adjectives — *Adjetivos interrogativos*

In English, *which* and *what* are used as interrogative adjectives to modify a noun and to ask a question. EXAMPLE: *Which* books do you want? *What* work have you done?

A. In Spanish the most common interrogative adjective is *qué*. It generally indicates that there is a choice of an unlimited number of objects.[2]

¿*Qué* ciudad es el centro del gobierno mexicano?	*What* city is the center of the Mexican government?

B. The adjective *qué* is also used non-interrogatively in exclamations with nouns to mean *What a . . . !* and with adjectives and adverbs to mean *How . . . !*

¡*Qué* contraste entre ustedes y nosotros!	*What a* contrast between you and us!
¡Ay, *qué* cansado estoy!	*How* tired I am!

C. The adjective *qué* is also used idiomatically with *más* and *tan* which modify the adjective following the noun.

¡*Qué* viaje *tan* magnífico! or ¡*Qué* magnífico viaje!	*What a* magnificent trip!
¡*Qué* pueblo *más* pintoresco!	*What a* picturesque town!

---

[1] The demonstrative pronouns are discussed in § 33.
[2] Very infrequently the adjective *cuál* is used interrogatively when a choice is to be made from a limited group.

D. The interrogative adjectives *cuánto, cuánta, cuántos, cuántas* are used to express *how much* or *how many*.

¿*Cuántos* habitantes tiene la capital?

How many inhabitants does the capital have?

17 / Cardinal Numerals — Numerales cardinales

A. The cardinal numerals are:

1	uno[1]	28	vientiocho
2	dos	29	veintinueve
3	tres	30	treinta
4	cuatro	31	treinta y uno
5	cinco	32	treinta y dos
6	seis	33	treinta y tres
7	siete	40	cuarenta
8	ocho	41	cuarenta y uno
9	nueve	42	cuarenta y dos
10	diez	50	cincuenta
11	once	60	sesenta
12	doce	70	setenta
13	trece	80	ochenta
14	catorce	90	noventa
15	quince	100	cien, ciento[2,3]
16	dieciséis	101	ciento uno
17	diecisiete	102	ciento dos
18	dieciocho	110	ciento diez
19	diecinueve	111	ciento once
20	veinte	112	ciento doce
21	veintiuno	120	ciento veinte
22	veintidós	145	ciento cuarenta y cinco
23	veintitrés	200	doscientos, –as[3]
24	veinticuatro	201	doscientos uno
25	veinticinco	250	doscientos cincuenta
26	veintiséis	300	trescientos, –as
27	veintisiete	400	cuatrocientos, –as

[1] The numerals *uno* and *veintiuno* become *un* and *veintiún* before a masculine noun, and the feminine form *veintiuna* sometimes becomes *veintiún* before a feminine noun: un país, una nación, veintiún países, veintiuna (veintiún) naciones.

[2] For the use of *cien* for *ciento*, see § 10 C.

[3] The adjective *ciento* is invariable, as for instance, *ciento cincuenta libros, ciento cincuenta mujeres*. But multiples of *ciento* agree in gender and number with the noun they modify, as, for instance, *doscientos libros, trescientas treinta mujeres*.

500	quinientos, –as	2001	dos mil uno
600	seiscientos, –as	3000	tres mil
700	setecientos, –as	100,000	cien mil
800	ochocientos, –as	1,000,000	un millón
900	novecientos, –as	2,000,000	dos millones
1000	mil	1,000,000,000,000	un billón
2000	dos mil		

B. Between 16 and 19 and 21 and 29, in addition to the connected forms (*dieciséis*, *veintiuno*, etc.) there exist alternate separated forms (*diez y seis*, *veinte y uno*, etc.). These separated forms are normally not used but are found in legal documents and other formal writing. Above 29, tens are connected to units by *y*. No connecting word is used to link hundreds or thousands to tens or units. (*ciento ocho, ciento treinta, doscientos sesenta, mil nueve, dos mil treinta y tres,* etc.)

C. The numerals *cien*[1] and *mil* are not preceded by a form of *uno* to express the English word *one*.

cien casas	one hundred houses
mil habitantes	one thousand inhabitants

But the plural forms *unos* and *unas* may precede *cien* and *mil* with the meaning of *some*.

unas cien casas	*some* hundred houses
unos mil habitantes	*some* thousand inhabitants

D. The words *millón* and *docena* are nouns in Spanish. They are preceded by the indefinite article or by a numeral and are followed by the preposition *de* when introducing a following noun.

un millón de habitantes	a million inhabitants
dos millones de personas	two million persons
una docena de huevos	a dozen eggs

E. In reading dates beyond 1000, *mil* and not a multiple of *ciento* must be used.

1492	mil cuatrocientos noventa y dos
1939	mil novecientos treinta y nueve

In expressing dates before Christ, the abbreviation *a. de Jc.* is used. There is no current abbreviation for A. D.

490 a. de Jc.	cuatrocientos noventa antes de Jesucristo

---

[1] For the use of *cien* for *ciento*, see § 10 C.

A. The ordinal[1] numerals are:

1st	primero[2]	12th	duodécimo
2d	segundo	13th	décimo tercero
3d	tercero[2]	14th	décimo cuarto
4th	cuarto	15th	décimo quinto
5th	quinto	16th	décimo sexto
6th	sexto	17th	décimo séptimo
7th	séptimo	18th	décimo octavo
8th	octavo	19th	décimo noveno
9th	noveno, nono	20th	vigésimo
10th	décimo	21st	vigésimo primero
11th	undécimo	22d	vigésimo segundo

B. Ordinals above *ten* are rarely used. They are replaced by cardinals, and when the cardinal is used for an ordinal, it is placed *after* the noun it modifies.

octava lección	eighth lesson
lección doce	twelfth lesson

C. Likewise to indicate kings and emperors Spanish uses ordinal numbers through *ten* and cardinal numbers for all others.

Napoleón III	Napoleón Tercero
Alfonso XIII	Alfonso Trece

D. Spanish dates are usually written without capitals and without commas. To indicate the day of the month Spanish uses an ordinal for the *first* day of the month and cardinals for *all others*.

1° de febrero de 1970	February 1, 1970
20 de agosto de 1982	August 20, 1982

E. To indicate centuries, Spanish uses ordinals and cardinals through *ten* and cardinals *beyond ten*.

el siglo séptimo   el siglo ocho   el siglo veinte
el décimo siglo de la era cristiana

---

[1] When abbreviating ordinals, the Spanish write a small ° to the right of the cardinal, as 1° (1st), 2° (2d), etc.

[2] For the apocopation of *primero* and *tercero*, see § 10 A.

THE ADVERB—EL ADVERBIO

An adverb is a word that modifies the meaning of a verb, an adjective, or another adverb.

He runs *fast*. (The adverb *fast* indicates how he runs.)
It is a *very* interesting book. (The adverb *very* intensifies *interesting*).
He reads *somewhat* slowly. (The adverb *somewhat* modifies *slowly*.)

19 / Formation of Adverbs — Formación de adverbios

In English most adverbs are formed by adding *–ly* to the corresponding adjective. EXAMPLE: slow (*adj.*), slowly (*adv.*)

A. In Spanish adverbs are often formed by adding *–mente* to the feminine form of the adjective.[1] *

ADJECTIVE	ADVERB	ADJECTIVE	ADVERB
exacto	exactamente	suave	suavemente
rápido	rápidamente	natural	naturalmente
completo	completamente	cortés	cortésmente

B. When two or more adverbs ending in *–mente* follow each other, only the last one in the series retains the termination *–mente*, the others taking the form that they would have had if *–mente* were to be added.

Las casas estaban *lujosa* y *suntuosa-mente* amuebladas.	The houses were furnished *luxuriously* and *sumptuously*.

C. In Spanish adjectives are sometimes used as adverbs.

Además viven *felices*.	Moreover they live *happily*.
Cojan ustedes un taxi e irán mucho más *cómodos*.	Take a taxi and you will travel much more *comfortably*.

D. Many Spanish adverbs have no corresponding adjective and do not end in *–mente*. Among these are *muy* (very), *pronto* (soon), *ahora* (now), etc.

---

[1] Adjectives which bear a written accent keep that accent when they become adverbs. EXAMPLES: rápido, rápidamente; cortés, cortésmente.

E. A number of adverbs may be converted into compound prepositions by the addition of the preposition *de*, as for instance, *cerca* (adverb) + *de* = *cerca de* (preposition). For a list of adverbs which may be converted into compound prepositions, see § 41 A.

20 / Comparison of Adverbs — *Comparación de adverbios*

A. Spanish adverbs, like adjectives,[1] are compared by placing *más*, *menos*, or *tan* before the positive form.

Roberto entiende *más fácilmente* que sus amigos.   Robert understands *more easily* than his friends.

B. The following adverbs are compared irregularly:

bien   mejor   mal   peor

21 / Ways of Using donde *and* ¿dónde? — *Modos de usar* donde *y* ¿dónde?

A. The preposition *de* is used with the relative *donde* and the interrogative ¿ *dónde* ? to express the English *from where* or *whence*, and in elegant Spanish style the prepositions *a* and *en* are used with these same words to express place to which and place in which. Colloquially, the Spanish tend not to use them.

¿ *De dónde* saca Roberto el dinero ?   *From where* does Robert take the money ?

¿ *(A) dónde* va Roberto ?   *Where* does Robert go ?

Ésta es la casa *(en)* donde vive.   This is the house *where* he lives.

B. The preposition *por* is used with *dónde* to ask *which way* one should go to get to a place. It may be expressed in English by *how, which way, by what route*.

¿ *Por dónde* se va a la calle de Lope ?   *How* does one get to Lope Street?

¿ *Por dónde* se sale del cine ?   *How* does one get out of the movies?

¿ *Por dónde* se entra en este edificio ?   *How* does one get into this building?

22 / The Negative — *La forma negativa*

An English sentence is made negative by means of the word *not*. EXAMPLE: Mexico is *not* a continent.

---

[1] For the comparison of adjectives, see § 12 A.

A. A Spanish sentence is made negative by placing *no* before the verb.

México *no* es un país de Sud Amé-   Mexico is *not* a country of South
rica.   America.

B. Ordinarily, *no* precedes all other words which come before the verb except the subject and its modifiers.

Roberto encuentra dos cartas, pero   Robert receives two letters, but he
no las lee.   does *not* read them.
Los amigos de Roberto *no* le oyen.   Robert's friends do *not* hear him.

C. In addition to *no*, the following negative words[1] are commonly used in Spanish:

NEGATIVE	MEANING	NEGATIVE	MEANING
nada	nothing	ninguno	no
nadie	no one	nunca	never[3]
ni[2] . . . ni	neither . . . nor	tampoco	neither, not . . . either

D. When the above negative words follow their verb, they require a *no* before the verb to complete their meaning.

Hay niños que *no* van *nunca* a la   There are children who *never* go to
escuela.   school.
Existen regiones donde *no* hay *nin-*   Regions exist where there is *no*
guna escuela.   school.
Los campesinos *no* saben *nada* de   The peasants do *not* know *anything*
higiene.   about hygiene.

But if these negative words precede their verb, they do not require a *no* to complete their meaning.

En algunas regiones *nadie* habla   In some regions *no one* speaks
español.   Spanish.
Naturalmente los maestros *tampoco*   Naturally the teachers do *not* earn
ganan mucho.   much *either*.

[1] For the meaning of the negative combination *no . . . más que*, see § 12 F 2.
[2] Sometimes only one *. . . ni . . .* is used. For instance: Las familias pobres *no* tienen dinero *ni* tiempo suficientes para la instrucción de sus hijos; or, Las familias pobres *no* tienen *ni* dinero *ni* tiempo suficientes para la instrucción de sus hijos.
[3] The negative word *jamás* which means *never* in the sense of *absolutely never* is rarely used in comparison to *nunca*.

106,361

E. In the compound tenses the *no* precedes the auxiliary verb and the negative word comes somewhere after the past participle, or the negative word **may** be used without *no* if it precedes the auxiliary verb.

Se negó a casarse con ella, diciendo que él *no había prometido nada*.	He refused to marry her, saying that he *had promised nothing*.
Nunca me *habían parecido* tan majestuosos y tan bellos los volcanes de Popocatepetl e Ixtaccihuatl.	*Never had* the volcanoes of Popocatepetl and Ixtaccihuatl *appeared* so majestic and so beautiful to me.

THE PRONOUN—EL PRONOMBRE

A pronoun is a word used to take the place of a noun. It is used when repeating the noun would seem awkward. EXAMPLE: First John went to Madrid and then *he* (meaning *John*) went to Toledo.

23 / Subject Personal Pronouns — Los pronombres personales usados como sujetos

A. The subject personal pronouns most needed by the foreigner in a Spanish-speaking country are:

yo	I	nosotros	we
él	he	⎰ellos[2]	
ella	she	⎱ellas	they
usted[1]	you	ustedes[3]	you

In Spanish *all* subject pronouns except *usted* and *ustedes* are omitted except for emphasis or for contrast of subjects. The pronouns *usted* and *ustedes* may be omitted when there is no doubt as to who the subject is, but it is more courteous to use them.

— ¿ Habla *usted* inglés ?	"Do *you* speak English?"
— Hablo muy poco, pero entiendo mucho.	"*I* speak very little, but *I* understand a great deal."

EMPHASIS

Según la tradición española, el marido es el amo de la casa; en casa manda *él*.	According to Spanish tradition, the husband is the master of the house; at home *he* commands.

[1] The pronoun *usted*, meaning *your grace* originally, is abbreviated *Ud.*, *Vd.*, and *V.*
[2] In Spanish there are two words for *they*. The pronoun *ellos* refers to masculine plural or masculine and feminine plural nouns; *ellas* refers to purely feminine plural nouns.
[3] The pronoun *ustedes* is abbreviated *Uds.*, *Vds.*, and *VV.*

Carlos canta en inglés, pero natu-	*Charles* sings in English, but natu-
ralmente *yo* todavía no escribo	rally *I* don't yet write poetry in
versos en esta lengua.	that language.

B. The pronoun *you* is ordinarily expressed by **usted** when speaking to one person. The pronoun **usted** has the same verb endings as a singular noun.

— ¿ Es *usted* norteamericano ?   "Are *you* a (North) American?"
— *Usted* habla español muy bien.   "*You* speak Spanish very well."

C. The pronoun *you* is ordinarily expressed by **ustedes** when speaking to more than one person. The pronoun **ustedes** has the same verb endings as a plural noun.

Ustedes son mis amigos y los invito   *You* are my friends, and I invite you
  a mi casa.   to my house.

D. When speaking to an intimate friend, a relative, a child, a pet, and some-times to a servant, the Spanish generally use the pronoun **tú** to express *you*. Students, soldiers doing military service, and others in the same general social class often speak to each other in the **tú** form. This **tú** form has a special set of verb endings[1]; the **tú** is often omitted and the verb ending alone indicates the subject of the sentence.

Tú me *enseñaste* las primeras pala-   *You taught* me the first words that
  bras que aprendí.   I learned.

E. The plural of *tú* is **vosotros,** and in Spain **vosotros** is used when speaking to several persons who would be addressed with *tú* individually. How-ever, the use of **vosotros** differs in various parts of the Spanish-speaking world. In Mexico, **vosotros** is not used at all, and **ustedes** serves as the plural of *tú*. In certain Latin American countries, *vos* is used as a singular intimate second person pronoun. The **vosotros** form has a special set of verb endings[1]; the **vosotros** is often omitted and the verb ending alone indicates the subject of the sentence.

¿ Cuándo *os vais* a ir *vosotros* ?   When are you going to leave?

F. Contrary to English usage, in sentences such as *It is I* (colloq. *It's me*), the person and number of *ser* agree with the personal pronoun, which is used as the subject.

---

[1] In addition to the special verb forms, which may be found throughout the paradigms in the GRAMMAR and especially in § 110, *tú* and *vosotros* have special object pronoun forms (§§ 24 D and 25 D), possessive adjective forms (§ 14 B, D), and possessive pro-noun forms (§ 32 B).

Soy yo.	It is I.
Es él.	It is he.
Es usted.	It is you.
Somos nosotros.	It is we.
Son ellos.	It is they.
Son ustedes.	It is you.

24 / Direct Object Personal Pronouns —

Los pronombres personales usados como complementos directos

In sentences like: He reads *them;* He pays *it;* She calls *you;* They hear *him,* the italicized pronouns are direct objects because they receive the direct action of the verbs *reads, pays, calls,* and *hear.* They are pronoun objects which take the place of some noun already understood.

A. In Spanish the third person direct object personal pronouns are:

PERSONS	THINGS	PERSONS AND THINGS
le him, you	lo [1] it (*masculine*)	los them, you (*masculine*)
la her, you	la it (*feminine*)	las them, you (*feminine*)

B. These pronouns take the place of noun objects. [2]

Roberto lee │*la carta.*│	Robert reads │*the letter.*│
Roberto *la* lee.	Robert reads *it.*
Los amigos oyen│*a Roberto.*│	The friends hear │*Robert.*│
Los amigos *le* oyen.	The friends hear *him.*
¿ Saluda Roberto │*a sus amigos ?*│	Does Robert greet │*his friends?*│
¿ *Los* saluda Roberto ?	Does Robert greet *them?*

C. The first person direct object pronouns are:

| me | me | nos | us |

| Como todos *me* entendieron, me quedé muy satisfecho. | As everyone understood *me,* I was very satisfied. |

---

[1] The pronoun *lo* is often used to refer to masculine persons, especially in Latin America.
[2] Notice that the pronoun objects in these examples come *before the verb.* For a discussion of the position of pronoun objects, see § 30 A.

D. The familiar second person direct object pronouns are:

te   you (*singular*)   os   you (*plural*)

Felipe *te* ve todos los días.	Philip sees *you* every day.
He pasado mucho tiempo *contigo*.	I spent a great deal of time with *you* .

25 / Indirect Object Personal Pronouns —

Los pronombres personales usados como complementos indirectos

In the sentences: I show *Charles* a book; We write *him* a letter; They give *us* a ride, the italicized words receive the indirect action of the verb. They are the indirect objects. They answer the question **to** or **for** *whom*. In each case, we might have said: I show a book **to** *Charles;* We write a letter to *him;* They give a ride **to** *us*, etc. The preposition **to**, understood or expressed, is the sign of the indirect object in English.

A. In Spanish the third person indirect object personal pronouns are:

le[1]   to him, to her, to you, to it
les   to them, to you

B. These pronouns indicate an indirect object referring to a person or thing already mentioned[2].

Carlos habla	a Roberto.		Charles speaks	to Robert.	
Carlos *le* habla.	Charles speaks *to him*.
¿ Da Felipe catorce boletos	a sus amigos ?		Does Philip give fourteen tickets	to his friends?	
¿ *Les* da boletos Felipe ?	Does Philip give *them* tickets?

C. The first person indirect object pronouns are exactly like the direct object pronouns:

me   to me   nos   to us

D. The familiar second person indirect object pronouns are exactly like the direct object pronouns.

te   to you (*singular*)   os   to you (*plural*)

---

[1] For the substitution of *se* for *le* and *les*, see § 31 B.

[2] Notice that the pronoun objects in these examples come *before the verb*. For a discussion of the position of pronoun objects, see § 30 A.

E. Since the following sentence may have several meanings:

Carlos *le* habla.
{
Charles speaks *to him.*
Charles speaks *to her.*
Charles speaks *to you.*
}

Spanish often clarifies such a sentence by the addition of *a* + the appropriate prepositional form.[1]

Carlos *le* habla *a él.*	Charles speaks *to him.*
Carlos *le* habla *a ella.*	Charles speaks *to her.*
Carlos *le* habla *a usted.*	Charles speaks *to you.*

This repetitive construction is also used for emphasis, especially where no clarification is necessary.

*A **mí** me* gustan las corridas.	*I* like bullfights.

It is regularly used where the noun indirect object precedes the verb.

A muchos mexicanos no *les* gustan las corridas.	The bullfights are not pleasing *to many Mexicans.*

Probably by extension of these same ideas, it is very common to find the indirect object pronoun construction even when the noun itself follows the verb.

Roberto *le* da el dinero *a Felipe.*	Robert gives the money *to Philip.*
El boletero *les* da *a los jóvenes* los boletos.	The ticket seller gives *the youths* the tickets.
Una criada entró con un plato muy grande y *se* lo dió *a Marta.*	A servant came in with a very large plate and gave it *to Martha.*

F. Indirect object nouns and pronouns are used together with the definite article + parts of the body or articles of clothing where English would use a possessive construction.[2]

La madre le lava la cara *a su niño.*	The mother washes *her child's* face.
La madre *le* lava la cara.	The mother washes *his* face.
Spinola *le*[3] pone la mano sobre el hombro del jefe del ejército vencido.	Spinola places his hand on the shoulder of the leader of the conquered army.

---

[1] For the prepositional forms of the pronouns, see § 29.
[2] See § 4 F.
[3] The *le* here, untranslatable, indicates that the act was to the advantage of the conquered chief.

G. The indirect object nouns and pronouns are often used idiomatically in Spanish to indicate that the action represented by the verb results in some advantage or disadvantage, gain or loss, to the person directly concerned in the action. The indirect object may then be roughly equivalent to the English expression *from* + *object*, *to* + *object*, or *for* + *object*, or may not be translated in English.

Toda la gente se va de vacaciones y los que nos quedamos unos días más tenemos tantas ganas de irnos que se *nos* hace el tiempo más largo de lo que es.	Everyone is going off on a vacation and those of us who are staying a few more days want so much to leave that time seems *for us* longer than it really is.
Ya *le* hemos quitado bastante tiempo *a nuestra visita al Prado.*[1]	We have taken enough time *from our visit to the Prado.*

26 / *Reflexive Pronouns — Pronombres reflexivos*[2]

Reflexive pronouns are those which are used as direct or indirect objects of the verb but refer to the subject. In English they are distinguished by the suffix *-self*. EXAMPLES: They wash *themselves*. She talks to *herself*.

A. Spanish reflexive pronouns are likewise used as direct or indirect objects of the verb. They *always* correspond to the subject of the sentence, and to fail to make them correspond is like saying in English: *He washes myself.*

DIRECT OBJECT	Nosotros *nos* divertimos.	We amuse *ourselves.*[3]
INDIRECT OBJECT	Nosotros *nos* hablamos.	We talk *to ourselves.*

B. The same set of reflexive pronouns is used for the direct as for the indirect objects. The common reflexive pronouns are:

me	myself	nos	ourselves
se	himself, herself yourself, oneself	se	themselves yourselves

C. The familiar second person reflexive pronouns are:

te	yourself	os	yourselves

---

[1] Here is an example of a noun indirect object reinforced by a pronoun indirect object denoting disadvantage or loss to that object.
[2] For the use of reflexive pronouns with verbs, see § 105.
[3] This is a literal translation. One usually says: *We have a good time.*

A. Any verb which takes an object may become reflexive by the presence of a reflexive object.

NON-REFLEXIVE	Felipe presenta a Carlos.	Philip introduces Charles.
REFLEXIVE	Felipe *se* presenta al norteamericano.	Philip introduces *himself* to the (North) American.
NON-REFLEXIVE	Yo lavo la mesa.	I wash the table.
REFLEXIVE	Yo *me* lavo.	I wash *myself*.

Note that the reflexive pronoun corresponds in person to the subject. Just as in English we say *I wash **myself*** and not *I wash **himself***, in Spanish they say *Yo me lavo*, and not *Yo se lavo*.

B. Some verbs are inherently reflexive, that is, they exist only in a reflexive form. Among these are:

arrepentirse	repent
atreverse	dare
quejarse	complain

C. Some verbs, transitive or intransitive, are used with the reflexive forms to give a more intensive meaning to the verb, often difficult to translate into English. Among these verbs are:

morir	morirse	die
quedar	quedarse	remain
pasear	pasearse	take a walk

D. Some verbs have a distinctly different meaning when used with a reflexive pronoun than when used without it. Among these are:

NON-REFLEXIVE FORM	MEANING	REFLEXIVE FORM	MEANING
caer	fall	caerse	fall (down)
comer	eat	comerse	eat up
decidir	decide	decidirse	make up one's mind
dormir	sleep	dormirse	go to sleep
estar	be	estarse	stay
ir	go	irse	go away
llevar	carry	llevarse	carry off
parecer	appear	parecerse	resemble
poner	put	ponerse [1]	put on

[1] The verb *ponerse* has several other meanings, one of which is *become*, which is taken up in § 104 C; *ponerse* + *a* + INFINITIVE means *begin to*.

E. The reflexive pronoun is used with the definite article to express possession with actions involving parts of the body or articles of clothing belonging to the subject of the sentence. English uses the possessive adjective in such cases. [1]

Pedro *se* quitó el sombrero.	Pedro took off *his* hat.
Me lavo la cara.	I wash my face.

F. When the reflexive pronoun is used in the sense of *each other*, it is known as a **reciprocal pronoun,** but its form in Spanish is exactly the same as if it were a reflexive pronoun.

Los chicos *se* ven en la facultad.	The boys see *each other* in the university.

However, since ambiguity might arise in a sentence like

Los chicos *se* hablan.	The boys talk *to themselves*.	REFLEXIVE MEANING
	The boys talk *to each other*.	RECIPROCAL MEANING

to make the meaning clearly reciprocal, the Spanish occasionally use forms of *uno a otro*. The reciprocal meaning of the above example might be clarified in one of the following ways:

Los chicos *se* hablan *uno a otro.*	(if there are only two boys)
Los chicos *se* hablan *unos a otros.*	(if there are more than two boys)

28 / The Pronoun se — El pronombre se

The third person[2] reflexive pronoun *se* is used in a certain number of special constructions in which the reflexive force of *se* is obscured and replaced by other concepts.

A. The pronoun *se* is used with transitive verbs as a substitute for the passive voice. The subject of the sentence is a thing and the verb agrees in number with the subject.

Esta avenida *se llama* el Paseo de la Reforma.	This avenue *is called* the Paseo de la Reforma.
En el paseo *se encuentran* árboles y flores.	On the boulevard *are found* trees and flowers.

B. If, however, the subject of the English sentence is (the equivalent of) a person or persons, *se* often seems to function as the subject of the Spanish

---

[1] See § 25 F.

[2] In the constructions explained in this section, only the *se* form is used. The first and second person reflexive pronouns cannot be used here.

sentence. This *se* may be rendered in English by *one, you, they, people* or by the passive voice. In such cases, the subject of the English sentence becomes the object of the Spanish sentence and is preceded by the personal *a*. The verb is always in the third person singular.

En el bosque *se escondió* a los soldados.	The soldiers *were hidden* in the woods.
En el cuadro *se ve* al jefe del ejército vencido.	In the picture *is seen* (*one sees, you see, people see*) the chief of the vanquished army.

C. The impersonal *se* is often used when there is no specific person or thing as the subject of the Spanish sentence. In such cases, *se* can be thought of as *one, you, they, people,* or rendered by the English gerund.

Por esa puerta *se va* al patio.	Through that door *one goes* (*you go, people go*) to the patio.
Al salir de Cuernavaca *se pasa* por un valle muy fértil.	On leaving Cuernavaca *one passes* through a very fertile valley.
Se baila mucho en México.	*Dancing* is very common in Mexico.

29 / Prepositional Pronoun Forms — *Pronombres después de preposiciones*

A. The common pronouns used after prepositions[1] are:

mí	me	nosotros	us
él	him, it	ellos	them (*masculine*)
ella	her, it	ellas	them (*feminine*)
usted	you (*singular*)	ustedes	you (*plural*)

Except for *mí*, these pronouns are exactly the same as the subject pronouns outlined in § 23 A.

¡ Qué contraste entre *ustedes* y *nosotros* !	What a contrast between *you* and *us!*

B. The familiar second person prepositional pronouns are:

ti	you (*singular*)	vosotros	you (*plural*)

C. The reflexive pronoun *se* has a special prepositional form *sí*.

---

[1] The subject pronouns are used after *menos, excepto,* and *salvo,* all of which mean *except.* EXAMPLE: Todos se fueron *menos yo.* All left *except me.*

<table>
<tr><td>Cuando la gente de Cataluña habla entre *sí*, suele usar el catalán.</td><td>When the people of Catalonia speak among *themselves*, they are accustomed to use Catalan.</td></tr>
</table>

D. There is a third person neuter prepositional form, *ello*, which refers to something indefinite without gender or number or to a previously mentioned idea.

<table>
<tr><td>Los indios de la costa tuvieron miedo de los caballos y de las armas de los blancos; por *ello*, no resistieron mucho.</td><td>The Indians of the coast were afraid of the horses and arms of the whites; for *that* (reason), they did not offer much resistance.</td></tr>
</table>

E. With the preposition *con* the pronouns *mí*, *ti*, and *sí* combine to form *conmigo*, *contigo*, and *consigo*.

<table>
<tr><td>He pasado mucho tiempo *contigo*.</td><td>I spent a great deal of time with *you*.</td></tr>
</table>

30 / Position of Object Pronouns — Colocación de pronombres usados como complementos

A. Object pronouns immediately precede their verb.[1]

<table>
<tr><td>Roberto *las* lee.</td><td>Robert reads *them*.</td></tr>
<tr><td>¿*Le* oyen sus amigos?</td><td>Do his friends hear *him*?</td></tr>
</table>

B. But object pronouns follow the verb and are joined to it when the verb is an affirmative imperative, an infinitive, or a present participle.

<table>
<tr><td>Permítan**me** decir**les** mi opinión.</td><td>Permit **me** to tell **you** my opinion.</td></tr>
<tr><td>Míren**las**.</td><td>Look at **them**.</td></tr>
<tr><td>Déjen**me** seguir.</td><td>Let **me** continue.</td></tr>
<tr><td>Madero, declarándo**se** candidato, **se** atrevió a protestar contra la reelección de Porfirio Díaz.</td><td>Madero, declaring **himself** a candidate, dared to protest against the reelection of Porfirio Díaz.</td></tr>
</table>

C. When the pronoun is joined to the verb form, that form retains its spoken stress and this stress is indicated by a written accent whenever the addition of the pronoun(s) would cause the basic rules for stress[2] to be violated.

---

[1] In literary style the object pronouns often follow indicative verbs at the beginning of sentences or clauses.

[2] The rules for stress are explained in PRONUNCIATION § 7.

Mire la playa.		Stress of *mire* is on the first syllable because it ends in a vowel.	
Mírela		Stress of *mírela* still on the first syllable. There is a written accent because the stress no longer comes on the next to the last syllable.	

D. Pronouns precede negative imperatives.

AFFIRMATIVE IMPERATIVE	MEANING	NEGATIVE IMPERATIVE	MEANING
Lléve*nos* usted.	Take *us*.	No *nos* lleve usted.	Don't take *us*.
Escríban*le* ustedes.	Write *to him*.	No *le* escriban ustedes.	Don't write *to him*.
Déme*lo* usted.	Give *it to me*.	No *me lo* dé usted.	Don't give *it to me*.

E. When an auxiliary verb is used with an infinitive or present participle which has object pronouns, *the object pronouns may be joined to the infinitive or present participle or they may precede the auxiliary verb.*

JOINED TO INFINITIVE OR PARTICIPLE	PRECEDING AUXILIARY	MEANING
Voy a enseñar*le* el camino.	*Le* voy a enseñar el camino.	I am going to show you the road.
Estoy esperándo*los*.	*Los* estoy esperando.	I am waiting for them.

31 / Order of Object Pronouns — *Orden de pronombres usados como complementos*

A. When there are two object pronouns, the indirect object precedes the direct object.

Felipe *me lo* dice.	Philip says *it to me*.
¿ *Nos lo* explica el profesor ?	Does the teacher explain *it to us?*

B. When both indirect and direct objects are third person the first of the pronoun objects becomes *se* whether it is singular or plural.

La criada ~~le~~ *se* *lo* da.	(Change *le* to *se*.)	The servant gives *it to him*.
Si ustedes quieren, ~~les~~ *se* *lo* presto.	(Change *les* to *se*.)	If you (*pl.*) wish, I (will) lend *it to you* (*pl.*).

A possessive pronoun is one which indicates possession. Possessive pronouns should be distinguished from possessive adjectives.

This is *your* pen.	Possessive adjective because *your* modifies *pen*.
It is *yours*.	Possessive pronoun because *yours* takes the place of *pen*.

A. The common possessive pronouns[1] are:

referring to singular nouns		referring to plural nouns		
MASCULINE	FEMININE	MASCULINE	FEMININE	
(el) mío	(la) mía	(los) míos	(las) mías	*mine*
(el) suyo	(la) suya	(los) suyos	(las) suyas	*his, hers, its, yours, theirs*
(el) nuestro	(la) nuestra	(los) nuestros	(las) nuestras	*ours*

B. The familiar second person forms of the possessive pronoun are:

referring to singular nouns		referring to plural nouns		
MASCULINE	FEMININE	MASCULINE	FEMININE	
(el) tuyo	(la) tuya	(los) tuyos	(las) tuyas	*yours (sing.)*
(el) vuestro	(la) vuestra	(los) vuestros	(las) vuestras	*yours (plur.)*

C. Possessive pronouns agree with their antecedents in gender and number and with the possessor in person. They do not depend on the gender of the possessor as is the case in English.

Mi casa es más grande que *la suya*.   My house is larger than *his*.

Here, the possessive pronoun, *la suya*, is feminine to agree with *casa* in spite of the fact that it refers to a masculine person.

D. The possessive pronoun is normally preceded by the definite article.

¿Qué te parece la Universidad de México comparada con *la tuya*?	What do you think of the University of Mexico compared with *yours*?

---

[1] The possessive pronouns are identical in form with the stressed forms of the possessive adjectives, which are explained in § 14 D.

But the article may be omitted after *ser* when it answers the question **whose.**

¿ De quién es este sombrero ?	Whose hat is this?
Este sombrero es *mío.*	This hat is *mine.*

The article is regularly used after *ser* and before the possessive pronoun to answer the question **which.**

¿ Cuál de esas casas es *la suya* ?	Which of those houses is *yours?*
Ésa a la derecha es *la mía.*	The one on the right is *mine.*

E. Since *suyo* means *his, hers, its, yours,* and *theirs,* its meaning may be clarified by using

article + *de* + prepositional form of pronoun[1]

$$
\left. \begin{array}{c} \text{el} \\ \text{la} \\ \text{los} \\ \text{las} \end{array} \right\} \quad \text{de} \quad \left\{ \begin{array}{l} \text{él} \\ \text{ella} \\ \text{usted} \\ \text{ellos} \\ \text{ellas} \\ \text{ustedes} \end{array} \right.
$$

Es natural que Madrid no sea una ciudad tan nueva como *las de ustedes.*	It is natural that Madrid should not be such a new city as *yours.*

33 / Demonstrative Pronouns — Pronombres demostrativos

In the sentence: "Here are two kinds of apples." "Give me *these,* not *those,*" *these* and *those* refer to *apples* and point out which ones. They are called *demonstrative pronouns.* In English, we often say *this one* or *that one* as well as *this* and *that.*

A. In Spanish the demonstrative pronouns correspond in form to the demonstrative adjectives,[2] but **they always bear a written accent** to distinguish them from the demonstrative adjectives. The demonstrative pronouns are:

SINGULAR		PLURAL		
MASCULINE	FEMININE	MASCULINE	FEMININE	
éste	ésta	éstos	éstas	*this, these*
ése	ésa	ésos	ésas	*that, those*
aquél	aquélla	aquéllos	aquéllas	*that, those*

[1] Compare with the way of clarifying the possessive adjective *su,* explained in § 14 C.
[2] For the demonstrative adjectives, see § 15.

As in case of the demonstrative adjectives, forms of *ése* (*that*) refer to objects near the person spoken to, and forms of *aquél* (*that*) refer to objects distant from both the speaker and the person spoken to.

Éstos son los frescos de Diego Rivera.	*These* are the frescos of Diego Rivera.
Aquélla es la catedral más grande de las Américas.	*That* is the largest cathedral of the Americas.

B. Forms of *éste* are often used in the sense of **the latter** and forms of *aquél* in the sense of **the former**. When both pronouns are used in the same sentence, the form of *éste* precedes the form of *aquél*.

Los ricos llevaban una vida de tal esplendor que no se fijaban en la miseria de los pobres; eran *éstos* víctimas de *aquéllos*.	The rich led a life of such splendor that they did not notice the poverty of the poor; the *latter* were victims of the *former*.

The English *the latter* is also often expressed by a form of *este último*.

C. The demonstrative pronouns *esto, eso* and *aquello* refer to an idea, situation, or previous statement, none of which has gender. These neuter pronouns are also used when the gender of an object has not yet been established or when the object itself has not been identified. These pronouns have no written accent because there is no corresponding adjective form with which they might be confused.

Se dice que la lengua de la mujer es más larga que la del hombre, pero *eso* no es verdad.	It is said that a woman's tongue is longer than a man's, but *that* isn't true.
Esto es demasiado para una sola lección.	*This* is too much for a single lesson.
Esto es una llave.	*This* is a key.

In the last example, *llave* has not yet been mentioned, and therefore the neuter form may be used. But one would say: *Ésta* es *mi* llave.

D. The forms of the definite article, *el, la, los, las,* are sometimes used as demonstrative pronouns.[1] In this case, they are always followed by *de* or *que*. In English they are expressed sometimes by a demonstrative pronoun, sometimes by *the one(s)*, sometimes by *he, she,* or *they*.

---

[1] The prepositions *a* and *de* contract with the definite article used as a demonstrative pronoun just as they do when it is used as an article. EXAMPLE: El número de muchachos es muy superior *al* de chicas. (The number of boys is very much superior *to that* of girls.)

El **que** no puede ver es ciego.	*He* **who** cannot see is blind.
Se dice que la lengua de la mujer es más larga que *la* **del** hombre, pero eso no es verdad.	It is said that the tongue of a woman is longer than *that* **of** a man, but that isn't true.
Las pirámides más grandes de México son *las* **de** San Juan de Teotihuacán.	The largest pyramids in Mexico are *those* **of** San Juan de Teotihuacán.

34 / Interrogative Pronouns — *Pronombres interrogativos*

A. The common interrogative pronouns are:

1. ¿ quién ? (*singular*) ¿ quiénes ? (*plural*) *who, whom* used to ask which person.

¿ *Quién* fue elegido presidente de México en 1876 ?	*Who* was elected president of Mexico in 1876?
¿ *Quiénes* eran esos ladrones?	*Who* were those thieves?
¿ A *quiénes* hablaban ustedes cuando entré?	*Whom* were you talking *to* when I came in?

2. ¿ cuál ? (*singular*) cuáles ? (*plural*) *which, which one(s), what, who* used to ask which persons or things.

¿*Cuáles* fueron las mejores películas del año pasado?	*What* were the best films of the past year?

3. ¿ qué ? (*singular and plural*)   *what* used to ask which thing.

¿ *Qué* tenían que hacer los pobres ?	*What* did the poor have to do?

4. ¿ de quién + *a form of* ser   *whose*

¿ *De quién* es este cuarto ?	*Whose* is this room?

5. ¿ cuánto ? ¿ cuánta ? ¿ cuántos ? ¿ cuántas ? *how much? how many?*

¿ *Cuánto* costó el coche ?	*How much* did the car cost?
¿ *Cuántos* salieron del país ?	*How many* left the country?

B. The English **What is . . . ?** and **What are . . . ?** are expressed in two ways in Spanish:

1. When the answer expected is equivalent to a definition, ¿ *Qué es* . . . ? and ¿ *Qué son* . . . ? are used.

¿ *Qué es* Taxco ?	*What is* Taxco?
¿ *Qué son* las matemáticas ?	*What is* mathematics?

2. When the answer expected is one of a number of possible choices,
¿ *Cuál es* . . . ? and ¿ *Cuáles son* . . . ? are used.

¿ *Cuál es* el país más montañoso de Norte América ?	*What* (which of all the countries in North America) *is* the most mountainous country in North America?
¿ *Cuáles son* los picos más altos de México ?	*What* (which of all the peaks in Mexico) are the highest peaks in Mexico?

35 / *The Relative Pronoun* que — *El pronombre relativo* que [1]

A relative pronoun connects a subordinate clause to a main clause. (The main clauses are in bold face and the relative pronoun is in italics.)

This is the house *which* we bought.
He is the man to *whom* we give the book.
Tell me *what* you are doing.

A. The most common relative pronoun is *que*. It may be either the subject or object of a verb and may refer either to persons or things. When used after a preposition, it refers only to things.

Los mexicanos *que* viven en la meseta tienen mucha energía.	The Mexicans *who* live on the plateau have a great deal of energy.
Conozco una calle *que* tiene muchas casas bonitas.	I know a street *that* has many lovely houses.
El Palacio de Bellas Artes es un enorme edificio donde está el gran teatro en *que* se dan los mejores conciertos de México.	The Palacio de Bellas Artes is an enormous building where there is the large theater in *which* are given the best concerts in Mexico.

B. The word *que* has several common uses besides its ordinary function as a relative.

   1. It is often found used in certain emphatic expressions and is not translatable.

---

[1] For the use of the definite article with *que*, see § 33 D. For the use of forms of *el que* instead of *el cual*, see § 37 C. For the neuter *lo que*, see § 5 F.

—¿No hay otra manera de ganarse la vida?	"Aren't there any other ways to earn a living?"
— ¡*Sí que* las hay!	"*Yes*, there are!"

2. It is similarly used preceding *sí* and *no* after verbs.

Le pregunté a María si quería acompañarme y contestó *que no*.	I asked Mary if she wanted to go with me, and she answered *no*.

3. When used at the beginning of a sentence, *que* often indicates or implies a previous clause not expressed but understood.

— ¿ Qué le parece, Roberto ?	"What do you think of it, Robert?"
— *Que* voy a seguir sus consejos.	"(I think) *that* I am going to follow your advice."

4. This *que* may be used as a conjunction usually meaning *for, since,* or *because.*

—Démelo, Roberto, por favor, *que* voy a enseñarle el camino.	"Please give it to me, Robert, *for* I am going to show you the road."

36 / The Relative Pronoun quien — El pronombre relativo quien

A. The relative pronoun *quien* is used after prepositions to refer to persons.

García Lorca escribió poemas sobre los gitanos, *con quienes* había vivido en Granada.	García Lorca wrote poems about the gypsies, *with whom* he had lived in Granada.
Nunca he visto otra vez a esos vecinos, *a quienes* había prestado mucho dinero.	I never again saw those neighbors, *whom* I had lent a great deal of money.

B. The relative pronoun *quien* is often used instead of *que* in parenthetical clauses.

Uno de los poetas españoles más célebres fue José de Espronceda, *quien* expresó su dolor y melancolía romántica.	One of the most famous Spanish poets was José de Espronceda, *who* expressed his sorrow and romantic melancholy.

C. The relative pronoun *quien* is used at the beginning of a sentence in the sense of *whoever,* or *he who, one who,* etc., especially in proverbial sayings.

Quien maltrata a una mujer no es bien mirado por los otros españoles.

He who mistreats a woman is not well regarded by other Spaniards.

37 / *The Relative Pronoun* cual — *El pronombre relativo* cual [1]

A. The relative pronouns *el cual, la cual, los cuales, las cuales* indicate more clearly than *que* the gender and number of the antecedent and often replace *que* in literary Spanish.

Muchas veces hemos visitado las ciudades del sur del país, *las cuales* son muy pintorescas.

Often we visited the cities of the south of the country, *which* are very picturesque.

B. A form of *el cual* replaces *que*

1. after compound prepositions of three syllables or more when referring to things.

Toledo parece una gran fortaleza dentro de *la cual* se destacan contra el cielo las torres de su Alcázar.

Toledo appears as a great fortress within *which* the towers of its Alcazar stand out against the sky.

2. when a relative clause is separated from the antecedent by an intervening noun. [2]

Al norte España está separada del resto de Europa por los altos Pirineos, una prolongación de *los cuales* se extiende a lo largo de la costa norte.

On the north Spain is separated from the rest of Europe by the high Pyrenees, a prolongation of *which* extends along the northern coast.

C. In literary Spanish *el que, la que, los que,* and *las que* are often used in the same places as *el cual,* etc., would be used.

Encima de una colina desde *la que* se puede ver el panorama de la Sierra Nevada construyeron la Alhambra.

On a hill from *which* can be seen the panorama of the Sierra Nevada they constructed the Alhambra.

En la universidad hay una organización a *la que* pertenecen todos los estudiantes españoles.

In the university there is an organization to *which* all the Spanish students belong.

---

[1] For the neuter *lo cual,* see § 5 E.

[2] In other words, if the relative pronoun could refer to two antecedents and it does refer to the first of the two, a form of *el cual* must be used as the relative pronoun.

The relative pronominal adjective *cuyo* shows possession at the same time that it connects a subordinate to a main clause. It agrees with the noun it modifies in gender and number.

Los labradores, *cuyos* métodos de trabajo nos parecieron muy primitivos, estaban recogiendo la cosecha.

The farmers, *whose* methods of work appeared very antiquated to us, were gathering the harvest.

The relative *cuyos* agrees with *métodos*, which it modifies, rather than with *labradores*, to which it refers.

Cervantes es un escritor *cuyas* obras se leen mucho.

Cervantes is a writer *whose* works are widely read.

The relative *cuyas* agrees with *obras*, which it modifies, rather than with *escritor*, to which it refers.

39 / Indefinites — El indefinido

A. The common indefinites are:

1. alguien   Used only as a pronoun meaning *someone*, it refers to a person not previously mentioned.

Alguien me dijo que debemos cambiar de coche.

Someone told me that we should change cars.

2. alguno[1]   Used both as a pronoun and an adjective. As a pronoun it is equivalent to *alguien* when referring to a person but it always refers to someone of a group already mentioned or understood.

PRONOUN

Algunos de los barrios de la ciudad son muy elegantes.

Some of the districts of the city are very elegant.

Hay muchas chicas en la escuela, y *algunas* estudian español.

There are many girls in the school, and *some* study Spanish.

[1] For the apocopation of *alguno*, see § 10 A.

En el Paseo de la Reforma hay *algunos* monumentos de la historia de México.

In Reform Boulevard there are *some* monuments of Mexican history.

3. algo   Used as a pronoun meaning *something* and as an adverb meaning *somewhat*.

Los niños indios aprenden *algo* de México y del resto del mundo.

The Indian children learn *something* of Mexico and of the rest of the world.

Algo más al sur del pueblo hay muy bellas playas.

Somewhat more to the south of the town there are very beautiful beaches.

Los labriegos son *algo* avaros.

The farmers are *somewhat* stingy.

B. There are three ways of expressing the indefinite English *one, they,* or *you:*

1. by the pronoun *uno.*

Uno tiene una cita a las cuatro y media y la persona llega a las cinco y cuarto y a veces no viene.

One has an appointment at half past four and the person arrives at a quarter after five and sometimes doesn't come.

2. by the third person plural of the verb.

Cada domingo *matan* seis toros.   Each Sunday *they kill* six bulls.

3. by the reflexive pronoun *se,* which is discussed in detail in § 28 C.

THE PREPOSITION[1]—LA PREPOSICIÓN

A preposition is a word used to introduce a phrase. EXAMPLES: The boy is *in* the house. The pencil is *on* the table. Robert is *with* his friend.

---

[1] For the use of the infinitive after prepositions, see § 80 D.

The following simple prepositions are very common in Spanish.

a	to; at; in	excepto	except, but
ante	before; in the presence of	hacia	toward
		hasta	as far as, to, until, up to
bajo	under, below	para	for; to, in order to
con	with	por	for; by; to; through; on account of
contra	against		
de	of; from; by; about (concerning)	salvo	except
		según	according to
desde	from; since	sin	without
durante	during	sobre	on, upon; about (concerning)
en	in; into; on, upon; at		
entre	between	tras	after

41 / Compound Prepositions — Preposiciones compuestas

In Spanish, certain adverbs, adjectives, and nouns are used with prepositions to form compound prepositions.

cerca (*adverb*) + de	cerca de
contrario (*adjective*) + a	contrario a
a + causa (*noun*) + de	a causa de

A. A number of adverbs may be converted into compound prepositions by the addition of the preposition *de*. The most common of these are:

ADVERB	MEANING	PREPOSITION	MEANING
además	besides	además de	besides
alrededor	around	alrededor de	around
antes	formerly	antes de	before
cerca	near	cerca de	near
debajo	underneath	debajo de	under
delante	in front	delante de	in front of
dentro	inside	dentro de	inside of
después	afterwards	después de	after
detrás	behind	detrás de	behind
encima	above	encima de	above
fuera	outside	fuera de	outside of

ADVERB	PREPOSITION
Además, tiene que saber algo de medicina.	En la meseta, *además de* la capital, hay muchas ciudades importantes.

B. The common compound prepositions with *de* are:

a causa de	because of	debajo de	under
a fin de	in order to	delante de	before, in front of
a fuerza de	by dint of	dentro de	within, inside of
a pesar de	in spite of	después de	after (*in time*)
acerca de	about, concerning	detrás de	behind (*in place*), after
además de	besides	en lugar de	instead of
al lado de	alongside of, beside	en vez de	instead of
alrededor de	around	encima de	above, on top of
antes de	before (*in time*)	fuera de	outside of
cerca de	near		

C. The most common compound prepositions with *a* are:

conforme a	according to	junto a	next to, close to
contrario a	contrary to	respecto a	in regard to
en cuanto a	as to, as for	tocante a	in regard to
frente a	opposite, facing		

42 / Possession — Posesión

English expresses possession by ——'s in the singular and ——s' in the plural or by the use of the preposition *of*. EXAMPLES: *Robert's* room, the *students'* teacher; the capital *of the country*.

Spanish expresses possession by placing the preposition *de* before a proper name or by *de* with the article or some other modifying word before a common noun. The preposition *de* with the article is also used with a title of respect.[1] The ——'s and ——s' do not exist in Spanish.

la casa *de la señora García*	*Mrs. García's* house
las guitarras *de los estudiantes*	*the students'* guitars
la puerta *del edificio*	the door *of the building*
la visita *de Roberto*	*Robert's* visit

---

[1] For the use of the article with titles of respect, see § 4 C.

The preposition *de* is used with unmodified nouns[1] to form adjectival phrases. The Spanish adjectival phrase is usually expressed in English by an adjective, which is often a noun used as an adjective.

corrida *de toros*	*bull*fight
libro *de consulta*	*reference* book
luna *de miel*	*honey*moon
lámina *de anatomía*	*anatomical* chart
compañía *de petróleo*	*oil* company
aceite *de oliva*	*olive* oil
hoz *de mano*	*hand* scythe
puerta *de entrada*	*entrance* door

44 / *The Personal* a — El a *personal*

A. In Spanish the preposition *a* is used before direct objects[2] referring to persons.[3] It is called the **personal** *a*.

También entiendo *a los turistas* que hablan inglés.	I also understand *the tourists* who speak English.
¿ Por qué admiran los mexicanos *a los norteamericanos* ?	Why do the Mexicans admire *the* (*North*) *Americans?*

This **personal** *a* is useful in certain sentences because it indicates which is the direct object and thus distinguishes it from the subject.[4] Consider the following examples:

¿ Admira Carlos *a María* ?	Does Charles admire *Mary?*
¿ Admira *a Carlos* María ?	Does Mary admire *Charles?*

---

[1] The preposition *de* may also be used with an infinitive to form an adjectival phrase as in *máquina de escribir*, which means *typewriter*.

[2] This **personal** *a* is not to be confused with the *a* which is the sign of the indirect object and which may be translated as *to*. EXAMPLE: Juan habla *a* María. John speaks *to* Mary (indirect object *a*).

[3] The preposition *a* sometimes precedes geographical names which are used as the direct object, but this is not a tendency in present-day Spanish. EXAMPLE: Para atacar *a* Inglaterra, Felipe II organizó una gran flota. The **personal** *a* also often precedes personified things. EXAMPLE: Vimos *a* su perro acercarse a Carlos.

[4] The necessity of distinguishing the subject from the object by *a* arises from the flexibility of Spanish word order. There is a discussion of this word order in §§ 54, 55.

But the verb *tener*, meaning *have*, ordinarily does not take the **personal** *a*.

Tengo *un hermano* que prepara el desayuno. I have *a brother* who gets breakfast.

B. When the personal direct object refers to an indefinite rather than to a definite person, the **personal** *a* is often omitted.

En las laderas de algunas montañas vimos *muchos indios* que cultivaban campos de maíz. On the sides of some mountains we saw many *Indians* who were cultivating cornfields.

Busco *una criada* que hable inglés. I am looking for *a servant* who speaks English.

45 / Uses of por **and** para — *Usos de las preposiciones* por y para

A. The preposition *por* is translated by *through, by, for, along,* and sometimes by other English prepositions. It has many uses, among which the most important are:

1. to express the English preposition *through*.

La luz entró *por* la ventana de mi cuarto. The light entered *through* the window of my room.

Volví al centro y di una vuelta *por* las calles. I went back downtown and took a walk *through* the streets.

2. to express the English preposition *by* after the passive voice. [1]

Este portal es cerrado *por* un portero hacia las diez de la noche. This door is closed *by* a porter about ten at night.

Esos ladrones fueron capturados *por* el policía ayer. Those robbers were captured *by* the policeman yesterday.

3. to express the English preposition *by* to indicate means. [2]

El mejor modo de viajar en España es *por* avión. The best way to travel in Spain is *by* airplane.

---

[1] With verbs expressing mental action and certain others, *de* often expresses agent. See § 87 C 2.

[2] However, *en* is used in expressions such as *en automóvil*.

4. to express *the reason for.*

Andalucía es célebre *por* sus corridas de toros.	Andalusia is famous *for* its bull-fights.
Juárez se distinguió *por* su absoluta honradez.	Juárez distinguished himself *by* his absolute honesty.
El hijo de nuestro primo no puede ir a Europa *por* falta de dinero.	Our cousin's son cannot go to Europe *because of* lack of money.
Por eso Roberto decidió tomar el cuarto.	*For* that reason Robert decided to take the room.

5. to express *for* meaning *in exchange for.*

Cambié algunos dólares *por* pesos mexicanos.	I exchanged some dollars *for* Mexican pesos.
Por poco dinero el viajero puede conseguir habitación para dormir.	*For* little money the traveler can get a room to sleep in.

6. sometimes to express duration of time. [1]

Iré a España *por* un mes.	I'll go to Spain *for* a month.

7. to express *for* meaning *in favor of, for the sake of,* or *in behalf of.* [2]

¿ Qué hizo Cárdenas *por* la educación ?	What did Cárdenas do *for* education?

8. to express the English *per* in expressions of rate or measure.

Muchos trenes salen solamente tres veces *por* semana.	Many trains leave only three times *per* week.
Salen en automóvil a setenta, ochenta o noventa kilómetros *por* hora.	They go out in a car at seventy, eighty or ninety kilometers *per* hour.
Suelen ser suspendidos un sesenta y cinco *por ciento* de los estudiantes.	Sixty-five *per cent* of the students usually fail.

9. meaning *to* after expressions of strong feeling or desire.

Tenía curiosidad *por* saber lo que decían.	I was curious *to* know what they were saying.

---

[1] The preposition *durante* often expresses duration of time. For the use of *hace, desde hace, desde que,* and *desde* to express *for* in time phrases, see § 59 B.

[2] This is almost like the use of *para* explained in § 45 B 2, and since the latter is more common, students should be cautious about using *por* with this meaning.

10. to indicate vague position.

Por todos lados se puede ver un paisaje magnífico.	*On* all sides a magnificent landscape can be seen.
Por todas partes oíamos hablar español.	Everywhere we heard Spanish spoken.
Atravesaron la carretera algunas vacas *por* delante de nuestro coche.	Some cows crossed the highway in front of our car.
Por aquí pasan centenares de vehículos al día.	Hundreds of vehicles per day pass *by* here.

11. with *estar* meaning *to be in favor of.*

Estamos *por* salir.	We are *in favor of* leaving.

12. in certain idiomatic expressions such as *por la mañana, por fin, por ejemplo, por lo general,* etc.

Por la noche salgo con mis amigos.	*At night* I go out with my friends.
Por lo general en estas estaciones hace buen tiempo.	*In general* in these seasons it is good weather.

13. after certain nouns and verbs.

La comida comienza *por* los entremeses.	The meal begins *with* relishes.

B. The preposition *para* is usually translated by *for* or *(in order) to.* It is used in the following cases:

1. to introduce an infinitive to express purpose. [1]

Los amigos le oyen y bajan *para* subir las maletas.	The friends hear him and go down *to* take up the suitcases.
Los estudiantes pasan a la sala *para* esperar a la señora García.	The students go into the living room *to* wait for Mrs. García.
Se acostumbra a tomar una taza de café *para* ayudar a hacer la digestión.	It is the custom to take a cup of coffee *to* help digest the food.

2. to express suitability, destination or use with nouns.

Mi padre acaba de comprar una nueva bicicleta *para* mi hermana mayor.	My father has just bought a new bicycle *for* my oldest sister.

---

[1] With verbs of motion, *a* often replaces *para.* EXAMPLE: Vamos a salir pronto *a* comer. We are soon going out *to* eat.

| No tenían caballos ni ruedas ni hierro *para* sus construcciones. | They had neither horses nor wheels nor iron *for* their constructions. |
| Acapulco es un lugar divino *para* los perezosos. | Acapulco is a divine place *for* the lazy. |

3. to express destination with place names.

| Salimos a las ocho de la mañana *para* Monterrey. | We left at eight o'clock in the morning *for* Monterrey. |

4. to indicate a definite point of time.

| Le aconsejé que pidiese las vacaciones *para* el mes de julio. | I advised him to ask for his vacation *for* the month of July. |
| Le invita a don Juan *para* el día siguiente. | He invites don Juan *for* the following day. |

5. with *estar* meaning *to be about to*.

| Estamos *para* salir. | *We are about to* leave. |

6. to express the English *for* meaning *considering (that)*.

| Durante la comida se bebe vino, que, *para* lo bueno que es, en España se compra por poco dinero. | During the meal they drink wine, which, *considering* its good quality, can be bought for little money in Spain. |

46 / Verbs Governing Nouns With or Without a Preposition —
Verbos empleados con o sin preposición

In Spanish verbs often require a preposition before a noun or in some cases no preposition at all where in English there might be an entirely different preposition.

| Jugamos *al* ajedrez. | We play chess. |
| Se ríe *de* su hermano. | He laughs *at* his brother. |

The following constructions occur frequently in Spanish.

acercarse *a* la escuela	approach the school
alejarse *de* la ciudad	go away from the city
apoderarse *de* la capital	seize the capital
aprovecharse *de* la oportunidad	take advantage of the opportunity
asomarse *a* la ventana	peer out of the window

asustarse *de* la luz	be afraid of the light
buscar un hotel	look for a hotel
cambiar *de* vestidos	change clothes
casarse *con* una señorita	marry a young lady
componerse *de* provincias	be composed of provinces
confiar *en* los amigos	trust friends
consistir *en* varios capítulos	consist of various chapters
contar *con* su ayuda	count on his help
cubrir *de* nieve	cover with snow
cuidar *de* los animales[1]	take care of the animals
depender *de* una persona	depend on a person
despedirse *de* la familia	take leave of the family
dirigirse *a* la escuela	go toward the school
enterarse *de* la existencia	inform oneself of the existence
entrar *en* la casa[2]	enter the house
escaparse *de* la cárcel	escape from the prison
esperar una carta	wait for a letter
fijarse *en* los detalles	notice the details
gozar *de* buena salud	enjoy good health
interesarse *por* la cultura[3]	be interested in culture
jugar *al* básquetbol	play basketball
llegar *a* un país	arrive in a country
mirar un retrato	look at a picture
parecerse *a* su padre	resemble his father
partir[4] *de* Málaga	leave Malaga
pensar *en* los problemas[5]	think of (about) the problems
pertenecer *a* los niños	belong to the children
quejarse *de* su suerte	complain about his lot
reirse *de* la muchacha	laugh at the girl
romper *con* una costumbre	break with a custom
salir *de* una casa	leave a house
servir *de* criado	serve as a servant
sonreir *a* una cosa	smile at a thing
soñar *con* una fortuna	dream of a fortune

---

[1] Likewise one can say: *cuidar los animales*

[2] The verb *entrar* is also followed by *a*. EXAMPLE: Felipe entró *al* comedor. (Philip entered the dining room.)

[3] The verb *interesarse* is followed by *en* especially when there is a financial interest. EXAMPLE: El señor se interesa *en* aquella fábrica. (The gentleman is interested in that factory.)

[4] But *dejar* (+ PLACE) or *salir de* (+ PLACE) are ordinarily used to express the verb *leave*. The verb *partir* is rarely used.

[5] But in questions in which one is asked what he thinks of something, *de* follows *pensar*. EXAMPLE: ¿ Qué piensa usted *de* esta muchacha ? (What do you think of this girl?)

In English some verbs are followed directly by a dependent infinitive, and others require a preposition to connect the verb to a dependent infinitive. In English we say:

I can read.	No preposition between *can* and *read*.
I want *to* read.	The preposition *to* connects *want* and *read*.
I insist *on* reading.	The preposition *on* connects *insist* and *reading*.

There is no rule that governs which construction is to be used. It must be learned with each verb.

In Spanish verbs are also connected to dependent infinitives in various ways. In Spanish they say:

Quiero leer.	No preposition between *quiero* and *leer*.
Voy *a* leer.	The preposition *a* connects *voy* and *leer*.
Trato *de* leer.	The preposition *de* connects *trato* and *leer*.
Insisto *en* leer.	The preposition *en* connects *insisto* and *leer*.

There are a few helpful principles which govern which prepositions are used in Spanish but no infallible rules. The preposition must be learned with each verb.

A. The most common verbs requiring *no* preposition before an infinitive are:

aconsejar	advise to	hacer[5]	have
acordar	agree to	impedir	prevent from
conseguir	succeed in	lograr	succeed in
deber[1]	ought to	mandar	order to
decidir[2]	decide to	merecer	deserve to
dejar[3]	let	necesitar	need to
desear	desire to	oír[6]	hear
esperar	hope to	olvidar[7]	forget to
gustar[4]	be pleasing	parecer	seem to

---

[1] For the meanings of *deber*, see § 99.

[2] Notice that *decidir* + **infinitive** means *decide; decidirse a* + **infinitive** means *make up one's mind*.

[3] Notice that *dejar* + **infinitive** means *let* or *allow to; dejar de* + **infinitive** means *stop doing something*.

[4] Occasionally the expression *gustar de* is used, meaning *be fond of*.

[5] For *hacer* + **infinitive** to make the causative construction, see § 102 D.

[6] The verb *oír* is used with the infinitives *decir* and *hablar* in sentences such as *Oí decir que . . .* and *Oí hablar español*.

[7] Note the following constructions with *olvidar*, all of which mean *I forgot to telephone: Olvidé telefonear. Me olvidé de telefonear. Se me olvidó telefonear.*

pensar [1]	intend to	recordar	remember to
poder	be able to, can	rehusar	refuse to
preferir	prefer to	resolver	resolve to
procurar	try to	saber	know how to
prohibir	forbid to	soler	be accustomed to
prometer	promise to	temer	fear to
querer	wish to	ver	see

B. Verbs of motion, verbs meaning *to begin*, and many others are followed by *a* before an infinitive. The most common of these are:

acertar a	happen to, succeed	entrar a [3]	enter to
acostumbrarse a	become accustomed to	enviar a	send to
acudir a	hasten to	invitar a	invite to
aguardar a	wait to	ir a	go to, be going to
alcanzar a	chance to, succeed in	llegar a	chance to, come to,
aprender a	learn to		succeed in
apresurarse a	hurry to	negarse a	refuse to
atreverse a	dare to	obligar a	oblige to
ayudar a	help to	oponerse a	be opposed to
bajar a	go down to	persuadir a	persuade to
comenzar a	begin to	ponerse a	begin to
correr a	run to	prepararse a	prepare oneself to
convidar a	invite to	principiar a	begin to
decidirse a [2]	decide to	resolverse a	resolve to
dedicarse a	devote oneself to	salir a	go out to
echarse a	begin to	venir a	come to
empezar a	begin to	volver a	—— again [4]
enseñar a	teach to		

C. The most common verbs which take *de* are:

acabar de [5]	finish	cesar de	stop
acordarse de	remember	cuidar de	take care to
alegrarse de	be glad to	deber de [6]	must, be probably

---

[1] Note that *Pienso salir* means *I intend to leave* and *Pienso en salir* means *I am considering leaving.*
[2] Notice that *decidir* + **infinitive** means *decide; decidirse a* + **infinitive** means *make up one's mind.*
[3] Distinguish between *entrar en* + **noun** and *entrar a* + **infinitive**.
[4] A form of *volver a* followed immediately by the infinitive means *to do something again. Volví a hacerlo = I did it again.*
[5] Note that *acabar de* expresses both the idea of finishing and the idiom *to have just.*
[6] For the meanings of *deber*, see § 99.

dejar de [1]	stop	olvidarse de [3]	forget
encargarse de	take it upon oneself to	tratar de	try to
haber de [2]	be going to	tratarse de	be a question of

D. The most common verbs which take *en* with a dependent infinitive are:

consentir en	consent to	pensar en	consider
consistir en	consist of	ocuparse en	busy oneself by
convenir en	agree to	quedar en	agree on
empeñarse en	insist on	tardar en	delay in, take long in
insistir en	insist on		

CONJUNCTIONS—CONJUNCIONES

A conjunction is a word which connects words, phrases, and clauses. Some of the commonest English conjunctions are *and, but, or,* and *if.*

48 / *The Conjunctions* y *and* o — *Las conjunciones* y *y* o

A. The conjunction *y* becomes *e* before words beginning with the sound of *i* (spelled *i-* or *hi-*).

Carlota se puso furiosa *e* **hi**zo un viaje a París.	Carlota became furious *and* made a trip to Paris.
Luego visitamos unas típicas casas *e* **i**glesias antiguas.	Then we visited some typical houses *and* ancient churches.

B. The conjunction *o* becomes *u* before words beginning with the sound of *o* (spelled *o-* or *ho-*).

La gente viaja con pollos *u* **o**tros animales.	The people travel with chickens *or* other animals.

49 / *The Conjunction* but — *La conjunción* but [4]

A. The usual word for *but* is **pero.**

---

[1] Notice that *dejar* + **infinitive** means *let* or *allow to; dejar de* + **infinitive** means *stop doing something.*

[2] For the meanings of *haber,* see § 101.

[3] Note the following constructions with *olvidar,* all of which mean *I forgot to telephone: Olvidé telefonear. Me olvidé de telefonear. Se me olvidó telefonear.*

[4] In the sentence *All came* **but** *John,* the word **but** is a preposition and may be expressed by *menos, excepto* or *salvo.* EXAMPLE: *Todos vinieron* **menos** *Juan.*

Bolivia y Venezuela son países de Sud América, *pero* México no es un país de Sud América. | Bolivia and Venezuela are countries of South America, *but* Mexico is not a country of South America.

B. The word **mas** also means *but;* however, it is found only in literary style.

Mas al ver a su antigua amada, se negó a casarse con ella. | *But* on seeing his former loved-one, he refused to marry her.

C. The word **sino** also means *but* and is used only after a negative statement which is contrasted with an affirmative statement containing no finite verb.

El cuadro más conocido del Greco **no** está en el Prado *sino* en la iglesia de Santo Tomé | The best known painting of El Greco is **not** in El Prado *but* in the church of Santo Tomé.

La verdad es que Jaime **no** tiene sólo una novia *sino* varias. | The truth is that James has **not** just one girl friend *but* several.

D. The expression **sino que** is likewise used only after a negative statement but is followed by a clause containing a finite verb.

El maestro **no** solamente daba muchas clases diarias *sino que* también trabajaba en una fábrica. | **Not** only did the teacher have many classes each day *but* he also worked in a factory.

50 / Uses of si — Modos de usar la conjunción si

A. The conjunction **si** ordinarily means *if*.

Si la meseta central no es tan alta como las montañas, es mucho más elevada que la costa. | If the central plateau is not as high as the mountains, it is much higher than the coast.

When **si**[1] means *if*, it is never followed by the future or conditional as it often is in English nor by the present subjunctive.

Si Felipe *estudiara*, aprendería fácilmente. | If Philip *would study*. he would learn easily.

---

[1] For tenses to use with *si* in a conditional sentence, see § 96.

B. The conjunction **si** may also mean *whether*.

A ver *si* podemos llevarlas esta tarde al cine.	Let's see *whether* we can take them to the movies this afternoon.
Sería difícil decir dónde hay más belleza, *si* en su mar o en su campo.	It would be difficult to say where there is more beauty, *whether* in its sea or in its fields.

C. One sometimes finds **si** used in exclamations to mean *why* or *but*.

— ¡ *Si* es la verdadera razón !	*"Why,* it's the real reason!"

D. The conjunction **si** may precede the future or conditional of probability[1] to heighten the idea of supposition or conjecture.

— ¿ *Si* le habrá visto en el paseo ?	*"I wonder if* he could have seen him on the boulevard?"

MISCELLANY—MISCELÁNEA

51 / *Time — La hora*

A. The days[2] of the week are:

lunes[3]	Monday	viernes	Friday
martes	Tuesday	sábado	Saturday
miércoles	Wednesday	domingo	Sunday
jueves	Thursday		

B. The months[2] of the year are:

enero	January	julio	July
febrero	February	agosto	August
marzo	March	septiembre	September
abril	April	octubre	October
mayo	May	noviembre	November
junio	June	diciembre	December

---

[1] For the future and conditional of probability, see §§ 66 B, 68 B.

[2] In Spanish the days of the week and the months of the year are not usually capitalized, but there is a tendency at present to capitalize them.

[3] In Spain Monday is considered the first and Sunday the last day of the week. On Spanish calendars Monday will be found as the first day of the week.

C. The seasons of the year are:

la primavera	spring
el verano	summer
el otoño	autumn
el invierno	winter

D. The Spanish tell time as follows:

¿ Qué hora es ?	What time is it?
Son las ocho.	It is eight o'clock.
Son las ocho y media.	It is half past eight.
Son las ocho y cuarto.	It is quarter after eight.
Son las ocho menos cuarto.	It is quarter to eight.
Son las ocho y cinco.	It is five minutes after eight.
Son las ocho menos cinco.	It is five minutes to eight.
Son las ocho de la mañana.	It is eight o'clock in the morning (8 A.M.).
Son las ocho de la noche.	It is eight o'clock in the evening (8 P.M.).
Es la una.	It is one o'clock.
Es la una y media.	It is half past one.
A las cuatro . . .	At four o'clock . . .

E. In timetables and some formal announcements, the Spanish use the twenty-four hour method of telling time, but in current conversation the twelve-hour method is employed. The Spanish do not use A.M. and P.M. They say *las nueve de la mañana, las dos de la tarde, las once de la noche.*

52 / Augmentatives and Diminutives — *Aumentativos y diminutivos*

The Spanish language contains a great number of suffixes which are added to words in order to express large size (augmentatives) and smallness (diminutives). These suffixes are used in colloquial speech with a wide variety of figurative meanings. The most common augmentative endings denoting large size, depreciation, etc., are –ón and –azo.

el hombre	el hombrón	*the big bad man* or *the big man*
el toro	el torazo	*the big mean bull* or *the mean bull*

The most common diminutive endings expressing smallness, affection, and a great number of special meanings are –ito, –cito, –ecito, –illo, –ecillo, and –cillo.

la casa	la casita	*the little house*
el pobre	el pobrecito	*the poor little thing*
el libro	el librito	*the little book*
la mano	la manecilla	*the little hand*

Diminutives are added to adjectives and adverbs as well as nouns.

María tiene la mano *pequeñita*.
Mary's hand is *very small*.

Ahorita[1] viene.
He is coming *right now*.

53 / The Use of ya — *Modo de usar* ya

The meaning of the adverb **ya** varies according to the tense with which it is used.

A. With past tenses it means *already*.

Encontramos una larga cola de gente que *ya* estaba esperando.
We found a long line of people who were *already* waiting.

B. With the present tense it often means *now* but may add an emphatic tone to the statement difficult to translate into English.

Ya sabes que antiguamente había un gran lago en el valle de México.
You (*indeed*) know that in olden days there was a large lake in the valley of Mexico.

Pero *ya* basta de ciudades.
But enough of cities *now*.

Ya entramos en el Paseo del Prado.
Now we are entering the Paseo del Prado.

C. With the future it often means *later* or *soon*.

Ya vendré.
I'll come *later*.

Ya sabré como debo hacerlo.
Then I'll know how I should do it.

D. The combination **ya no** means *no longer*.

Pero *ya no* puedo escribirle más por hoy.
But I can *not* write *any more* for today.

E. The combination **ya que** means *since*.

Ya que he viajado algo por España, puedo decirle muchas cosas sobre los trenes españoles.
Since I have traveled somewhat through Spain, I can tell you many things concerning the Spanish trains.

---

[1] The diminutive *ahorita* is very current in Mexico but not in Spain.

Ordinary Spanish word order is much more flexible than English word order. The following English sentence might be said in four different ways in Spanish:

Robert meets two students
in front of the house.

> Roberto encuentra a dos estudiantes delante de la casa.
>
> Roberto encuentra delante de la casa a dos estudiantes.
>
> Encuentra Roberto a dos estudiantes delante de la casa.
>
> Delante de la casa encuentra Roberto a dos estudiantes.

This word order tends to make the Spanish language very colorful, but it also renders it more difficult for an English-speaking person to read.

The following hints concerning affirmative word order may be helpful.

A. The subject often follows the verb, especially when it is longer than the predicate.

Cerca de la ciudad colonial de Taxco **se fabrican y se venden** *muchos artículos de plata.*

Near the colonial city of Taxco *many articles of silver* **are manufactured and sold.**

Existen *casi cien dialectos indios.*

Almost a hundred Indian dialects **exist**

B. In dependent clauses the subject generally follows its verb.

Pero también hay muchos barrios donde **viven** *los obreros* en casas bastante elegantes.

But there are also many districts where *the workingmen* **live** in rather elegant houses.

El mexicano emplea algunas palabras que no **usan** *los españoles.*

The Mexican employs some words that *the Spanish* **do** not **use.**

C. The two parts of a compound tense are not separated.

Los mexicanos **siempre** *han tenido* gran habilidad artística.

The Mexicans *have* **always** *had* great artistic ability.

D. Frequently the adjective *otro* does not immediately precede its noun but places other adjectives such as numerals, *mucho,* and *poco* between itself and the noun.

| Delante de la puerta hay **otros** *dos* estudiantes. | In front of the door are *two* **other** students. |

E. Contrary to English usage, cardinal numerals precede ordinals.

| Estudiamos las **diez** *primeras* lecciones. | We are studying the *first* **ten** lessons. |

55 / Interrogative Word Order — La frase interrogativa

A. The ordinary way of making a declarative sentence interrogative is to place the verb before the subject.[1]

STATEMENT	QUESTION
La capital tiene muchos habitantes.	¿ **Tiene** *la capital* muchos habitantes ?
Usted vive cerca de la universidad.	¿ **Vive** *usted* cerca de la universidad ?

B. In questions the word order is often

$$\text{VERB} + \begin{cases} \text{ADVERB} \\ \text{NOUN OBJECT} \\ \text{PREDICATE ADJECTIVE} \end{cases} + \text{SUBJECT}$$

STATEMENT	QUESTION
Felipe canta bien.	¿ Canta bien Felipe ?
Las casas mexicanas tienen patios.	¿ Tienen patios las casas mexicanas ?
Las calles mexicanas son muy estrechas.	¿ Son muy estrechas las calles mexicanas ?

C. But a subject which is shorter than the noun object and its modifiers normally follows the verb immediately. Much in interrogative word order depends on the rhythm of the sentence.

STATEMENT	QUESTION
La gente pobre vive en las afueras de las ciudades mexicanas.	¿ Vive la gente pobre en las afueras de las ciudades mexicanas ?
Su padre tiene su silla en el patio.	¿ Tiene su padre su silla en el patio ?

---

[1] For the punctuation of an interrogative sentence, see PRONUNCIATION § 4 B 1.

D. The placing of the expressions *¿ verdad ?* or *¿ no es verdad ?* or simply *¿ no ?* after a declarative sentence turns it into a question.[1]

La puntualidad es muy importante ¿ verdad ?   Punctuality is very important, *isn't it?*

THE VERB—EL VERBO

A verb is a word which shows action or state of being. Every complete sentence must have a verb. EXAMPLES: The boy *runs*. We *ate* dinner. He *is* tired. They *will seem* interested.

I. Organization of the Spanish Verb — Organización del verbo español

56 / The Spanish Verb — El verbo español

A. The Spanish verb[2] is divided into three main groups of regular verbs known as conjugations:

> 1. *-ar* verbs
> 2. *-er* verbs
> 3. *-ir* verbs

B. The tenses of the verbs are formed on stems. Regular verbs have only one stem, which might be called the *infinitive stem*. Irregular verbs have an infinitive stem and sometimes several other stems. These stems are discussed in § 109 A, B.

C. The *infinitive stem* of a verb is found by taking the infinitive ending *-ar*, *-er*, or *-ir* from the infinitive.

INFINITIVE	INFINITIVE STEM
hablar	habl–
comer	com–
vivir	viv–

---

[1] The Spanish *¿ verdad ?* is equivalent to the French *n'est-ce pas ?* and the German *nicht wahr ?*

[2] For the conjugation of the verbs, see § 110.

A. The Spanish verb is divided into simple and compound tenses, as follows:

SIMPLE TENSES	COMPOUND TENSES
present	perfect
imperfect	pluperfect
preterite	preterite perfect
future	future perfect
conditional	conditional perfect

B. These tenses are commonly translated as follows:

Simple Tenses

TENSE	SPANISH 3D PERSON SINGULAR FORM	ENGLISH TRANSLATION
present	habla	he speaks, he is speaking, he does speak
imperfect	hablaba	he spoke, he was speaking
preterite	habló	he spoke, he did speak
future	hablará	he will speak
conditional	hablaría	he would speak

Compound Tenses

perfect	ha hablado	he has spoken
pluperfect	había hablado	he had spoken
preterite perfect	hubo hablado	he had spoken
future perfect	habrá hablado	he will have spoken
conditional perfect	habría hablado	he would have spoken

II. Formation and Use of Tenses and Other Parts of the Verb — Formación y empleo de los tiempos y otras partes del verbo

58 / *Formation of the Present Tense — Formación del presente* [1]

A. The *–ar* verbs form their present tense by adding to the infinitive stem [2] (——) the following endings:

---

[1] The present of reflexive verbs will be found in § 105 B, the present of radical-changing verbs in § 106 A, the present of orthographical-changing verbs in § 107, and the conjugation of models of all types of verbs in § 110.

[2] The formation of the infinitive stem is explained in § 56 C.

yo ——o		nosotros ——amos	
tú ——as		vosotros ——áis	
él[1] ——a		ellos[2] ——an	

B. The *-er* verbs form their present tense by adding to the infinitive stem[2] (——) the following endings:

yo ——o		nosotros ——emos	
tú ——es		vosotros ——éis	
él[1] ——e		ellos[2] ——en	

C. The *–ir* verbs form their present tense by adding to the infinitive stem[3] (——) the following endings:

yo ——o		nosotros ——imos	
tú ——es		vosotros ——ís	
él[1] ——e		ellos[2] ——en	

D. The following common verbs are irregular in the present and must be learned if one is to speak Spanish correctly. Many of these verbs are irregular only in the *yo* form, but a few of them, such as *ir* and *ser*, are irregular throughout.

caer	dar	decir	estar	haber	hacer	ir
caigo	doy	digo	estoy	he	hago	voy
caes[4]	*das*	*dices*	*estás*	*has*	*haces*	*vas*
cae	da	dice	está	ha	hace	va
caemos	damos	decimos	estamos	hemos	hacemos	vamos
caéis[4]	*dais*	*decís*	*estáis*	*habéis*	*hacéis*	*vais*
caen	dan	dicen	están	han	hacen	van

oír	poder	poner	querer	saber	salir
oigo	puedo	pongo	quiero	sé	salgo
oyes	*puedes*	*pones*	*quieres*	*sabes*	*sales*
oye	puede	pone	quiere	sabe	sale
oímos	podemos	ponemos	queremos	sabemos	salimos
oís	*podéis*	*ponéis*	*queréis*	*sabéis*	*salís*
oyen	pueden	ponen	quieren	saben	salen

[1] In all tables and paradigms, the *él* form represents equally the *ella* and *usted* forms, which are always identical.

[2] In all tables and paradigms, the *ellos* form represents equally the *ellas* and *ustedes* forms, which are always identical.

[3] The formation of the infinitive stem is explained in § 56 D.

[4] The *tú* and *vosotros* forms are given in italics to permit students who are not learning them to disregard them in studying these paradigms.

GRAMMAR § 58

ser	tener	traer	valer	venir	ver
soy	tengo	traigo	valgo	vengo	veo
eres	*tienes*	*traes*	*vales*	*vienes*	*ves*
es	tiene	trae	vale	viene	ve
somos	tenemos	traemos	valemos	venimos	vemos
sois	*tenéis*	*traéis*	*valéis*	*venís*	*veis*
son	tienen	traen	valen	vienen	ven

59 / Uses of the Present Tense — Modo de usar el presente

A. In Spanish as in English the present is used to express an action which is taking place in the present or which takes place in general.

El indio que *vive* en la ciudad *habla* español. — The Indian who *lives* in the city *speaks* Spanish.

Escribo poesías, pero no *soy* buen poeta. — I *write* poetry, but I *am* not a good poet.

But in English there are three ways of expressing a present action, which may all be expressed in Spanish by the simple present.

TYPES OF PRESENT TENSE

	in English	*in Spanish*
SIMPLE	he eats	
PROGRESSIVE [1]	he is eating	come
EMPHATIC	he does eat	

B. 1. Consider the tenses of the following sentences.

Llueve desde ayer. — It *has been raining* since yesterday.

Marta *canta* desde hace dos horas — Martha *has been singing* for two hours.

Hace diez minutos que Roberto *habla*. — Robert *has been talking* for ten minutes.

In each sentence, the action began in the past and is continuing in the present. In each case, Spanish uses the *present tense*, English the *present perfect*. Thus, we may say:

---

[1] Spanish has also a progressive form similar to the English progressive form, which is explained in § 83 A, B.

The present tense is used with a certain number of expressions of time, such as **desde, desde hace, desde que,** and **hace ... que** (which are equivalent to *for* or *since* in English) to express an action which has begun in the past and is continuing in the present. English ordinarily uses the present perfect to express such actions.

2. Consider the nature and position of the time expressions in the following sentences.

Usted trabaja **desde 1960.**	You have been working **since 1960.**
Estamos aquí **desde esta mañana.**	We have been here **since this morning.**
¿**Desde cuándo** estudia usted francés ?	**Since when** have you been studying French?
Desde el principio del siglo XX millares de campesinos llegan a Barcelona.	**Since the beginning of the twentieth century** thousands of farmers have been arriving in Barcelona.

Note that when **desde** is followed by a definite point of time, such as a definite year, a definite part of the day, etc., it conserves its literal meaning *since*.

* * *

3.

Estamos aquí **desde hace una hora.**	We have been here **for an hour.**
Aprendo francés **desde hace dos meses.**	I have been learning French **for two months.**

The expression **desde hace**[1] (rendered in English by *for*) usually comes after the verb and is followed by a statement of space of time involved.

* * *

Hace una hora que estamos aquí.	We have been here **for an hour.**
Hace dos meses que aprendo francés.	I have been learning French **for two months.**

The expression **Hace ... que**[2] (rendered in English by *for*) usually comes at the beginning of the sentence. The space of time is stated between **hace** and **que**.

---

[1] Literally, *desde hace* means *since it makes*, so that literally, the first sentence above would be translated: *We are here since it makes an hour*, therefore, *We have been here* **since an hour ago.** (See § 102 B.)

[2] Literally, *Hace ... que* means *it makes that*, so that literally, the first sentence above would be translated: *It makes an hour that we are here.*

A. The *-ar* verbs form their imperfect tense by adding to the infinitive stem (——) the following endings:

yo ——aba	nosotros ——ábamos
tú ——abas	vosotros ——ábais
él ——aba	ellos ——aban

B. The *-er* and *-ir* verbs form their imperfect tense by adding to the infinitive stem (——) the following endings:

yo ——ía	nosotros ——íamos
tú ——ías	vosotros ——íais
él ——ía	ellos ——ían

C. Only three verbs are irregular in the imperfect. They are:

ir	ser	ver
iba	era	veía
ibas	*eras*	*veías*
iba	era	veía
íbamos	éramos	veíamos
ibais	*erais*	*veíais*
iban	eran	veían

61 / Uses of the Imperfect Tense — *Modo de usar el imperfecto*

A. The imperfect tense is called so because basically it indicates an incomplete action or state of being. The imperfect is used for background, accessory or incidental actions which set the scene for the principal actions. Note in the following example how the italicized verbs, which are in the imperfect, form a background for what happened but do not actually indicate the principal actions.

A la mañana siguiente me desperté temprano. La luz *entraba* por la ventana de mi cuarto y los pájaros *cantaban* fuera; de vez en cuando un automóvil *pasaba* por la carretera. Me levanté en seguida y cuando bajé, vi que el profesor y su esposa ya *estaban* en el comedor. *Comían* huevos con jamón, porque en el hotel donde *estábamos paraban* muchos norteamericanos y el dueño *sabía* que a los turistas les gustan mucho los huevos con jamón.

---

[1] The Spanish often call this tense the *pretérito imperfecto*.

B. Three common ways in which the imperfect forms a background for the principal actions are:

1. to express a condition, often a description or a state of mind during a period of time in the past.

Vimos muchos indios que *culti-vaban* campos de maíz y todos ellos *estaban* vestidos con sara-pes que *llevaban* encima de sus típicos trajes blancos.	We saw many Indians who *were cultivating* fields of corn and they all *were* dressed in serapes which they *wore* over their typical white suits.

2. to express a continued[1] past action which is interrupted by some other action. This is ordinarily expressed in English by *was* or *were* and the present participle.

El profesor y su esposa *comían* cuando Roberto entró en el comedor.	The teacher and his wife *were eating* when Robert entered the dining room.

3. to express a customary, habitual, or repeated action in past time. This is ordinarily expressed in English by *used to* or *would* with the infinitive.

Los niños *pasaban* la mañana trabajando en la clase y la tarde jugando a la pelota.	The children *spent* (*used to spend*) the morning working in class and the afternoon playing ball.
Mi tío *salía* a las siete de la mañana para llegar a la fábrica a las ocho y *volvía* a casa por la noche.	My uncle *left* (or *used to leave* or *would leave*) at seven o'clock in the morning in order to get to the factory at eight and *returned* (or *used to return* or *would return*) home at night.

C. The imperfect is used with **hacía . . . que, desde hacía,** and **desde que** (which are equivalent to *for* or *since* in English) to express an action which began in the remote past and continued up to a given time in the past when something else took place. English uses the pluperfect progressive to express this concept.

---

[1] Learners often believe erroneously that all continued past actions should be in the imperfect. This is false. The criterion for the imperfect is not whether the action was continued (for all actions, however short, are continued over some period of time), but whether the action did or did not have a definite beginning and end in the particular situation at hand. If the beginning or end existed, then the imperfect would not be used.

Expulsaron a los moros que *habitaban* en España **desde hacía casi ochocientos años.**	They expelled the Moors who *had been living* in Spain **for almost eight hundred years.**
Desde hacía algunos años los barcos españoles y portugueses *hacían* viajes de exploración.	**For some years** the Spanish and Portuguese boats *had been making* voyages of exploration.
Hacía ya algunos años que el protestantismo *se extendía* por Europa.	**For some years** now protestantism *had been spreading* over Europe.

62 / Formation of the Preterite — Formación del pretérito [1]

A. The *-ar* verbs form their preterite tense by adding to the infinitive stem (——) the following endings:

yo ——é	nosotros ——amos
tú ——aste	vosotros ——asteis
él ——ó	ellos ——aron

B. The *-er* and *-ir* verbs form their preterite tense by adding to the infinitive stem (——) the following endings:

yo ——í	nosotros ——imos
tú ——iste	vosotros ——isteis
él ——ió	ellos ——ieron

C. But there are a number of common irregular verbs in the preterite, and these verbs add their endings to a special stem, different from the infinitive stem, which is called the *preterite stem*.

1. Three of these verbs are completely irregular and must be learned without rule. They are:

dar	**ir**	**ser**
di [2]	fui [2]	fui [2]
diste	*fuiste*	*fuiste*
dio [2]	fue [2]	fue [2]
dimos	fuimos	fuimos
disteis	*fuisteis*	*fuisteis*
dieron	fueron	fueron

---

[1] The Spanish often call this tense the *pretérito indefinido*. The preterite of radical-changing verbs will be found in § 106 B, the preterite of orthographical-changing verbs in § 107, and the conjugation of models of all types of verbs in § 110.

[2] Formerly, these forms were written with an accent: *dí, dió, fuí, fué.*

2. The other irregular verbs form their preterites by adding to their special preterite stems (——) the following endings:

yo ——e	nosotros ——imos
tú ——iste	vosotros ——isteis
él ——o	ellos ——ieron

These verbs with their special preterite stems are:

INFINITIVE	PRETERITE STEM	PRETERITE	
		yo	*ellos*
andar	anduv–	anduve	anduvieron
caber	cup–	cupe	cupieron
decir	dij–	dije	dijeron[2]
-ducir[1]	–duj–	–duje	–dujeron[2]
estar	estuv–	estuve	estuvieron
haber	hub–	hube	hubieron
hacer	hic–	hice[3]	hicieron
poder	pud–	pude	pudieron
poner	pus–	puse	pusieron
querer	quis–	quise	quisieron
saber	sup–	supe	supieron
satisfacer	satisfic–	satisfice[4]	satisficieron
tener	tuv–	tuve	tuvieron
traer	traj–	traje	trajeron[2]
venir	vin–	vine	vinieron

63 / Uses of the Preterite — Modos de usar el pretérito

A. The preterite is the past tense which is used to recount the successive main actions in a narrative. Note in the following example how the italicized forms show a series of successive actions, each one of which contributes to forwarding the narrative.

Los oficiales me *hablaron* en español, los *entendí* perfectamente, y les *contesté* en el mismo idioma. No *abrieron* más que una de mis maletas, y a

---

[1] This stem represents all verbs in *-ducir*, such as *conducir*, *introducir*, and *traducir*. For a more complete discussion of these verbs, see § 107 F.

[2] When the preterite stem ends in *-j-*, the *-i-* of the *-ieron* ending is absorbed in the *-j-*.

[3] The third person singular preterite of *hacer* is *hizo*. This is to preserve a uniform sound throughout the tense.

[4] The third person singular preterite of *satisfacer* is *satisfizo*. This is to preserve a uniform sound throughout the tense.

los cinco minutos *salí* de la aduana, *cambié* algunos dólares por pesos mexicanos, y *me encaminé* hacia el centro de Nuevo Laredo.

B. The preterite is often used to state a fact which, in the speaker's mind, is a completed whole regardless of duration.

La civilización más avanzada del valle de México *fue* la de los toltecas.	The most advanced civilization of the valley of Mexico *was* that of the Toltecs.

64 / Combined Uses of the Preterite and the Imperfect —
Modo de usar combinados el pretérito y el imperfecto

In narration there are usually two types of actions: those which recount the main events of the story and those which give background to what happens but have little to do with the actual forwarding action of the story. The main events are in the preterite, the background actions are in the imperfect.

In the following example the italicized verbs, which are in the imperfect, create a background for the main action. The verbs in boldface, which are in the preterite, narrate what happened and are main actions. Keep in mind that it is the speaker who determines which actions or states are background, which are forwarding narration.

En la facultad de medicina los estudiantes *entraban* y *salían*, los profesores *explicaban* sus materias, y en los laboratorios se *estudiaban* las ciencias biológicas. Por fin **salió** Carlos y **saludó** a su amigo Roberto que le *esperaba* fuera.

— ¿ Quiere usted ver el interior de la facultad ?

— ¡ Cómo no !

Después de pasar por varios laboratorios interesantes, los amigos **entraron** en una clase — un aula donde *se enseñaba* anatomía. Detrás de la mesa del profesor *había* una lámina de anatomía y una pizarra, y delante de la mesa *estaban* los asientos de los estudiantes.

— Debe de ser muy interesante el estudio de la medicina — **dijo** Roberto.

B. The use of the imperfect and the preterite to express mental and physical states is of particular importance.

MENTAL STATES

Imperfect	*Preterite*
The imperfect describes a state of mind not specifically limited in time.	The preterite often indicates a change of state of mind.

Pedro *sabía* que usted llegaría mañana.

Peter *knew* that you would arrive tomorrow.

Yo *pensaba* que usted lo haría.

I *thought* that you would do it.

María *tenía miedo* de que usted saliera.

Mary *was afraid* that you would go out.

Creía que lo harían.

I *thought* that they would do it.

Pedro **supo** por Jorge que usted llegaría mañana.

Peter **found out** from George that you would arrive tomorrow.

De repente **pensé** que usted lo haría.

Suddenly **it occurred to me** that you would do it.

María **tuvo miedo** de que usted saliera.

Mary **became afraid** that you would go out.

Creí que lo harían.

I *once thought* that they would do it.

PHYSICAL STATES

Imperfect

The imperfect describes a physical state which forms a background for something else which happened.

Yo *tenía mucho calor* cuando volvimos a casa.

I *was very warm* when we returned home.

Hacía frío anoche cuando llegamos a casa.

It was cold last night when we arrived home.

Preterite

The preterite often describes the beginning of a physical state which may be expressed in English by *got* or *became*.

Tuve mucho calor cuando volvimos a casa.

I **became very warm** when we returned home.

Hizo frío anoche después de que volvimos a casa.

It **got cold** last night after we arrived home.

When the physical state is definitely limited in time, it is normally expressed by the preterite even though it takes place over a period of time.

Hizo calor toda la semana.

Tuve dolor de cabeza durante tres días.

It was warm the whole week.

I had a headache for three days.

65 / Formation of the Future — *Formación del futuro*

In English the future is formed by the use of the auxiliary verbs *shall* and *will* and is conjugated: *I shall speak, you will speak, he will speak,* etc.[1]

---

[1] Current American usage conjugates the future: *I will speak, you will speak, he will speak,* etc., or *I'll speak, you'll speak, he'll speak,* etc.

A. In Spanish the future is formed by adding to the infinitive a set of endings [1] which are really the present of *haber* without the *h-*: (*h*)*e*, (*h*)*as*, (*h*)*a*, (*h*)*emos*, (*hab*)*éis*, (*h*)*an*. In the following table the —— represents the infinitive.

yo ——é	nosotros ——emos
tú ——ás	vosotros ——éis
él ——á	ellos ——án

B. The endings of the future are always the same, but there are eleven common verbs which have slightly irregular stems. These verbs are:

1. those that drop the greater part of their stem:

decir	hacer
diré	haré
dirás	*harás*
dirá	hará
diremos	haremos
diréis	*haréis*
dirán	harán

2. those that drop the *-e-* of the infinitive ending:

haber	poder	querer	saber
habré	podré	querré	sabré
habrás	*podrás*	*querrás*	*sabrás*
habrá	podrá	querrá	sabrá
habremos	podremos	querremos	sabremos
habréis	*podréis*	*querréis*	*sabréis*
habrán	podrán	querrán	sabrán

3. those that insert *-d-* between the stem and the *-r* of the infinitive for reasons of pronunciation:

poner	salir	tener	valer	venir
pondré	saldré	tendré	valdré	vendré
pondrás	*saldrás*	*tendrás*	*valdrás*	*vendrás*
pondrá	saldrá	tendrá	valdrá	vendrá
pondremos	saldremos	tendremos	valdremos	vendremos
pondréis	*saldréis*	*tendréis*	*valdréis*	*vendréis*
pondrán	saldrán	tendrán	valdrán	vendrán

---

[1] The future like all other Spanish tenses except the present, the imperfect, and the preterite is in reality a compound tense. We can trace it back to before 1000 A.D. and it was sometimes written as two words (*hablar he*, etc.) as late as the sixteenth century.

A. The Spanish future, like the English, expresses actions which will take place at some future time.

Desde ahora *hablaremos* de cosas más interesantes.	From now on *we'll speak* of more interesting things.

B. The Spanish future is often used to indicate what the speaker feels is probably true in the present.

Como oigo sonar el teléfono, supongo que ya me *estará esperando* abajo.	As I hear the telephone ringing, I suppose that *he must* already *be waiting for* me down below.
Este señor *tendrá* mucho dinero.	This man *must have* (*probably has*) a great deal of money.

C. In interrogative sentences, the Spanish future may indicate conjecture or supposition.

¿ Qué *harán* allá ?	What *can they be* *do you suppose they are* *doing* there?

67 / Formation of the Conditional — *Formación del condicional* [1]

In English the conditional is formed by the use of the auxiliary verbs *should* and *would* and is conjugated: *I should speak, you would speak, he would speak*, etc. [2]

A. In Spanish the conditional is formed by adding to the infinitive the endings [3] which are added to the infinitive stem to form the imperfect of *-er* and *-ir* verbs. In the following table, the —— represents the infinitive.

yo ——ía	nosotros ——íamos
tú ——ías	vosotros ——íais
él ——ía	ellos ——ían

---

[1] The Spanish often call the conditional *el modo potencial*.

[2] Current American usage conjugates the conditional: *I would speak, you would speak, he would speak*, etc., or *I'd speak, you'd speak, he'd speak*, etc.

[3] These endings are in reality shortened forms of the imperfect indicative of the verb *haber*.

B. The endings of the conditional are always the same, but the eleven common verbs which are irregular in the future[1] have the same irregularities in the conditional. The verbs, with the *yo* form of the conditional are:

INFINITIVE	CONDITIONAL	INFINITIVE	CONDITIONAL
	yo		*yo*
decir	diría	poner	pondría
hacer	haría	salir	saldría
haber	habría	tener	tendría
poder	podría	valer	valdría
querer	querría	venir	vendría
saber	sabría		

68 / Uses of the Conditional — Modo de usar el condicional

A. The conditional is used to express a future action depending upon another action which is usually in the past.

Diego le prometió a Inés que a su regreso *se casaría* con ella.	Diego promised Inez that on his return he *would marry* her.

B. The conditional often conveys the idea of conjecture or probability in the past.

Alguien llamó a la puerta. *¿ Sería Roberto ?*	Someone knocked at the door. *Could it be* Robert?
Un pretendiente, pensando que ella *tendría* otro amante, la espió durante día y noche.	A suitor, thinking that she *must have (probably had)* another lover, spied on her day and night.

C. The conditional is often used in the result clause of a contrary-to-fact condition when the verb in the if-clause is in the imperfect subjunctive.[2]

Si el suelo español fuese más rico, seguramente *habría* más comida.	If the Spanish soil were richer, there *would* certainly *be* more food.
Si hubiera más minerales y más energía eléctrica, el país *gozaría* de más ventajas y la gente *sería* menos pobre.	If there were more minerals and more electric power, the country *would enjoy* more advantages and the people *would be* less poor.

---

[1] For the verbs which are irregular in the future, see § 65 B.
[2] For the discussion of conditional sentences, see § 96.

A compound tense is one which is made up of an auxiliary and some part of the main verb. EXAMPLES: *we have seen, they had eaten, I shall find.*

In Spanish the principal compound tenses and their composition is as follows:

Perfect	Perfecto	present of *haber*	past
Pluperfect	Pluscuamperfecto	imperfect of *haber*	participle
Preterite Perfect	Pretérito Perfecto	preterite of *haber*	+ of
Future Perfect	Futuro Perfecto	future of *haber*	main
Conditional Perfect	Condicional Perfecto	conditional of *haber*	verb

70 / Formation of the Perfect — Formación del perfecto

In English the perfect tense is composed of the **present tense** of the auxiliary verb *have* and the **past participle** of the main verb.

I have spoken	we have spoken
you have spoken	you have spoken
he has spoken	they have spoken

In Spanish the perfect tense is composed of the **present tense** of the auxiliary verb *haber* and the **past participle** of the main verb.

hablar	comer	vivir
he hablado	he comido	he vivido
has hablado	*has comido*	*has vivido*
ha hablado	ha comido	ha vivido
hemos hablado	hemos comido	hemos vivido
habéis hablado	*habéis comido*	*habéis vivido*
han hablado	han comido	han vivido

71 / Uses of the Perfect — Modo de usar el perfecto

A. The Spanish perfect is used in general as the English perfect.

Estos artistas *han pintado* la historia de México en los muros de los edificios públicos.

These artists *have painted* the history of Mexico on the walls of the public buildings.

B. Especially in conversation the Spanish perfect is often used to express a simple past action.

En una tarde *he visto* muchas casas. In one afternoon I *saw* many houses.

C. In general, the perfect is used when the action is within a given unit of time, usually linked to the present, such as *esta mañana, esta semana, este año,* and the preterite when the action is before that unit of time, such as *ayer, la semana pasada, el año pasado,* etc.

Esta mañana *he escrito* dos cartas.	This morning I *wrote* two letters.
Ayer *escribí* dos cartas.	Yesterday I *wrote* two letters.

72 / Formation of the Pluperfect — Formación del pluscuamperfecto

In English the pluperfect tense is composed of the **past tense** of the auxiliary verb *have* and the **past participle** of the main verb.

I had spoken	we had spoken
you had spoken	you had spoken
he had spoken	they had spoken

In Spanish the pluperfect tense is composed of the **imperfect** of the auxiliary verb *haber* and the **past participle** of the main verb.

hablar	comer	vivir
había hablado	había comido	había vivido
habías hablado	*habías comido*	*habías vivido*
había hablado	había comido	había vivido
habíamos hablado	habíamos comido	habíamos vivido
habíais hablado	*habíais comido*	*habíais vivido*
habían hablado	habían comido	habían vivido

73 / Use of the Pluperfect — Modo de usar el pluscuamperfecto

The pluperfect is used to indicate a past action which took place before another past action.

México *había ganado* su independencia pero la mayoría de sus habitantes todavía no tenían libertad.	Mexico *had won* her independence but the majority of her inhabitants did not yet have liberty.

74 / Formation of the Preterite Perfect — Formación del pretérito perfecto

The preterite perfect is a compound tense consisting of the **preterite** of the auxiliary verb *haber* and the **past participle**. It does not exist in English, which generally uses the pluperfect to express the same type of action.

hablar	comer	vivir
hube hablado	hube comido	hube vivido
hubiste hablado	*hubiste comido*	*hubiste vivido*
hubo hablado	hubo comido	hubo vivido
hubimos hablado	hubimos comido	hubimos vivido
hubisteis hablado	*hubisteis comido*	*hubisteis vivido*
hubieron hablado	hubieron comido	hubieron vivido

75 / Use of the Preterite Perfect — Modo de usar el pretérito perfecto

The preterite perfect is used in literary style with conjunctions of time such as *apenas, cuando, después (de) que, luego que*, etc., to indicate an action which took place immediately before another action when this second action is expressed by the preterite.

Muchos novelistas, después de que *hubieron observado* las costumbres del pueblo español, **escribieron** no solamente para distraer a sus lectores sino también para que éstos se enteraran de los problemas nacionales.	Many novelists, after they *had observed* the customs of the Spanish people, **wrote** not only to amuse their readers but also so that the latter might become aware of the national problems.

76 / Formation of the Future Perfect — Formación del futuro perfecto

In English the future perfect tense is composed of the **future** of the auxiliary verb *have* and the **past participle** of the main verb. It is conjugated: *I shall have spoken, you will have spoken, etc.*

In Spanish the future perfect tense is composed of the **future** of the auxiliary verb *haber* and the **past participle** of the main verb.

hablar	comer	vivir
habré hablado	habré comido	habré vivido
habrás hablado	*habrás comido*	*habrás vivido*
habrá hablado	habrá comido	habrá vivido
habremos hablado	habremos comido	habremos vivido
habréis hablado	*habréis comido*	*habréis vivido*
habrán hablado	habrán comido	habrán vivido

77 / Uses of the Future Perfect — Modo de usar el futuro perfecto

A. The Spanish future perfect, like the English, is used to indicate an action which will have taken place when another action occurs.

Habremos acabado nuestro trabajo cuando usted llegue.	*We shall have finished* our work when you arrive.

B. The future perfect frequently expresses what was probably true in the past up to and including the present.

Y tengo tanta sed que creo que hoy ya *habré bebido* más de tres litros de agua.	And I am so thirsty that I believe that today I *must have* already *drunk* (*probably have drunk*) more than three quarts of water.

78 / Formation of the Conditional Perfect — *Formación del condicional perfecto*

In English the conditional perfect tense is composed of the **conditional** of the auxiliary verb *have* and the **past participle** of the main verb. It is conjugated: *I should have spoken, you would have spoken, etc.*

In Spanish the conditional perfect tense is composed of the **conditional** of the auxiliary verb *haber* and the **past participle** of the main verb.

hablar	comer	vivir
habría hablado	habría comido	habría vivido
habrías hablado	*habrías comido*	*habrías vivido*
habría hablado	habría comido	habría vivido
habríamos hablado	habríamos comido	habríamos vivido
habríais hablado	*habríais comido*	*habríais vivido*
habrían hablado	habrían comido	habrían vivido

79 / Uses of the Conditional Perfect — *Modo de usar el condicional perfecto*

A. The conditional perfect indicates the probability of a past action which took place before another past action.

¿ Nos *habrían oído* ?	*Could* they *have heard* us?

B. The conditional perfect is often used in the result clause of a contrary-to-fact condition.[1]

Si no hubieras pasado tanto tiempo	If you had not spent so much time

---

[1] For the discussion of conditional sentences, see § 96.

hablando por teléfono, *habríamos podido* ir al supermercado.

talking over the telephone, *we would have been able* to go to the supermarket.

80 / *The Infinitive — El infinitivo*

In English the infinitive is the general form of the verb normally preceded by *to*. EXAMPLES: *to work, to live, to have*. No specific person or time is indicated by the infinitive form. On the other hand, other forms of the verb have endings which indicate person and time. EXAMPLES: he *works*, you *will live*, we *had*.

A. In Spanish the infinitive ends in *-ar*, *-er*, or *-ir*.

trabajar	to work
tener	to have
vivir	to live

B. In Spanish the infinitive is often used after an adjective or a verb to complete the meaning of the sentence.

Es *más fácil* **trabajar** en un clima agradable.

It is *easier* **to work** in an agreeable climate.

¿*Quiere* usted **ver** el cuarto y **hablar** con la señora García?

Do you *want* **to see** the room and **(to) speak** with Mrs. García?

C. In Spanish the infinitive is used as a verbal noun. In English we use either the infinitive or the gerund.

(*El*) *viajar* es muy divertido.

To travel } is very amusing.
Traveling }

Los mexicanos ricos imitaban a los franceses en su manera de *vivir*.

The rich Mexicans imitated the French in their manner of *living*.

D. In English the **gerund** follows a preposition. In Spanish an **infinitive** follows a preposition.

En México es costumbre discutir el precio con el chofer *antes de* **subir** al coche.

In Mexico it is customary to discuss the price with the chauffeur *before* **getting into** the taxi.

Después de **lavarse** bajan otra vez.

After **washing themselves** they go down again.

Muchas gracias *por* **habernos enseñado** la ciudad.

Many thanks *for* **having shown us** the city.

E. In Spanish the contraction *al* + **infinitive** corresponds to the English *on* + **gerund**

Al **llegar** delante de su casa, Alfredo   *On* **arriving** in front of his house,
me invitó a entrar.   Alfred invited me to come in.

81 / Formation of the Present Participle — *Formación del gerundio*

In English the verbal form ending in *–ing* is called a present participle if it is used as an adjective and a gerund if it is used as a noun.

PRESENT PARTICIPLE   Robert saw Philip *writing* a letter.
GERUND   *Writing* a letter is not always easy.

A. In Spanish this present participle or gerund ends in *–ndo*. The present participle of *–ar* verbs adds *–ando* to the infinitive stem; the present participle of *–er* and *–ir* verbs adds *–iendo* to the infinitive stem.

INFINITIVE	PRESENT PARTICIPLE	
hablar	hablando	speaking
comer	comiendo	eating
vivir	viviendo	living

B. Four verbs have irregular present participles: [1]

INFINITIVE	PRESENT PARTICIPLE	
decir	diciendo	saying
ir	yendo	going
poder	pudiendo	being able
venir	viniendo	coming

82 / Uses of the Present Participle — *Modo de usar el gerundio*

A. The present participle is a verbal adjective, that is, it modifies a noun or pronoun but functions largely as a verb. It does not agree with the word it modifies — its form never changes.

Los hombres, *esperando* salir de viaje,   The men, *hoping* to take a trip,
compraron un coche.   bought a car.

---

[1] The *–ir* radical-changing verbs have irregular present participles in *–i–* and *–u–*: *pedir—pidiendo; dormir—durmiendo* (§ 106 C); verbs in *–aer, –eer,* and *–uir* have present participles in *–yendo: caer—cayendo; leer—leyendo; construir—construyendo* (§ 107 J, K). Reflexive verbs add the reflexive object to the present participle: *acostarse—acostándose.*

Although the present participle *esperando* modifies a plural noun, it retains its singular form.

B. The present participle expresses the condition under which an act takes place. It often refers to the subject of the sentence.

Las chicas pasaron muchas horas *hablando* de su viaje por España.   The girls spent a lot of time *talking* about their trip through Spain.

C. In contrast to English, the Spanish present participle is *not* used as a pure adjective. The English present participle used as an adjective must be expressed by a *que* clause in Spanish.

La chica *que canta* es mi hermana.   The girl *singing* is my sister.

D. The present participle is used with the verb *estar* to form the progressive tenses. This is explained in § 83.

83 / Progressive Forms — Formas de estar con el gerundio

In English a progressive form of a tense is one that shows clearly that an action is continuing. These progressive forms are made up of a combination of some form of the verb *be* and the **present participle** of the main verb.

I *am writing* a letter.   They *will be traveling* in Spain this summer.
He *was studying* this morning.   We *have been eating* fruit.

A. In Spanish the progressive forms are made up of a combination of some form of the verb *estar* and the **present participle**[1] of the main verb.

estoy hablando   I am speaking
estábamos comiendo   we were eating

B. The progressive form stresses the continuity of the action.

Encontramos una larga cola de gente que ya *estaba esperando* para sacar billetes.   We met a long line of people who *were* already *waiting* to get tickets.

C. The verbs *ir, venir, seguir,* and *andar* are sometimes used with the present participle to indicate continued action. Each of these verbs imparts different meanings.

---

[1] Verbs of motion such as *ir, venir, entrar,* and *salir* are not normally used in the progressive form. The simple tenses of those verbs are preferred.

1. *seguir* means to keep on or to continue.

Al día siguiente *seguimos* via-jando hacia el sur.	On the following day we *continued* **traveling** toward the south.

2. *ir* indicates that the progression is gradual or emphasizes the fact that it is beginning.

Según nos alejábamos del mar, *íbamos* **entrando** en la imponente llanura.	As we moved away from the sea, we *gradually began* **entering** the imposing plain.

3. *venir* indicates that an act begun in the past has progressed toward the present.

Desde el año pasado *viene* **pidiendo** dinero.	Since last year he *has kept on* **asking** for money.

4. *andar* emphasizes that the act is performed in a busy manner or indicates aimlessness or carelessness of action.

Anda **buscando** flores.	He *goes around* **looking for** flowers.

84 / Formation of the Past Participle — Formación del participio pasado

In English the past participle of regular verbs is formed by adding *-ed* to the infinitive. EXAMPLE: jump, *jumped;* live, *lived.*

A. In Spanish the past participle of *-ar* verbs adds *-ado* to the infinitive stem, the past participle of *-er* and *-ir* verbs adds *-ido* to the infinitive stem.

INFINITIVE	PAST PARTICIPLE	
hablar	hablado	spoken
comer	comido	eaten
vivir	vivido	lived

B. The common verbs with irregular past participles are:

INFINITIVE	PAST PARTICIPLE		INFINITIVE	PAST PARTICIPLE	
abrir	abierto	opened	**morir**	muerto	died, dead
cubrir	cubierto	covered	**poner**	puesto	put
decir	dicho	said	**resolver**	resuelto	resolved
descubrir	descubierto	discovered	**satisfacer**	satisfecho	satisfied
escribir	escrito	written	**ver**	visto	seen
hacer	hecho	done	**volver**	vuelto	returned

A. The past participle[1] is often used as an adjective. In such cases it agrees in gender and number with the noun it modifies.

Los coches *fabricados* en Rusia no son parecidos a los de los otros países europeos.	The cars *made* in Russia are not like those of the other European countries.
La pirámide del Sol está *construida* de piedra volcánica.	The pyramid of the Sun is *constructed* of volcanic stone.

B. Like other adjectives, some past participles may be used as nouns. EXAMPLES: aficionado, empleado, significado, resultado, llegada, entrada, salida.

C. The past participle is used to form the compound tenses. In this case participle never changes in form.

La muchacha ha *hablado*. Los niños han *venido*. Las flores habían *crecido*.

D. The past participle is used with the verb *ser* to form the passive voice. This is explained in § 86.

86 / *Formation of the Passive Voice — Formación de la voz pasiva*

A sentence in the active voice is one in which the subject *is acting;* a sentence in the passive voice is one in which the subject *is acted upon.* In English the passive voice is composed of some form of the auxiliary verb *be* and the **past participle.**

ACTIVE	PASSIVE
The dog *bites* the man.	The man *is bitten* by the dog.
Robert *bought* the car.	The car *was bought* by Robert.

A. The Spanish passive voice is formed just as the English, that is, by some form of the auxiliary verb *ser* and the **past participle.**

---

[1] For the use of *estar* with the past participle, see § 98 C.

ACTIVE	PASSIVE
Un autor muy conocido *escribió* ese poema.	Ese poema *fue escrito* por un autor muy conocido.
Los indios *cultivaban* los campos.	Los campos *eran cultivados* por los indios.
Cortés *fundó* Veracruz.	Veracruz *fue fundada*[1] por Cortés.

B. The tenses of the passive correspond to the tenses of the verb *ser* which are used.

INDICATIVE

PRESENT	son comprados	they are bought
IMPERFECT	eran comprados	they were bought
PRETERITE	fueron comprados	they were bought
FUTURE	serán comprados	they will be bought
CONDITIONAL	serían comprados	they would be bought
PERFECT	han sido comprados	they have been bought
PLUPERFECT	habían sido comprados	they had been bought
PRETERITE PERFECT	hubieron sido comprados	they had been bought
FUTURE PERFECT	habrán sido comprados	they will have been bought
CONDITIONAL PERFECT	habrían sido comprados	they would have been bought

SUBJUNCTIVE

PRESENT	sean comprados	(that) they be bought
IMPERFECT	{ fueran comprados / fuesen comprados	(that) they were bought
PERFECT	hayan sido comprados	(that) they have been bought
PLUPERFECT	{ hubieran sido comprados / hubiesen sido comprados	(that) they had been bought

C. The past participle of the verb in the passive voice agrees with the subject of the clause.

¿Cuándo fueron *construidos* estos templos ?	When were these temples *constructed?*

87 / Uses of the Passive Voice — *Modo de usar la voz pasiva*

A. English and Spanish both use the passive voice in sentences in which the subject is acted upon rather than acting.

---

[1] Most cities are considered feminine in Spanish.

| Las pirámides *fueron construidas* por los toltecas. | The pyramids *were constructed* by the Toltecs. |

B. Spanish uses the passive voice rather infrequently and most often in the preterite. There are many cases where it would be awkward to use the passive voice in Spanish. Two ways of avoiding the passive voice are:

1. by the use of the *se* construction.[1]

| El águila y la serpiente *se con- servan* en la bandera nacional de la república. | The eagle and the serpent *are con- served* in the national flag of the republic. |
| *Se dice* que la civilización· más avanzada del valle de México fue la de los toltecas. | *It is said* that the most advanced civilization of the valley of Mexico was that of the Toltecs. |

2. by the third person plural of the verb.

| Cada domingo *matan* seis toros. | Each Sunday $\begin{cases} \textit{they kill} \text{ six bulls.} \\ \text{six bulls } \textit{are killed.} \end{cases}$ |

C. After forms of the passive voice, the English preposition *by* is expressed

1. by **por** usually if the action is real.

| ¿*Por* quién fue pintado ese cuadro? | *By* whom was that picture painted? |
| Nuestros hijos fueron bautizados *por* el Padre Romero. | Our sons were baptized *by* Father Romero. |

2. by **de** when the action is only apparent and indicates rather a condi- tion or state; also by *de* with certain verbs such as *acompañar, preceder, rodear,* and *seguir.*

| Juárez era admirado *de* todos. | Juárez was admired *by* all. |
| A unos setenta kilómetros al sur de Madrid se encuentra la ciudad de Toledo rodeada *de* antiguas murallas. | At some seventy kilometers to the south of Madrid is the city of Toledo surrounded *by* ancient walls. |

---

[1] For a discussion of this *se* CONSTRUCTION, see § 28 A. Note that whenever the English passive states a general condition without mentioning by whom it is done, Spanish tends to use the *se* CONSTRUCTION, whereas a specific act done by a certain person is expressed by the passive. EXAMPLES: *Se venden* casas todos los días. (Houses *are sold* every day.) Las casas *fueron vendidas* por mi padre. (The houses *were sold* by my father.)

A. The present subjunctive of most verbs is formed by adding the following endings to the stem obtained by dropping the *-o* from the first person singular present indicative. In the following conjugations this stem is represented by —————.

-ar verbs		*-er* and *-ir* verbs	
yo —————e		yo —————a	
tú —————es		tú —————as	
él —————e		él —————a	
nosotros —————emos		nosotros —————amos	
vosotros —————éis		vosotros —————áis	
ellos —————en		ellos —————an	

B. Note the subjunctive of the following verbs:

INFINI-TIVE	1ST PERSON SINGULAR PRESENT INDICATIVE	PRESENT SUBJUNCTIVE	INFINI-TIVE	1ST PERSON SINGULAR PRESENT INDICATIVE	PRESENT SUBJUNCTIVE
caer	*caigo*	caiga, etc.	salir	*salgo*	salga, etc.
decir	*digo*	diga, etc.	tener	*tengo*	tenga, etc.
hacer	*hago*	haga, etc.	traer	*traigo*	traiga, etc.
oír	*oigo*	oiga, etc.	valer	*valgo*	valga, etc.
poder	*puedo*	pueda, etc. [2]	venir	*vengo*	venga, etc.
poner	*pongo*	ponga, etc.	ver	*veo*	vea, etc.

C. The following verbs do not follow the above rule. Notice their present subjunctives.

	dar	estar	haber	ir	saber	ser
yo	dé	esté	haya	vaya	sepa	sea
tú	*des*	*estés*	*hayas*	*vayas*	*sepas*	*seas*
él	dé	esté	haya	vaya	sepa	sea
nosotros	demos	estemos	hayamos	vayamos	sepamos	seamos
vosotros	*deis*	*estéis*	*hayáis*	*vayáis*	*sepáis*	*seáis*
ellos	den	estén	hayan	vayan	sepan	sean

[1] The present subjunctive of radical-changing verbs will be found in § 106 D, the present subjunctive of orthographical-changing verbs in § 107, and the conjugation of models of all types of verbs in § 110.

[2] The first and second person plural present subjunctive of *poder* are *podamos* and *podáis*.

A. All verbs form their imperfect subjunctives by adding a set of endings to the stem which is obtained by dropping *-ron* from the third person plural preterite.

INFINITIVE	3D PERSON PLURAL PRETERITE	STEM OF IMPERFECT SUBJUNCTIVE
hablar	hablaron	habla–
comer	comieron	comie–
dormir	durmieron	durmie–
decir	dijeron	dije–
saber	supieron	supie–
ser	fueron	fue–

B. The following two sets of endings are added to the stem obtained by taking the *-ron* from the third person plural preterite. This stem is represented by ——.

THE *-ra* ENDINGS	THE *-se* ENDINGS
yo ——ra	yo ——se
tú ——ras	tú ——ses
él ——ra	él ——se
nosotros —́—ramos	nosotros —́—semos
vosotros ——rais	vosotros ——seis
ellos ——ran	ellos ——sen

C. As to the choice between the *-ra* and the *-se* endings of the imperfect subjunctive,

1. the *-ra* endings may always be used; the *-se* endings may not be used in the conclusion of a contrary-to-fact condition[1] but may be used in all other cases where an imperfect subjunctive is required;

2. the *-ra* endings are used both in Spain and in Latin America; the *-se* endings are used in Spain but rarely in Latin America.

---

[1] For the use of the imperfect subjunctive in the conclusion of conditional sentences, see page 101, note 2.

The perfect subjunctive is a combination of the present subjunctive of the auxiliary verb *haber* and the **past participle** of the main verb.

yo haya hablado	nosotros hayamos hablado
tú hayas hablado	*vosotros hayáis hablado*
él haya hablado	ellos hayan hablado

The pluperfect subjunctive is a combination of the imperfect subjunctive of the auxiliary verb *haber* and the **past participle** of the main verb.

THE *-ra* ENDINGS	THE *-se* ENDINGS
yo hubiera hablado	yo hubiese hablado
tú hubieras hablado	*tú hubieses hablado*
él hubiera hablado	él hubiese hablado
nosotros hubiéramos hablado	nosotros hubiésemos hablado
vosotros hubierais hablado	*vosotros hubieseis hablado*
ellos hubieran hablado	ellos hubiesen hablado

The two principal modes of Spanish as of English are the indicative and the subjunctive. The indicative states a fact objectively; it expresses reality. EXAMPLE: He *goes* to school.

The subjunctive is a subjective mode concerned with the speaker's feeling toward the fact rather than with the fact itself. EXAMPLE: They insist that he *go* to school. Although the subjunctive has almost disappeared from English, it is still used:

USE	EXAMPLES
1. in contrary-to-fact conditions	If he *were* here, we could discuss the problem.
2. in wishes	I wish she *were* here. Long *live* the king!
3. after certain verbs and expressions which indicate the attitude of a speaker toward an action.	I suggest that he *do* his work. We insist that he *study*. It is necessary that he *be* here. It is possible that he *may leave*.

The subjunctive is used far more in Spanish than in English. For that reason a Spanish subjunctive is often expressed in English not by a subjunctive but rather by a form of the indicative, the conditional, or even the infinitive.

SPANISH SUBJUNCTIVE	ENGLISH EQUIVALENT
Me alegro de que *esté* aquí.	I am glad that he *is* here.
Es preciso que lo *haga.*	It is necessary that he *should do* it.
Quiero que *venga*	I want him *to come.*

Care must be taken on the one hand in rendering the Spanish subjunctive in English and on the other in recognizing which English constructions require a subjunctive in Spanish.

Basically the Spanish subjunctive expresses

1. the attitude or feeling of the speaker toward a state or action
2. a condition contrary-to-fact

It is used specifically:

A. in commands [1]

Miren las calles estrechas.	*Look at* the narrow streets.
Subamos por esta calle.	*Let us go up* by this street.
Que me *salgan* muchos clientes como ustedes.	May many customers like you *come* to me.

B. after certain impersonal expressions *where not the fact but an opinion concerning the fact* is stated.[2] The commonest of these impersonal expressions are:

es posible que	it is possible that
es probable que	it is probable that
es necesario que	it is necessary that
es preciso que	it is necessary that
es importante que	it is important that
basta con que	it is sufficient that
es imposible que	it is impossible that
es natural que	it is natural that
vale más que	it is better that
puede ser que	it may be that
importa que	it is important that
es raro que	it is seldom that

---

[1] All imperatives except the affirmative *tú* and *vosotros* imperatives are subjunctives in form. For a discussion of the imperative, see § 95.
[2] But after impersonal expressions in which certainty is emphasized the indicative is used. Examples of such expressions are *es cierto que, es claro que, es verdad que, es seguro que,* etc.

Es probable que por aquí **pasen** centenares de vehículos al día.	*It is probable* that hundreds of vehicles per day pass by here.
Basta con que **nos acordemos** de esta fuente.	*It is sufficient* that we remember this fountain.
Es natural que no **sea** tan nueva como la de ustedes.	*It is natural* that it is not as new as yours.

C. after verbs and expressions of feeling and emotion such as *tener miedo* (be afraid), *temer* (fear), *alegrarse* (be glad), *sentir* (regret), *esperar* (hope), *ser lástima* (be too bad), etc., which indicate the attitude or feeling of the speaker toward a state or action.

Temo que **tengan miedo** de mí.	*I fear* that they are afraid of me.
Espero que **te diviertas** mucho allí.	*I hope* that you are having a good time there.
Es una lástima que usted no **haya podido** tratar a una chica.	*It is too bad* that you haven't been able to meet a girl.

D. after verbs and expressions of doubt, denial, uncertainty, and disbelief.

Dudo que me **hagan** caso.	*I doubt* that they pay any attention to me.

The verb *creer* is followed by the indicative when it is affirmative and by the subjunctive when it is negative.

Creo que **es** más fácil entender que hablar.	*I believe* that it is easier to understand than to talk.
No creo que usted **haya estado** en España el tiempo suficiente para conocerla bien.	I *do not believe* that you have been in Spain long enough to know it well.

E. in relative clauses where there is doubt or denial of the existence or attainability of the antecedent.

Quiero relacionarme con *una chica* que **salga** conmigo.	I want to get acquainted with *a girl* who will go out with me.
Usted ha de buscar *una persona* que lo **presente** a ella.	You must look for *a person* who will present you to her.
No hay cosa que más **moleste** que ir a pasar una temporada a cualquier sitio.	*There is nothing* that is more annoying than to go to pass some time in some place or other.

F. after verbs of *commanding, requesting, wishing, permitting, forbidding, preventing, advising, persuading, suggesting, inviting, insisting, compelling,* and the like, all of which express the attitude or feeling of the speaker toward the action in question.

Yo le *aconsejé* que **pidiese** las vacaciones para el mes de julio.	I *advised* him to ask for his vacation for the month of July.
Él *prefiere* que se las **den** en agosto.	He *prefers* to have them give it to him in August.[1]
Mi hermano y su esposa *querían* que **fuésemos** todos a Francia.	My brother and his wife *wanted* us all to go to France.[2]
El gobierno no *permite* que **se saque** dinero.	The government doesn't *permit* money to be taken out.
Mi marido *había sugerido* que **hiciéramos** un viaje a Santander.	My husband *had suggested* that we take a trip to Santander.

G. **always** after the following conjunctions:

a menos que	unless	con tal que	provided **that**
a fin (de)[3] que	in order that	para que	in order that
antes (de)[3] que	before	sin que	without
como si	as if		

Voy a hablar a mi marido *para que* **vayamos** uno de estos días.	I am going to talk to my husband *in order that* we may go one of these days.
Tienen que tapar las calles con toldos *a fin de que* el sol no **penetre**.	They have to cover the streets with canvas *in order that* the sun does not penetrate.
Este verano tendré una buena ocasión de conocer mejor Andalucía *a menos que* luego **cambie** de ideas.	This summer I will have a good opportunity to know Andalusia better *unless* he changes his mind then.

H. after the following conjunctions when the action has not yet taken place at the time of the action of the main verb:

cuando	when	hasta que	until
después (de) que	after	luego que	as soon as
en cuanto	as soon as	tan pronto como	as soon as

ACTION NOT YET TAKEN PLACE — SUBJUNCTIVE

Lo decidiremos *cuando* mi marido **regrese** de su viaje de negocios.	We will decide it *when* my husband returns from his business trip.

---

[1] The literal translation would be: *He prefers that they give them to him in August.*
[2] The literal translation would be: *My brother and his wife wanted that we all go to France.*
[3] In these expressions the *de* is sometimes used and sometimes not used.

Lo decidimos *cuando* mi marido **regresó** de su viaje de negocios.

We decided it *when* my husband returned from his business trip.

ACTION NOT YET TAKEN PLACE — SUBJUNCTIVE

Saldremos *en cuanto* **sepamos** el lugar exacto.

We will leave *as soon as* we know the exact place.

ACTION ALREADY TAKEN PLACE — INDICATIVE

Salimos *en cuanto* **supimos** el lugar exacto.

We left *as soon as* we knew[1] the exact place.

I. The indicative is used with *aunque* (although), *de manera que* (so that as a result), and *de modo que* (so that as a result) when it is a question of a fact. The subjunctive is used with *aunque* when the truth of the statement of the clause is not conceded and after *de manera que* (so that, in order that) and *de modo que* (so that, in order that) when they indicate purpose.

SIMPLE FACT — INDICATIVE

Aunque **hablo** mucho, Carlos no cambia.

Although I **speak** a great deal, Carlos does not change.

Pedro *condujo* muy rápidamente, *de modo que* **llegaron** a tiempo.

Pedro drove very rapidly, *so that (as a result)* they **arrived** in time.

CONCESSION — SUBJUNCTIVE

Aunque **hable** mucho, Carlos no cambiará.

Although I **may speak** a great deal, Carlos will not change.

UNFULFILLED PURPOSE — SUBJUNCTIVE

Pedro condujo muy rápidamente *de modo que* **llegaran** a tiempo.

Pedro drove very rapidly *so that (in order that)* they **would arrive** in time.

J. after expressions such as *acaso*, *tal vez*, and *quizá(s)*, all of which mean perhaps, when there is sufficient doubt in the mind of the speaker.

Quizá **vayamos** a Valencia.

Perhaps we'll go to Valencia.

K. in clauses introduced by *cualquiera*, with *querer* and *deber* in softened statements, in wishes with *ojalá*, in expressions such as *por más . . . que*, *por muy . . . que*, and *por mucho . . . que* (*no matter how much*), in stating alternatives, etc.

---

[1] or *learned*, since *saber* usually has the meaning of *learned* in the preterite.

Quisiera[1] ir a España.	I should like to go to Spain.
¡ *Ojalá* se **cumplan** tus palabras !	*May* your words be fulfilled.
Por mucho que las **mirase** nunca me cansaría.	*No matter how much* I looked at them, I'd never get tired.

L. in contrary-to-fact conditions.[2]

Si los españoles no **tuviesen** que luchar tanto por la vida, serían más felices.	If the Spanish **did** not **have** to struggle so much for a living, they would be happier.
Si Francia e Inglaterra **se hubiesen atrevido** a enviar ayuda a los republicanos, acaso éstos **hubieran ganado.**	If France and England **had dared** to send aid to the republicans, perhaps the latter **would have won.**

93 / Sequence of Tenses — Concordancia de los tiempos

In English the sequence of tenses may be illustrated by sentences such as

He *says* that he **will come.**	The main verb *says* is naturally followed by the verb **will come** in the subordinate clause.
He *said* that he **would come.**	The main verb *said* is naturally followed by the verb **would come** in the subordinate clause.

In Spanish a set of principles govern the tenses used in the subordinate clauses. The tense of the subjunctive used in the subordinate clause depends upon the tense used in the main clause.

A. The present subjunctive is used in a subordinate clause after the present indicative, future, and imperative in the main clause to relate an action which takes place at the same time as or after the action of the main verb.

Me alegro   (*I am glad*)
Me alegraré (*I shall be glad*) } de que Roberto **venga** (*that Robert is coming*).
Alégrese   (*Be glad*)

B. The perfect subjunctive[3] is used in subordinate clauses after the present

---

[1] The form *quisiera* is expressed in English by *I should like* as opposed to *quiero* which is much stronger and means *I want*.
[2] Contrary-to-fact conditions are taken up in detail in § 96 B.
[3] In most constructions the imperfect subjunctive could also be used under the conditions outlined in this section, and the example would then read: *Me alegro de que Roberto viniera*, etc.

indicative, future, and imperative in the main clause to relate an action which has gone on before the action of the main verb.

Me alegro   (*I am glad*)
Me alegraré (*I shall be glad*) } de que Roberto **haya venido** (*that Robert has come*).
Alégrese   (*Be glad*)

C. The imperfect subjunctive is used after any past tense[1] or the conditional to relate an action which took place at the same time or after the action of the main verb.

Me alegraba   (*I was glad*)
Me alegré   (*I was glad*)
Me he alegrado   (*I was glad*)   } de que Roberto **viniera**
Me había alegrado (*I had been glad*)   (*that Robert was coming*).
Me alegraría   (*I would be glad*)
Me habría alegrado (*I should have been glad*)

D. The pluperfect is used after any past tense[1] or the conditional to relate an action which had taken place before the action of the main verb.

Me alegraba   (*I was glad*)
Me alegré   (*I was glad*)
Me he alegrado   (*I was glad*)   } de que Roberto **hubiera**
Me había alegrado (*I had been glad*)   **venido** (*that Robert had*
Me alegraría   (*I should be glad*)   *come*).
Me habría alegrado (*I should have been glad*)

E. Thus, under the conditions described above, the sequence of tenses in Spanish sentences with subordinate clauses requiring subjunctive may be outlined as follows:

MAIN CLAUSE		SUBORDINATE CLAUSE (*in subjunctive*)
present future imperative	que	present[2] perfect[3, 4]
all past tenses conditional	que	imperfect[2] pluperfect[3]

[1] When the perfect tense is equivalent to the preterite, it is followed by the sequence outlined in C and D; otherwise it is followed by the sequence outlined in A and B.

[2] This tense of the subjunctive is used when the action of the subordinate clause takes place at the same time as or after the action of the main clause.

[3] This tense of the subjunctive is used when the action of the subordinate clause takes place before the action of the main clause.

[4] The imperfect subjunctive may also be used here.

A. Usually the subjunctive is found in a subordinate clause whose subject is different from that of the main clause. Where the subject of the subordinate clause would be the same as the subject of the main clause in English, an infinitive construction usually replaces the subjunctive clause in Spanish. Study the following examples.

I am glad that *you* are in Spain.	Me alegro de que **usted esté** en España.
I am glad that *I* am in Spain.	Me alegro de **estar** en España.
I will write you before *he* comes.	Le escribiré antes de que **venga.**
I will write you before *I* come.	Le escribiré antes de **venir.**
We bought the book in order that *he* might learn the words.	Compramos el libro para que **aprendiera** las palabras.
We bought the book in order that *we* might learn the words.	Compramos el libro para **aprender** las palabras.

B. Many conjunctions which are followed by the subjunctive have corresponding prepositions which are followed by the infinitive.

CONJUNCTION FOLLOWED BY SUBJUNCTIVE	PREPOSITION FOLLOWED BY INFINITIVE
antes (de)[1] que	antes de
a fin (de)[1] que	a fin de
después (de)[1] que	después de
hasta que	hasta
para que	para
sin que	sin

Calisto y Melibea se encuentran *sin que* **se den** cuenta de estas relaciones los padres de la joven.	Calisto y Melibea se encuentran *sin* **darse** cuenta de la presencia de sus padres.
Calisto and Melibea meet *without* the girl's parents knowing of these meetings.	Calisto and Melibea meet *without* knowing of the presence of her parents.
Los niños de estas familias trabajan *para que* sus padres **tengan** dinero.	Los niños de estas familias trabajan *para* **ganar** dinero.
The children of these families work *so that* their parents may have money.	The children of these families work *to* earn money.

---

[1] In these expressions the *de* is sometimes used and sometimes not used.

Discutí el precio con el chofer *antes de que* mis amigos **subieran** al coche.

I discussed the price with the chauffeur *before* my friends got into the taxi.

Discutí el precio con el chofer *antes de* **subir** al coche.

I discussed the price with the chauffeur *before* getting into the taxi.

C. Either the subjunctive construction or the infinitive may be used with the verbs *aconsejar, dejar, hacer,*[1] *impedir, mandar, permitir,* and *prohibir.*

SUBJUNCTIVE CLAUSE

El profesor manda *que escribamos los ejercicios.*

Le aconseja a mi amigo *que escuche la música.*

Mi padre impidió *que yo fuera al cine.*

Dejo a mis amigos *que usen mi automóvil.*

INFINITIVE CONSTRUCTION

El profesor *nos* manda *escribir los ejercicios.*

Le aconseja a mi amigo *escuchar la música.*

Mi padre *me* impidió *ir al cine.*

Dejo a mis amigos *usar mi automóvil.*

D. Where a subjunctive clause has a pronoun subject after an impersonal expression, the infinitive construction may also be used.

SUBJUNCTIVE CLAUSE

Es imposible que *yo* **vaya** allí el mes próximo.

Es preciso que *usted* **aprenda** a bailar.

INFINITIVE CONSTRUCTION

Me es imposible **ir** allí el mes próximo.

Le es preciso *a usted* **aprender** a bailar.

The impersonal constructions *Es imposible ir allí el mes próximo*, and *Es preciso aprender a bailar*, are also very common.

95 / The Imperative — El imperativo [2]

In English the imperatives or command-forms are distinguished by the absence of a subject. EXAMPLES: *Get* the book. *Write* a letter. *Let's go to* Madrid.

---

[1] These constructions are used with *hacer* when it is used in the causative construction. See § 102 D.

[2] The *usted*-**imperatives** of radical-changing verbs are formed according to the rule given in B, as are the imperatives of the orthographical-changing verbs. For the imperatives of reflexive verbs, see § 105 D.

A. One commonly used imperative in Spanish is the *usted*-imperative, that is, the imperative which is used when addressing a person with *usted*. In polite speech the pronouns *usted* and *ustedes* are used with these imperatives, but in familiar conversation they are often omitted.

B. The *usted*-imperatives are formed by adding the following endings to the stem obtained by dropping the *-o* from the first person singular present indicative. In the following table this stem is represented by ——

-ar verbs	*-er* verbs	*-ir* verbs
——e Ud.	——a Ud.	——a Ud.
——en Uds.	——an Uds.	——an Uds.
hable Ud.	coma Ud.	viva Ud.
hablen Uds.	coman Uds.	vivan Uds.

C. Notice the imperative of the following verbs:

INFINITIVE	1ST PERSON SINGULAR PRESENT INDIC.	IMPERATIVE	INFINITIVE	1ST PERSON SINGULAR PRESENT INDIC.	IMPERATIVE
caer	*caigo*	caiga Ud.	salir	*salgo*	salga Ud.
decir	*digo*	diga Ud.	tener	*tengo*	tenga Ud.
hacer	*hago*	haga Ud.	traer	*traigo*	traiga Ud.
oír	*oigo*	oiga Ud.	valer	*valgo*	valga Ud.
poder	*puedo*	pueda Ud.	venir	*vengo*	venga Ud.
poner	*pongo*	ponga Ud.	ver	*veo*	vea Ud.

D. The *usted*-imperatives of the following verbs cannot be formed from the present stem:

INFINITIVE	IMPERATIVE	
dar	dé Ud.	den Uds.
estar	esté Ud.	estén Uds.
ir	vaya Ud.	vayan Uds.
saber	sepa Ud.	sepan Uds.
ser	sea Ud.	sean Uds.

E. In English there is a first person plural imperative which may be called the *let's*-imperative. EXAMPLES: Let's speak. Let's eat. Let's live. In Spanish the corresponding imperative may be expressed in two ways:

1. by the first person plural of the present subjunctive. This form usually corresponds as to stem to the *usted*-imperatives. [1]

INFINI- TIVE	*usted*- IMPERATIVE	*let's*- IMPERATIVE	INFINI- TIVE	*usted*- IMPERATIVE	*let's*- IMPERATIVE
hablar	hable	hablemos	dar	dé	demos
comer	coma	comamos	decir	diga	digamos
vivir	viva	vivamos	ir	vaya	vamos [2]
caer	caiga	caigamos	ser	sea	seamos

Entremos por estas calles de la derecha.　　*Let's enter* these streets at the right.

2. by the use of *vamos a* + **infinitive.**

Pero *vamos a dejar* la Gran Vía en este ángulo.　　But *let's leave* the *Gran Vía* at this turn.

F. There are also *tú-* and *vosotros*-imperatives. Each uses one set of forms in the affirmative and an entirely different set in the negative. The pronouns are usually not used with these forms. In the affirmative, the following endings are added to the infinitive stem (——) to form the imperatives:

	-ar **verbs**	*-er* **verbs**	*-ir* **verbs**
(tú)	——a	——e	——e
(vosotros)	——ad	——ed	——id
(tú)	habla	come	vive
(vosotros)	hablad	comed	vivid

The following verbs have irregular affirmative *tú*-imperatives.

INFINI- TIVE	*tú*- IMPERATIVE	INFINI- TIVE	*tú*- IMPERATIVE	INFINI- TIVE	*tú*- IMPERATIVE
decir	di	poner	pon	tener	ten
hacer	haz	salir	sal	valer	val
ir	ve	ser	sé	venir	ven

All *vosotros*-imperatives are regular.

G. In the negative the *tú-* and *vosotros*-imperatives are simply present subjunc-

---

[1] But the first person plural subjunctive of radical-changing verbs does not have the present stem. For the subjunctive of radical-changing verbs, see § 106 D.

[2] The *let's*-imperative of *ir* is *vamos*, not the first person plural subjunctive *vayamos*. This is the only exception in Spanish to the general rule of translating the *let's*-imperative with the present subjunctive.

tives and have the same stem and endings as the present subjunctive.[1]
The ―― represents the stem on which the subjunctive is formed.

	-ar verbs	*-er* verbs	*-ir* verbs
(tú)	no ――es	no ――as	no ――as
(vosotros)	no ――éis	no ――áis	no ――áis
(tú)	no hables	no comas	no vivas
(vosotros)	no habléis	no comáis	no viváis

96 / Conditions – Condiciones

A condition is characterized by the conjunction *if*. It consists of two parts: the **condition** and the **conclusion**. Examples: If it rains, they will not come. If he were there, he would meet Mr. Smith.

A. There are many types of conditions. Often Spanish uses the same combination of tenses in the two parts of a conditional sentence as English.

Si la meseta no *es* tan alta como las montañas, *es* mucho más elevada que la costa.	If the plateau *is* not as high as the mountains, it *is* much higher than the coast.
Si la amistad *es* muy grande, *consentirá* en ir con usted.	If the degree of friendship *is* very great, she *will consent* to go with you.

B. Contrary-to-fact conditions, that is, those which deal with a situation which is not true or which was not true, use the subjunctive in the *si*-clause and the conditional[2] in the conclusion, as follows:

si-CLAUSE IMPERFECT SUBJUNCTIVE	CONCLUSION CONDITIONAL[2]
Si el suelo español *fuese*[3] más fértil, seguramente *habría* más comida.	If the Spanish soil *were* more fertile, *there would* certainly *be* more food.
Si *hubiese* más fábricas en España, los españoles *tendrían* un nivel de vida más alto.	If there *were* more factories in Spain, the Spanish *would have* a higher standard of living.

---

[1] For the present subjunctive forms of verbs, see § 88.
[2] The *-ra* form of the imperfect subjunctive may be used in the conclusion of this type of condition instead of the conditional. The above examples could read: Si el suelo español fuese más fértil, seguramente *hubiera* más comida. Si hubiese más fábricas en España, los españoles *tuvieran* un nivel de vida más alto.
[3] or *fuera*

si-CLAUSE	CONCLUSION
PLUPERFECT SUBJUNCTIVE	CONDITIONAL PERFECT [1]

Si el general Franco no *hubiese*[2] *tenido* tropas moras, no *habría triunfado* tan pronto.	If General Franco *had* not *had* Moorish troops, he *would* not *have triumphed* so soon.
Si las otras naciones no *hubiesen*[3] *intervenido*, el gobierno *habría podido* suprimir la revolución.	If the other nations *had* not *intervened*, the government *would have been able* to put down the revolution.

C. The construction . . . *como si* . . . is regularly followed by the imperfect or pluperfect subjunctive.

La señora García habla **como si** *tuviera* mucho que hacer.	Mrs. García speaks **as if** she *had* a great deal to do.

D. The conjunction *si*, meaning **if**, never takes the future, conditional, or present subjunctive.

Si usted *compra* el libro, su hermano lo leerá.	If you *will buy*[4] the book, your brother will read it.

III. Uses of Certain Verbs — Modo de usar ciertos verbos

97 / *Uses of the Verb* ser — *Modo de usar el verbo* ser

Spanish has two verbs which mean **to be,** *ser* and *estar*. They cannot, however, be used interchangeably. Each one has certain functions.

The verb *ser* is used:

A. with predicate nouns[5] to tell *what* something or someone *is*.

Bolivia y Venezuela *son* países de Sud América.	Bolivia and Venezuela *are* countries of South America.
Felipe *es* un estudiante mexicano.	Philip *is* a Mexican student.

---

[1] The *-ra* form of the pluperfect subjunctive may be used in the conclusion of this type of condition instead of the conditional perfect. The above examples could read: Si el general Franco no hubiese tenido tropas moras, no *hubiera triunfado* tan pronto. Si las otras naciones no hubiesen intervenido, el gobierno *hubiera podido* suprimir la revolución.

[2] or *hubiera tenido*.   [3] or *hubieran intervenido*

[4] In English this is really not a future, for it means *If you are willing to buy;* we can also say simply *If you buy the book, your brother will read it.*

[5] A predicate noun is a noun used after the verb *to be* or its Spanish equivalent.

B. to indicate origin, ownership, and material.

Yo *soy* de Guadalajara y José *es* de Oaxaca.	I *am* from Guadalajara and Joseph *is* from Oaxaca.
Las universidades *son* del Estado.	The universities *are* government-owned.
Las casas *son* de adobe.	The houses *are* of adobe.

C. with the past participle to form the true[1] passive voice.[2]

El alumno *es* **examinado** sobre todo lo que ha aprendido.	The pupil *is* **examined** on all that he has learned.
Los indios *fueron* **maltratados** y tuvieron que trabajar como esclavos.	The Indians *were* **mistreated** and had to work like slaves.

D. meaning *to happen, to take place.*

Este examen *es* en junio.	This examination *takes place* in June.

E. with adjectives to express an inherent quality of the subject.[3] It answers the question *What kind of?*

Estos barrios *son* elegantes.	These districts *are* elegant.
El clima *es* agradable.	The climate *is* agreeable.
El tiempo *es* seco.	The weather *is* dry.
El terreno *es* bajo.	The land *is* low.
La cena *es* ligera.	The dinner *is* light.

98 / Uses of the Verb estar — *Modo de usar el verbo* estar

The verb *estar* indicates by nature a temporary or transitory state or condition. It is used:

A. to express position or location, whether it is permanent or temporary.

Tampico también *está* en el este de México.	Tampico also *is* in the east of Mexico.

B. with the present participle to make up the progressive forms[4] of the tenses.

Le *estoy* **escribiendo** desde mi hotel.	I *am* **writing** you from my hotel.

---

[1] For the apparent or pseudo-passive voice, see § 98 C.
[2] For a discussion of the formation of the passive voice, see § 86.
[3] Compare with § 98 D.   [4] For the progressive forms, see § 83.

C. with the past participle to indicate a state or condition which has come about as a result of some previous action.[1]

La pirámide del Sol *está* **construida** de piedra volcánica.	The pyramid of the Sun *is* **constructed** of volcanic stone.
Ellos *estaban* **vestidos** con sarapes.	They *were* **dressed** in serapes.
La taquilla todavía *estaba* **cerrada.**	The ticket window *was* still **closed.**

D. with adjectives to indicate a state or condition subject to change.[2] It answers the question *In what condition?*

¡ Qué cansado *estoy* !	How tired I *am!*
Felipe *está* muy alegre esta noche.	Philip *is* very happy tonight.

E. A number of adjectives therefore change their meaning when used with *ser* or *estar*.

ADJECTIVE	MEANING WITH *ser*	MEANING WITH *estar*
aburrido	boring	bored
alto	tall, high	in a high position
bajo	short, low	in a low position
bueno	good (character)	in good health, well
callado	taciturn	silent
cansado	tiresome	tired
cierto	true	sure
enfermo	invalid, patient	sick
limpio	cleanly	clean
listo	clever	ready
loco	silly	crazy
malo	bad (character)	sick
nuevo	newly-made	unused
triste	dull, deplorable	sad

99 / *Meanings of the Verb* deber — *Diversos significados del verbo* deber

The verb *deber* offers many difficulties in interpreting the exact value of the various tenses.

---

[1] The combination of *estar* + **past participle** is known as the apparent or pseudo-passive as compared with the real passive which is made up of a form of *ser* + **past participle** and which is discussed in §§ 86, 87. The two may be contrasted by considering this real passive: *La puerta* **fue abierta,** (*The door was opened*) which indicates the action, and this apparent passive: *La puerta* **estaba abierta,** (*The door was open*) which indicates the resultant state.

[2] Contrast with § 97 E.

A. Used with a noun or pronoun object the verb *deber* means **owe**.

¿ Cuánto *debe* usted ?   How much do you *owe?*
Debo mil pesetas.   I *owe* a thousand pesetas.

B. Followed by a dependent infinitive the present of *deber* may express either necessity or obligation.

Debemos terminar la fiesta.   We $\begin{cases} must \\ ought\ to \end{cases}$ bring an end to the holiday.

C. The forms *debía, debería,* or *debiera* express obligation in a less forceful and less direct fashion than the present of *deber*. [1]

Cuando alguien les dice que *deberían*   When someone tells them that they
    cambiar de métodos, ellos se ríen   *should* change methods, they
    de él.   laugh at him.

D. The form **must have** [2] may be expressed in two ways:

1. present of *deber* + **perfect infinitive**

Usted *debe* **haber trabajado**   You *must* **have worked** a great deal.
    mucho.

2. perfect of *deber* + **present infinitive**

He *debido* **soñar** contigo.   I *must have* **dreamed** of you.

E. A form of *deber de* + **infinitive** often expresses probability. [3]

Debe de **ser** muy interesante el   The study of medicine *must* **be**
    estudio de la medicina.   (*probably is*) very interesting.

But *deber de* + **infinitive** sometimes expresses simple obligation or necessity as in § 99 B.

100 / *Constructions with* gustar (*like*), faltar (*lack*), quedar (*remain*) —

Modo de usar gustar, faltar, quedar

These three verbs are similar in that in Spanish a thing is the subject of the sentence and a person is the indirect object, whereas in English a person

---

[1] This idea of obligation is expressed in English by *should* or *ought to*.
[2] The future perfect (§ 77 B) is also used to express *must have* + *past participle.*
[3] The future (§ 66 B) is also used to express probability.

is the subject and a thing is the direct object. Therefore, in expressing these sentences in Spanish, it is necessary to reword the English sentence, or better still to learn the Spanish pattern without thinking of the English.

A. Note the following sentences with *gustar:*

ORDINARY ENGLISH SENTENCE	REWORDING OF ENGLISH SENTENCE	SPANISH
I like books.	Books are pleasing to me.	A mí me gustan los libros.
He likes books.	Books are pleasing to him.	A él le gustan los libros.
She likes books.	Books are pleasing to her.	A ella le gustan los libros.
You (sing.) like books.	Books are pleasing to you.	A usted le gustan los libros.
Robert likes books.	Books are pleasing to Robert.	A Roberto le gustan los libros.
We like books.	Books are pleasing to us.	A nosotros nos gustan los libros.
They like books.	Books are pleasing to them.	A ellos les gustan los libros.
You (pl.) like books.	Books are pleasing to you.	A ustedes les gustan los libros.
The boys like books.	Books are pleasing to the boys.	A los muchachos les gustan los libros.

Thus, to express the English sentence *I like books* in Spanish, we make the object of the English sentence, which is *books*, the subject of the Spanish sentence. The subject of the English sentence, *I*, becomes the indirect object of the Spanish sentence. By rewording the English sentence *Books are pleasing to me*, it can be put directly into Spanish: *A mí me gustan los libros*, or simply *Me gustan los libros*, which is less emphatic. Equally correct is *Me gustan a mí los libros*. But note that the subject of the Spanish sentence comes at the end and that *gustar* agrees with it in number.

B. The verbs *faltar* (lack) and *quedar* (remain) follow the same pattern.

ORDINARY ENGLISH SENTENCE	REWORDING OF ENGLISH SENTENCE	SPANISH
I lack[1] energy.	Energy is lacking to me.	A mí me falta energía.
He has silver left.	Silver remains to him.	A él le queda plata.

101 / Uses of the Verb haber — *Modo de usar el verbo* haber

The verb *haber* is usually an auxiliary verb used to form the perfect, pluperfect, future perfect, conditional perfect, and preterite perfect in conjunction with the past participle of the main verb. For the formation of these tenses, see §§ 70, 72, 74, 76, 78.

---

[1] This sentence also means *I need energy.*

A. The special form *hay* means both **there is** and **there are.**

En este parque *hay* una colina.   In this park *there is* a hill.
Pero *hay* también muchos barrios   But *there are* also many poor dis-
    pobres.   tricts.

B. The word *hay* has a corresponding form in other tenses, and this form is used with both singular and plural nouns. The forms in the other tenses are:

TENSE	SPANISH FORM	ENGLISH
IMPERFECT	había	there was, there were
PRETERITE	hubo	there was, there were[1]
FUTURE	habrá	there will be
CONDITIONAL	habría	there would be
PERFECT	ha habido	there has been, there have been
PLUPERFECT	había habido	there had been

C. The forms of *hay* outlined above are used **with *que* to express necessity** impersonally and in a general sense.

Para conocer a chicas en bailes, *hay*   To get acquainted with girls at
    que tener mucha habilidad.   dances *it is necessary* to have a
    great deal of skill.

D. The forms of *haber* + *de* + infinitive express the idea of what is going to happen, what is probably true, or of mild necessity.

Si alguna vez *he de* casarme con una   If some time I *am to* marry a Spanish
    española, ya sabré cómo debo   girl, I'll already know how I
    hacerlo.   should do it.

102 / *Uses of the Verb* hacer — *Modo de usar el verbo* hacer

The verb *hacer* is used in a great number of idiomatic expressions.

A. It is used in the following expressions of weather:

¿Qué tiempo hace?   What kind of weather is it?
Hace buen tiempo.   It is good weather.
Hace mal tiempo.   It is bad weather.
Hace calor.[2]   It is hot.

---

[1] The preterite form *hubo* sometimes means *there took place.*
[2] Note the expressions *Hace **mucho** calor* and *Hace **mucho** frío,* meaning *It is very hot* and *It is very cold.*

Hace frío. [1]	It is cold.
Hace fresco.	It is cool.
Hace sol. [2]	It is sunny.
Hace viento. [2]	It is windy.

These expressions can be used in any tense of *hacer.*

B. The form *hace* is used with time expressions and a past tense of the main verb to express the English **ago.**

| *Hace algunos años* la gente viajaba en tranvías. | *Some years ago* people used to travel in street cars. |

C. The forms *hace . . . que* and *desde hace* are used with the present, [3] and *hacía . . . que* and *desde hacía* with the imperfect [4] in sentences expressing extent of time.

D. In every language there is some way of expressing the idea of *having something done.* Grammatically, this is called the **causative construction.** In Spanish this construction is expressed with *hacer* + **infinitive** or *mandar* + **infinitive**

| La *hicieron* montar en coche con ellas. | They *had* her get into the coach with them. |

103 / *Uses of the Verb* tener — *Modo de usar el verbo* tener

A. Forms of the verb *tener* + *que* + **infinitive** express the idea of *to have to* + **infinitive.**

| El maestro *tiene que hablar* algún dialecto indio. | The teacher *has to speak* some Indian dialect. |
| También *tuvieron que poner* agua en el radiador. | They also *had to put* water in the radiator. |

B. The verb *tener* is used in many idiomatic expressions of which the subject is a person or a thing.

| El emperador *tuvo miedo.* | The emperor *was afraid.* |
| Este examen *tiene lugar* en la universidad. | This examination *takes place* in the university. |

---

[1] Note the expressions *Hace **mucho** calor* and *Hace **mucho** frío,* meaning *It is very hot* and *It is very cold.*
[2] The verb *haber* may also be used with *sol* and *viento.* One can say: *Hay sol* and *Hay viento.*
[3] For this construction, see § 59 B.
[4] For this construction, see § 61 C.

The following expressions are used with *tener*. They are given in the infinitive form, but they are normally used in any person and any tense.

tener —— años[1]	to be —— years old	tener hambre[3]	to be hungry
tener calor[2]	to be hot	tener lugar	to take place
tener la culpa	to be to blame	tener miedo[2]	to be afraid
tener cuidado	to take care	tener prisa[3]	to be in a hurry
tener deseos (de)	to desire (to)	tener razón[4]	to be right
tener éxito	to be successful	tener sed[3]	to be thirsty
tener frío[2]	to be cold	tener sueño[2]	to be sleepy
tener ganas (de)	to feel like	tener vergüenza[3]	to be ashamed

104 / *Ways of Expressing the English Verb* become *in Spanish —*

Modo de expresar el verbo inglés become *en español*

The English verb *become* is used in a variety of senses. Among the most common Spanish equivalents are:

A. *hacerse:* to become as a result of one's efforts. It is generally used with a predicate noun.[5]

   Juárez *se hizo* abogado.   Juárez *became* a lawyer.

B. *llegar a ser:* to become, indicating the final step in a series or culmination of a process. It is used with a predicate noun.[5]

   Juárez *llegó a ser* presidente.   Juárez *became* president.

C. *ponerse:* to become temporarily. It is used with a predicate adjective.[5]

   Carlota *se puso* furiosa.   Carlota *became* furious.

D. *volverse:* to become as a result of a fundamental and deep-seated change.

   Carlota *se volvió* loca.   Carlota *became* mad.

---

[1] ¿Cuántos años tiene usted? = *How old are you?* Tengo veinte años = *I am twenty years old.*

[2] The English *very* is expressed by *mucho*. Tengo **mucho** calor. Tiene **mucho** sueño.

[3] The English *very* is expressed by *mucha*. ¿Tiene usted **mucha** hambre? Tenga **mucha** sed.

[4] The expression *to be wrong* may be expressed in Spanish either by *no tener razón* or by *estar equivocado*, which means *to be mistaken.*

[5] A predicate noun is a noun used in the predicate of the sentence as the complement of a copulative or linking-verb. EXAMPLE: Robert becomes a *doctor*. A predicate adjective is an adjective used in the same way. EXAMPLE: Robert becomes *tired*.

IV. Special Types of Verbs — Categorías especiales de verbos

105 / *Reflexive Verbs — Verbos reflexivos*

A. A reflexive verb is one which has a reflexive object, that is, an object which refers to the subject.

ORDINARY VERB

El estudiante *presenta* a su amigo.   The student *introduces* his friend.

REFLEXIVE VERB

El estudiante *se presenta* al extran-   The student *introduces himself* to the
jero.   foreigner.

B. Verbs become reflexive when used with reflexive objects. They are conjugated exactly like ordinary verbs except that they are accompanied by the reflexive objects which, in Spanish, normally precede the verb. [1]

yo me presento	I introduce myself
él ⎫ ella ⎬ se presenta usted ⎭	he introduces himself she introduces herself you introduce yourself
nosotros nos presentamos	we introduce ourselves
ellos ⎫ ellas ⎬ se presentan ustedes ⎭	they introduce themselves they introduce themselves you introduce yourselves

C. Verbs such as *presentar* (introduce) and *presentarse* (introduce oneself) offer no difficulty as to meaning, but other reflexive verbs may be divided into the following types:

1. those which take on a plainly reflexive sense when used with the reflexive pronoun but whose English equivalent is not generally reflexive:

SPANISH FORM	ENGLISH EQUIVALENT	IDIOMATIC ENGLISH EQUIVALENT
me acuesto	I put myself to bed.	I go to bed.
me divierto	I amuse myself.	I have a good time.
me levanto	I get myself up.	I get up.
me siento	I seat myself.	I sit down.

2. those whose meaning becomes more intense or changes entirely in the reflexive form. These verbs are listed in § 27 C, D.

---

[1] But the reflexive object ordinarily follows and is joined to infinitives, present participles, and affirmative imperatives, as explained in § 30 B, C.

3. those which do not exist without the reflexive object and are therefore inherently reflexive. A few of these are listed in § 27 B.

D. Reflexive verbs are conjugated like ordinary verbs except that they are accompanied by the reflexive objects. A model reflexive verb is conjugated in § 110, no. 4. But reflexive verbs require special attention in the imperative:

1. In the affirmative commands the reflexive pronoun follows the verb and is joined to it.

   a. The *usted*-imperatives are

levántese usted	levántense ustedes

   The stress remains where it would if there were no reflexive pronoun and it must therefore be indicated by a written accent when it violates the basic rules stated in PRONUNCIACIÓN § 7 A, B.

   b. the *let's*-imperative is

   levantémonos

   which is a combination of *levantemos* + *nos*. The final –*s* of the verbal ending –*mos* is dropped before the addition of the reflexive pronoun *nos*.

   c. the *tú*-imperative is

   levántate

   d. the *vosotros*-imperative is

   levantaos

   which is a combination of *levantad* + *os*. The final –*d* of the verbal ending –*ad*, –*ed*, or –*id* is dropped before the addition of the reflexive pronoun *os*.[1]

2. In the negative commands the reflexive pronoun precedes the verb and the forms offer no special irregularities.

   a. the *usted*-imperatives are

no se levante usted	no se levanten ustedes

   b. the *let's*-imperative is

   no nos levantemos

   c. the *tú*-imperative is

   no te levantes

   which is really the present subjunctive form.

---

[1] But the *vosotros*-imperative of *irse* is *idos*.

d. the *vosotros-* **imperative** is

no os levantéis

which is really the present subjunctive form.

106 / *Radical-Changing Verbs — Verbos que cambian la vocal radical* [1]

In Spanish certain verbs change the vowel[2] of their infinitive stem[3] under certain conditions. Such verbs are called *radical-changing*[4] verbs. These stem-vowel changes take place in

(1) the present indicative, the present subjunctive, and certain imperatives of all radical-changing verbs;

(2) the preterite, imperfect subjunctive, and present participle of *-ir* radical-changing verbs.

Radical-changing verbs are indicated in the vocabularies by placing the vowel-change in parentheses after the infinitive. EXAMPLES: *cerrar (ie); contar (ue); pedir (i)*. When there are two changes both changes are indicated in the final vocabulary. EXAMPLES: *dormir (ue, u); pedir (i, i)*. This means that the stem-vowel of *dormir* changes to *ue* in certain forms of the present and to *u* in certain forms of the preterite, and in the present participle and the imperfect subjunctive.

A. In the present indicative, radical-changing verbs with a stem-vowel which is *-o-* change the *-o-* to *-ue-;* some radical-changing verbs with a stem-vowel which is *-e-* change the *-e-* to *-ie-;* others change the *-e-* to *-i-.* These changes occur only in those forms which when pronounced are stressed on the stem-vowel. Thus changes take place in the *yo, tú, él,* and *ellos* forms of the present of all radical-changing verbs, but there is no change in the *nosotros* or *vosotros* forms.

	cerrar	volver	pedir
yo	cierro	vuelvo	pido
tú	*cierras*	*vuelves*	*pides*
él	cierra	vuelve	pide
nosotros	cerramos	volvemos	pedimos
vosotros	*cerráis*	*volvéis*	*pedís*
ellos	cierran	vuelven	piden

[1] The Spanish call these verbs simply *verbos irregulares.*
[2] This is always the last vowel in the infinitive stem. In the radical-changing verb *despertar (ie)*, the stem is *despert-* and it is the second *-e-* which changes.
[3] The infinitive stem is the stem which remains when *-ar, -er,* or *-ir* is taken from the infinitive.
[4] The radical of a verb is its stem.

B. In the preterite there is no change in the stem-vowel of *-ar* and *-er* radical-changing verbs. In the *él* and *ellos* forms of the preterite of *-ir* radical-changing verbs, the *-o-* of the stem becomes *-u-* and *-e-* of the stem becomes *-i-*.

	cerrar	volver	pedir	dormir
yo	cerré	volví	pedí	dormí
tú	*cerraste*	*volviste*	*pediste*	*dormiste*
él	cerró	volvió	pidió	durmió
nosotros	cerramos	volvimos	pedimos	dormimos
vosotros	*cerrasteis*	*volvisteis*	*pedisteis*	*dormisteis*
ellos	cerraron	volvieron	pidieron	durmieron

C. There is no change in the stem-vowel of the present participle of *-ar* and *-er* radical-changing verbs. In the present participles of *-ir* radical-changing verbs, the *-o-* of the stem becomes *-u-* and the *-e-* of the stem becomes *-i-*.

INFINITIVE	cerrar	volver	pedir	dormir
PRESENT PARTICIPLE	cerrando	volviendo	pidiendo	durmiendo

The same change takes place in the irregular verbs *decir* and *poder:*

INFINITIVE	decir	poder
PRESENT PARTICIPLE	diciendo	pudiendo

D. In the present subjunctive the *-ar* and *-er* radical-changing verbs make exactly the same vowel changes and in the same forms as they do in the present indicative. The *-ir* radical-changing verbs also make these changes and in addition in the *nosotros* and *vosotros* forms, they change *-o-* to *-u-* and *-e-* to *-i-*.

	cerrar	volver	pedir	dormir
yo	cierre	vuelva	pida	duerma
tú	*cierres*	*vuelvas*	*pidas*	*duermas*
él	cierre	vuelva	pida	duerma
nosotros	cerremos	volvamos	pidamos	durmamos
vosotros	*cerréis*	*volváis*	*pidáis*	*durmáis*
ellos	cierren	vuelvan	pidan	duerman

E. The radical changes in the imperative are illustrated in the following examples:

	cerrar	volver	pedir	dormir
(usted)	cierre	vuelva	pida	duerma
	no cierre	no vuelva	no pida	no duerma
(ustedes)	cierren	vuelvan	pidan	duerman
	no cierren	no vuelvan	no pidan	no duerman
(tú)	cierra	vuelve	pide	duerme
	no cierres	no vuelvas	no pidas	no duermas
(vosotros)	cerrad	volved	pedid	dormid
	no cerréis	no volváis	no pidáis	no durmáis

F. Radical-changing verbs may be divided into three classes:

Class I — All radical-changing verbs in –ar and –er;

Class II — Radical-changing verbs in –ir which change –e– in the stem to –ie– and –o– in the stem to –ue– in the present indicative.

Class III — Radical-changing verbs in –ir which change –e– in the stem to –i–.

G. The following table summarizes the changes of the stem-vowel in the radical-changing verbs:

Class	I	II	III
INFINITIVE ENDING	–ar and –er	–ir	–ir
yo, tú, él, ellos forms of present indicative and present subjunctive; tú, usted and ustedes imperatives	e changes to ie o changes to ue	e changes to ie o changes to ue	e changes to i
nosotros and vosotros forms of present subjunctive; nosotros and negative vosotros imperatives	no change	e changes to i o changes to u	e changes to i
present participle	no change	e changes to i o changes to u	e changes to i
él and ellos forms of preterite	no change	e changes to i o changes to u	e changes to i

For reasons of pronunciation some Spanish verbs have spelling changes in certain forms. Languages were not written until long after they were spoken, and also certain consonants which were pronounced uniformly in Latin developed to one sound when followed by certain vowels and to another sound when followed by other vowels. A single consonant sound may sometimes be written in several ways depending on the vowel sound that follows it. For example, the consonant sound *k* is written k in *kilómetro*, qu in *querer*, and c in *colonia*. To maintain a uniform sound before different vowels, then, the following changes occur in writing:

A. Verbs in –zar
z (pronounced *th* or *s*)[2] changes to c before e.
Verbs in –zar change –z– to –c– in the first person singular of the preterite, in the present subjunctive, and in the *usted*- and *let's*-imperatives.[3]

cruzar *cross*

PRES. IND.	cruzo, *cruzas*, cruza, cruzamos, *cruzáis*, cruzan
PRETERITE	crucé, *cruzaste*, cruzó, cruzamos, *cruzasteis*, cruzaron
PRES. SUBJ.	cruce, *cruces*, cruce, crucemos, *crucéis*, crucen
IMPERATIVE	cruce usted, crucemos, crucen ustedes

Other verbs in –zar are *alcanzar, avanzar, comenzar, empezar, rezar*, etc.

B. Verbs in –gar
g (pronounced hard *g*)[4] changes to gu before e.
Verbs in –gar change –g– to –gu– in the first person singular of the preterite, in the present subjunctive, and in the *usted* and *let's* imperatives.[5]

llegar *arrive*

PRES. IND.	llego, *llegas*, llega, llegamos, *llegáis*, llegan
PRETERITE	llegué, *llegaste*, llegó, llegamos, *llegasteis*, llegaron

---

[1] Also called ORTHOGRAPHICAL CHANGING VERBS.
[2] See the discussion of the pronunciation of c and z on pages 145 and 146.
[3] These three imperatives are really present subjunctives which are repeated in these tables for the convenience of the learner. Changes in the *tú*-imperative are the same as those of the *tú* form of the present indicative. The *vosotros*-imperative undergoes no spelling-changes.
[4] See the discussion of the pronunciation of g on pages 146 and 147.
[5] These three imperatives are really present subjunctives which are repeated in these tables for the convenience of the learner. Changes in the *tú*-imperative are the same as those of the *tú* form of the present indicative. The *vosotros* imperative undergoes no spelling-changes.

PRES. SUBJ.   llegue, *llegues*, llegue, lleguemos, *lleguéis*, lleguen
IMPERATIVE   llegue usted, lleguemos, lleguen ustedes

Other verbs in –**gar** are *pagar* and *jugar*. [1]

C. Verbs in –**car**
   c (pronounced *k*) [2] changes to **qu** before **e**.
   Verbs in –**car** change –**c**– to –**qu**– in the first person singular of the preterite, in the present subjunctive, and in the *usted-* and *let's*-imperatives. [3]

colocar   *put, place*

PRES. IND.   coloco, *colocas*, coloca, colocamos, *colocáis*, colocan
PRETERITE   coloqué, *colocaste*, colocó, colocamos, *colocasteis*, colocaron
PRES. SUBJ.   coloque, *coloques*, coloque, coloquemos, *coloquéis*, coloquen
IMPERATIVE   coloque usted, coloquemos, coloquen ustedes

Other verbs in –**car** are *acercarse, dedicar, explicar, indicar, sacar,* etc.

D. Verbs in –**ger** and –**gir**
   g (pronounced *j*) [4] changes to **j** before **a** and **o**.
   Verbs in –**ger** and –**gir** change –**g**– to –**j**– in the first person singular of the present indicative and throughout the present subjunctive and the imperative. [3]

dirigir   *direct*

PRES. IND.   dirijo, *diriges*, dirige, dirigimos, *dirigís*, dirigen
PRETERITE   dirigí, *dirigiste*, dirigió, dirigimos, *dirigisteis*, dirigieron
PRES. SUBJ.   dirija, *dirijas*, dirija, dirijamos, *dirijáis*, dirijan
IMPERATIVE   dirija usted, dirijamos, dirijan ustedes

Other verbs in –**ger** and –**gir** are *coger, escoger,* and *exigir*.

E. Verbs in VOWEL + –**cer** [5]
   c (pronounced *th* or *s*) changes to **zc** before **a** and **o**.
   Verbs in VOWEL + –**cer** change –**c**– to –**zc**– in the first person singular of the present indicative and throughout the present subjunctive and the imperative. [3]

---

[1] The verb *jugar* is also radical-changing. The –*u*– changes to –*ue*–.
[2] See the discussion of the pronunciation of **c** on pages 145 and 146.
[3] These three imperatives are really present subjunctives which are repeated in these tables for the convenience of the learner. Changes in the *tú*-imperative are the same as those of the *tú* form of the present indicative. The *vosotros*-imperative undergoes no spelling-changes.
[4] See the discussion of the pronunciation of **g** on pages 146 and 147.
[5] Verbs in CONSONANT + –**cer** are few and unimportant. The **c** changes to **z** before **a** and **o**. This change is made in the first person singular of the present indicative and throughout the present subjunctive and imperative. EXAMPLE: *vencer = conquer.*

conocer *be acquainted with*

PRES. IND.	conozco, *conoces*, conoce, conocemos, *conocéis*, conocen
PRETERITE	conocí, *conociste*, conoció, conocimos, *conocisteis*, conocieron
PRES. SUBJ.	conozca, *conozcas*, conozca, conozcamos, *conozcáis*, conozcan
IMPERATIVE	conozca usted, conozcamos, conozcan ustedes

Other verbs in VOWEL + –cer are *merecer, ofrecer,* and *reconocer.*

F. Verbs in –ducir

c (pronounced *th* or *s*) changes to zc before a and o.

Verbs in –ducir change –c– to –zc– in the first person singular of the present indicative and throughout the present subjunctive and imperative.[1] The preterite of verbs in –ducir have a preterite stem in –duj–.

traducir *translate*

PRES. IND.	traduzco, *traduces*, traduce, traducimos, *traducís*, traducen
PRETERITE	traduje, *tradujiste*, tradujo, tradujimos, *tradujisteis*, tradujeron
PRES. SUBJ.	traduzca, *traduzcas*, traduzca, traduzcamos, *traduzcáis*, traduzcan
IMPERATIVE	traduzca usted, traduzcamos, traduzcan ustedes

Other verbs in –ducir are *conducir, introducir, producir,* and *reducir.*

G. Verbs in –guar

gu (pronounced *gw*) changes to gü before e.

Verbs in –guar change –gu– to –gü– in the first person singular of the preterite and throughout the present subjunctive and the imperative.[1]

averiguar *find out*

PRES. IND.	averiguo, *averiguas*, averigua, averiguamos, *averiguáis*, averiguan
PRETERITE	averigüé, *averiguaste*, averiguó, averiguamos, *averiguasteis*, averiguaron
PRES. SUBJ.	averigüe, *averigües*, averigüe, averigüemos, *averigüéis*, averigüen
IMPERATIVE	averigüe usted, averigüemos, averigüen ustedes

H. Verbs in –guir

gu (pronounced hard *g*) changes to g before a and o.

Verbs in –guir change –gu– to –g– in the first person singular of the present indicative and throughout the present subjunctive and the imperative.[1]

---

[1] These three imperatives are really present subjunctives which are repeated in these tables for the convenience of the learner. Changes in the *tú*-imperative are the same as those of the *tú* form of the present indicative. The *vosotros*-imperative undergoes no spelling-changes.

distinguir *distinguish*

PRES. IND.	distingo, *distingues*, distingue, distinguimos, *distinguís*, distinguen
PRETERITE	distinguí, *distinguiste*, distinguió, distinguimos, *distinguisteis*, distinguieron
PRES. SUBJ.	distinga, *distingas*, distinga, distingamos, *distingáis*, distingan
IMPERATIVE	distinga usted, distingamos, distingan ustedes

Another verb in **-guir** is *seguir*.

I. Verbs in **-iar** and **-uar**

In many verbs the **-i-** and **-u-** are not accented in the present indicative and subjunctive. EXAMPLE: *cambiar: cambio, cambias, cambia,* etc. However, in many verbs in **-iar** and **-uar**, the **-i-** and **-u-** bear the stress and a written accent in the singular and third person plural of the present indicative and subjunctive and in the imperative.

variar *vary*

PRES. IND.	varío, *varías*, varía, variamos, *variáis*, varían
PRETERITE	varié, *variaste*, varió, variamos, *variasteis*, variaron
PRES. SUBJ.	varíe, *varíes*, varíe, variemos, *variéis*, varíen
IMPERATIVE	varíe usted, variemos, varíen ustedes

Other verbs in **-iar** which are accented are *confiar, criar, enviar, fiar, guiar,* etc.

continuar *continue*

PRES. IND.	continúo, *continúas*, continúa, continuamos, *continuáis*, continúan
PRETERITE	continué, *continuaste*, continuó, continuamos, *continuasteis*, continuaron
PRES. SUBJ.	continúe, *continúes*, continúe, continuemos, *continuéis*, continúen
IMPERATIVE	continúe usted, continuemos, continúen ustedes

Other verbs in **-uar** which are accented are *acentuar, atenuar, efectuar, situar,* etc.

J. Verbs in **-aer** and **-eer**

In verbs in **-aer** and **-eer**, when unaccented **-i-** falls between two vowels, it changes to **-y-**. This change occurs in the present participle, the third person singular and plural of the preterite, and throughout the imperfect subjunctive.

caer *fall*

PRES. PART.   cayendo
PRETERITE   caí, *caíste*, cayó, caímos, *caísteis*, cayeron
IMPERF. SUBJ. $\begin{cases} \text{cayera, } cayeras, \text{ cayera, cayéramos, } cayerais, \text{ cayeran} \\ \text{cayese, } cayeses, \text{ cayese, cayésemos, } cayeseis, \text{ cayesen} \end{cases}$

leer *read*

PRES. PART.   leyendo
PRETERITE   leí, *leíste*, leyó, leímos, *leísteis*, leyeron
IMPERF. SUBJ. $\begin{cases} \text{leyera, } leyeras, \text{ leyera, leyéramos, } leyerais, \text{ leyeran} \\ \text{leyese, } leyeses, \text{ leyese, leyésemos, } leyeseis, \text{ leyesen} \end{cases}$

K. Verbs in **–uir**

Verbs ending in **–uir** (except those in **–guir** and **–quir**) and the verb *oír*[1] insert y before any vowel in the ending except **i**. Also, when the un-accented **–i–** falls between two vowels, it changes to **–y–**. These changes take place in the present indicative and the subjunctive throughout the singular and in the third person plural, in the present participle, in the third person singular and plural of the preterite, and throughout the imperfect subjunctive.

construir *construct*

PRES. IND.   construyo, *construyes*, construye, construimos, *construís*,
                                         construyen
PRES. PART.   construyendo
PRES. SUBJ.   construya, *construyas*, construya, construyamos,
                                  construyáis, construyan
PRETERITE   construí, *construiste*, construyó, construimos, *construisteis*,
                                       construyeron
IMPERF. SUBJ. $\begin{cases} \text{construyera, } construyeras, \text{ construyera, construyéramos,} \\ \qquad\qquad\qquad\qquad construyerais, \text{ construyeran} \\ \text{construyese, } construyeses, \text{ construyese, construyésemos,} \\ \qquad\qquad\qquad\qquad construyeseis, \text{ construyesen} \end{cases}$

---

108 / Irregular Verbs — Verbos irregulares

A. An irregular verb is one which deviates in some way from the general pattern given for the formation of the various tenses of the –ar, –er, and –ir verbs.

---

[1] For the conjugation of *oír*, see § 110, no. 22.

B. Tenses of verbs are formed on certain basic stems which should be learned for each verb. All these stems together are called the *principal parts of the verb* and are explained in § 109.

V. The Conjugation of the Verb — Conjugación del verbo

109 / *Principal Parts of Verbs — Enunciado del verbo*

A. In order to be able to conjugate a Spanish verb in all its tenses, one must be acquainted with all possible stems. The stems of the regular verbs may all be derived from the infinitive; the stems of irregular verbs are sometimes derived from the infinitive, but often they are different from the infinitive. The different stems to which endings are added are called the *principal parts*. Each of the principal parts furnishes the stem for certain tenses.

B. The following principal parts are used to indicate the stem for the listed tenses:

1. *infinitive*

    The *future* and *conditional* are formed by adding the proper endings directly to the infinitive.

2. *infinitive stem*[1]

    The *present indicative*, and *imperfect indicative*, and the *present participle* are formed by adding the proper endings to the infinitive stem.[2]

3. *first person singular present indicative*[3]

    The *present subjunctive* and the *usted*, *let's*, and **negative** *tú* and *vosotros* **imperatives** are formed by adding the proper endings to this stem.

4. *preterite*

    The *preterite* is formed by adding the proper endings to the preterite stem. The *imperfect subjunctive* is formed by adding the proper endings to the stem obtained by dropping *–ron* from the third person plural of the preterite.

---

[1] The infinitive stem is the part of the verb which is left when the *–ar*, *–er*, or *–ir* is taken from the infinitive.

[2] The singular and the third person plural of the present of radical-changing verbs as well as the present participle of *–ir* radical-changing verbs deviate from the infinitive stem. See § 106 A, C for these forms.

[3] This stem is found by taking the final *–o* from the first person singular present indicative.

5. *past participle*

The *perfect, pluperfect, preterite perfect, future perfect,* and *conditional perfect indicative,* and the *perfect* and *pluperfect subjunctive* are formed by using the proper tense of the auxiliary verb *haber* with the past participle.

C. The conjugation of the irregular verb *poner* by principal parts will illustrate how this outline can be used to organize one's knowledge of a verb.

INFINITIVE	INFINITIVE STEM	FIRST PERSON SINGULAR PRESENT	PRETERITE	PAST PARTICIPLE
poner	*pon–*	*pongo*	*pusieron*	*puesto*

future	present indicative	present subjunctive	preterite	perfect
pondré	pongo	ponga	puse	he puesto, etc.
pondrás	pones	pongas	pusiste	
pondrá	pone	ponga	puso	**pluperfect**
pondremos	ponemos	pongamos	pusimos	había puesto, etc.
pondréis	ponéis	pongáis	pusisteis	
pondrán	ponen	pongan	pusieron	**preterite perfect**
				hube puesto, etc.

condi-tional	imperfect indicative	formal imperative	imperfect subjunctive	future perfect
pondría	ponía	ponga Ud.	pusiera	habré puesto, etc.
pondrías	ponías	pongamos	pusieras	
pondría	ponía	pongan Uds.	pusiera	**conditional perfect**
pondríamos	poníamos		pusiéramos	
pondríais	poníais	**familiar negative imperatives**	pusierais	habría puesto, etc.
pondrían	ponían		pusieran	
				perfect subjunctive
	present participle	no pongas	*or*	haya puesto, etc.
	poniendo	no pongáis		
			pusiese	**pluperfect subjunctive**
			pusieses	
	familiar affirmative imperatives		pusiese	hubiera puesto, etc.
	pon		pusiésemos	*or*
	poned		pusieseis	
			pusiesen	hubiese puesto, etc.

INFINITIVES AND PARTICIPLES	INDICATIVE			
	PRESENT	IMPERFECT	PRETERITE	FUTURE
1. −ar verbs hablar (*to speak*) hablando hablado	hablo *hablas* habla hablamos *habláis* hablan	hablaba *hablabas* hablaba hablábamos *hablabais* hablaban	hablé *hablaste* habló hablamos *hablasteis* hablaron	hablaré *hablarás* hablará hablaremos *hablaréis* hablarán
	PERFECT	PLUPERFECT	PRETERITE PERFECT	FUTURE PERFECT
	he hablado *has hablado* ha hablado hemos hablado *habéis hablado* han hablado	había hablado *habías hablado* había hablado habíamos hablado *habíais hablado* habían hablado	hube hablado *hubiste hablado* hubo hablado hubimos hablado *hubisteis hablado* hubieron hablado	habré hablado *habrás hablado* habrá hablado habremos hablado *habréis hablado* habrán hablado
	PRESENT	IMPERFECT	PRETERITE	FUTURE
2. −er verbs comer (*to eat*) comiendo comido	como *comes* come comemos *coméis* comen	comía *comías* comía comíamos *comíais* comían	comí *comiste* comió comimos *comisteis* comieron	comeré *comerás* comerá comeremos *comeréis* comerán
	PERFECT	PLUPERFECT	PRETERITE PERFECT	FUTURE PERFECT
	he comido *has comido* ha comido hemos comido *habéis comido* han comido	había comido *habías comido* había comido habíamos comido *habíais comido* habían comido	hube comido *hubiste comido* hubo comido hubimos comido *hubisteis comido* hubieron comido	habré comido *habrás comido* habrá comido habremos comido *habréis comido* habrán comido
	PRESENT	IMPERFECT	PRETERITE	FUTURE
3. −ir verbs vivir (*to live*) viviendo vivido	vivo *vives* vive vivimos *vivís* viven	vivía *vivías* vivía vivíamos *vivíais* vivían	viví *viviste* vivió vivimos *vivisteis* vivieron	viviré *vivirás* vivirá viviremos *viviréis* vivirán
	PERFECT	PLUPERFECT	PRETERITE PERFECT	FUTURE PERFECT
	he vivido *has vivido* ha vivido hemos vivido *habéis vivido* han vivido	había vivido *habías vivido* había vivido habíamos vivido *habíais vivido* habían vivido	hube vivido *hubiste vivido* hubo vivido hubimos vivido *hubisteis vivido* hubieron vivido	habré vivido *habrás vivido* habrá vivido habremos vivido *habréis vivido* habrán vivido

CONDITIONAL	SUBJUNCTIVE		IMPERATIVE
PRESENT CONDITIONAL	**PRESENT**	**IMPERFECT**	
hablaría	hable	hablara [1]	*habla* (*tú*)
hablarías	*hables*	*hablaras*	*no hables* (*tú*)
hablaría	hable	hablara	hable Ud.
hablaríamos	hablemos	habláramos	hablemos (nosotros)
hablaríais	*habléis*	*hablarais*	*hablad* (*vosotros*)
hablarían	hablen	hablaran	*no habléis* (*vosotros*)
			hablen Uds.
CONDITIONAL PERFECT	**PERFECT**	**PLUPERFECT**	
habría hablado	haya hablado	hubiera [1] hablado	
habrías hablado	*hayas hablado*	*hubieras hablado*	
habría hablado	haya hablado	hubiera hablado	
habríamos hablado	hayamos hablado	hubiéramos hablado	
habríais hablado	*hayáis hablado*	*hubierais hablado*	
habrían hablado	hayan hablado	hubieran hablado	
PRESENT CONDITIONAL	**PRESENT**	**IMPERFECT**	
comería	coma	comiera [1]	*come* (*tú*)
comerías	*comas*	*comieras*	*no comas* (*tú*)
comería	coma	comiera	coma Ud.
comeríamos	comamos	comiéramos	comamos (nosotros)
comeríais	*comáis*	*comierais*	*comed* (*vosotros*)
comerían	coman	comieran	*no comáis* (*vosotros*)
			coman Uds.
CONDITIONAL PERFECT	**PERFECT**	**PLUPERFECT**	
habría comido	haya comido	hubiera [1] comido	
habrías comido	*hayas comido*	*hubieras comido*	
habría comido	haya comido	hubiera comido	
habríamos comido	hayamos comido	hubiéramos comido	
habríais comido	*hayáis comido*	*hubierais comido*	
habrían comido	hayan comido	hubieran comido	
PRESENT CONDITIONAL	**PRESENT**	**IMPERFECT**	
viviría	viva	viviera [1]	*vive* (*tú*)
vivirías	*vivas*	*vivieras*	*no vivas* (*tú*)
viviría	viva	viviera	viva Ud.
viviríamos	vivamos	viviéramos	vivamos (nosotros)
viviríais	*viváis*	*vivierais*	*vivid* (*vosotros*)
vivirían	vivan	vivieran	no viváis (*vosotros*)
			vivan Uds.
CONDITIONAL PERFECT	**PERFECT**	**PLUPERFECT**	
habría vivido	haya vivido	hubiera [1] vivido	
habrías vivido	*hayas vivido*	*hubieras vivido*	
habría vivido	haya vivido	hubiera vivido	
habríamos vivido	hayamos vivido	hubiéramos vivido	
habríais vivido	*hayáis vivido*	*hubierais vivido*	
habrían vivido	hayan vivido	hubieran vivido	

[1] For the alternate imperfect and pluperfect subjunctives in *-se*, see pages 89-90.

INFINITIVES AND PARTICIPLES	INDICATIVE				
	PRESENT	IMPERFECT	PRETERITE	PERFECT	FUTURE
4. reflexive verb lavarse (*to wash oneself*) lavándose lavado	me lavo *te lavas* se lava nos lavamos *os laváis* se lavan	me lavaba *te lavabas* se lavaba nos lavábamos *os lavabais* se lavaban	me lavé *te lavaste* se lavó nos lavamos *os lavasteis* se lavaron	me he lavado *te has lavado* se ha lavado nos hemos lavado *os habéis lavado* se han lavado	me lavaré *te lavarás* se lavará nos lavaremos *os lavaréis* se lavarán
5. radical-changing verb[1] cerrar (*to close*) cerrando cerrado	cierro *cierras* cierra cerramos *cerráis* cierran	cerraba *cerrabas* cerraba cerrábamos *cerrabais* cerraban	cerré *cerraste* cerró cerramos *cerrasteis* cerraron	he cerrado *has cerrado* ha cerrado hemos cerrado *habéis cerrado* han cerrado	cerraré *cerrarás* cerrará cerraremos *cerraréis* cerrarán
6. radical-changing verb[2] contar (*to tell, to count*) contando contado	cuento *cuentas* cuenta contamos *contáis* cuentan	contaba *contabas* contaba contábamos *contabais* contaban	conté *contaste* contó contamos *contasteis* contaron	he contado *has contado* ha contado hemos contado *habéis contado* han contado	contaré *contarás* contará contaremos *contaréis* contarán
7. radical-changing verb[3] dormir (*to sleep*) durmiendo dormido	duermo *duermes* duerme dormimos *dormís* duermen	dormía *dormías* dormía dormíamos *dormíais* dormían	dormí *dormiste* durmió dormimos *dormisteis* durmieron	he dormido *has dormido* ha dormido hemos dormido *habéis dormido* han dormido	dormiré *dormirás* dormirá dormiremos *dormiréis* dormirán

[1] This is a model for *–ar* and *–er* radical-changing verbs whose stem-vowel is *–e–*.
[2] This is a model for *–ar* and *–er* radical-changing verbs whose stem-vowel is *–o–*.
[3] This is a model for *–ir* radical-changing verbs in which *–e–* changes to *–ie–* and *–o–* changes to *–ue–* in the present.

CONDITIONAL	SUBJUNCTIVE			IMPERATIVE
	PRESENT	IMPERFECT		
me lavaría	me lave	me lavara	me lavase	*lávate* (*tú*)
te lavarías	*te laves*	*te lavaras*	*te lavases*	*no te laves* (*tú*)
se lavaría	se lave	se lavara	se lavase	lávese Ud.
nos lavaríamos	nos lavemos	nos laváramos	nos lavásemos	lavémonos (nosotros)
os lavaríais	*os lavéis*	*os lavarais*	*os lavaseis*	*lavaos* (*vosotros*)
se lavarían	se laven	se lavaran	se lavasen	*no os lavéis* (*vosotros*)
				lávense Uds.
cerraría	cierre	cerrara	cerrase	*cierra* (*tú*)
cerrarías	*cierres*	*cerraras*	*cerrases*	*no cierres* (*tú*)
cerraría	cierre	cerrara	cerrase	cierre Ud.
cerraríamos	cerremos	cerráramos	cerrásemos	cerremos (nosotros)
cerraríais	*cerréis*	*cerrarais*	*cerraseis*	*cerrad* (*vosotros*)
cerrarían	cierren	cerraran	cerrasen	*no cerréis* (*vosotros*)
				cierren Uds.
contaría	cuente	contara	contase	*cuenta* (*tú*)
contarías	*cuentes*	*contaras*	*contases*	*no cuentes* (*tú*)
contaría	cuente	contara	contase	cuente Ud.
contaríamos	contemos	contáramos	contásemos	contemos (nosotros)
contaríais	*contéis*	*contarais*	*contaseis*	*contad* (*vosotros*)
contarían	cuenten	contaran	contasen	*no contéis* (*vosotros*)
				cuenten Uds.
dormiría	duerma	durmiera	durmiese	*duerme* (*tú*)
dormirías	*duermas*	*durmieras*	*durmieses*	*no duermas* (*tú*)
dormiría	duerma	durmiera	durmiese	duerma Ud.
dormiríamos	durmamos	durmiéramos	durmiésemos	durmamos (nosotros)
dormiríais	*durmáis*	*durmierais*	*durmieseis*	*dormid* (*vosotros*)
dormirían	duerman	durmieran	durmiesen	*no durmáis* (*vosotros*)
				duerman Uds.

INFINITIVES AND PARTICIPLES	INDICATIVE				
	PRESENT	IMPERFECT	PRETERITE	PERFECT	FUTURE
8. radical-changing verb[1] pedir (*to ask for*) pidiendo pedido	pido *pides* pide pedimos *pedís* piden	pedía *pedías* pedía pedíamos *pedíais* pedían	pedí *pediste* pidió pedimos *pedisteis* pidieron	he pedido *has pedido* ha pedido hemos pedido *habéis pedido* han pedido	pediré *pedirás* pedirá pediremos *pediréis* pedirán
9. andar[2] (*to go, to walk*) andando andado	ando *andas* anda andamos *andáis* andan	andaba *andabas* andaba andábamos *andabais* andaban	anduve *anduviste* anduvo anduvimos *anduvisteis* anduvieron	he andado *has andado* ha andado hemos andado *habéis andado* han andado	andaré *andarás* andará andaremos *andaréis* andarán
10. caber (*to fit*) cabiendo cabido	quepo *cabes* cabe cabemos *cabéis* caben	cabía *cabías* cabía cabíamos *cabíais* cabían	cupe *cupiste* cupo cupimos *cupisteis* cupieron	he cabido *has cabido* ha cabido hemos cabido *habéis cabido* han cabido	cabré *cabrás* cabrá cabremos *cabréis* cabrán
11. caer (*to fall*) cayendo caído	caigo *caes* cae caemos *caéis* caen	caía *caías* caía caíamos *caíais* caían	caí *caíste* cayó caímos *caísteis* cayeron	he caído *has caído* ha caído hemos caído *habéis caído* han caído	caeré *caerás* caerá caeremos *caeréis* caerán
12. conducir (*to lead*) conduciendo conducido	conduzco *conduces* conduce conducimos *conducís* conducen	conducía *conducías* conducía conducíamos *conducíais* conducían	conduje *condujiste* condujo condujimos *condujisteis* condujeron	he conducido *has conducido* ha conducido hemos conducido *habéis conducido* han conducido	conduciré *conducirás* conducirá conduciremos *conduciréis* conducirán

[1] This is a model for *–ir* radical-changing verbs in which *–e–* changes to *–i–* in the present.
[2] From this point on, all verbs are irregular and in alphabetical order.

CONDITIONAL	SUBJUNCTIVE			IMPERATIVE
	PRESENT	IMPERFECT		
pediría	pida	pidiera	pidiese	*pide (tú)*
pedirías	*pidas*	*pidieras*	*pidieses*	*no pidas (tú)*
pediría	pida	pidiera	pidiese	pida Ud.
pediríamos	pidamos	pidiéramos	pidiésemos	pidamos (nosotros)
pediríais	*pidáis*	*pidierais*	*pidieseis*	*pedid (vosotros)*
pedirían	pidan	pidieran	pidiesen	*no pidáis (vosotros)*
				pidan Uds.
andaría	ande	anduviera	anduviese	*anda (tú)*
andarías	*andes*	*anduvieras*	*anduvieses*	*no andes (tú)*
andaría	ande	anduviera	anduviese	ande Ud.
andaríamos	andemos	anduviéramos	anduviésemos	andemos (nosotros)
andaríais	*andéis*	*anduvierais*	*anduvieseis*	*andad (vosotros)*
andarían	anden	anduvieran	anduviesen	*no andéis (vosotros)*
				anden Uds.
cabría	quepa	cupiera	cupiese	*cabe (tú)*
cabrías	*quepas*	*cupieras*	*cupieses*	*no quepas (tú)*
cabría	quepa	cupiera	cupiese	quepa Ud.
cabríamos	quepamos	cupiéramos	cupiésemos	quepamos (nosotros)
cabríais	*quepáis*	*cupierais*	*cupieseis*	*cabed (vosotros)*
cabrían	quepan	cupieran	cupiesen	*no quepáis (vosotros)*
				quepan Uds.
caería	caiga	cayera	cayese	*cae (tú)*
caerías	*caigas*	*cayeras*	*cayeses*	*no caigas (tú)*
caería	caiga	cayera	cayese	caiga Ud.
caeríamos	caigamos	cayéramos	cayésemos	caigamos (nosotros)
caeríais	*caigáis*	*cayerais*	*cayeseis*	*caed (vosotros)*
caerían	caigan	cayeran	cayesen	*no caigáis (vosotros)*
				caigan Uds.
conduciría	conduzca	condujera	condujese	*conduce (tú)*
conducirías	*conduzcas*	*condujeras*	*condujeses*	*no conduzcas (tú)*
conduciría	conduzca	condujera	condujese	conduzca Ud.
conduciríamos	conduzcamos	condujéramos	condujésemos	conduzcamos (nosotros)
conduciríais	*conduzcáis*	*condujerais*	*condujeseis*	*conducid (vosotros)*
conducirían	conduzcan	condujeran	condujesen	*no conduzcáis (vosotros)*
				conduzcan Uds.

INFINITIVES AND PARTICIPLES	INDICATIVE				
	PRESENT	IMPERFECT	PRETERITE	PERFECT	FUTURE
13. conocer *(to be acquainted with)* conociendo conocido	conozco *conoces* conoce conocemos *conocéis* conocen	conocía *conocías* conocía conocíamos *conocíais* conocían	conocí *conociste* conoció conocimos *conocisteis* conocieron	he conocido *has conocido* ha conocido hemos conocido *habéis conocido* han conocido	conoceré *conocerás* conocerá conoceremos *conoceréis* conocerán
14. construir *(to construct)* construyendo construido	construyo *construyes* construye construimos *construís* construyen	construía *construías* construía construíamos *construíais* construían	construí *construiste* construyó construimos *construisteis* construyeron	he construido *has construido* ha construido hemos construido *habéis construido* han construido	construiré *construirás* construirá construiremos *construiréis* construirán
15. dar *(to give)* dando dado	doy *das* da damos *dais* dan	daba *dabas* daba dábamos *dabais* daban	di[1] *diste* dio[1] dimos *disteis* dieron	he dado *has dado* ha dado hemos dado *habéis dado* han dado	daré *darás* dará daremos *daréis* darán
16. decir *(to say)* diciendo dicho	digo *dices* dice decimos *decís* dicen	decía *decías* decía decíamos *decíais* decían	dije *dijiste* dijo dijimos *dijisteis* dijeron	he dicho *has dicho* ha dicho hemos dicho *habéis dicho* han dicho	diré *dirás* dirá diremos *diréis* dirán
17. estar *(to be)* estando estado	estoy *estás* está estamos *estáis* están	estaba *estabas* estaba estábamos *estabais* estaban	estuve *estuviste* estuvo estuvimos *estuvisteis* estuvieron	he estado *has estado* ha estado hemos estado *habéis estado* han estado	estaré *estarás* estará estaremos *estaréis* estarán

[1] Formerly the forms *di* and *dio* were written *dí* and *dió*.

CONDITIONAL	SUBJUNCTIVE			IMPERATIVE
	PRESENT	IMPERFECT		
conocería	conozca	conociera	conociese	*conoce (tú)*
conocerías	*conozcas*	*conocieras*	*conocieses*	*no conozcas (tú)*
conocería	conozca	conociera	conociese	conozca Ud.
conoceríamos	conozcamos	conociéramos	conociésemos	conozcamos (nosotros)
conoceríais	*conozcáis*	*conocierais*	*conocieseis*	*conoced (vosotros)*
conocerían	conozcan	conocieran	conociesen	*no conozcáis (vosotros)*
				conozcan Uds.
construiría	construya	construyera	construyese	*construye (tú)*
construirías	*construyas*	*construyeras*	*construyeses*	*no construyas (tú)*
construiría	construya	construyera	construyese	construya Ud.
construiríamos	construyamos	construyéramos	construyésemos	construyamos (nosotros)
construiríais	*construyáis*	*construyerais*	*construyeseis*	*construid (vosotros)*
construirían	construyan	construyeran	construyesen	*no construyáis (vosotros)*
				construyan Uds.
daría	dé	diera	diese	*da (tú)*
darías	*des*	*dieras*	*dieses*	*no des (tú)*
daría	dé	diera	diese	dé Ud.
daríamos	demos	diéramos	diésemos	demos (nosotros)
daríais	*deis*	*dierais*	*dieseis*	*dad (vosotros)*
darían	den	dieran	diesen	*no deis (vosotros)*
				den Uds.
diría	diga	dijera	dijese	*di (tú)*
dirías	*digas*	*dijeras*	*dijeses*	*no digas (tú)*
diría	diga	dijera	dijese	diga Ud.
diríamos	digamos	dijéramos	dijésemos	digamos (nosotros)
diríais	*digáis*	*dijerais*	*dijeseis*	*decid (vosotros)*
dirían	digan	dijeran	dijesen	*no digáis (vosotros)*
				digan Uds.
estaría	esté	estuviera	estuviese	*está (tú)*
estarías	*estés*	*estuvieras*	*estuvieses*	*no estés (tú)*
estaría	esté	estuviera	estuviese	esté Ud.
estaríamos	estemos	estuviéramos	estuviésemos	estemos (nosotros)
estaríais	*estéis*	*estuvierais*	*estuvieseis*	*estad (vosotros)*
estarían	estén	estuvieran	estuviesen	*no estés (vosotros)*
				estén Uds.

INFINITIVES AND PARTICIPLES	INDICATIVE				
	PRESENT	IMPERFECT	PRETERITE	PERFECT	FUTURE
18. haber *(to have)*[1] habiendo habido	he *has* ha hemos *habéis* han	había *habías* había habíamos *habíais* habían	hube *hubiste* hubo hubimos *hubisteis* hubieron	he habido *has habido* ha habido hemos habido *habéis habido* han habido	habré *habrás* habrá habremos *habréis* habrán
19. hacer *(to make, to do)* haciendo hecho	hago *haces* hace hacemos *hacéis* hacen	hacía *hacías* hacía hacíamos *hacíais* hacían	hice *hiciste* hizo hicimos *hicisteis* hicieron	he hecho *has hecho* ha hecho hemos hecho *habéis hecho* han hecho	haré *harás* hará haremos *haréis* harán
20. ir *(to go)* yendo ido	voy *vas* va vamos *vais* van	iba *ibas* iba íbamos *ibais* iban	fui[2] *fuiste* fue[2] fuimos *fuisteis* fueron	he ido *has ido* ha ido hemos ido *habéis ido* han ido	iré *irás* irá iremos *iréis* irán
21. leer *(to read)* leyendo leído	leo *lees* lee leemos *leéis* leen	leía *leías* leía leíamos *leíais* leían	leí *leíste* leyó leímos *leísteis* leyeron	he leído *has leído* ha leído hemos leído *habéis leído* han leído	leeré *leerás* lerrá leeremos *leeréis* leerán
22. oír *(to hear)* oyendo oído	oigo *oyes* oye oímos *oís* oyen	oía *oías* oía oíamos *oíais* oían	oí *oíste* oyó oímos *oísteis* oyeron	he oído *has oído* ha oído hemos oído *habéis oído* han oído	oiré *oirás* oirá oiremos *oiréis* oirán

[1] The verb *haber* is used mainly as an auxiliary verb.
[2] Formerly the forms *fui* and *fue* were written *fuí* and *fué*.

CONDITIONAL	SUBJUNCTIVE		IMPERATIVE
	PRESENT	IMPERFECT	
habría	haya	hubiera hubiese	*he (tú)*
habrías	*hayas*	*hubieras hubieses*	*no hayas (tú)*
habría	haya	hubiera hubiese	haya Ud.
habríamos	hayamos	hubiéramos hubiésemos	hayamos (nosotros)
habríais	*hayáis*	*hubierais hubieseis*	*habed (vosotros)*
habrían	hayan	hubieran hubiesen	*no hayáis (vosotros)*
			hayan Uds.
haría	haga	hiciera hiciese	*haz (tú)*
harías	*hagas*	*hicieras hicieses*	*no hagas (tú)*
haría	haga	hiciera hiciese	haga Ud.
haríamos	hagamos	hiciéramos hiciésemos	hagamos (nosotros)
haríais	*hagáis*	*hicierais hicieseis*	*haced (vosotros)*
harían	hagan	hicieran hiciesen	*no hagáis (vosotros)*
			hagan Uds.
iría	vaya	fuera fuese	*ve (tú)*
irías	*vayas*	*fueras fueses*	*no vayas (tú)*
iría	vaya	fuera fuese	vaya Ud.
iríamos	vayamos	fuéramos fuésemos	vamos (nosotros)
iríais	*vayáis*	*fuerais fueseis*	*id (vosotros)*
irían	vayan	fueran fuesen	*no vayáis (vosotros)*
			vayan Uds.
leería	lea	leyera leyese	*lee (tú)*
leerías	*leas*	*leyeras leyeses*	*no leas (tú)*
leería	lea	leyera leyese	lea Ud.
leeríamos	leamos	leyéramos leyésemos	leamos (nosotros)
leeríais	*leáis*	*leyerais leyeseis*	*leed (vosotros)*
leerían	lean	leyeran leyesen	*no leáis (vosotros)*
			lean Uds.
oiría	oiga	oyera oyese	*oye (tú)*
oirías	*oigas*	*oyeras oyeses*	*no oigas (tú)*
oiría	oiga	oyera oyese	oiga Ud.
oiríamos	oigamos	oyéramos oyésemos	oigamos (nosotros)
oiríais	*oigáis*	*oyerais oyeseis*	*oíd (vosotros)*
oirían	oigan	oyeran oyesen	*no oigáis (vosotros)*
			oigan Uds.

INFINITIVES AND PARTICIPLES	INDICATIVE				
	PRESENT	IMPERFECT	PRETERITE	PERFECT	FUTURE
23. poder (*can, to be able*) pudiendo podido	puedo *puedes* puede podemos *podéis* pueden	podía *podías* podía podíamos *podíais* podían	pude *pudiste* pudo pudimos *pudisteis* pudieron	he podido *has podido* ha podido hemos podido *habéis podido* han podido	podré *podrás* podrá podremos *podréis* podrán
24. poner (*to put*) poniendo puesto	pongo *pones* pone ponemos *ponéis* ponen	ponía *ponías* ponía poníamos *poníais* ponían	puse *pusiste* puso pusimos *pusisteis* pusieron	he puesto *has puesto* ha puesto hemos puesto *habéis puesto* han puesto	pondré *pondrás* pondrá pondremos *pondréis* pondrán
25. querer (*to wish, to love*) queriendo querido	quiero *quieres* quiere queremos *queréis* quieren	quería *querías* quería queríamos *queríais* querían	quise *quisiste* quiso quisimos *quisisteis* quisieron	he querido *has querido* ha querido hemos querido *habéis querido* han querido	querré *querrás* querrá querremos *querréis* querrán
26. saber (*to know*) sabiendo sabido	sé *sabes* sabe sabemos *sabéis* saben	sabía *sabías* sabía sabíamos *sabíais* sabían	supe *supiste* supo supimos *supisteis* supieron	he sabido *has sabido* ha sabido hemos sabido *habéis sabido* han sabido	sabré *sabrás* sabrá sabremos *sabréis* sabrán
27. salir (*to leave*) saliendo salido	salgo *sales* sale salimos *salís* salen	salía *salías* salía salíamos *salíais* salían	salí *saliste* salió salimos *salisteis* salieron	he salido *has salido* ha salido hemos salido *habéis salido* han salido	saldré *saldrás* saldrá saldremos *saldréis* saldrán

CONDITIONAL	SUBJUNCTIVE			IMPERATIVE
	PRESENT	IMPERFECT		
podría	pueda	pudiera	pudiese	
podrías	*puedas*	*pudieras*	*pudieses*	
podría	pueda	pudiera	pudiese	
podríamos	podamos	pudiéramos	pudiésemos	
podríais	*podáis*	*pudierais*	*pudieseis*	
podrían	puedan	pudieran	pudiesen	
pondría	ponga	pusiera	pusiese	*pon (tú)*
pondrías	*pongas*	*pusieras*	*pusieses*	*no pongas (tú)*
pondría	ponga	pusiera	pusiese	ponga Ud.
pondríamos	pongamos	pusiéramos	pusiésemos	pongamos (nosotros)
pondríais	*pongáis*	*pusierais*	*pusieseis*	*poned (vosotros)*
pondrían	pongan	pusieran	pusiesen	*no pongáis (vosotros)*
				pongan Uds.
querría	quiera	quisiera	quisiese	*quiere (tú)*
querrías	*quieras*	*quisieras*	*quisieses*	*no quieras (tú)*
querría	quiera	quisiera	quisiese	quiera Ud.
querríamos	queramos	quisiéramos	quisiésemos	queramos (nosotros)
querríais	*queráis*	*quisierais*	*quisieseis*	*quered (vosotros)*
querrían	quieran	quisieran	quisiesen	*no queráis (vosotros)*
				quieran Uds.
sabría	sepa	supiera	supiese	*sabe (tú)*
sabrías	*sepas*	*supieras*	*supieses*	*no sepas (tú)*
sabría	sepa	supiera	supiese	sepa Ud.
sabríamos	sepamos	supiéramos	supiésemos	sepamos (nosotros)
sabríais	*sepáis*	*supierais*	*supieseis*	*sabed (vosotros)*
sabrían	sepan	supieran	supiesen	*no sepáis (vosotros)*
				sepan Uds.
saldría	salga	saliera	saliese	*sal (tú)*
saldrías	*salgas*	*salieras*	*salieses*	*no salgas (tú)*
saldría	salga	saliera	saliese	salga Ud.
saldríamos	salgamos	saliéramos	saliésemos	salgamos (nosotros)
saldríais	*salgáis*	*salierais*	*salieseis*	*salid (vosotros)*
saldrían	salgan	salieran	saliesen	*no salgáis (vosotros)*
				salgan Uds.

INFINITIVES AND PARTICIPLES	INDICATIVE				
	PRESENT	IMPERFECT	PRETERITE	PERFECT	FUTURE
28. ser (*to be*) siendo sido	soy *eres* es somos *sois* son	era *eras* era éramos *erais* eran	fui[1] *fuiste* fue[1] fuimos *fuisteis* fueron	he sido *has sido* ha sido hemos sido *habéis sido* han sido	seré *serás* será seremos *seréis* serán
29. tener (*to have*) teniendo tenido	tengo *tienes* tiene tenemos *tenéis* tienen	tenía *tenías* tenía teníamos *teníais* tenían	tuve *tuviste* tuvo tuvimos *tuvisteis* tuvieron	he tenido *has tenido* ha tenido hemos tenido *habéis tenido* han tenido	tendré *tendrás* tendrá tendremos *tendréis* tendrán
30. traer (*to bring*) trayendo traído	traigo *traes* trae traemos *traéis* traen	traía *traías* traía traíamos *traíais* traían	traje *trajiste* trajo trajimos *trajisteis* trajeron	he traído *has traído* ha traído hemos traído *habéis traído* han traído	traeré *traerás* traerá traeremos *traeréis* traerán
31. valer (*to be worth*) valiendo valido	valgo *vales* vale valemos *valéis* valen	valía *valías* valía valíamos *valíais* valían	valí *valiste* valió valimos *valisteis* valieron	he valido *has valido* ha valido hemos valido *habéis valido* han valido	valdré *valdrás* valdrá valdremos *valdréis* valdrán
32. venir (*to come*) viniendo venido	vengo *vienes* viene venimos *venís* vienen	venía *venías* venía veníamos *veníais* venían	vine *viniste* vino vinimos *vinisteis* vinieron	he venido *has venido* ha venido hemos venido *habéis venido* han venido	vendré *vendrás* vendrá vendremos *vendréis* vendrán
33. ver (*to see*) viendo visto	veo *ves* ve vemos *veis* ven	veía *veías* veía veíamos *veíais* veían	vi[1] *viste* vio[1] vimos *visteis* vieron	he visto *has visto* ha visto hemos visto *habéis visto* han visto	veré *verás* verá veremos *veréis* verán

[1] The forms *fui, fue, vi,* and *vio* were formerly written *fuí, fué, ví,* and *vió.*

CONDITIONAL	SUBJUNCTIVE			IMPERATIVE
	PRESENT	IMPERFECT		
sería	sea	fuera	fuese	*sé (tú)*
serías	*seas*	*fueras*	*fueses*	*no seas (tú)*
sería	sea	fuera	fuesç	sea Ud.
seríamos	seamos	fuéramos	fuésemos	seamos (nosotros)
seríais	*seáis*	*fuerais*	*fueseis*	*sed (vosotros)*
serían	sean	fueran	fuesen	*no seáis (vosotros)*
				sean Uds.
tendría	tenga	tuviera	tuviese	*ten (tú)*
tendrías	*tengas*	*tuvieras*	*tuvieses*	*no tengas (tú)*
tendría	tenga	tuviera	tuviese	tenga Ud.
tendríamos	tengamos	tuviéramos	tuviésemos	tengamos (nosotros)
tendríais	*tengáis*	*tuvierais*	*tuvieseis*	*tened (vosotros)*
tendrían	tengan	tuvieran	tuviesen	*no tengáis (vosotros)*
				tengan Uds.
traería	traiga	trajera	trajese	*trae (tú)*
traerías	*traigas*	*trajeras*	*trajeses*	*no traigas (tú)*
traería	traiga	trajera	trajese	traiga Ud.
traeríamos	traigamos	trajéramos	trajésemos	traigamos (nosotros)
traeríais	*traigáis*	*trajerais*	*trajeseis*	*traed (vosotros)*
traerían	traigan	trajeran	trajesen	*no traigáis (vosotros)*
				traigan Uds.
valdría	valga	valiera	valiese	*val (tú)*
valdrías	*valgas*	*valieras*	*valieses*	*no valgas (tú)*
valdría	valga	valiera	valiese	valga Ud.
valdríamos	valgamos	valiéramos	valiésemos	valgamos (nosotros)
valdríais	*valgáis*	*valierais*	*valieseis*	*valed (vosotros)*
valdrían	valgan	valieran	valiesen	*no valgáis (vosotros)*
				valgan Uds.
vendría	venga	viniera	viniese	*ven (tú)*
vendrías	*vengas*	*vinieras*	*vinieses*	*no vengas (tú)*
vendría	venga	viniera	viniese	venga Ud.
vendríamos	vengamos	viniéramos	viniésemos	vengamos (nosotros)
vendríais	*vengáis*	*vinierais*	*vinieseis*	*venid (vosotros)*
vendrían	vengan	vinieran	viniesen	*no vengáis (vosotros)*
				vengan Uds.
vería	vea	viera	viese	*ve (tú)*
verías	*veas*	*vieras*	*vieses*	*no veas (tú)*
vería	vea	viera	viese	vea Ud.
veríamos	veamos	viéramos	viésemos	veamos (nosotros)
veríais	*veáis*	*vierais*	*vieseis*	*ved (vosotros)*
verían	vean	vieran	viesen	*no veáis (vosotros)*
				vean Uds.

PRONUNCIATION, ETC.

SPELLING AND PUNCTUATION—

ORTOGRAFÍA Y PUNTUACIÓN

1 / *The Alphabet — El alfabeto*

A. There are thirty letters in the Spanish alphabet. They are

LETTER	NAME	LETTER	NAME
a	a	n	ene
b	be	ñ	eñe
c	ce	o	o
ch	che	p	pe
d	de	q	cu
e	e	r	ere
f	efe	rr	erre
g	ge	s	ese
h	hache	t	te
i	i	u	u
j	jota	v	ve *or* uve
k	ka	w	ve doble *or* doble u
l	ele	x	equis
ll	elle	y	i griega *or* ye
m	eme	z	zeta

B. Most of the letters of the Spanish alphabet are the same as those of the English alphabet. However, in Spanish, *k* and *w* are used only in words of foreign origin, and in addition to the other letters, Spanish has *ch*, *ll*, *ñ*, and *rr*, which are usually considered separate letters and are so alphabetized.[1]

C. The Spanish alphabet, like the English, is divided into vowels (*vocales*) and consonants (*consonantes*). The vowels are *a*, *e*, *i*, *o*, and *u*. The letter *y* is a vowel when final in a word, as in *soy*, *estoy*, and *Monterrey*, and in the conjunction *y* (*and*). All other letters are consonants.

D. The vowels are divided into two groups:

strong vowels	*a, e, o*
weak vowels	*i, u*

---

[1] Since *rr* never begins a word, it is not alphabetized as a separate letter.

In addition to the letters of the alphabet, an accent mark (´) is used in Spanish.

A. Spanish words do not normally bear an accent, but whenever the stress[1] does not fall in the usual place, this accent indicates which syllable of a word is stressed.

América	México	país	nación	también

B. Interrogative words[2] always bear a written accent.

¿ qué ?	¿ cuántos ?	¿ cuál ?	¿ quién ?
¿ dónde ?	¿ cuándo ?	¿ cuáles ?	¿ cómo ?

C. The written accent is used to distinguish between two words spelled alike but different in meaning.

de	*of*	dé	*give*
el	*the*	él	*he*
mas	*but*	más	*more*
se	*himself*, etc.	sé	*I know*
si	*if*	sí	*yes; self*
solo	*alone* (adj.)	sólo	*only* (adv.)

3 / Other Spelling Signs — Otros signos ortográficos

Two other signs are used to aid spelling and pronunciation of Spanish words.

A. The diaeresis (··) (*diéresis o crema*) is used over *u*[3] in combinations of *–güe–* and *–güi–* to show that the *u* is pronounced. EXAMPLES: antigüedad, vergüenza, lingüístico.

B. The hyphen (-) (*guión*) is used, as in English, to separate parts of a word at the end of a line.

---

[1] For the rules for stress, see § 7 of this section.
[2] Some of these same words bear the written accent when used in exclamations. EXAMPLES: ¡ Cómo no ! ¡ Qué viaje tan magnífico !
[3] For the use of *–u–* after *–g–*, see § 12 of this section under the discussion of *g* (+ *ue*, + *ui*).

A. Spanish punctuation marks (*signos de puntuación*) are:

(.)	punto	(··)	diéresis o crema
(,)	coma	(*)	asterisco
(;)	punto y coma	(-)	guión
(:)	dos puntos	(—)	raya
(¿)	principio de interrogación	( )	paréntesis
(?)	fin de interrogación	(« »)	comillas
(¡)	principio de admiración	(. . .)	puntos suspensivos
(!)	fin de admiración		

B. In many respects, Spanish punctuation is approximately the same as English. The most notable differences are:

1. An inverted question mark precedes questions.

¿ Qué es México ?	What is Mexico?
Cuando Roberto llegó a la capital ¿ qué hizo ?	When Robert arrived in the capital, what did he do?

2. An inverted exclamation point precedes exclamations.

¡ Qué magnífico país !	What a magnificent country!

3. In Spanish, no comma is used between the last two words in a series, where in English it usually is.

La criada trae naranjas, plátanos y uvas.	The servant brings oranges, bananas, and grapes.

4. Dashes are ordinarily used to indicate a change of speaker, although lowered quotation marks are also used occasionally.

— ¿ No es usted norteamericano ? — pregunta Felipe.	"Aren't you an American?" asks Phillip.
— Sí, señor — contesta Roberto —. Yo soy norteamericano.	"Yes, sir," answers Robert. "I am an American."

C. In Spanish, capital letters are not used as frequently as in English. Small letters are used in the following cases where English requires capitals:

1. for *yo* (*I*) in the interior of a sentence;
2. to begin the days[1] of the week and the months of the year;

---

[1] Many Spanish-speaking people now use capitals for days of the week and months of the year.

Fuimos a Barcelona el miércoles.	We went to Barcelona on Wednesday.
Hace frío en enero.	It is cold in January.

3. to begin nouns or adjectives of nationality and names of languages;

la cultura mexicana	Mexican culture
la lengua inglesa	the English language
aprender francés	to learn French
los españoles y los mexicanos	the Spaniards and the Mexicans

4. usually to begin any but the first word of titles

El águila y la serpiente	*The Eagle and the Serpent*
Los de abajo	*The Underdogs*

5 / Division of Words into Syllables — Silabeo

Not many of us are sure where to divide English words into syllables. Spanish words may be divided more easily because six rules may be applied to govern their division.

A. A single consonant between vowels always goes with the following vowel.

A-mé-ri-ca	bo-ni-tas	ciu-dad
Mé-xi-co	tie-ne	ca-pi-tal
ca-si	u-na	pe-ro
na-ción	pri-mi-ti-vo	a-ve-ni-da

B. Two consonants of which the second is l or r generally both belong in the following syllable. The single consonantal sounds ch, ll, and rr also go with the following syllable.

ki-ló-me-tros	re-pú-bli-ca	ca-lles
o-tro	Ve-ra-cruz	ba-rrios
a-gra-da-ble	im-pe-ne-tra-ble	mu-cho

C. In other combinations of two consonants, the first consonant goes with the preceding and the second consonant with the following syllable.

con-ti-nen-te	par-te	gran-de
nor-te	tam-bién	ha-bi-tan-tes
par-que	na-tu-ral-men-te	cul-tu-ra

D. Combinations of three consonants are generally divided after the first consonant.

siem-pre	mez-cla	es-cri-bir
en-tre	en-cuen-tran	in-fluen-cia
san-gre	in-dus-trial	cen-tral

E. Two adjacent strong vowels[1] form two separate syllables.

pa-se-o	mu-se-o	ma-es-tro
o-es-te	le-e	hé-ro-e

F. Adjacent strong and weak vowels[1] or two weak vowels normally combine to form a single syllable. This combination of two vowels is called a *diphthong*.

Co-lom-bia	na-cio-nes	ciu-dad
go-bier-no	es-ta-tua	cau-sa

6 / Importance of Knowing How to Divide a Word into Syllables — Importancia del silabeo

It is important for you to know how to divide a Spanish word into syllables for the following reasons:

A. Spaniards generally pronounce consonants with the following rather than the preceding syllable. Whereas in English we say "A-mer-i-ca," the Spaniard says "A-mé-ri-ca," and whereas we say "ge-og-ra-phy," the Spaniard says "ge-o-gra-fí-a."
B. It is necessary to follow these rules for syllabication in separating words at the end of a line.
C. The spoken stress on a Spanish word is governed by rules which involve syllables. Unless you know how to divide a word into syllables, you cannot be sure where to stress new words which you have never heard.

THE PRONUNCIATION OF SPANISH-- LA PRONUNCIACIÓN DEL ESPAÑOL

In English, every polysyllabic word has one syllable which is stressed more than others. EXAMPLES: tre-**men**'-dous, **sum**'-ma-rize. There is no way of telling where the accent of an English word falls except by looking the word up in the dictionary. In Spanish, there are convenient rules for determining the stressed syllable.

---

[1] For the explanation of strong and weak vowels, see § 1 D of this section.

A. Words ending in a consonant, except –n or –s, are stressed on the last syllable.

capital	nacional	español	separar
existir	ciudad	trabajar	metal

B. Words ending in a vowel or –n or –s are stressed on the next to the last syllable.

norte	naciones	edificios	cultura
continente	gobierno	primitivo	una
habitantes	parte	hablan	joven

C. Words whose stress is not in conformity with these rules bear a written accent on the stressed vowel.

América	nación	árbol	México
públicos	también	millón	república

D. In a combination of a strong and weak vowel[1] or of two weak vowels, the strong vowel or the second of two weak vowels is normally stressed in an accented syllable.

gobierno	doscientos	estudiar	puerto
tiempo	viejo	bien	construido

E. In combinations of a strong and weak vowel, when the weak vowel is stressed, there is always a written accent which divides the two vowels into separate syllables. Otherwise, the combination becomes a diphthong of one syllable with the stress on the strong vowel.

país	mayoría	río	continúa
aún	frío	baúl	envíe

8 / *Regional Differences in Spanish Pronunciation —*

Diferencias regionales de pronunciación española

Spanish is spoken in many different parts of the world, including Spain, Spanish Morocco, Mexico, Central and South America, parts of the United

---

[1] For the explanation of strong and weak vowels, see § 1 D of this section.

States, and numerous islands. Each of these regions has its own peculiar way of pronouncing Spanish, just as in diverse sections of the United States the pronunciation of English differs from that of England, Canada, and Australia.

The Spanish spoken in that part of Spain known as *Castile* and by educated Spaniards in most parts of the country is called *Castilian*. This pronunciation of Castile, the political and cultural center of the Hispanic world for many centuries, is to Spanish approximately what standard usage in Southern England is to our language.

The main differences in pronunciation among the Spanish-speaking regions of the world involve a few basic sounds and numerous variations in intonation.

The main differences in sound are:

A. the pronunciation of c *followed by* e *or* i and of z in all positions.

    1. In some parts of Spain and in most other parts of the Spanish-speaking world, c *followed by* e *or* i and z in all words are pronounced like s in the English word *send*.

    2. In Castilian, c *followed by* e *or* i and z in all words are pronounced somewhat like th in the English word *thin*.

B. the pronunciation of ll

    1. In some parts of Spain and in many other parts of the Spanish-speaking world, ll is pronounced like the English y in *young*.

    2. In still other parts of the Spanish-speaking world, ll (and also the consonant y) are pronounced at times like s in *pleasure* and at times like j in *judge*.

    3. In Castilian, ll is pronounced approximately like lli in the English word *million*.

Intonation[1] is the rising and falling of the voice when reading or speaking. The intonation of English spoken in England differs from that of English spoken in the United States, and, within the borders of the United States, the intonation heard in Michigan is quite different from that heard in Mississippi. Likewise, the intonation of Spanish spoken in Spain differs from that spoken in Mexico, and the intonation heard in Guadalajara, Mexico differs from that of Mexico City. In other words, each Spanish-speaking region has its peculiar intonation.

---

[1] The various types of intonation are too numerous to discuss, and they can, in any case, only be learned through imitation. Imitate your teacher's intonation.

The ability to pronounce individual syllables or words well does not in itself constitute a good pronunciation. Words generally occur in breath-groups which make up sentences, and in order to speak or read aloud correctly, it is necessary to practice pronouncing entire phrases and sentences, keeping in mind the *meaning* of what one is pronouncing. Words pronounced in logical breath-groups tend to be joined more closely together and may cause a regrouping of syllables. One does not say *Norte | América | es | un | continente*, but *Norte América es un continente*.

The following rules generally govern the linking of words within a breath-group:

A. The final vowel in one word tends to form one syllable with the initial vowel of the following word. EXAMPLES: Norte América, millones de habitantes, algunos de estos barrios, una avenida muy ancha, sobre esta colina se encuentra un castillo, no es la única ciudad importante

B. The final consonant of one word is often linked with the initial vowel of the following word. EXAMPLES: es un continente, ciudad importante, calor insoportable, son elegantes

10 / *The Vowels — Las vocales*

Pronounce the English word *fate*. Note that you say "f-a-ee-t." The *a* is made up of the sound *a* plus the glide-sound *ee*. Spanish vowels do not have the glide-sound. Their pronunciation is constant, the jaws, lips, and tongue being held in the same position throughout the time required for making the sound. The Spanish-speaking person would pronounce *fate* "f-ā-t," which would cause it to sound foreign, for it would be too abrupt. You must pronounce your Spanish vowels without the glide-sound to make them sound truly Spanish.

In Spanish, as in English, a vowel in a stressed syllable is much clearer than it is in an unstressed syllable. However, even in an unstressed syllable, the Spanish vowel is never slurred. In the English word *Alaska*, the second *a* is given the most force and the first and last *a* become *uh* in English. In Spanish, *Alaska* would be sounded so that each *a* was pronounced approximately as the English *a* in *father*, but the first and last *a* would be said rapidly whereas the second *a* would be said more slowly and more distinctly.

a

a is pronounced as the English **a** in *father*.

varios	la	paseo	Reforma
grande	ciudad	América	una
parte	calles	también	nación

e

e has two basic sounds in Spanish.

When it ends a syllable or is followed in the syllable by **d, m, n** or **s,** it is comparable to the English **e**[1] in *they*.

México	América	es	que
pero	continente	Norte	parte

In all other cases, it is comparable to the English **e** in *bet*.

el	puerto	del	selva
aspectos	cerca	gobierno	hotel

i

i and *y* as vowel (*y* generally when it stands alone or at the end of a word) are pronounced as English **i** in *police*.

Chile	América	primitivo	Paraguay
divide	continente	y	Uruguay
interesante	México	hay	estoy

o

o has two basic sounds in Spanish.

When it ends a syllable, it is comparable to the English **o** in *spoke*.

sobre	no	bonitas	México
como	colonia	pero	paseo

In all other cases, it is comparable to the English **o** in *for*.

Norte	son	Reforma	árbol
continente	nación	importante	bosque

---

[1] This Spanish *e* is actually between the English **e** in *they* and the English **e** in *met*.

u is pronounced as English **u** in *rule*.

un	muchos	una	europea
Sud	públicos	única	Chapultepec
ciudad	cultura	algunos	unidos

11 / Diphthongs — Diptongos

A diphthong[1] is a combination of two vowels in the same syllable. Whether the diphthong is in an accented or unaccented syllable, the stress falls on the strong vowel or the second of two weak vowels.

también	gobierno	nadie	Colombia
nación	aunque	aislados	varios
tiene	seis	europea	edificios
hay	siete	serie	continuo

12 / The Consonants — Las consonantes

b, v

b and *v* are pronounced exactly alike in Spanish and have two basic sounds. At the beginning of a breath-group or following *m* or *n*, they are comparable to English **b** in *boat*.

bonitos	barrios	va	venden
bellas	Colombia	veces	ver
también	ve	varios	enviar

In other cases, *b* and *v* are somewhat like English **b** without the firm closing of the lips.

gobierno	adobe	divide	civilización
Orizaba	habitantes	elevada	primitiva

c (+ e *and* + i),   z

c *before* e *and* i and z in all positions are pronounced alike. In Mexico and most parts of Spanish America, they are pronounced as English **c** in *city*. In most of Spain, these letters are lisped and sound like English **th** in *thin*.

nación	ciudad	zona	Venezuela
centro	veces	civilizaciones	Orizaba
principal	edificios	mestizos	Veracruz

---

[1] For an explanation of the diphthong, see § 5 F in this section.

c (+ a, + o, + u),   c (+ *consonant*),   k,   qu

k, qu, *and* **c** *before* **a, o,** *and* **u** *or a consonant* have the sound of the English **k.**

América	capital	que	bosque
continente	frecuente	quiere	aquí
cultura	encuentra	parque	kilómetro

ch

ch is pronounced as the **ch** in the English *church.*

mucho	Chile	Chapultepec	charlar

d

When at the beginning of a breath-group or following *l* or *n*, the Spanish *d* is similar to English **d** in *do* but with the tip of the tongue more forward and touching the upper front teeth.

de	diferentes	después	donde
dos	denso	dinero	indio
dar	día	indicar	aldea

In other positions, it is comparable to English **th** in *they*.   Between vowels and in final position in a word, it is often scarcely audible in rapid conversation.

ciudad	adobe	sud	hablado
elevada	médicos	usted	comido
Estados Unidos	agradable	facultad	vivido

f

f is pronounced as **f** in the English word *fool.*

edificios	Reforma	famoso	Felipe
diferentes	fácil	fábrica	filosofía

g (+ e *and* i), j

g *before* **e** *and* **i** and **j** in all positions have no English equivalent.   They are pronounced like the **ch** in the German word *ach.*[1]

región	energía	José	trabajar
general	ingeniero	extranjero	bajo
vegetación	higiene	Guadalajara	justicia

---

[1] Students who have difficulty making the sound of the Spanish **j** can obtain an approximation but not an equivalent of the sound by pronouncing the sound of the English **h** very forcefully.

g (+ a, + o, + u, + ue, + ui), g (+ *consonant*)

g *before* a, o, *and* u *or a consonant* has a sound similar to that of the g in the English word *garden* when at the beginning of a breath-group or following n. The letter g followed by a consonant has a similar sound. The g between vowels is much weaker (the back of the tongue does not shut off the passage of air).

grande	algo	segundo	pregunta
gobierno	lengua	agua	elegante
algunas	González	luego	antigua

In order to indicate the hard sound of the g when followed by e or i, a silent u is inserted between the g and the e or i.

guerra	llegué	guitarra	águila

h is always silent as English h in *hour*.

habitantes	hablan	higiene	historia
hay	hasta	ahora	hotel

l

l constitutes a special difficulty since it does not correspond to the English l. It approaches initial l in *least*. Imitate your instructor's *l* and avoid making the l of the English word *fell*.

Colombia	la	españoles	película
Chile	capital	del	los

ll

ll is pronounced like y in the English word *young* in Mexico, many parts of South America, and in some parts of Spain.
ll is pronounced at times like s in *pleasure* and at times like j in *judge* in Argentina, Uruguay, and neighboring countries. [1]
ll is pronounced approximately like lli in the English word *million* in most parts of Spain.

millones	llaman	llegan	lleva
bella	lluvia	ella	llanura
calles	castillo	llueve	llenar

---

[1] The letter *y* (consonant) is pronounced as the *ll* in these countries.

m

m is pronounced as **m** in the English word *meet*.

muy	América	también	llaman
mucho	México	mexicano	mezcla

n

n is pronounced approximately like **n** in the English word *never*. [1]

norte	también	nación	son
un	continente	tiene	naturalmente

ñ

ñ is pronounced approximately like **ni** in the English word *onion*.

españoles	señor	niños	mañana
montañas	señorita	años	dueño

p

p is pronounced approximately as in the English word *speak*.

parte	pero	capital	primitiva
país	pues	públicos	aspectos

r

r (except at the beginning of a word or after *n*, *l*, or *s*) differs from English **r** in that the tongue quickly touches the roof of the mouth near the front teeth somewhat like **d** in the English word *meadow*.

diferentes	América	pobres	parques
norte	parte	grande	centro
pero	cultura	varios	primitiva

rr

rr always and *r* at the beginning of a word or after *n*, *l*, or *s* are strongly trilled.

Reforma	sierra	terreno	alrededor
región	Monterrey	guitarra	honrado
residencia	barrios	desarrollar	Enrique

---

[1] Before *b*, *p*, and *v*, however, *n* is pronounced as **m**. EXAMPLES: **en**viar, **en**vidia.

s is pronounced somewhat[1] like **s** in the English word **s***ea*.[2]

país	aspectos	presidente	desde
casi	Sud América	residencia	mismo
Paseo	presente	señor	desgraciadamente

t

t is pronounced as **t** in the English word *too* but with the tongue touching the back of the upper front teeth.

norte	parte	habitantes	primitiva
continente	también	centro	tiene

x

x has two basic sounds in Spanish.[3]
Before a vowel or *h*, it sounds somewhat like the English combination **gs**.[4]

exactamente	existen	examen	éxito

Before a consonant, it is comparable to the **s** in the English word *best*.

extranjero	explica	extraña	excelente
exclamar	expresión	exportación	extender

---

[1] There are several types of *s* in the various parts of the Spanish-speaking world, but the English *hissed* **s** is a fair approximation except for the specialist.

[2] *s* before *b, d, g, l, m, n,* and *v* is pronounced like the weak English *z*-sound in *boy*s. EXAMPLES: desde, mismo.

[3] In certain Mexican words, especially in proper names, *x* is pronounced like the Spanish *j*. EXAMPLES: México, Oaxaca, Texas. An initial *x* in Mexican words is pronounced like *s*. EXAMPLE: Xochimilco.

[4] Be careful not to pronounce the *x* as **gz.**

PEQUEÑOS OBSTÁCULOS EN ESPAÑOL PROVENIENTES DEL INGLÉS

Almost every English-speaking person who is still in the process of learning the language makes certain errors in Spanish because of the influence of English vocabulary and English constructions. To eliminate such errors, one must first become aware that they exist, then set about to learn how Spanish expresses such words and constructions.

The following 113 English sentences contain words and constructions which present problems when expressed in Spanish. The English list is alphabetized by the italicized keyword which entails the difficulty. The Spanish list gives the correct way of expressing the English sentences in Spanish.

To study these sentences, it is suggested that the student cover the Spanish list, then try to write the Spanish equivalent of a limited number of the English sentences, check his sentence against the Spanish list in the book, then learn the correct form of sentences in which he has made errors.

1. Charles has *about* eight books.
2. Charles writes a letter *about (concerning)* his class.
3. Charles will meet Mary *at about* five o'clock.
4. Charles gives *advice* to Mary.
5. Charles runs *after* the car.
6. Charles leaves *after* the meal.
7. Charles will leave *after* he speaks.
8. Charles leaves *after* Mary has spoken.
9. Charles studies his lesson *again*.

10. Charles *agrees* with Mary.
11. Charles and Mary *agree* on the importance of Spanish.
12. Charles has *another* book.
13. Charles *approaches* Mary.
14. Charles *arrives in* Spain.

1. Carlos tiene *cerca de* ocho libros.
2. Carlos escribe una carta *acerca de* su clase.
3. Carlos encontrará a María *a eso de* las cinco.
4. Carlos da *consejos* a María.
5. Carlos corre *tras* el coche.
6. Carlos sale *después de* la comida.
7. Carlos saldrá *después de* hablar.
8. Carlos sale *después (de) que* María ha hablado.
9. Carlos estudia su lección *otra vez*. Carlos estudia su lección *de nuevo*. Carlos *vuelve a* estudiar su lección.
10. Carlos *está de acuerdo* con María.
11. Carlos y María *están de acuerdo* sobre la importancia del español.
12. Carlos tiene *otro* libro.
13. Carlos *se acerca a* María.
14. Carlos *llega a* España.

15. Mary is not *as* tall *as* Charles.
16. Charles interprets it *as a* sign of good luck.
17. *As* Charles walks toward the square, he meets Mary.

18. Charles *asks Mary for a book.*
19. Charles *asks her for a book.*
20. Charles *asks Mary a question.*
21. Charles admires Mary *because* of her intelligence.
22. Charles admires Mary *because* she is intelligent.
23. Charles leaves *before* he has finished his work.
24. Charles leaves *before* Mary arrives.
25. Charles reads, *but* Mary works.
26. Charles does not study history *but* literature.
27. Charles does not read *but* works.
28. All come *but (except)* Charles.
29. Charles reads *but (only)* two books.
30. Don Juan is the most important *character* in the play.
31. Charles has a violent *character.*
32. Charles goes *down* the river.
33. Charles *enters* the room.
34. Charles has *everything* he needs.
35. Charles *feels* good.

36. Charles listens *first.*
37. *At first* Charles doesn't understand.
38. Charles has been singing *for* an hour.
39. Charles sang *for* an hour.
40. Charles sings, *for (because)* he is happy.
41. Charles takes the book away *from* Mary.
42. Charles *has* a book.
43. Charles *has* read a book.
44. Charles *hears of* the war.

15. María no es *tan* alta *como* Carlos.
16. Carlos lo interpreta *como* señal de buena suerte.
17. *Mientras (cuando)* Carlos camina hacia la plaza, encuentra a María.

18. Carlos *pide un libro a María.*
19. Carlos *le pide un libro.*
20. Carlos *hace una pregunta a María.*
21. Carlos admira a María *a causa* de su inteligencia.
22. Carlos admira a María *porque* es inteligente.
23. Carlos sale *antes de* terminar su trabajo.
24. Carlos sale *antes (de) que* María llegue.
25. Carlos lee, *pero* María trabaja.
26. Carlos no estudia historia *sino* literatura.
27. Carlos no lee *sino que* trabaja.
28. Todos vienen *menos* Carlos.
29. Carlos *no* lee *más que* dos libros.
30. Don Juan es el *personaje* más importante de la comedia.
31. Carlos tiene el *carácter* violento.
32. Carlos va río *abajo.*
33. Carlos *entra en* el cuarto.
34. Carlos tiene *todo lo que* necesita.
35. Carlos *se siente* bien.
Carlos *está* bien.
36. Carlos escucha *primero.*
37. *Al principio* Carlos no entiende.
38. Carlos canta *desde hace* una hora. *Hace* una hora *que* Carlos canta.
39. Carlos cantó *durante* una hora.
40. Carlos canta, *porque* está alegre.
41. Carlos *le* quita *a* María el libro.
42. Carlos *tiene* un libro.
43. Carlos *ha* leído un libro.
44. Carlos *oye hablar de* la guerra.

45. Charles is (*at*) *home*.
46. Charles goes *home*.
47. Charles leaves *home*.
48. Charles gets up at six *in the* morning.
49. Charles studies *in the* morning and goes to school *in the* afternoon.
50. Charles *intends* to go to Spain.
51. Charles *is interested in* painting.
52. Charles *introduces* me to Mary.
53. Charles *knocks* at the door.
54. Charles *knows* that Mary is at home.
55. Charles *knows* Mary.
56. Charles *knows how* to dance.
57. *Charles lacks* friends.
58. The *last* day Charles left for Spain.
59. *Last night* Charles worked.
60. *Last* week Charles traveled.
61. Charles *laughs at* Mary.
62. Charles *leaves* the school.
63. Charles *leaves* the pencil on the desk.
64. Charles *looks at* the flowers.
65. Charles *looks for* a book.
66. Charles *loves* Mary.
67. Charles *is in love with* Mary.
68. Charles *falls in love with* Mary.
69. Charles *marries*.
    Charles *gets married*.
70. Charles *marries* Mary.
71. Charles *is married*.

72. Charles *is married to* Mary.
73. What *does* "despacio" *mean*?
74. Charles *must* (*has to*) work.
75. Charles *must* (probably) study a great deal.
76. Charles *must* (ought to) study more.
77. *What is* Charles' *name*?

45. Carlos está *en casa*.
46. Carlos va *a casa*.
47. Carlos sale *de casa*.
48. Carlos se levanta a las seis *de la* mañana.
49. Carlos estudia *por la* mañana y va a la escuela *por la* tarde.
50. Carlos *piensa* ir a España.
51. Carlos *se interesa por* la pintura.
52. Carlos me *presenta* a María.
53. Carlos *llama* a la puerta.
54. Carlos *sabe* que María está en casa.
55. Carlos *conoce* a María.
56. Carlos *sabe* bailar.
57. *A Carlos le faltan* amigos.
58. El *último* día Carlos salió para España.
59. *Anoche* Carlos trabajó.
60. La semana *pasada* Carlos viajó.
61. Carlos *se ríe de* María.
62. Carlos *sale de* la escuela.
63. Carlos *deja* el lápiz en el escritorio.
64. Carlos *mira* las flores.
65. Carlos *busca* un libro.
66. Carlos *quiere* a María.
67. Carlos *está enamorado de* María.
68. Carlos *se enamora de* María.
69. Carlos *se casa*.

70. Carlos *se casa con* María.
71. Carlos *está casado*.
    Carlos *es casado*.
72. Carlos *está casado con* María.
73. ¿ Qué *quiere decir* « despacio » ?
74. Carlos *tiene que* trabajar.
75. Carlos *debe de* estudiar mucho.
    Carlos *estudiará* mucho.
76. Carlos *debe* estudiar más.

77. ¿ *Cómo se llama* Carlos ?

78. I know a boy *named* Charles.

79. *The next* morning Charles left.

80. *Next* week Charles will leave.

81. Charles *passes* the house.
82. Charles *plays* football and chess.

83. Charles *plays* the guitar.
84. Charles *resembles* his mother.
85. Charles *returns* to Madrid.

86. Charles *returns* the money.
87. Charles is sleeping *since (because)* he is tired.
88. Charles has been sleeping *since* yesterday.
89. Charles *is sitting (seated)* on a chair.
90. Charles *is sitting (seating himself)*.

91. Charles *spends* a great deal of money.
92. Charles *spends* a month in Madrid.
93. Charles *takes* a pencil from the table.
94. Charles *takes* Mary to the dance.
95. Charles *takes* a course.
96. Charles *takes* a walk.

97. Charles *tells* a story.
98. Charles *tells* of his trip.
99. Charles *thinks of* Mary.
100. What *does* Charles *think of* the book?
101. Charles doesn't have enough *time*.
102. Charles calls three *times*.
103. What *time* is it?
104. Charles *has a good time*.
105. Charles goes *up* the street.

78. Conozco a un chico *llamado* Carlos.

79. *A la* mañana *siguiente* Carlos salió.

80. Carlos saldrá la semana *que viene*. Carlos saldrá la semana *próxima*.

81. Carlos *pasa por delante de* la casa.
82. Carlos *juega al* fútbol y *al* ajedrez.

83. Carlos *toca* la guitarra.
84. Carlos *se parece a* su madre.
85. Carlos *vuelve* a Madrid. Carlos *regresa* a Madrid.

86. Carlos *devuelve* el dinero.
87. Carlos duerme *porque* está cansado.

88. Carlos duerme *desde* ayer.

89. Carlos *está sentado* en una silla.

90. Carlos *se sienta*.

91. Carlos *gasta* mucho dinero.

92. Carlos *pasa* un mes en Madrid.

93. Carlos *toma* un lápiz de la mesa.

94. Carlos *lleva* a María al baile.
95. Carlos *sigue* un curso.
96. Carlos *da* un paseo (una vuelta). Carlos *(se) pasea*.
97. Carlos *cuenta* una historia.
98. Carlos *habla* de su viaje.
99. Carlos *piensa en* María.
100. ¿ Qué le *parece* a Carlos el libro ?

101. Carlos no tiene bastante *tiempo*.

102. Carlos llama tres *veces*.
103. ¿ Qué *hora* es ?
104. Carlos *se divierte*.
105. Carlos va calle *arriba*.

106. Charles takes his *vacation* in June.

107. Charles *waits for* the letter.

108. Charles *wants Mary to leave.*

109. Charles is *with* Mary.

110. The mountain is covered *with* snow.

111. Charles *wonders* what Mary is doing.

112. Charles *would write* if he had time.

113. Charles *would write (used to write)* every day.

106. Carlos toma sus *vacaciones* en junio.

107. Carlos *espera* la carta.

108. Carlos *quiere que María salga.*

109. Carlos está *con* María.

110. La montaña está cubierta *de* nieve.

111. Carlos *se pregunta* qué hace María.

112. Carlos *escribiría* si tuviera tiempo.

113. Carlos *escribía* todos los días.

EXERCISES

1 / Forms of the Indefinite Article — Formas del artículo indeterminado

1 Place *un, una, unos* or *unas* in front of each noun. (§1 A, B)

1 Buscamos . . . apartamento. 2 Necesito . . . pesos. 3 Aquí hay . . . sillas. 4 ¿Qué buscas Pedro, . . . pluma? 5 El señor Muñoz busca . . . abogado. 6 Gregorio quiere comprar . . . camisas nuevas. 7 ¿Puede decirme dónde hay . . . farmacia? 8 Mañana María traerá . . . discos populares. 9 Aquí hay . . . teléfono. 10 ¿Qué es esto? Es . . . libro de arte.

2 Write the following sentences in Spanish, using a form of the indefinite article for the indicated words. (§1 A, B)

1 Is there **a** restaurant here? 2 There is **a** drugstore on the corner. 3 (*tú*) Do you have **some** interesting books? 4 Where can I buy **some** stamps? 5 There is **a** café over there. 6 (*Ud.*) Did you find **some** chairs?

2 / Forms of the Definite Article — Formas del artículo determinado

1 Place *el, la, los* or *las* in front of each noun. (§2 A, B)

1 ¿Puedo hablar con . . . jefe de la compañía? 2 . . . chocolate está caliente. 3 Quiero hablar con . . . ingeniero Flores. 4 . . . oficina no está lejos. 5 ¿Viene . . . amiga de Felipe? 6 Busco . . . apartamento del señor Miró. 7 . . . calles de este barrio son anchas. 8 ¿Son grandes . . . coches europeos? 9 ¿Llegan . . . secretarias a las ocho? 10 . . . padres de Julio viven cerca de aquí.

2 Write the following sentences in Spanish, using the appropriate form of the definite article. (§2 A, B)

1 (*tú*) Are you going to buy **the** house? 2 **The** doctor isn't here. 3 Where are **the** records? 4 Here is **the** letter. 5 (*Uds.*) Do you prefer **the** theatre or **the** cinema? 6 Where are **the** girls?

3 / Contractions of the Definite Article — Contracciones del artículo determinado

1 Rewrite each sentence, replacing the indicated noun with the ones given in parentheses. Make the contraction if necessary. (§3 A, B)

≫ Carlos viene de la **oficina**. (colegio)
Carlos viene **del colegio**.

a) Carlos viene de la **oficina**. (1 hotel, 2 aeropuerto, 3 capital, 4 parque, 5 baile, 6 conferencia)

b) Los amigos salen de la **clase.** (1 escuela, 2 apartamento, 3 casa, 4 coche, 5 cine, 6 fábrica)

c) Voy a la **fiesta.** (1 centro, 2 estación, 3 mercado, 4 cuarto, 5 cocina, 6 patio)

d) Le escribo a **María.** (1 chico, 2 alumno, 3 señor, 4 profesor, 5 señorita, 6 secretaria)

4 / Uses of the Article — Modos de usar los artículos

1 Complete each sentence with the appropriate form of the definite article *el, la, los, las* if it is needed. (§4 A)

1 Soy de México pero aprendo . . . inglés. 2 La señorita Cruz enseña . . . español. ¿Es fácil . . . español? 3 Se habla . . . francés en Francia y en algunos otros países. ¿Hablas . . . francés? 4 En Colombia algunas personas no leen . . . español pero lo hablan perfectamente.

2 Write the following sentences in Spanish. Use the definite article where needed. (§4 B)

1 Baseball is popular in Mexico. 2 Children are always curious. 3 (*Ud.*) Do you prefer cats or dogs? 4 Coffee and tea are favorite beverages in the United States.

3 Complete each sentence with the appropriate form of the definite article if it is needed. (§4 C)

1 --¿Está aquí . . . señor Gómez? ¡Ah, . . . señor Gómez, buenos días! 2 --Buenas tardes, . . . señorita Sandoval. ¿Es posible hablar con . . . señora Flores? 3 --¿Cómo está usted, . . . señora Donoso? ¿Quiere ver a . . . señora Muñoz?

4 Complete each sentence with the appropriate form of the indefinite article if it is needed. (§4 D)

1 Mi madre es . . . secretaria. Trabaja para el Ministerio de Economía. 2 Después de la guerra el Coronel Miranda llegó a ser . . . senador. 3 El nuevo presidente del instituto es . . . abogado muy conocido. También es . . . doctor de filosofía y letras. 4 Fernando es . . . mexicano pero vive en Texas. 5 Cuando se casó mi hermana se hizo . . . católica. Ahora sus hijos son . . . católicos también.

5 Complete each sentence with the appropriate form of the definite article if it is needed. (§4 A, B, C, D)

1 --¿Está presente . . . señorita Moreno? Buenos días, . . . señorita Moreno. 2 En el Canadá hablan . . . inglés y . . . francés. ¿Crees que . . . inglés y . . . francés son

lenguas difíciles? 3 Mi tío es . . . médico. . . . médicos trabajan muchas horas. 4 La abuela de Carmen es . . . francesa pero entiende . . . inglés.

6 Write these sentences in Spanish. In some cases you will need to use either the indefinite article or the definite article. In other cases the article is not necessary. (§4 A, B, C, D)

1 European cars are economical but American cars are more comfortable. 2 --Good morning, Mr. Torres. Is[1] Mrs. Torres at home? 3 (**Ud.**) You don't have to know English. I speak French. 4 Goodbye, Don Pablo. 5 (**tú**) White wine is very cheap in Spain. Do you like white wine? 6 My father is a lawyer. I want to be a lawyer too. 7 I like French, but I prefer to study Spanish. 8 Who is Mr. Carrera? Is he a Spaniard or a Cuban? 9 Mr. García is an American. He speaks English and Spanish. 10 John is a student. He wants to be an engineer.

7 Answer each question in a complete sentence. Use the definite article where it is needed before days of the week. (See §51 for the days of the week) (§4 E)

1 ¿Qué día es hoy? 2 ¿Qué día es mañana? 3 ¿Cuál es el primer día de la semana en los Estados Unidos? 4 ¿Qué días de la semana tienes clases? 5 ¿Qué días de la semana no tienes clases? 6 ¿Qué día va la gente a la iglesia?

8 Write the following sentences in Spanish, using the definite article with the days of the week when necessary. (§4 E)

1 Is today[2] Monday or Tuesday? 2 We go to the park on Sundays. 3 Is Robert coming Friday or Saturday? 4 (**tú**) Which[3] day is your birthday, Wednesday or Thursday? 5 Mr. Romero pays me every Friday.

9 Write the appropriate definite article which goes before each part of the body. (§4 F)

1 . . . cabeza (*head*)
2 . . . pelo (*hair*)
3 . . . ojo (*eye*) . . . ojos
4 . . . nariz (*nose*)
5 . . . cara (*face*)
6 . . . brazo (*arm*) . . . brazos
7 . . . mano (*hand*) . . . manos
8 . . . dedo (*finger*) . . . dedos
9 . . . pierna (*leg*) . . . piernas

10 . . . oreja (*ear*) . . . orejas
11 . . . boca (*mouth*)
12 . . . diente (*tooth*) . . . dientes
13 . . . lengua (*tongue*)
14 . . . pie (*foot*) . . . pies
15 . . . dedo (*toe*) . . . dedos
16 . . . estómago (*stomach*)
17 . . . corazón (*heart*)

[1] *estar*   [2] *¿Hoy es*   [3] *¿Qué*

Las partes del cuerpo

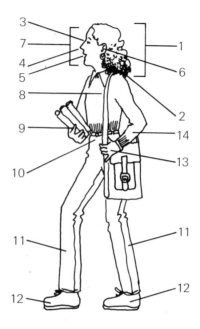

10 Write the part of the body identified by each number. Each part should be accompanied by the appropriate definite article. (§4 F)

11 Write the appropriate definite article which goes before each article of clothing. (§4 F)

1 . . . camisa (*shirt*)

2 . . . pantalones (*trousers*)

3 . . . ropa interior (*underwear*)

4 . . . calcetín (*sock*) . . . calcetines

5 . . . zapato (*shoe*) . . . zapatos

6 . . . media (*stocking*) . . . medias

7 . . . vestido (*dress*)

8 . . . blusa (*blouse*)

9 . . . falda (*skirt*)

10 . . . suéter (*sweater*)

11 . . . abrigo (*coat*)

12 . . . guante (*glove*) . . . guantes

13 . . . sombrero (*hat*)

12 Write the following sentences in Spanish using a form of the definite article. (§4 F)

1 Charles is putting on[1] **his** shirt. 2 I put on[1] **my** shoes and **my** socks. 3 Albert said that he broke[2] **his** arm and **his** nose in the accident. 4 When Domingo has nothing to do he puts **his** hands in **his** pockets. 5 John is taking off[3] **his** hat and **his** gloves. 6 Pepito always eats with **his** hands.

[1] to put on = *ponerse*   [2] *se rompió*   [3] to take off = *quitarse*

13 Complete each sentence with the appropriate form of the definite article if it is needed. (§4 G)

1 Madrid, . . . capital de España, tiene parques bonitos. 2 El policía, . . . hombre alto y delgado, me indicó la farmacia. 3 Un compañero de escuela, . . . chico rubio y amable, me enseñó a nadar. 4 El 4 de julio, . . . día de la independencia de los Estados Unidos, corresponde al 16 de setiembre, . . . día de la independencia mexicana.

14 Complete each sentence with the appropriate form of the indefinite or definite article if it is needed. (§4 H, I)

1 . . . Estados Unidos son una nación grande de . . . Norte América. 2 . . . Canadá es . . . otra nación de . . . Norte América pero no es tan grande. 3 En . . . cierta región de . . . España se habla catalán. 4 ¿Conoces los países de . . . Sud América como . . . Colombia y . . . Venezuela? 5 Hay pocas diferencias entre el español de . . . Argentina y el de . . . Uruguay. 6 . . . Bolivia es . . . otro país donde se habla español.

15 Write these sentences in Spanish, omitting the indefinite or the definite article when necessary. (§4 G, H, I)

1 My friend Alice is going to Chile. Another friend (f.) went there[1] last summer.
2 Cervantes, **the** famous Spanish writer, died in 1616. 3 The scientist is going to Brazil in order to[2] look for **a** certain type of mineral. Another scientist is going too.
4 Saltillo, **a** city in the north of Mexico, is famous for[3] its sarapes. 5 **A** certain group of students always goes there on Fridays.[4]

5 / *The Neuter Article* lo — *El artículo neutro* lo

1 Translate these sentences into Spanish using *lo* + <u>adjective</u>. (§5 A)

1 **The important thing** is to remember the tickets. 2 **The difficult thing** is to arrive early. 3 **The bad thing** is that we don't have a car. 4 The climate is **the best thing** about this region. 5 **The main** (principal) **thing** is to find the street.

2 Translate these sentences into Spanish using *lo.* (§5 D)

1 **That business of** finding their house was difficult. 2 (*tú*) Can you tell me **that matter about** your aunt? 3 **The affair of** the rebellion is interesting. 4 (*Ud.*) Do you know[5] **that business about** Mr. Arango?

[1] *allá*
[2] in order to = *para*
[3] *para*

[4] on Fridays = *los viernes*
[5] *saber*

3 Translate into Spanish using *lo cual* or *lo que.* Either may be used in each case. (§5 E)

1 Carlos said that the prices are high, **which** is true. 2 Mr. Fernández speaks English well, **which** surprises me. 3 Domingo has very serious ideas, **which** is rare for[1] a child of his age. 4 I can't go, **which** means that Pepe has to go alone.

4 Translate into Spanish using *lo que.* (§5 F)

1 (*tú*) I want to know **what** you are doing. 2 She explained **what** John said in the letter. 3 (*tú*) Do you know **what** you prefer to do? 4 (*Ud.*) Do you remember **what** the doctor said?

5 Complete each sentence with *lo, lo de,* or *lo que* as necessary. (§5 A, B, C, D, E, F)

1 Me interesa . . . las elecciones. Por . . . menos vamos a tener elecciones libres esta vez. 2 Los Incas eran muy poderosos hasta la llegada de Pizarro quien . . . cambió todo. 3 . . . ir al mercado todos los días es casi necesario. Por . . . general es necesario comprar algunas cosas cada día. . . . malo es que a veces no hay tiempo. 4 Nuestro equipo ganó en el partido de fútbol, . . . me gustó mucho. 5 Haga usted . . . quiera con el dinero. Sé . . . haría yo. 6 A . . . largo del río se ven las casas de los pobres.

6 / Gender of Nouns — *Género de los nombres*

1 Rewrite these sentences changing the possessive (*mi, tu, su*) to the definite article *el, la, los, las.* (§6 A)

1 Aquí está **su** oficina. 2 Son **mis** nuevos vecinos. 3 ¿Dónde está **tu** bicicleta? 4 Ahí están **tus** llaves. 5 ¿Cuándo son **sus** exámenes?

2 Identify the gender of each noun by placing the appropriate indefinite article before it. (§6 B)

1 . . . ciudad	8 . . . mapa
2 . . . problema	9 . . . probabilidad
3 . . . decisión	10 . . . legumbre
4 . . . costumbre	11 . . . programa
5 . . . sistema	12 . . . dificultad
6 . . . amistad	13 . . . canción
7 . . . oposición	14 . . . actividad

[1] *para*

3 Write the following sentences in Spanish, using the appropriate form of the in-definite or definite article with the noun. (§6 A, B)

 1 The city has **a problem** with **the pollution.** 2 **The inauguration** took place during **the month** of June. 3 (*Uds.*) Do you have **a map** of **the university**? 4 **The siesta** is still **a custom** in many parts of Mexico.

7 / Plural of Nouns — Plural de los nombres

1 Write the plural of each article and noun. (§7 A, B)

 1 la economía 2 el atleta 3 el tocadiscos 4 el avión 5 el joven ·6 la ley 7 la pared 8 el papel 9 el tren 10 la flor

2 Write the singular of the noun and give the English translation. (§7 C)

 1 las voces 2 las veces 3 las actrices 4 las luces 5 unos lápices 6 unos jueces 7 unas cruces 8 unos peces

3 Write the following sentences in Spanish, using the appropriate form of the in-definite or definite article. (§7 A, B, C)

 1 (*tú*) Did you lose **a pencil**? 2 We saw **the lights** of **the plane** in **the night**. 3 **The actress** spoke with[1] **a** clear **voice**. 4 Often (many times) we take **the train** to Madrid. 5 **A judge** must know **the laws** very well.

8 / Agreement of Adjectives — Concordancia de los adjetivos

1 Complete each sentence, making the adjective in parentheses agree with the noun(s). (§8 A, B)

 1 Prefiero la camisa . . . (amarillo). 2 Paco es un muchacho muy . . . (alto). 3 Anoche escuchamos unas canciones muy . . . (bonito). 4 Aquí vienen los atletas . . . (famoso). 5 Las calles y los parques de esta ciudad son . . . (limpio). 6 Rafael tiene cuatro perritos para vender. Uno es . . . (blanco) y los otros son . . . (blanco) y . . . (negro). 7 Vamos a pasar tres días . . . (entero) en Lima. 8 Algunos programas de radio son . . . (bueno). 9 Esas chicas . . . (rubio) se llaman Isabel y María. 10 Concha dice que sus dos hijos y su hija menor están . . . (enfermo) hoy.

9 / Forms of the Adjectives — Formas de los adjetivos

1 Rewrite these phrases, substituting the noun in parentheses for the indicated noun. Make any other changes necessary. (§9 A)

 1 el **chico** contento (chica) 2 un **cuento** largo (historia) 3 el **edificio**

[1]with = *en*

EXERCISES § 7

moderno (estatua) 4 un **animal** magnífico (obra) 5 un **vestido** rojo (camisa) 6 el
río ancho (avenida)

2 Write the plural of these phrases, making any necessary changes in agreement.
(§9 A, B)

    1 la montaña hermosa 2 un reloj viejo 3 un día especial 4 una pregunta fácil
5 la hija menor 6 el baile alegre 7 un trabajo útil 8 una muchacha inteligente

3 Rewrite each sentence, changing the subject to the plural. Make any other changes
necessary. (§9 A, B, C)

    1 La chica morena es bonita. 2 Un amigo de Tomás es español. 3 ¿El hijo
mayor va a la universidad? 4 Una joven inglesa busca trabajo aquí. 5 El problema
de Enrique es difícil. 6 La voz del niño era muy alta.

4 Complete with the necessary form of each adjective in parentheses. (§9 A, B, C)

    a) Necesito una camisa . . . (nuevo) para celebrar mi cumpleaños. Prefiero los
colores . . . (oscuro). La semana . . . (pasado) vi . . . (mucho) ropa . . . (fino) en esa
tienda . . . (pequeño) del centro. Creo que voy allí.

    b) --¿Cómo se llama esa chica . . . (español)? --Ah, sí esa muchacha . . . (moreno).
Se llama Carmen. Su familia vive cerca de nosotros. Su padre es . . . (español) pero su
madre es . . . (francés). Son todos muy . . . (amable).

5 Write these sentences in Spanish. (§9 A, B, C)

    1 The Retiro is a famous park in Madrid. 2 The streets of Lima are wide and
beautiful. 3 Does Lima have many modern buildings? 4 I have an uncle and two
aunts in California. They're Americans. 5 (*tú*) I prefer short novels. Do you read
many interesting books?   6 In Seville we lived in a typical house with white walls
and a red roof.

10 / Apocopation of Adjectives — Apócope de los adjetivos

1 Rewrite each sentence, replacing the indicated noun with the ones given in parentheses. Make the necessary changes in the preceding adjective. (§10 A)

≫ Tengo una **abuela** en Costa Rica. (amigo, hermanos)
Tengo **un amigo** en Costa Rica.
Tengo **unos hermanos** en Costa Rica.

a) Tengo una **abuela** en Costa Rica. (1 abuelo, 2 primas, 3 primos, 4 tío)

b) Vamos a llegar durante la primera **semana**. (1 día, 2 mes, 3 hora)

c) ¿Hay alguna **tienda** por aquí? (1 restaurantes, 2 banco, 3 peluquería, 4 fábricas)

d) Es buena **muchacha.** (1 muchacho, 2 profesoras, 3 compañeros, 4 jefe)

2 Complete each sentence with the appropriate form of the adjective(s) in parentheses. (§10 A, B)

1 Miguel tiene . . . (uno) apartamento . . . (pequeño) en la Calle Rosario. 2 Ayer comimos una . . . (grande) comida en casa. 3 Mario, ¿tienes . . . (alguno) fotografías de tus vacaciones? 4 Mi abuela está . . . (enfermo). Los médicos dicen que está en muy . . . (malo) condición. 5 Mi tío Gregorio me mandó un paquete . . . (grande). 6 Van a construir . . . (alguno) edificio público allí en la esquina. 7 Ya no había . . . (ninguno) periódico para leer. 8 Enrique Zamora fue el . . . (último) nombre en la lista.

3 Rewrite each sentence, replacing the indicated portion with each of the items in parentheses. Make any other changes necessary. (§10 C, D)

a) Voy a pedirle unos **veinte** pesos a don Federico. (100, 150, 200, 105)

b) Somos de la ciudad de Santa **Cruz.** (1 Juan, 2 Francisco, 3 Tomás, 4 Sebastián)

4 Write these sentences in Spanish. (§10 A, B, C, D, E)

1 My brother lives in **Saint Augustine.** He is the **third** child (son) in[1] the family. 2 Ramón Jiménez is a **great** poet. **Some** poems are[2] in English. 3 Paul wants **a hundred** dollars for[3] his bike. I think that it's a **good** bike.

11 / Position of Adjectives — Colocación de los adjetivos

1 Translate these sentences into Spanish, putting the adjective in the proper place. (§11 B)

1 (*tú*) Do you prefer **French** wine? 3 I think that she's a **pretty** girl! 3 We ate in an **Italian** restaurant. 4 Mrs. Macías prepared **hot** chocolate. 5 I bought a **blue** shirt yesterday.

[1] *de*
[2] *estar*
[3] *por*

2 Rewrite these sentences, placing the adjective(s) in parentheses either before or after the indicated noun. (§11 A, B)

≫ Había **gente** en el restorán. (poca)
Había **poca gente** en el restorán.
≫ Caminamos por las **calles**. (silenciosas)
Caminamos por las **calles silenciosas**.

1 (exacta) No recordamos la **dirección**. 2 (interesantes) Raúl tiene muchas **ideas**. 3 (última) Entré y me senté en la **silla**. 4 (cruel) ¿La corrida de toros le parece un **arte**? 5 (comercial) Pasamos por una **calle** del pueblo. 6 (antiguo) Estamos en un **barrio** de la capital. 7 (clásica) ¿Te gusta esta **música**? 8 (primera...blanca) Elena vive en esa **casa**. 9 (muchos...nuevos) ¿Hay **apartamentos** en esta ciudad?

3 Translate these sentences into Spanish, placing the indicated adjective either before or after the noun as necessary. (§11 D, E, F)

1 (m.) **How many** friends are coming? 2 **These** photographs are old. 3 **What** day is tomorrow? 4 **His** daughter works here. 5 (*Ud.*) I talked with a friend of **yours**. 6 The **two** brothers are engineers. 7 The **fourteenth** day, we left Quito. 8 I live in the **second** house from the corner. 9 (*tú*) **How much** money do you have? 10 **This** coat is **mine**! 11 The policeman asked me **some** questions.

4 Translate these sentences into Spanish, placing the adjective according to the intended meaning. (§11 G)

a) 1 Edward was a great man. 2 Edward was a big man.
b) 1 I bought a brand-new car! 2 I bought a new (used) car.
c) 1 This poor child, he's tired. 2 This poor (poverty-stricken) child needs clothing.
d) 1 It's a sheer (utter) lie! 2 It's pure water.

12 / Comparison of Adjectives — Comparación de adjetivos

1 Complete the sentence using the comparative expression *más...que...* (§12 A)

≫ Yo soy alta pero Luisa es ....
Yo soy alta pero Luisa es **más alta que yo**.

1 La biología es difícil pero la química es .... 2 El clima de aquí es agradable pero el clima de Arizona es .... 3 Susana es delgada pero Alicia es .... 4 San Francisco es grande pero Los Angeles es .... 5 Manuel es aplicado pero Antonio es .... 6 Estuve muy ocupado ayer pero hoy estoy ....

2 Translate these sentences into Spanish using the comparative expression *más* (*menos*) ...*que* .... (§12 A)

1 Robert is more ambitious than I (me). 2 The actor seems less nervous than before. 3 That dress is less typical than many others. 4 Inez[1] is less practical than her sister. 5 This coffee is[2] stronger than yesterday.

3 Rewrite these sentences in order to express the superlative. (§12 A, B)

≫ Es un museo famoso de Madrid.
  Es el museo más famoso de Madrid.

1 Es una iglesia antigua de mi pueblo. 2 Es un coche económico de los Estados Unidos. 3 Es un deporte popular de México. 4 Es un caballo fino de su tío Jaime. 5 Para nosotros es un programa divertido. 6 La paella es un plato famoso de Valencia.

4 Translate these sentences into Spanish using the superlative. (§12 B)

1 Santiago is the largest city in[3] Chile. 2 Today is the longest day of the year. 3 (*Ud.*) What[4] is the least interesting part of your work? 4 (*tú*) What was[5] the most horrible moment of your life? 5 (*tú*) What was[5] the most interesting part of your trip?

5 Complete these sentences using the comparative with *mejor, peor, mayor, menor.* (§12 C)

1 Aunque el camino que va a San Luis es malo, este camino es .... 2 Santos es buen poeta pero García es.... 3 Carlos es un muchacho grande pero Julio es el hermano .... 4 Aunque este restaurante es muy malo, el otro es.... 5 Pepita es una niña pequeña. Es la hija...de la familia. 6 Margarita es una niña buena pero Mariana es....

6 Use the irregular adjectives of comparison in writing these sentences in Spanish. (§12 A, B, C)

1 It's a very **good** coat. It's the **best** coat that I have. 2 Steve is a **big** boy. He's the **oldest** boy in[3] the family. 3 This wine is very **good**. (*tú*) Do you think it's the **best**

[1] *Inés*
[2] *estar*
[3] *de*

[4] *¿Cuál*
[5] What was = *¿Cuál fue*

wine from Spain? 4 Today was a very **bad** day. I think that it was the **worst** day of my life. 5 Is Adelita the **youngest** daughter of the family? 6 It was a very **bad** trip. It was the **worst** trip to Europe in ten years.

7 Translate these sentences into Spanish using the emphatic *-ísimo* construction. (§12 D)

1 This color is **very ugly**. 2 The Andes are **extremely high** mountains. 3 This song is **very beautiful**. 4 Their dog is **extremely fat**.

8 Translate into Spanish using *de* or *que* to express "than." (§12 F)

1 Susan has more **than** twenty records. I have only (no more **than**) twelve. 2 John read more **than** five books this week. 3 Mary and Julia have less time **than** we. 4 I have only (no more **than**) ten minutes. 5 Charles sold more **than** fifty tickets. I sold only (didn't sell more **than**) thirty-five.

9 Combine the two sentences to make the comparison of equality using *tan . . . como . . . .* (§12 G)

≫ Gregorio llega tarde. Felipe llega tarde también.
  Felipe llega **tan** tarde **como** Gregorio.

1 El café de Brasil es bueno. El café de Colombia es bueno también. 2 Lima es una ciudad moderna. México es una ciudad moderna también. 3 La ropa aquí cuesta poco dinero. La ropa allá cuesta poco dinero también. 4 La película fue divertida. La novela fue divertida también. 5 Yo estoy cansada. ¿Usted está cansada también? 6 Mi padre es un hombre generoso. Mi tío es un hombre generoso también.

10 Write these sentences in Spanish, using the comparative of equality *tan . . . como . . . .* (§12 G)

1 My son wants to be[1] **as** big **as** I (me). 2 Don Fernando is **as** old **as** my grandfather. 3 These chairs are **as** hard **as** the others. 4 Albert is **as** handsome **as** his father. 5 This book is **as** interesting **as** they said[2].

11 Complete each sentence with the equivalent of "than," using *del que, de la que, de los que, de las que, de lo que* as needed. (§12 H, I)

1 Ana es menos joven . . . parece. 2 La casa era más pequeña . . . describían en

[1] to be = *ser*
[2] *dijeron*

la carta. 3 El hombre que robó la ropa parecía más joven . . . veo en la foto. 4 Mi abuelo es menos viejo . . . yo pensaba. 5 El político creía que era más famoso . . . era. 6 Estas son las frutas más frescas . . . hemos comprado. 7 Estos apartamentos son los más cómodos . . . hemos visto.

13 / Adjectives Used as Nouns — Adjetivos usados como nombres

1 Rewrite the sentence omitting the noun so that the adjective takes its place.

1 La primera señora comenzó a hablar. 2 Los hombres ricos comen allí. 3 La chica morena acaba de llegar. 4 Los muchachos mayores trabajan en la fábrica.

14 / Possessive Adjectives — Adjetivos posesivos

1 Write the Spanish translation of the possessive adjective in parentheses. (§14 A, B)

1 ¿Dónde están (*my*) . . . gafas? 2 Aquí vienen (*our*) . . . compañeros. 3 Estos pobres chicos no conocen a (*their*) . . . padres. 4 ¿Tienes (*your*) . . . documentos, Antonio? 5 (*our*) . . . apartamento está cerca de aquí. 6 (Ud.) Ahí está (*your*) . . . reloj. 7 Los jóvenes llegan a (*their*) . . . trabajo temprano. 8 Concha, ¿puedes darme (*your*) . . . número de teléfono?

2 Rewrite these sentences, clarifying the meaning of *su* or *sus*. (§14 C)

≫ **Sus** padres están de vacaciones. (*his*)
  Los padres **de él** están de vacaciones.

1 **Sus** tíos son muy amables. (*her*) 2 Creo que **su** dirección es la Calle Potosí. (*theirs, m.*) 3 Recibimos **su** carta la semana pasada. (*theirs, f.*) 4 ¿**Su** primo es pintor? (*his*) 5 ¿Cuándo llegan **sus** invitados a comer? (*your, pl.*)

3 Rewrite these sentences using the stressed form of the possessive adjective. (§14 D, E)

≫ **Su** trabajo es muy duro.
  El trabajo **suyo** es muy duro.

1 **Sus** documentos están con la policía. 2 **Nuestras** maletas están allí en el rincón. 3 **Su** amiga se fue a California. 4 ¿**Tu** coche es nuevo? 5 **Mis** problemas son complicados, ¿verdad? 6 **Nuestros** productos son importados. 7 ¿**Su** abrigo es de Francia? 8 **Tu** pregunta es muy complicada.

4 Write the following sentences in Spanish using the stressed form of the possessive adjective. (§14 D, E)

1 These books are **mine**. 2 (*tú*) Are the records on the table **yours**? 3 A cousin (m.) of **ours** is a dentist. 4 (*Ud.*) Is this coffee **yours** or **mine?** 5 Some friends (m.) of **theirs** are going to have a party. 6 A friend of **ours** (f.) is going with us. 7 (*Ud.*) Is this money **yours**? No, it's not **mine**. 8 Are these letters **theirs**?

15 / Demonstrative Adjectives — Adjetivos demostrativos

1 Rewrite each sentence, replacing the indicated noun with the nouns given in parentheses. Make any other necessary changes. (§15 A, B, C, D)

≫ Esta **avenida** es hermosa. (parque, casa)
Este parque es hermoso.
Esta casa es hermosa.

a) Esta **avenida** es bonita. (1 canciones, 2 pintura, 3 sombrero, 4 animales)

b) Prefiero ese **queso** blanco. (1 camisas, 2 color, 3 flores, 4 papeles)

c) ¿Van a visitar aquel **lugar** famoso? (1 edificios, 2 playa, 3 iglesia, 4 hacienda)

2 Write the Spanish translation of the demonstrative adjective in parentheses. (§15 A, B, C, D)

1 (*that*) . . . sofá que tienes, ¿es cómodo? 2 i(*these*) . . . naranjas son jugosas! 3 Algunas de (*those*) . . . ruinas en España son de la época de los romanos. 4 No puedo comer toda (*this*) . . . carne. 5 Voy a comprar (*those*) . . . zapatos ahí. 6 (*those*) . . . países allá en el oriente producen una gran cantidad de petróleo.

3 Translate these sentences into Spanish using the demonstrative adjectives. (§15 A, B, C, D)

1 **That** man on the left[1] is called Mr. Cruz. 2 **These** shoes are very cheap. 3 **This** painting is very modern. 4 **That** city is the largest in[2] Mexico. 5 **Those** children are hungry. 6 We'll discuss **those** questions tomorrow. 7 **That** girl never comes here. 8 (*Ud.*) Did you see Macchu Picchu? I visited **that** place last year.

[1] on the left = *a la izquierda*
[2] *de*

16 / *Interrogative Adjectives — Adjetivos interrogativos*

1 Complete each sentence with the Spanish equivalent of the English interrogative adjective in parentheses.   (§16 A, D)

≫ ¿... (*What*) vestido te gusta más?
  ¿**Qué** vestido te gusta más?

1 ¿... (*What*) países se encuentran en Sud América? 2 ¿... (*How many*) boletos compraron ellas para el viaje? 3 ¿... (*What*) nombre busca usted? 4 ¿... (*How many*) personas vienen a comer esta noche? 5 ¿... (*How much*) café quiere usted comprar? 6 ¿... (*How much*) electricidad usamos este mes? 7 ¿... (*How many*) personas asistieron a la reunión anoche? 8 ¿... (*How many*) hermanos tiene Roberto?

2 Translate the following sentences using the interrogatives *qué, cuánto, cuánta, cuántos, cuántas.* (§16 A, D)

1 (*Ud.*) **How much** money do you earn here? 2 **How many** names are there on the list? 3 (*tú*) **What** sport do you prefer, Alice? 4 (*Ud.*) **What** book do you need? 5 (*tú*) **How much** clothing did you sell? 6 **How many** times did Philip call?

3 Translate the following exclamations using *qué.* (§16 B, C)

1 **What** a surprise! 2 (*tú*) **How** pretty you are[1], Ann! 3 **What** a man!
4 **How** nervous I am[2]! 5 **How** cold it is[3]! 6 **How** horrible! 7 **What** a movie! 8 **How** tired I am[2]!

17 / *Cardinal Numerals — Numerales cardinales*

1 (§17A, B, C, D, E)

a) Write the numbers in Spanish from one to twenty.
b) Count by tens to one hundred.
c) Count by hundreds to one thousand
d) Write the following numbers: 16, 22, 34, 40, 73, 96, 101, 1976
e) Write the following in arabic numbers: *once, quince, veintisiete, sesenta y nueve, ciento cinco, quinientos, mil setecientos trece.*

2 Translate the following sentences into Spanish. (§17 A, B, C, D, E)

1 My aunt lives approximately[4] one hundred kilometers from here. 2 We need

[1] *estás*
[2] *estoy*
[3] *está*
[4] *aproximadamente a*

a dozen eggs and some five kilos of sugar.   3 This city has five million inhabitants.
4 Three Americans arrived at[1] the moon in 1969.

18 / Ordinal Numerals — Numerales ordinales

1 Write the ordinal numbers from first to tenth in Spanish.   (§18 A)

2 Translate the following sentences into Spanish.   (§18 A, B, C, D, E)

1 My grandparents came from Spain September 1, 1965.   2 The last chapter is
the fifteenth.   3 (*tú*) Have you read much French literature of the twentieth
century?   4 Queen Elizabeth II has three children.   5 It's my second trip to Mexico.

19 / Formation of Adverbs — Formación de adverbios

1 Complete each sentence by changing the adjective in parentheses to an adverb.
(§19 A, B)

≫ (inmediato) Tráigame ese paquete . . . .
Tráigame ese paquete **inmediatamente**.

1 (probable) Don Alberto dice que . . . lloverá esta noche.   2 (general) . . .
comíamos en casa cuando vivíamos en Santiago.   3 (ansioso) Esperamos . . . la
llegada de mi padre.   4 (rápido / fácil) Encontramos la casa . . . y . . . .

2 Translate into Spanish.   (§19 A, B)

1 I am **completely** lost.   2 Charles works **rapidly** and **professionally.**   3 We
spoke very **briefly** with the doctor.   4 **Unfortunately** I can't go tomorrow.
5 **Fortunately** no one is[2] sick today.   6 My father always arrives **exactly** on time[3].

3 Complete these sentences, with the Spanish equivalent of each adverb given in
parentheses.   (§19 D)

≫ Voy a salir . . . . (*soon*)
Voy a salir **pronto**.

a) Voy a salir . . . . (*now, early, afterwards*)
b) Don Antonio trabajó muy . . . . (*late, slowly, quickly*)

[1]*llegar a*
[2]*nadie está*
[3]on time = *a tiempo*

1 Rewrite these sentences using the comparative expression *más...que....*
The comparison is always with the item in parentheses. (§20 A)

≫ Carlos aprende las matemáticas fácilmente. (Pedro)
Carlos aprende las matemáticas **más fácilmente que Pedro.**

1 José llega a su trabajo puntualmente. (sus hermanos) 2 En las carreras Ramón maneja su coche rápidamente. (los otros) 3 Aquellos artistas pueden expresarse libremente. (nosotros) 4 Me parece que en la iglesia los padres cantan claramente. (los niños) 5 Creo que el señor Gómez habla sinceramente. (los otros políticos)

2 Translate these sentences into Spanish using *más (menos)...que....* (§20 A)

1 Mrs. García greeted us **more** courteously today **than** yesterday. 2 I see Victor now **less** frequently **than** last year. 3 Governor Sánchez speaks **more** sincerely **than** the other officials. 4 Alice sings **more** clearly and perfectly **than** the other girls.

3 Complete these sentences, using the comparative of the adverb of the first clause. (§20 B)

≫ Aunque Cecilia canta bien, Mariana canta . . . .
Aunque Cecilia canta bien, Mariana canta **mejor.**

1 Me siento mal hoy pero ayer me sentí . . . . 2 Usted lo expresó bien, Roberto, pero es posible expresarlo . . . . 3 Yo juego mal a las cartas pero Francisco juega . . . . 4 Este año el equipo de fútbol salió bien pero el año pasado salió . . . .

4 Use the irregular adverbs of comparison in writing these sentences in Spanish. (§20 B)

1 Robert writes **badly**. He writes **worse** than I. 2 This car runs[1] **well**. It runs **better** than the other one. 3 Michael doesn't play tennis **well**. He will play **better** next year.

21 / *Ways of Using* donde *and* ¿dónde? *— Modos de usar* donde *y* ¿dónde?

1 Write the Spanish translation for the word in parentheses according to the context of the sentence. (§21 A, B)

1 --Carlos, ¿(*where*) . . . vives? --Vivo (*where*) . . . la Avenida Flores cruza con la Calle Miró. 2 Mario quiere vivir en el campo, (*where*) . . . no hay tanta contaminación

[1]*funciona*

del aire. 3 ¿(*where*) . . . está Susana? 4 ¿(*where*) . . . fue Vicente? 5 Nosotros vamos a Badajoz (*where*) . . . tenemos parientes. 6 ¿(*where*) . . . está mi paraguas? 7 ¿(*from where*) . . . viene el señor Gutiérrez? 8 ¿(*which way*) . . . se puede subir la escalera? 9 ¿(*by what route*) . . . salgo de esta calle? 10 Vamos a una tienda (*where*) . . . venden muebles importados. 11 Paco no quiere decirme (*from where*) . . . viene.

2 Translate into Spanish using *donde, ¿dónde?, de donde, ¿de dónde?, ¿adónde?* or *¿por dónde?* (§21 A, B)

1 (*tú*) Charles, **where** are you going? 2 (*Ud.*) Are you going to Paris? **From where** are you leaving? 3 **Where** is[1] the telephone? 4 (*Uds.*) Do you remember the store **where** we saw the French paintings? 5 Do the children know **where** to go? 6 I found a place **where** they sell old books. 7 **Where** does the novel take place? 8 **How** (by what route) did the thief come in? 9 (*Ud.*) **Where** did you work last year? 10 (*tú*) Are you going out? **Where?** 11 (*Uds.*) **How** (by what route) did you go out of the city? 12 John comes **from where** they speak Catalan.

22 / The Negative — La forma negativa

1 Rewrite these sentences making them negative. (§22 A, B)

1 Este chico se llama Carlos. 2 Le escribo a mi novia cada semana. 3 A Pepe le gusta la música. 4 Jaime sabe tocar la guitarra. 5 La comida está preparada. 6 He visto al abogado.

2 For each blank, write the Spanish word that is *opposite* in meaning to the word given. The English translation is given in parentheses. (§22 C)

1 alguien	(*someone; somebody*)	. . .	(*no one*)
2 algo	(*something*)	. . .	(*nothing*)
3 siempre	(*always*)	. . .	(*never*)
4 también	(*also*)	. . .	(*neither; not either*)
5 o . . . o	(*either . . . or*)	. . .	(*neither . . . nor*)
6 alguno	(*some; any*)	. . .	(*no; none*)

3 Make these sentences negative by changing the indicated word to a negative. (§22 C, D)

≫ **Alguien** me lo dijo.
  Nadie me lo dijo.

1 Juan **también** fue al centro. 2 Francisco **siempre** nos ayuda con el trabajo.

[1]*está*

3 ¿**Alguien** quiere más café? 4 **Siempre** llueve aquí por la tarde. 5 Jorge **también** está aquí. 6 **O** los vecinos **o** los amigos tienen la llave.

4 Rewrite these sentences, placing the indicated negative after the verb. Make any other changes necessary. (§22 D)

≫ **Nadie** va conmigo.
  No va **nadie** conmigo.

1 **Nunca** trabajamos los domingos. 2 Yo **tampoco** voy. 3 **Nada** sabemos de las elecciones. 4 **Nadie** estuvo en la oficina ayer. 5 Mi esposo **nunca** hizo el servicio militar.

5 Translate these sentences into Spanish. Give special attention to the indicated negative forms. (§22 A, B, C, D)

1 (*tú*) I **never** received your letter. 2 **Neither** my sister **nor** I heard[1] the telephone. 3 **No one** comes here. 4 John knows **nothing** about music[2]. 5 (*tú*) --Do you have any cousins (f.)? --No, I don't have **any**[3] cousins. 6 Henry is not going to the cinema. We are not going **either**. 7 In my family **no**[3] child is lazy.

6 Make these sentences negative. (§22 E)

1 El profesor Ruiz estaba hablando cuando entramos. 2 Richardo me ha pedido mucho dinero. 3 Hemos visto al señor Flores esta mañana. 4 Si hubieran llegado antes de las nueve me habrían visto[4]. 5 El documento ha sido firmado por todos los diplomáticos.

23 / *Subject Personal Pronouns — Los pronombres personales usados como sujetos*

1 Write the pronoun subject of each of the following sentences. (§23 A, B, C, D)

≫ ¿Vas al cine? **Tú**

1 Como en casa todos los días. 2 Miguel y Jorge son amigos de Antonio.
3 Vivimos en Francia con mis abuelos. 4 Veo a Enrique cada día. 5 Se llama Rosa. 6 ¿Cecilia y Enrique son de los Estados Unidos? 7 Las secretarias llegan temprano en la oficina. 8 ¿Vuelves a trabajar mañana? 9 Es un hombre muy inteligente. 10 Tenemos que salir muy pronto.

---

[1]*oímos*
[2]*de música*
[3]singular
[4]You will have to use a negative in both clauses.

2 Rewrite these sentences, replacing the indicated subjects with subject pronouns. Do not use the *vosotros* as a subject. (§23 A, B, C, D)

≫ **Luisa y Elena** son hermanas.
Ellas son hermanas.

1 **Manuel y Vicente** acaban de salir. 2 **Usted y yo** vamos a ganar el partido de tenis. 3 **El doctor González** trabaja aquí. 4 ¿**Tú y Rodrigo** pueden acompañarme al café? 5 **La señora García** tiene tres hijos. 6 ¿**Usted y su esposa** van a Europa? 7 **Mi hermano y yo** pasamos mucho tiempo en el patio. 8 **Las dos chicas** son muy amables.

3 Translate these sentences into Spanish, using the subject pronouns for emphasis or clarity. (§23 A)

1 (formal) How are **you** Mr. Diaz? 2 (formal) --Are **you** Mexican? --No, **I** am Colombian. 3 Mr. Giménez and Miss Guzmán are Spaniards. **He** is from Madrid and **she** is from Seville. 4 Charles wants to go to the party. **I** don't want to go. 5 Robert reads more than **we**. 6 **I** live in an apartment but **they** (m.) live with their parents. 7 Susan and Paul are cousins. **She** goes to the university and **he** works.

4 Translate these sentences into Spanish, giving special attention to the indicated personal pronoun. (§23 F)

1 (*tú*) --Is that **you**, Charles? --Yes, it is **I** (it's me). 2 It is **they** who[1] want to visit Lima. 3 (*Ud.*) Who called? Was it[2] **you** or Mary? 4 --Who is it? --It is **we** (It's us).

24 / Direct Object Personal Pronouns —
Los pronombres personales usados como complementos directos

1 Rewrite the second sentence in each item, replacing the indicated noun object with the third person direct object personal pronoun *le, la, lo, la, los, las*. (§24 A, B)

≫ Tengo una camisa nueva. Compré **la camisa nueva** ayer.
La compré ayer.

1 Emilio tiene abuelos en Toledo. Visita **a sus abuelos** de vez en cuando.
2 Juanita, ¿compraste algunos discos? ¿Llevas **los discos** contigo? 3 Me gusta la fruta. Siempre compro **la fruta** ahí en esa tienda. 4 Acaba de regresar Alicia. Llamo **a Alicia** esta noche. 5 ¿Te gustan estas pinturas de Picasso? Nosotros admiramos mucho **estas pinturas**. 6 Jaime nos mandó una tarjeta desde Córdoba. Escribió

[1]*que*
[2]was it = *fue*

su última tarjeta el martes.   7 El señor Gutiérrez es buen amigo nuestro. ¿Invitamos **al señor Gutiérrez** a la boda?   8 Ya viene Gloria. Desde aquí vemos **a Gloria.**   9 El coche no funciona bien. ¿Dejamos **el coche** en el garaje?   10 Nos gusta mucho la paella. Muchas veces yo preparo **la paella** en casa.   11 No me interesa ese programa de televisión. Vi **ese programa de televisión** el año pasado.   12 Fernando quiere acompañarnos al centro. Veo **a Fernando** ahí con Paco y Víctor.

2 Complete each sentence with the Spanish equivalent of the English direct object pronoun in parentheses. (§24 C, D)

≫ (*me*) El señor Pérez . . . saluda todos los días.
El señor Pérez **me** saluda todos los días.

1 (*us*) ¿Este autobús . . . llevará al centro?   2 (*me*) Creo que Joaquín no . . . vio ayer en la fiesta.   3 (*you*-tú) ¿Tus padres . . . dejaban salir por la noche?   4 (*me*) Tu esposo . . . dijo que iba a regresar por la tarde.   5 (*you*-tú) El señor Romero . . . conoce porque estuvo aquí el año pasado.   6 (*us*) Carlos dice que . . . vio en el teatro anoche.   7 (*me*) Los padres . . . necesitan en casa ahora.   8 (*us*) El señor Martínez . . . invitó a tomar café.   9 (*me*) El coronel . . . mandó avanzar con los otros soldados. 10 (*us*) Hablamos con Domingo por teléfono pero no . . . entendió bien.

3 Write these sentences in Spanish giving special attention to the direct object pronoun. (§24 A, B, C, D)

1 John wants to use my car. He needs **it** tomorrow.   2 Charles prefers classical music. He listens to **it** all the time.[1]   3 Mr. García congratulated **me** yesterday. 4 We left **them** (f.) at[2] the airport.   5 (*Ud.*-m.) Alice understands **you** perfectly in Spanish.   6 That policeman greets **us** every day[3].   7 (*tú*) I don't believe **you.** It's impossible.   8 My grandparents live in Laredo. I visit **them** each year.   9 I see Andrew[4] every day[3]. I know **him** well.

25 / Indirect Object Personal Pronouns —
Los pronombres personales usados como complementos indirectos

1 Complete these sentences with the Spanish equivalent of the English words in parentheses. Use *le* or *les*. (§25 A, B)

≫ (*to him*) Jaime . . . explica el problema.
Jaime **le** explica el problema.

1 (*to her*) Isabel . . . leyó el telegrama.   2 (*to them*) Mario . . . enseña las fotos. 3 (*for her*) La criada . . . abre la puerta.   4 (*to them*) La señora . . . escribe cada

---

[1]all the time = *todo el tiempo*
[2]*en*

[3]every day = *todos los días*
[4]*a Andrés*

mes. 5 (*to you*–Uds.) Don Carlos . . . manda saludos. 6 (*to you*–Ud.) ¿Roberto . . . explicó la razón por qué no pudimos ir?

2 Complete these sentences with the Spanish equivalent of the English words in parentheses. Use *me, te,* or *nos.* (§25 C, D)

≫ (*to me*) Mi padre . . . da dinero cada mes.
Mi padre **me** da dinero cada mes.

1 (*to us*) La criada . . . sirve la cena a las seis. 2 (*for me*) Mis padres . . . compraron este abrigo. 3 (*to you*–tú) ¿El señor Ruiz . . . habló de sus viajes? 4 (*to me*) Este mozo . . . trajo el menú. 5 (*to you*–tú) El doctor . . . dará unas medicinas mañana. 6 (*to us*) El policía . . . indicó el Banco Nacional. 7 (*to me*) El señor Pérez . . . hablaba de los equipos de fútbol. 8 (*to us*) Mis padres siempre . . . leían las noticias del periódico.

3 Write these sentences in Spanish, using the indirect object personal pronouns *me, te, le, nos, les.* . (§25 A, B, C, D)

1 (*Ud.*) Does the company pay **you** every week? 2 We sent **them** a list of books. 3 Carmen always asks **me** for[1] money. 4 (*tú*) I will write **to you** soon. 5 (*tú*) Jim tells **us** that you have to leave at ten. 6 Paul is showing **me** his new car. 7 Louise called. I talked **to her** about the tickets. 8 Our friends (m.) came at eight. We prepared a dinner **for them**.

4 Rewrite these sentences, clarifying the meaning by adding *a* + the appropriate prepositional pronoun. This form should immediately follow the verb. (§25 E)

≫ (*to her*) Felipe le escribe todos los días.
Felipe le escribe **a ella** todos los días.

1 (*from you*–Ud.) Le pido un favor. 2 (*to her*) El médico le describió la operación. 3 (*to you*–Ud.) El banco le da dos semanas para pagar el dinero. 4 (*to them*–m.) Rosa les dio unos regalos de Europa. 5 (*to you*–Uds.) Les diré la fecha de la conferencia.

5 Translate the following sentences into Spanish using the indirect object pronoun *le* and giving special attention to the indicated portions. (§25 F)

≫ The mother **washes her child's face.**
La madre le lava la cara a su niño.

1 Mr. Moreno **cuts my son's hair.** 2 The mother **puts the coat on her child.** 3 Mrs. González **takes off Johnny's shoes.**

[1]Do not translate *for.*

1 Write the reflexive pronoun corresponding to the subject pronoun in each sentence. (§26 A, B, C)

≫ Manuel . . . pone el sombrero cuando sale de la casa.
Manuel **se** pone el sombrero cuando sale de la casa.

1 A veces (yo) . . . duermo viajando por avión. 2 ¿(tú) . . . sientas siempre en el mismo lugar? 3 Víctor . . . encuentra delante de la estatua de don Quijote.
4 Cecilia . . . burla de su hermano menor. 5 (nosotros) . . . quedaremos en Caracas dos semanas. 6 ¿(ustedes) . . . despiertan siempre a la misma hora?

2 Rewrite these sentences substituting the subject in parentheses for the indicated subject. Make any other changes necessary. (§26 A, B, C)

≫ **Nosotros** nos acostamos a las once. (Felipe)
Felipe se acuesta a las once.

1 **Yo** siempre me lavo antes de comer. (Lorenzo) 2 ¿**Tú** te sientes mejor hoy? (los niños) 3 **Esa rubia** se llama Mariana. (yo) 4 **Los padres** se preocupan por el mal tiempo. (nosotros) 5 **Javier** se queja mucho de su trabajo. (las secretarias)
6 ¿Se despiertan **los campesinos** cuando se levanta el sol? (tú)

3 Write the appropriate form of the verb in parentheses, including the reflexive pronoun *me, te, se,* or *nos.* (§26 A, B, C)

1 (levantarse) Las enfermeras . . . a las cuatro. 2 (preocuparse) Ana y tú . . . demasiado por el dinero.[1] 3 (sentarse) ¿Por qué no . . . (nosotros) en el patio?
4 (divertirse) Los muchachos . . . mucho en la playa. 5 (interesarse) Señor Palacios, ¿. . . usted por los deportes?

27 / *Uses of the Reflexive Forms — Modos de usar las formas reflexivas*

1 Each sentence below has a direct object. Replace the indicated direct object with a reflexive object. (§27 A)

≫ La madre viste **a su hija.**
La madre **se** viste.

1 Casi siempre lavo **a mi perro** en la bañera. 2 El cómico divirtió **a la gente.**
3 ¿Tú bañas **al niño** todos los días? 4 Nosotros acostamos **al bebé** temprano. 5 Yo preparé **a los atletas** para el partido de fútbol. 6 ¿Levantaste **a tus hermanas** a las seis?

---

[1]The *vosotros* form would probably be used here in Spain.

2 Write these sentences in Spanish, using the reflexive form of the verb.
(§27 B, C, D)

1 My brother always **goes to bed** at ten. 2 Does John **complain** about[1] the
neighbors? 3 (*tú*) Is your sister **getting married** in August? 4 (*Uds.*) **Did you
eat up** all the bread? 5 Who **carried off** my coat? 6 Mary **resembles** her mother.
7 Mrs. Guzmán **fell down** in the street. 8 (*tú*) **Dare you**[2] ask for more
dessert?

3 Write these sentences in Spanish using the reciprocal pronoun *se*. (§27 F)

1 Alice and Tom **write to each other** a lot. 2 Do Steven and Tony **know**[3] **each
other**? 3 Do the cousins **see each other** much? 4 Those cats **hate each other**.
5 The neighbors **visit each other** a lot. 6 The children **help each other** in school.
7 My wife and my mother-in-law **talk to each other** every day.

4 Clarify the following sentences by adding the *uno a otro* construction. (§27 F)

≫ María y José se miran cuando gritan.
  María y José se miran **uno a otro** cuando gritan.

1 Alfredo y Vicente se ayudan mucho. 2 Los jóvenes no se entienden[4]. 3 Esos
dos atletas se estiman. 4 Esos dos enemigos se engañan mucho.

28 / *The Pronoun* se — *El pronombre* se

1 Complete these sentences with the Spanish equivalent of the English verb in
parentheses. Use the *se* construction for the passive voice. (§28 A)

≫ (*is found*) El Lago Titicaca . . . en Sud América.
  El Lago Titicaca **se encuentra** en Sud América.

1 (*is heard*) El idioma catalán . . . en las calles de Barcelona. 2 (*are sold*) En
esta tienda . . . muebles importados. 3 (*is written*) México . . . a veces con *x* y a
veces con *j*. 4 (*are observed*) Las estrellas . . . con la ayuda de un telescopio.
5 (*are examined*) Los animales . . . en la clínica. 6 (*is prepared*) La comida
española . . . con mucho aceite de oliva. 7 (*were discussed*) . . . muchas ideas en la
reunión de ayer. 8 (*was inaugurated*) Ayer . . . el nuevo estadio de fútbol.

---

[1] *de*
[2] to dare = *atreverse a*
[3] to know = *conocer*
[4] Use the plural *unos a otros*.

2 Write these sentences in Spanish using the impersonal *se* construction. (§28 B)

≫ **One calls** the waiter by clapping his hands.
  Se llama al camarero con una palmada.

  1 **One sees** many American tourists in Spain. 2 **One gets to know** the people well in the small towns. 3 **One employs** a maid if the family is large. 4 **One invites** all his[1] friends to a wedding.

3 Rewrite these sentences, changing the verb from the third person plural to the passive construction using *se*. (§28 C)

≫ Producen mucha carne en la Argentina.
  Se produce mucha carne en la Argentina.

  1 Dicen que Alonso se hizo médico. 2 Cierran esta tienda a las nueve de la noche.
3 Solicitan dinero para el proyecto público. 4 Celebran el Día de los Reyes el 6 de enero. 5 Todavía usan el aqueducto romano en Segovia. 6 Venden ropa fina en esa tienda. 7 Comen mucho maíz en México. 8 Empiezan la construcción en marzo.

29 / Prepositional Pronoun Forms — *Pronombres después de preposiciones*

1 Rewrite each sentence, using a prepositional pronoun instead of the indicated noun. (§29 A)

≫ Este telegrama es para **Catalina.**
  Este telegrama es para ella.

  1 Según **Jorge y Ramón**, la conferencia empezará a las diez. 2 ¿Quiénes van a la fiesta además de **Luisa y usted**? 3 A pesar de lo que dicen tú y María, voto por **don Alonso García.** 4 Los policías estaban cerca de **la actriz** para protegerla. 5 Un hombre guapo se sentó frente a **Carmen y Candia.** 6 Todos comían menos **Gonzalo y yo.**

2 Translate these sentences into Spanish using the proper prepositional pronoun. (§29 A, B, C)

  1 (*tú*) Rose, I can't go without **you.** 2 (*Ud.*) Is Fernando eating with **you**?
3 Are they talking about **me**? 4 (m.) A dog was running after[2] **them.** 5 A tall man sat down in front of **us.** 6. Is this letter for **me**? 7 (*tú*) I come to **you** because I need help.

[1]*los*
[2]*tras*

3 Complete these sentences by writing the Spanish equivalent of the English preposition and prepositional pronoun in parentheses. (§29 E)

≫ (*with you*-tú) Quiero ir al centro . . . .
Quiero ir al centro **contigo.**

1 (*with me*) Don Rafael ha viajado mucho . . . . 2 (*with you*-tú) ¿Gerardo va al cine . . .? 3 (*to himself*) El señor Gómez habla . . . mismo. 4 (*with me*) Clara discute mucho la política . . . . 5 (*with you*-tú) ¿Cuántos años vivió Alfonso . . .? 6 (*with him*) Cuando salió para Madrid Lorenzo llevaba quinientos pesos . . . .

30 / Position of Object Pronouns — *Colocación de pronombres usados como complementos*

1 Rewrite these sentences, substituting a direct object pronoun for the indicated noun object. (§30 A)

≫ Mariana escucha **la música.**
Mariana **la** escucha.

1 Pilar no recuerda **los nombres extranjeros.** 2 No entiendo **el capítulo once.** 3 Doña Elisa mira **a sus hijos.** 4 ¿Buscas **a tu marido?** 5 Siempre veo **a Laura** en el colegio.

2 Rewrite each sentence, changing the indicated portion to a pronoun and joining it to the verb. Place an accent over the stressed syllable when necessary. (§30 B, C)

a) Imperative

≫ Mire **el nuevo coche.**
Mírelo.

1 Esperen **a nuestras compañeras** por favor. 2 Abra **la puerta.** 3 Escuchen **a sus padres.** 4 Traiga **la ropa sucia.** 5 Pida **la lista** mañana.

b) Infinitive

≫ Quiero ver **a don Agustín.**
Quiero verlo.

1 ¿Piensas avisar **a Alfredo** de las noticias? 2 Alonso dice que va a vender **los boletos.** 3 Ana desea empezar **el trabajo** el lunes. 4 Vamos a buscar **la cuenta** en la oficina. 5 Jaime prefiere ver **la revista.**

c) Present participle

≫ Estamos mirando **las fotos.**
Estamos mirándolas.

1 ¿Estás preparando **la comida?** 2 Estoy esperando **a mis suegros.** 3 Estamos

escuchando **el programa de radio**. 4 Mi hermana está leyendo **las noticias**. 5 María está explicando **la película**.

3 Rewrite these sentences, making each one negative. Make any other changes necessary. (§30 D)

≫ Tráigame más café por favor.
   No me traiga más café por favor.

   1 Espérenos en casa. 2 Dígame lo que pasó en la reunión. 3 El señor Oviedo tiene el documento. Pídaselo. 4 Doña Claudia quiere ver las fotos. Déselas.

4 Rewrite these sentences, placing the object pronoun(s) before the auxiliary verb. (§30 E)

≫ Vamos a explicarles nuestras ideas.
   Les vamos a explicar nuestras ideas.

   a) 1 Quiero presentarle a mi esposa. 2 ¿Piensas devolverlas mañana, Carlos?
3 El jefe va a contestarle por carta. 4 Las secretarias pueden mandárselos inmediatamente.

   b) 1 Estamos terminándolo ahora mismo. 2 Alicia está escribiéndoselo. 3 Mis niños necesitan zapatos. Estoy comprándoselos. 4 Su coche no funciona bien. Están arreglándolo.

5 Translate these sentences into Spanish, giving special attention to the indicated object pronouns. (§30 A, B, C, D, E)

   1 Our parents live in Santiago. We are going to visit **them** in June. 2 (*Ud.*) --Mrs. Macías, wait **for me** here. 3 Where are the books? I can't find **them**. 4 It's too much money. I can't accept **it**. 5 A policeman helped[1] **us** find the museum. 6 (*Uds.*) Mr. Robles is the guide. Follow **him**, please. 7 (*tú*) You lost your purse? Can you describe **it**? 8 My wife is preparing a special meal **for us**! 9 (*Uds.*) This chapter is important. Study **it** carefully!   10 The house is very modern. They are constructing **it** now.

31 / *Order of Object Pronouns — Orden de pronombres usados como complementos*

   1 Rewrite these sentences changing the indicated direct object to an object pronoun. (§31 A)

≫ Víctor me da **el dinero**.
   Víctor me **lo** da.

---

[1]to help = *ayudar a*

1 María siempre nos prepara **el postre**. 2 ¿La recepcionista te dio **el número**? 3 Mis abuelos siempre me mandan **regalos**. 4 ¿Susana te enseñó **su blusa nueva**?

2 Rewrite these sentences changing the indicated noun object to an object pronoun. Make the necessary changes in the indirect object pronoun. (§31 A, B)

≫ El chico le vendió **el periódico**.
El chico **se lo** vendió.

1 El señor Ramírez le escribió **su dirección**. 2 Fernando les explicó **las dificultades de la lección**. 3 Jaime, ¿por qué no le pediste **el permiso** al señor Muñoz? 4 Amalia le preparó **la cena**. 5 La enfermera le compró **las medicinas** en la farmacia. 6 El señor Losa le mandó **los libros**.

3 Translate these sentences into Spanish, paying special attention to the indicated object pronouns. (§31 A, B)

1 I sent **it** (f.) **to them**. 2 Philip asked **us for them** (f.). 3 (*tú*) When did you give **it** (m.) **to her**? 4 (*tú*) I will show **it** (f.) **to you** tomorrow.

32 / Possessive Pronouns — *Pronombres posesivos*

1 Rewrite these sentences, replacing the indicated words with a possessive pronoun. (§32 A, B, C, D)

≫ **El coche suyo** es verde.
El suyo es verde.

1 **Los hijos míos** nacieron en España. 2 ¿Es enfermera también **la prima suya**? 3 ¿Es de color **el televisor suyo**? 4 **La finca nuestra** está a ocho kilómetros de la ciudad. 5 ¿Viven en Bogotá **los padres suyos**? 6 **Las cartas mías** siempre son breves.

2 Rewrite these sentences, replacing the indicated words with a possessive pronoun. (§32 A, B, C, D)

≫ **Mi casa** es la segunda de la esquina.
La mía es la segunda de la esquina.

1 **Nuestro mapa** no indica ese pueblo. 2 ¿Prefieren **sus hijos** la música clásica? 3 ¿Sabe **su tía** preparar la paella? 4 **Mi pueblo** tiene dos mil habitantes. 5 **Tu suéter** está en la silla, Alicia. 6 **Nuestros padres** viven cerca de aquí. 7 ¿Tiene **tu hija** quince años? 8 Todas **mis camisas** ya son viejas.

3 Rewrite the second sentence in each item, replacing the indicated words with a possessive pronoun. (§32 A, B, C, D)

≫ Traje mis libros. ¿Trajiste **tus libros**?
  ¿Trajiste **los tuyos**?

1 Los hijos del señor Paredes van al colegio San Andrés. ¿Adónde van **sus hijos**?
2 Mi secretaria no sabe alemán. ¿Sabe alemán **su secretaria**? 3 No tenemos nuestras fotos. Carmen, ¿tienes **nuestras fotos**? 4 Busco mis cigarillos. Rosa, ¿has visto **mis cigarillos**? 5 Tengo mi pasaporte. Julio, ¿tienes **tu pasaporte**?

4 Answer each question using the Spanish equivalent of the English in parentheses. (§32 A, B, C, D)

≫ ¿De quién es este paquete? (*It's yours.*–tú)
  Es tuyo.

1 ¿De quién son estos papeles? (*They are mine.*) 2 ¿De quiénes son estos libros? (*They are his.*) 3 ¿De quiénes son esos juguetes en la calle? (*They are theirs.*–m.) 4 ¿De quién es esa casa a la izquierda? (*It's ours.*)

5 Complete these sentences with the Spanish equivalent of the English words in parentheses. (§32 A, B, C, D)

1 La guitarra de Roberto es más nueva que . . . (*mine*). 2 La hija de los Gómez es mayor que . . . (*ours*). 3 (*tú*) El coche de nuestros vecinos anda más rápido que . . . (*yours*). 4 El reloj que compró mi padre es más caro que . . . (*mine*). 5 Los ríos de España son menos navegables que . . . (*ours*). 6 (*tú*) Las fotos que tomamos en Europa son más interesantes que . . . (*yours*).

6 Clarify the meaning of the possessive pronouns in the following sentences according to the English in parentheses. (§32 E)

≫ (*yours*–Ud.) Mi abrigo no es del mismo color que **el suyo**.
  Mi abrigo no es del mismo color que **el de usted**.

1 (*hers*) Jaime y yo mandamos cada invitación menos **la suya**. 2 (*theirs*–m.) Nuestras escuelas no son como **las suyas**. 3 (*yours*–Ud.) Aquí están mis libros. ¿Dónde están **los suyos**? 4 (*theirs*–m.) Rosa traerá a su hija y a **la suya** también. 5 (*his*) Pablo dice que nuestros problemas son tan graves como **los suyos**. 6 (*hers*) Carmen saludó a mis padres pero no vio a **los suyos**.

1 Rewrite the following sentences replacing the indicated demonstrative adjective and noun with a demonstrative pronoun. Remember the demonstrative pronoun takes an accent. (§33 A)

≫ **Esta foto** es de mi hermano mayor.
   Ésta es de mi hermano mayor.

   1 **Ese hombre** se llama señor Fariñas. 2 ¡Miren **esos retratos** de Goya! 3 ¡Ay, **esa chica** me vuelve loca!   4 **Estos zapatos** me quedan bien, ¿verdad?   5 **Aquellos países** están más lejos de los Estados Unidos que España.

2 Complete these sentences with the Spanish equivalent of the English demonstrative pronouns in parentheses. Use the forms of *éste* and *ése.* (§33 A)

   1 Vamos a otra tienda, (*this one*) . . . es muy cara. 2 ¿Es (*this*) . . . el lugar donde vivió el Presidente Cárdenas?   3 ¿Crees que (*this*) . . . fue una buena película? 4 Prefiero estas naranjas, (*those*) . . . no. 5 Señora Soler, ¿son (*these*) . . . sus hijos? 6 Este coche azul es nuestro, (*that one*) . . . es de mi vecino.

3 Translate these sentences into Spanish, giving special attention to the indicated portions. (§33 A)

   1 (*tú*) Victor, where are your new ties? **These** are old ones. 2 (*Ud.*) —Doctor Flores, is **this** your office or is it **that one**?   3 **Those** are my children.   4 Of all the cities in[1] Spain, I like **that one**. 5 (*tú*) Is **this** your telephone number?

4 Complete the following sentences with the Spanish equivalent of the English in parentheses. Remember that the forms of *éste* and *aquél* must agree with the subject to which they refer and that *éste* precedes *aquél.* (§33 B)

   1 García Lorca y José Martí son poetas muy conocidos en la literatura española. . . . (*The latter*) era de Cuba y . . . (*the former*) era de Andalucía. 2 María Hernández y Carmen Losa vienen a visitarme en el verano. . . . (*The latter*) es mi prima y . . . (*the former*) era mi compañera de clase.   3 El señor Ortega y su esposa viven en San Juan y Concha vive con su hermana. . . . (*The latter*) era nuestra sirvienta y . . . (*the former*) eran nuestros vecinos.

5 Translate the following sentences into Spanish using *esto* or *eso* for the indicated portions. (§33 C)

   1 Robert, **this** is a gift. 2 Mary wants to be a famous actress. **This** is very difficult! 3 Susan, what is **that**? 4 **This** is very good!

[1]*de*

6 Translate these sentences into Spanish paying special attention to the indicated portions. (§33 D)

1 These streets are[1] wider than **the ones** downtown. 2 Philip's new car is[1] more economical than **the one** that he sold. 3 (m.) **Those who** arrived late waited a long time[2]. 4 Mary's ideas are[1] better than **those of** her boy friends. 5 **He who** loses his passport has to obtain another.

34 / Interrogative Pronouns — *Pronombres interrogativos*

1 Complete these sentences, with the Spanish equivalent of the English in parentheses. (§34 A)

1 (*to whom*) Alicia, ¿ . . . mandaste una tarjeta? 2 (*which*) ¿ . . . es tu coche, éste? 3 (*what*) Rosa, ¿ . . . piensas hacer mañana? 4 (*how much*) ¿ . . . cuesta un litro de gasolina aquí? 5 (*who*-pl.) ¿ . . . asistieron a la reunión anoche? 6 (*whose*-pl.) ¿ . . . son estas maletas? 7 (*which ones*) ¿ . . . son tus canciones favoritas? 8 (*how many*) Tengo cinco boletos. ¿ . . . quieres?

2 Translate the following sentences into Spanish, giving special attention to the indicated portions. (§34 A)

1 (*tú*) **Which** of the dresses do you prefer? 2 **Who** called on the telephone[3]? 3 **How many** (*estudiantes*[4]) are there at[5] the university? 4 **What** can we do? 5 (*Ud.*) **How much** (*dinero*[4]) did you pay for the book? 6 **Whose** dog is this? [6] 7 **How many** (*personas*[4]) live in Mendoza? 8 **Who** (pl.) are coming to the party?

3 Change each of the following statements to a question. Begin each question with *qué* or *cuál(es)* in accordance with the meaning. (§34 B)

≫ Es el número de teléfono de Ana.
    ¿Cuál es el número de teléfono de Ana?

1 Es la ciudad más grande de España. 2 Son tus actores favoritos. 3 Es el jai-alai. 4 Es la capital de Chile. 5 Son los días de vacaciones. 6 Son estos dos edificios a la derecha.

4 Translate these sentences into Spanish using *qué* or *cuál(es)*. (§34 B)

1 (*Ud.*) **What** is your address? 2 **What** is a Creole? 3 **What** are the best restaurants of Malaga? 4 **What** is Barcelona?

[1]*ser*
[2]a long time = *mucho tiempo*
[3]on the telephone = *por teléfono*

[4]Do not include in your translation.
[5]*en*
[6]. . . *es este perro?*

35 / The Relative Pronoun que — El pronombre relativo que

1 Rewrite the two sentences, joining them with *que*. Omit the indicated portion when joining the two sentences. (§35 A)

≫ Aquí está la camisa nueva. Compré **la camisa nueva** ayer.
Aquí está la camisa nueva **que** compré ayer.

1 Elena es mi tía. **Elena** vive en Monterrey. 2 El señor Castillo es el juez. Vimos **al señor Castillo** anoche. 3 ¿Has leído esta novela? ¿**Esta novela** ganó el premio literario? 4 Esos son paquetes de ropa. **Los paquetes** llegaron hoy. 5 Ésta es la carretera. **Esta carretera** va hasta Santa Cruz. 6 Hay más de treinta mil jóvenes aquí. **Los jóvenes** van a la universidad.

2 Translate these sentences into Spanish using the relative pronoun *que*. (§35 A)

1 Mary is the girl **who** plays[1] the piano. 2 I bought a car **that** is economical. 3 This is the same program **that** we saw before. 4 There is a bus **which** goes to the beach.

36 / The Relative Pronoun quien — El pronombre relativo quien

1 Complete each sentence, with *que, quien* or *quienes* as required. (§36 A)

≫ El señor Ruiz es el hombre de . . . hablé.
El señor Ruiz es el hombre de **quien** hablé.
≫ Ése es el aeropuerto . . . construyeron el año pasado.
Ése es el aeropuerto **que** construyeron el año pasado.

1 Aquí está la avenida . . . me indicó el policía. 2 ¿Es Alicia la muchacha a . . . mandaste la tarjeta? 3 El tenis es un deporte . . . me gusta mucho. 4 Margarita y Susana son las chicas para . . . dimos la fiesta anoche. 5 El plato . . . nos trajo el mozo era típico de Andalucía. 6 Los jóvenes con . . . jugamos fútbol son muy hábiles. 7 Las cartas . . . escribía Luis eran muy breves.

2 Translate these sentences into Spanish using *quien* or *quienes*. (§36 B)

1 My father, **who** was born in Toledo, is a[2] doctor. 2 Mr. Silva, **who** called yesterday, is the mayor of the city. 3 My daughter, **who** speaks Spanish and French, travels a lot. 4 His parents, **who** live in Monterrey, are coming here.

[1] *tocar*
[2] Do not include in your translation.

3 Begin each of these Spanish proverbs with *quien.* Write the English translation for each proverb. (§36 C)

≫ . . . busca, halla.
   Quien busca, halla. *He who seeks, finds.*

1 . . . ríe después, ríe más. 2 . . . mucho habla, mucho yerra. 3 . . . mal anda, mal acaba. 4 . . . trabaja y canta, sus males espanta. 5 . . . mucho abarca, poco aprieta.

37 / *The Relative Pronoun* cual — *El pronombre relativo* cual

1 Complete the following sentences with *el cual, la cual, los cuales,* or *las cuales.* The relative pronoun refers to the first of two antecedents. (§37 A)

≫ El hermano de Ana, . . . nos habló ayer, vive en Valladolid.
   El hermano de Ana, **el cual** nos habló ayer, vive en Valladolid.

1 La vecina de mi tío, . . . vive en la esquina, tiene cuatro perros. 2 Los vinos españoles, de . . . hablaba mi padre a menudo, nunca se vendían en México. 3 Sacamos unas fotos en Francia y Alemania . . . son muy interesantes. 4 Ayer conocí a la hija del señor Ramírez, . . . es muy inteligente. 5 Compré un regalo para mi esposa, . . . es muy grande.

2 Complete these sentences with a form of *el cual.* The English relative pronoun is given in parentheses. (§37 B)

1 En la carretera vimos unos toros y caballos detrás de . . . (*which*) venían algunos coches y camiones. 2 El huracán se llevó varias casas del pueblo, partes de . . . (*which*) se encontraron muy lejos de allí. 3 En el centro de Madrid se encuentra el Hotel Plaza enfrente de[1] . . . (*which*) se ve la estatua de don Quijote. 4 La Organización Estudiantil, unos miembros de . . . (*which*) no vinieron a la reunión anoche, nombró a un nuevo presidente.

3 Complete each sentence with *el que, la que, los que* or *las que.* The English relative pronoun is given in parentheses. (§37 C)

≫ Encima de una colina desde . . . (*which*) se ve la Sierra Nevada, los moros construyeron la Alhambra.
   Encima de una colina desde **la que** se ve la Sierra Nevada, los moros construyeron la Alhambra.

1 En Pamplona vendían unos vinos excelentes por . . . (*which*) pagamos relativamente poco. 2 En la noche vimos unas casas hacia . . . (*which*) nos dirigimos. 3 Para ir a Barcelona tomamos un tren en . . . (*which*) había mucho ruido. 4 Durante las

---

[1]*De* contracts with the article here: *del.*

vacaciones, visitamos unos seis países europeos, . . . (*which*) están en la europa oriental. 5 Tengo un examen mañana para . . . (*which*) no quiero prepararme. 6 Salgo con una muchacha por . . . (*which*) no estoy interesado.

4 Complete each sentence with the appropriate relative pronoun *que, quien,* or a form of *el cual* or *el que.* (§§36, 37)

1 Alberto Cuevas es un buen amigo a . . . escribo mucho. 2 . . . dice que María vive en esta casa está equivocado. 3 En la plaza se reunió una gran multitud de gente dentro de . . . se veía el gobernador Sánchez. 4 ¡Para la cena trajeron a la sala unas mesas encima de . . . había toda clase de comida! 5 Éste es un reloj . . . me dio mi padre. 6 Nuestro hermano mayor, . . . estudiaba ingeniería, está casado. 7 Mi tío Enrique acaba de comprar una casa detrás de . . . piensa cultivar toda clase de frutas. 8 Javier Losa es un amigo . . . trabaja conmigo.

5 Translate these sentences into Spanish using *que, quien,* or a form of *el cual* or *el que* for the indicated portions. (§§35, 36, 37 A, B, C)

1 Where is the record **that** Gregory bought? 2 Charles is the man with **whom** I work. 3 The Cafe Victoria is an old restaurant in **which** many students meet in order to[1] eat and to talk. 4 We visited the Church of St. Mary near **which** we found a good hotel. 5 My uncle, **who** is a captain in the Army, speaks three languages.

38 / *The Relative Adjective* cuyo — *El adjetivo relativo* cuyo

1 Complete each sentence with the appropriate form of *cuyo* (whose). (§38)

≫ Cecilia es una chica . . . ideas siempre son buenas.
Cecilia es una chica **cuyas** ideas siempre son buenas.

1 Ése es el chico . . . nombre no recuerdo. 2 Conozco a una muchacha . . . padres son de Chile. 3 La señora Oviedo, . . . marido está enfermo, no puede venir hoy. 4 Victoria Muñoz es la artista . . . cuadros vimos en el café. 5 ¿Dónde vive ahora tu tía . . . casa se quemó? 6 Cervantes es un autor . . . obras me gustan mucho. 7 ¿Habló con los padres . . . hijo se perdió?

2 Translate these sentences into Spanish using a form of *cuyo* for the indicated portions. (§38)

1 Concha is the woman **whose** sons died in the war. 2 Where is the hotel **whose** restaurant serves Italian food? 3 How is the boy **whose** leg was broken[2]? 4 Who is

[1]*para*
[2]*se rompió*

that doctor **whose** house we bought?   5 Juan Ramón Jiménez is a writer **whose**
poetry is very famous.   6 Mr. Duran is the man **whose** daughter married Charles.
7 John is the boy **whose** stories[1] are always amusing.

39 / Indefinites — El indefinido

1 Write the Spanish indefinite that is opposite in meaning to the word given. The
English translation of these opposites is given in parentheses. (§39 A)

1 nada (*nothing*)	. . . (*something*)
2 ninguno (*none*)	. . . (*some*)
3 nadie (*no one*)	. . . (*someone; somebody*)

2 Write these sentences in Spanish. (§39 A)

1 (*Ud.*) Can you tell me **something** about your family?   2 **Someone** forgot their
books.   3 Joe is **somewhat** curious about[2] his new neighbors.   4 **Some** of my friends
(m.) are French.   5 **Someone** said that Mary is[3] ill.   6 **Some** American cities have
Spanish names.   7 I see **something** on the roof.   8 (*tú*) --Pete, have you seen the new
cars[4]? --Yes, I've seen **some**.

3 Rewrite these sentences, changing the verb from the passive *se* construction to the
third person plural. (§39 B)

≫ **Se dice** que Fernando es capitán en el ejército.
   Dicen que Fernando es capitán en el ejército.

1 **Se abre** este parque a las siete de la mañana.   2 **Se importa** mucho café a los
Estados Unidos.   3 **Se pide** el pasaporte en la frontera.   4 **Se habla** mucho francés
en Montreal.   5 **Se cierra** este restaurante a las dos de la mañana.

4 Write these sentences in Spanish, giving special attention to the indicated portions.
(§39 B)

1 **One** has to arrive early in order to buy[5] a ticket.   2 **They say** that the new cars[4]
are more expensive.   3 **They close** the office at six.   4 **You** need to exchange dollars
for[6] pesos in Mexico.   5 **One** has to practice a lot in order to be[5] a[7] musician.
6 **They produce** fine silver in Taxco.

[1]*cuentos*
[2]*acerca de*
[3]*estar*
[4]*coches nuevos*
[5]*para* + infinitive
[6]*por*
[7]Don't translate.

40 / Simple Prepositions — Preposiciones simples

1 Complete these sentences with the Spanish equivalent of each preposition given in parentheses. (§40)

≫ El perro corrió . . . la niña. (*after, toward*)
El perro corrió **tras** la niña.
El perro corrió **hacia** la niña.

a) El perro corrió . . . la niña. (*with, up to*)
b) Los pájaros cantaban . . . los árboles del jardín. (*from, between, under, in*)
c) Todo el mundo llegó, . . . Amalia. (*except, according to, but*)

2 Complete each sentence with the Spanish equivalent of the preposition in parentheses. (§40)

1 --Buenos días, ¿está tu madre . . . (*at*) casa? 2 --Señor Fernández, sus cartas están . . . (*on*) la mesa. 3 Compré un regalo . . . (*for*) Elena. 4 ¿Cuándo jugaremos al fútbol . . . (*against*) los alemanes? 5 El senador Muñoz ha llegado . . . (*from*)[1] Santa Cruz. 6 ¿Podemos salir . . . (*through*) esta puerta? 7 . . . (*according to*) Mario, es una película . . . (*about*)[2] la guerra. 8 Los soldados estaban . . . (*under*) el mando del coronel Jiménez. 9 Carlos y Antonio han esperado . . . (*since*) las tres. 10 . . . (*during*) nuestras vacaciones fuimos . . . (*as far as*) Córdoba.

41 / Compound Prepositions — Preposiciones compuestas

1 Complete these sentences, with the Spanish equivalent of the English in parentheses. You will need a Spanish compound preposition in each case. (§41 A, B)

1 Hay algunos barrios pobres . . . (*around*) la Ciudad de Lima. 2 Luisa, ¿por qué no vienes con nosotras . . . (*instead of*[3]) estudiar? 3 Tenemos un árbol grande . . . (*in front of*) nuestra casa y . . . (*along side*) la casa tenemos un patio. 4 No jugaron el partido de béisbol . . . (*because of*) la lluvia. 5 . . . (*near*) la capital se encuentran las Pirámides de Teotihuacán. 6 Carmen está . . . (*outside of*) la casa. 7 Podemos descansar . . . (*after*) terminar nuestro trabajo. 8 El avión está . . . (*above*) las nubes. 9 Mi perro duerme . . . (*underneath*) mi silla. 10 Los papeles están . . . (*inside of*) el[4] cajón.

---

[1]Use *de* or *desde.*
[2]Use *de* or *sobre.*
[3]Use either possible preposition.
[4]There is a contraction here, *de + el = del.*

2 Write the Spanish compound prepositions which are opposite in meaning to the ones given below. The English translations of these opposites are given in parentheses. (§41 A, B)

≫ debajo de (*under*)   **encima de** (*above, on top of*)

1 detrás de (*behind-in place; after*)   . . . (*in front of; before*)
2 lejos de (*far from*)   . . . (*near*)
3 antes de (*before-in time*)   . . . (*after-in time*)
4 dentro de (*within; inside of*)   . . . (*outside of*)

3 Complete these sentences with the Spanish equivalent of the English prepositions in parentheses. (§41 C)

1 . . . (*as for*) Carolina, ella sale para los Estados Unidos el viernes. 2 El Banco Nacional está . . . (*opposite*) la Iglesia de Santa Teresa. 3 Juana me escribió . . . (*in regard to*[2]) las joyas de su tía. 4 La fábrica de ropa está . . . (*next to*) la carretera.

4 Translate these sentences into Spanish, giving special attention to the indicated portion. (§41 A, B, C)

1 (*tú*) Robert, do you live **near** the school? 2 **In spite of** her age, my grandmother married again! 3 My car is[1] **in front of** the store. 4 **As for** Susan and Charles, they will come at seven. 5 The garage is[1] **behind** the house. 6 (*tú*) Philip, can you work today **instead of**[2] tomorrow? 7 **Besides** washing the clothes, I have to prepare the dinner. 8 **In regard to** the letter, it's on the table. 9 Two children (m.) sat down **opposite** the statue.

42 / Possession — Posesión

1 Translate these sentences into Spanish using *de* to show possession. (§42)

≫ Here is **George's car.**
    Aquí está **el coche de Jorge.**

1 Here is[1] **Mr. Castillo's house.** 2 Today is[3] **Alice's birthday.** 3 Here is[1] **Charles' watch.** 4 **Joe's sister** is[3] very pretty! 5 **The hotel's elevator** does not work[4].

[1] *estar*
[2] Use either possible preposition.
[3] *ser*
[4] *funcionar*

43 / The Preposition de Used with Nouns — La preposición de usada con nombres

1 Write the following sentences in Spanish, including the preposition **de** when translating the indicated portion. (§43)

≫ The **bullfights** begin in May.
Las **corridas de toros** empiezan en mayo.

1 This **typewriter** works[1] well.   2 Mary works in a **beauty parlor.**   3 The **gasoline station** is[2] on the corner.   4 I need to buy the **English book.**   5 My father works for[3] the **insurance company.**

44 / The Personal a — El a personal

1 Rewrite each sentence, replacing the indicated direct object with the ones given in parentheses. Make any other changes necessary. (§44 A)

≫ Buscamos **la Iglesia San Martín.** (María, casa)
Buscamos **a** María.
Buscamos la casa.

a) Buscamos **la Iglesia San Martín.** (1 señor Blanco[4], 2 señorita Muñoz, 3 parque, 4 hotel, 5 Ricardo, 6 niño[4])

b) Veo **el coche.** (1 mis compañeras, 2 periódicos, 3 chicos, 4 soldados, 5 casa, 6 muchachas)

2 Complete each sentence with the <u>personal</u> *a* if it is needed. (§44 A)

≫ Esperamos . . . José.
Esperamos **a** José.
≫ Veo . . . la farmacia en la esquina.
Veo la farmacia en la esquina.

1 No conozco . . . Elena Martínez.   2 Constanza, ¿entiende usted bien . . . la profesora Salazar?   3 Juan no puede ver . . . el número de la casa.   4 No oímos . . . la música.   5 Visitamos . . . mis abuelos los domingos.   6 Delia, ¿conoces . . . la señora Mercedes?   7 Mario y yo esperamos . . . un taxi.

3 Translate these sentences into Spanish. Include the <u>personal</u> *a* in your translation where necessary. (§44 A, B)

1 Tony admires Carmen.   2 Charles admires the new car.   3 I see my boss every day[5].   4 I don't know Mr. González.   5 (*tú*) Ann, do you see the bus?   6 Pepe has two uncles.

[1]*funcionar*
[2]*estar*
[3]*para*

[4]You will need the contraction here, *a* + *el* = *al.*
[5]*todos los días*

1 Answer the following questions. Include *por* plus the words in parentheses in your response. (§45 A)

≫ ¿Por dónde entró el ladrón? (la ventana)
   El ladrón entró **por la ventana.**
≫ ¿Cómo va Alberto a Madrid? (avión)
   Alberto va a Madrid **por avión.**

1 ¿Por qué es célebre Taxco? (sus artículos de plata) 2 ¿Cómo podemos salir de este edificio? (esa puerta) 3 Lucía, ¿cuándo llega el correo aquí? (la mañana) 4 ¿Por quién fue construido este edificio? (la Compañía Hércules) 5 ¿Por cuántos días va a estar aquí Roberto? (unos cinco días) 6 ¿Por dónde pasean los amantes los domingos? (el río)

2 Answer the following questions. Include *para* plus the words in parentheses in your response. (§45 B)

≫ ¿Para qué fueron Manuel y Alberto a la capital? (buscar trabajo)
   Manuel y Alberto fueron a la capital **para buscar trabajo.**
≫ ¿Para dónde sale Enrique? (clase)
   Enrique sale **para clase.**

1 ¿Para cuándo tienen que terminar la construcción de la casa? (primero de agosto) 2 ¿Para quién trabaja Mario? (el Banco Central) 3 ¿Para qué necesita Paco estas herramientas? (arreglar su coche) 4 ¿Para cuándo necesitan ellos la ropa lavada? (mañana) 5 ¿Para quiénes son estos paquetes? (Alicia y Mariana) 6 ¿Para qué estudia Jorge? (ser médico) 7 ¿Para qué es este vaso? (vino)

3 Complete each sentence with *por* or *para* as needed. Indicate which division of §45 A and B explains the particular use of *por* and *para*. (§45 A, B)

≫ Mi novia compró un disco nuevo . . . mi cumpleaños.
   Mi novia compró un disco nuevo **para** mi cumpleaños. (rule 2)

1 Don Fernando sale mañana . . . la capital. 2 Mis tíos estuvieron con nosotros . . . una semana. 3 . . . ir a Santa Cruz hay que tomar un camino peligroso. 4 . . . la mañana mi madre se levantaba temprano . . . preparar el desayuno. 5 . . . conservar la gasolina no debemos manejar más de a noventa kilómetros . . . hora. 6 Entramos en Monterrey . . . la carretera principal. 7 El ministro fue recibido . . . el presidente y otros distinguidos oficiales del gobierno francés. 8 La invitación es . . . el sábado a las ocho. 9 El ruido de los coches entró . . . la ventana de la casa. 10 La Argentina es todavía famosa . . . el tango. 11 No puedo jugar ahora, Juanito. Estoy . . . (*about to*) ir al trabajo. 12 Felipe y yo tenemos clases . . . la mañana. Vamos al café . . . la tarde. 13 Gracias . . . darme tu libro, Ana. 14 El señor Murillo quiere comprar nuestra casa. Por eso estoy aquí, . . . vendérsela. 15 Jaime cree que perdió su cartera . . . aquí. 16 Guillermo pagó un buen precio . . . su motocicleta.

4 Translate into Spanish using *por* or *para*. (§45 A, B)

1 The message is **for** Mary. 2 **In order to** arrive at 8:00, John leaves early. 3 Thanks **for** everything, Charles. 4 Let's go **by way of** Miraflores Street. 5 **For** a Frenchman, Paul speaks English very well! 6 My parents will leave **for** Europe tomorrow. They're going **by** plane. 7 (*tú*) Julia, can you finish **by** 9:00? 8 Jim paid sixty pesos **for** the tickets. 9 Pepe has to study **in the evening**. 10 I'll call **in the morning**.

46 / Verbs Governing Nouns With or Without a Preposition — *Verbos empleados con o sin preposición*

1 Complete these sentences with the Spanish preposition which accompanies the verb in each case. (§46)

1 Esteban se despidió . . . sus amigos en la fiesta. 2 Paco, ¿quieres jugar . . .[1] tenis? 3 Poco a poco el tren se alejó . . . la capital. 4 Fernando se aprovechó . . . la oportunidad de hablar con don Alberto. 5 Susana, ¿piensas mucho . . . tu futuro viaje a Colombia? 6 A las seis nos dirigimos . . . la plaza central. 7 Mi esposa soñó . . . ladrones anoche. 8 Graciela, ¿te interesas mucho . . . la política? 9 El niño se acercó . . . los perros. 10 Los jóvenes cambiaron . . . vestidos para ir a la playa.

2 Complete these sentences, with the Spanish equivalent of the English in parentheses. A preposition should follow each verb in Spanish. (§46)

1 Creo que Elena . . . (*resembles*) su hermana. 2 Generalmente . . . (*I leave*) la casa a las siete. 3 Luis y yo . . . (*arrived at*) la reunión un poco tarde. 4 La sangría . . . (*consists of*) vino tinto, frutas y azúcar. 5 Anoche Lorenzo . . . (*entered*) el patio. 6 El bebé . . . (*smiles at*) su mamá cuando ella le habla. 7 Mi esposa . . . (*is afraid of*) los aviones. 8 Esta bicicleta . . . (*belongs to*) José. 9 Mi tía . . . (*married*) un español. 10 El jefe de la compañía . . . (*trusts*) Antonio y mí.

3 Translate these sentences into Spanish. The indicated portions must include a preposition in Spanish. (§46)

1 Raymond **counts**[2] **on** his parents for[3] money. 2 Dr. Campos **leaves** his office at six. 3 Tom **thinks about** his work. 4 Susan **dreams of** her boy friend. 5 This painting **belongs to** Margaret. 6 The two children (m.) **entered** my room. 7 Our trip **depends on** the plane strike[4]. 8 (*tú*) John, do you want **to play** cards?

---

[1] There will be a contraction here, *a* + *el* = *al*.
[2] This verb is radical-changing.
[3] *para*
[4] *huelga de aviones*

47 / *Verbs Followed by Dependent Infinitives With or Without a Preposition —*
Verbos seguidos de infinitivos con o sin preposición

1 Complete these sentences with the preposition *a* if it is needed. (§47 A, B)

1 Por la tarde empezó . . . llover. 2 Ramón, te invito . . . comer conmigo esta
noche. 3 Vicente dice que no desea . . . jugar al fútbol hoy. 4 Mi hermana mayor
me enseñó . . . tocar la guitarra. 5 Antonio y Salvador prefieren . . . vivir en un
apartamento. 6 Julia espera . . . comprar un coche en enero. 7 Debo . . . escribir
unas cartas esta noche. 8 Jorge y Víctor se pusieron . . . discutir la economía de
España. 9 Pablo, ¿quieres . . . tomar más café? 10 Luis se sentó y volvió . . . leer
su periódico. 11 Isabel decidió . . . hacerse enfermera. 12 Diego prometió . . .
llevarme a la feria.

2 Complete these sentences with the Spanish equivalent of the English in parentheses.
Each translation must include a Spanish preposition. (§47 C, D)

1 Los Romero . . . (*insist on*) visitarme en setiembre. 2 Doña Amalia . . . (*is glad*)
ver a sus nietos otra vez. 3 . . . (*we tried*) entender al extranjero pero no pudimos.
4 . . . (*I stopped*) fumar el mes pasado. 5 La esposa del doctor Miró . . . (*busies
herself by*) ayudar en la clínica. 6 Mis tíos . . . (*are thinking of*) la compra de la nueva
casa. 7 Eduardo y yo . . . (*agree on*[1]) reunirnos en el Café Mago mañana. 8 Tu
carta . . . (*took three days*) llegar aquí.

3 Translate these sentences into Spanish. The indicated portions must include a
preposition in Spanish. In some cases there is no corresponding English preposition.
(§47 B, C, D)

1 Rose **helps** prepare the dinner. 2 **I am going** to buy a new shirt. 3 Charles
wants **to devote himself to** studying. 4 Alice and Steve **tried to** call yesterday.
5 (*tú*) John, why do you **insist on** paying the bill? 6 Mary **forgot to**[2] give me her
address! 7 Pete **learned how** to swim last summer.

48 / *The Conjunctions* y *and* o — *Las conjunciones* y *y* o

1 Rewrite these sentences. Add the conjunction *y* or *e* as required, and the words in
parentheses. (§48 A)

≫ Mi prima Alicia habla alemán. (inglés)
  Mi prima Alicia habla alemán **e** inglés.

1 Gerardo estudia geografía. (historia) 2 La Pampa es una región muy fértil.
(inmensa en Sud América) 3 Paco es un chico alto. (moreno) 4 Ramón irá al cine
esta noche. (Carlos irá también) 5 El señor Palacios es un senador joven. (idealista)

[1]*quedar*. . .
[2]Use the reflexive form, *olvidarse* plus the preposition.

2 Rewrite these sentences. Add the conjunction *o* or *u* as required, and the words in parentheses. (§48 B)

≫ Diego, ¿cuántos boletos tienes, siete? (ocho)
Diego, ¿cuántos boletos tienes, siete **u** ocho?

1 Quiero saber si la oficina está vacía. (ocupada) 2 Elena, ¿quieres tomar café? (té) 3 Carmen, ¿prefieres plata? (oro) 4 ¿Qué fue la víctima, mujer? (hombre) 5 ¿Viene el señor Delgado hoy? (mañana)

49 / The Conjunction but — *La conjunción* but

1 Complete each sentence with either *pero* or *sino* as required. (§49 A, C)

1 Susana quiere visitar México . . . no tiene el dinero necesario. 2 ¡Amalia Gutiérrez no es mi tía . . . mi abuela! 3 La gente del Brasíl no habla español . . . portugués. 4 Mi apartamento no es muy grande . . . es cómodo. 5 El señor García no llega hoy . . . mañana. 6 Esperamos a Julia . . . ella no vino.

2 Complete each sentence with either *sino* or *sino que.* (§49 C, D)

1 La palabra "chocolate" no es de origen español . . . azteca. 2 No sólo hizo mucho viento anoche . . . llovió bastante. 3 Nuestro equipo de fútbol no sólo ganó muchos partidos . . . ganó el campeonato chileno. 4 Manuel Ocampo no sólo es un hombre sincero . . . además sabe cumplir con sus obligaciones. 5 Para mí, la historia no es aburrida . . . interesante.

3 Translate these sentences into Spanish, paying special attention to the indicated portions. (§49 A, C, D)

1 Anthony is not from Spain **but** from Italy. 2 Ann wants to go **but** she is[1] sick. 3 I not only wrote a letter **but** I also called by telephone! 4 Mary and I are tired (f.) **but** happy. 5 The telegram is not for[2] Paul, **but** for[2] Robert.

50 / Uses of si — *Modos de usar la conjunción* si

1 Complete each sentence with the Spanish equivalent of the English word in parentheses. (§50 A, B)

1 A ver . . . (*whether*) venden cigarillos en esta tienda. 2 . . . (*if*) llueve, no iremos a la playa hoy. 3 Carolina, . . . (*if*) necesitas algo, llámame por favor. 4 Yo no sé . . . (*whether*) Alonso viene hoy o mañana. 5 Señora Cruz, ¿sabe usted . . . (*whether*) el lunes es el cumpleaños de Ana?

[1]*estar*
[2]*para*

2 Translate these sentences into Spanish, paying special attention to the indicated portions. (§50 A, B)

1 (*tú*) **If** you come, can you come early?   2 I want to see the book tomorrow, **if** it's possible.   3 We don't know **whether** we won or lost the game.   4 **If** Mary goes, Alice will go with her.

51 / *Time — La hora*

JUNIO

lunes	martes	miércoles	jueves	viernes	sábado	domingo
					1	2
3	4	5	6	7	8	9
10	11	12	13	14	15	16
17	18	19	20	21	22	23
24	25	26	27	28	29	30

1 Use the Spanish calendar above to answer the following questions in complete sentences in Spanish[1].   (See §4 E for use of the definite article with days of the week)   (§51 A)

≫ ¿Qué día es el veintitrés de junio?
El veintitrés de junio es domingo.

1 ¿Qué día es el 5 de junio?   2 ¿Qué día es el 21 de junio?   3 ¿Qué día es el 17 de junio?   4 ¿Qué día es el 1° de junio?   5 ¿Qué día es el 30 de junio?   6 ¿Qué día es el 12 de junio?   7 ¿Qué día es el 6 de junio?

2 Answer the following questions in complete sentences in Spanish.   (§51 B, C)

≫ ¿En qué mes empieza la primavera?
La primavera empieza en marzo.

1 ¿En qué mes celebramos la independencia de los Estados Unidos?   2 ¿En qué mes celebramos la Navidad?   3 ¿Cuáles son los tres meses del verano?   4 ¿Cuáles son los tres meses del otoño?   5 ¿Cuáles son los tres meses del invierno?   6 ¿Cuáles

[1]On Spanish calendars the first day of the week is Monday.

son los tres meses de la primavera?   7 ¿En qué mes celebramos los cumpleaños de Jorge Washington y Abrahán Lincoln?   8 ¿Cuál es el primer mes del año?   9 ¿Cuál es el último mes del año?   10 ¿Qué mes tiene 28 días?

3 Translate these sentences into Spanish.   (See §18 D for expressing dates in Spanish.) (§51 B, C)

1 John and I will go to Europe for[1] **the summer.** We will return in **August.**   2 (*tú*) Susan, which[2] season do you prefer, **the spring** or **the autumn?**   3 My parents will go to Miami for[1] **the winter.** They will leave in **January** or **February.**   4 Generally there is snow here in **October** or **November.**   5 My birthday is[3] in **April** and our aniversary is[3] in **May.**

4 Answer the question *¿Qué hora es?* by writing the time indicated by each of these clocks. (§51 D)

(A.M.)
Son las nueve de la mañana.

(P.M.)
Son las ocho de la noche.

 1

 2

 3

 4

(A.M.)   (P.M.)   (A.M.)   (A.M.)

The A.M. / P.M. equivalents may be omitted when indicating the times below.

 5

 6

 7

 8

[1]*por*
[2]*qué*
[3]*ser*

5 Translate these sentences into Spanish, paying special attention to the indicated portions. (§51 D, E)

1 Rose, **what time is it?** 2 **It's five o'clock in the afternoon.** 3 **It's a quarter after one.** 4 **Is it eight o'clock** or **is it nine o'clock?** 5 **It's half past one in the morning!** I have to go home[1]!

52 / Augumentatives and Diminutives — Aumentativos y diminutivos

1 Rewrite these nouns below, adding the diminutive ending *-ito.*

≫ una casa	**una casita**	(*a little house*)
1 un libro	. . .	(*a little book*)
2 un viejo	. . .	(*a little old man*)
3 mi abuela	. . .	(*my dear old grandmother*)
4 Juan	. . .	(*Johnny*)
5 un momento	. . .	(*just a moment (second)*)
6 un perro	. . .	(*a puppy*)

53 / The Use of ya — Modo de usar ya

1 Complete these sentences with the Spanish equivalent of the English in parentheses, using *ya, ya no,* or *ya que.* (§53 A, B, C, D, E)

1 Manuel . . . (*already*) salió para la oficina. Volverá a las seis. 2 Hoy es mi cumpleaños. i . . . (*now*) tengo veintidós años! 3 . . . (*since*) estamos en Granada, debemos visitar la Alhambra. 4 Son las nueve en punto. . . . (*now*) empezará la película. 5 Creo que doña Blanca . . . (*no longer*) vive en esta calle. 6 Fernando, ¿ . . . (*now*) estás listo[2] para ir a clase? 7 Jorge, ¿ . . . (*already*) leíste este artículo sobre España? 8 . . . (*since*) Carlos se fue a la universidad, no lo vemos por aquí. 9 El cielo está muy oscuro. . . . (*soon*) va a llover.

2 Translate these sentences into Spanish using *ya, ya no,* or *ya que* for the indicated portion. (§53 A, B, C, D, E)

1 Carmen **already** ate. She's in her room. 2 We **no longer** talk of the war. 3 **Soon** I will write the letter. 4 My son **already** knows how to read! 5 Susan **no longer** takes the bus at eight o'clock.

[1] *a casa*
[2] *estar listo* = to be ready

1 Rewrite these sentences so that the word order is: subject + verb + remainder. (§54 A, B)

≫ Murió mi padre después de la guerra civil.
   Mi padre murió después de la guerra civil.

1 Llegarán los invitados a las ocho a comer. 2 Enfrente del parque vive la familia Salazar. 3 Cerca del pueblo se encuentra el Lago de Junín. 4 Llamó María para hablar con su mamá. 5 Llegaron dos policías para hacerme preguntas sobre el accidente. 6 Fuera de la ciudad, donde cultivan olivos, fuimos a pasear por el río.

2 Translate these sentences into Spanish. Remember that verbs in compound tenses are not separated in Spanish. (§54 C)

1 I **have** never **read** that book. 2 Charles **has** always **lived** with us. 3 We **had** never **seen** that movie. 4 My grandfather **had** always **hoped** to visit Spain. 5 (*tú*) --Pepita, you **have** scarcely **eaten** your supper[1]! 6 We **have** generally **started** our work at eight o'clock.

3 Rewrite these sentences, including the adjective in parentheses. Follow the rule for the placement of the adjective in parentheses in relation to *otro*. (§54 D)

≫ Delante de la puerta hay otros estudiantes. (dos)
   Delante de la puerta hay **otros dos** estudiantes.

1 Había otros pasajeros en el coche de Antonio. (tres)   2 Federico nos dio unos muebles y otras cosas. (pocas)   3 El barrio de San Isidro tiene otras escuelas. (cuatro)

55 / *Interrogative Word Order — La frase interrogativa*

1 Make these sentences interrogative by placing the verb before the subject. (§55 A)

≫ Enrique va a la universidad.
   ¿**Va Enrique** a la universidad?

1 Jaime llega a las once y media. 2 Pepe come con sus padres. 3 Pablo trabaja los sábados. 4 Fernando gana mucho dinero en la fábrica. 5 Carolina espera a su novio. 6 Sus dos hijas están casadas. 7 Rafael es estudiante en la universidad. 8 El correo llega por la tarde.

[1] *la cena*

2 Make these sentences interrogative as shown in the examples in §55 B. (§55 B)

1 Antonio juega mal al tenis. 2 Consuelo habla bien el inglés. 3 Los obreros necesitan más tiempo. 4 Muchas familias toman café y pan para el desayuno. 5 Esta iglesia es muy moderna. 6 La secretaria inglesa habla varias lenguas. 7 Los muchachos salen al centro todos los días. 8 Muchas familias norteamericanas tienen un coche. 9 La compañía de petróleo vende gasolina y otros productos.

3 Make these sentences interrogative by placing *¿verdad?* at the end. (§55 D)

≫ Pablo es mexicano.
  Pablo es mexicano, ¿verdad?

1 Ésta es una novela aburrida. 2 Josefa tiene dos hermanos. 3 Amalia sabe la dirección. 4 Mañana es viernes. 5 Jaime compró la radio nueva. 6 Esta silla es muy cómoda.

4 Translate these interrogative sentences into Spanish, paying careful attention to the word order. (§55 A, B, C, D)

1 Does Mendoza have an airport? 2 Does Robert work in the drugstore? 3 Is flamenco music very traditional? 4 Are the American movies very violent? 5 Is Mr. Murillo very angry? 6 The game begins at two o'clock, doesn't it? 7 (*tú*) Does your brother have two cars? 8 Do tourists come here during the summer? 9 Does Susan dance well? 10 (*tú*) Mary, do you see their flowers?

56 / *The Spanish Verb — El verbo español*

-ar Infinitive	Infinitive Stem	*-er* Infinitive	Infinitive Stem	*-ir* Infinitive	Infinitive Stem
hablar	habl-	comer	com-	vivir	viv-
comprar	compr-				

1 Make a chart like the one above and place the following regular verbs in their respective conjugations (*-ar, -er, -ir*). Also write the infinitive stem for each verb. (§56 A, B, C)

Regular verbs: hablar, comer, vivir, comprar, vender, escribir, insistir, llegar, estudiar, leer, trabajar, creer, necesitar, responder, pasear, entrar, escuchar, abrir, ver, correr, recibir, prometer.

1 Write the English translation of the indicated verb in each sentence below. Also identify the tense of the verb. All of the verbs in this exercise are in the simple tenses. (§57 A, B)

≫ La abuela **contestó** el teléfono.   *answered, preterite*
≫ Carmen **iría** al parque pero no tiene el tiempo.   *would go, conditional*

1 Mi tía Elena **llamará** mañana. 2 Pablo **vendría** a la fiesta pero no conoce a mis amigos. 3 La criada **volverá** mañana a las ocho. 4 Consuelo **escuchaba** los discos. 5 Estas cartas **llegaron** hoy. 6 Don Miguel **leía** su periódico. 7 **Vimos** el partido de fútbol ayer. 8 Alicia, ¿**eres** tú la hija menor?

2 Write the English translation of the indicated verb in each sentence. Also identify the tense of the verb. All the verbs in this exercise are in a compound tense. (§57 A, B)

≫ Mario **ha terminado** la cena.   *has finished, perfect*
≫ Pepito **había caído** de su bicicleta.   *had fallen, pluperfect*

1 Luisa, ¿**has mandado** las invitaciones? 2 Eran las ocho. Todos los obreros **habrían salido** si no hubiera llovido tanto. 3 Paco, ¡**habríamos llegado** más temprano pero perdimos tu dirección! 4 ¿Quién **ha traído** este perro? 5 Vicente **había esperado** media hora.

3 Translate these sentences into Spanish. The indicated verbs are in both simple and compound tenses. (§57 A, B)

1 Charles **has sold** his car. 2 **I would have insisted** but **they had bought** the tickets. 3 Ellen **opened** the gift. 4 The boys **were studying** history. 5 The maid always **prepares** the breakfast. 6 Our plane **will leave** at two o'clock. 7 **I have written** the letter. 8 (*tú*) George, **did you read** this chapter?

58 / *Formation of the Present Tense — Formación del presente.*

1 Complete these sentences with the appropriate form of the verb in parentheses. The verb in parentheses is always in the infinitive. Therefore you will need to add the appropriate ending to the infinitive stem. (§58 A)

≫ (llegar) Antonio . . . a la oficina a las nueve.
  Antonio **llega** a la oficina a las nueve.

1 (buscar) (yo) . . . una buena secretaria. 2 (trabajar) El doctor López . . . en la clínica. 3 (necesitar) (tú) ¿ . . . una pluma, Pedro? 4 (hablar) Carmen . . . español y portugués. 5 (enseñar) Señora Cruz, ¿ . . . usted música? 6 (entrar) Los políticos . . . en la cámara de representantes. 7 (esperar) (yo) . . . a mi compañero Alberto.

8 (pasear) Los novios . . . por el Parque Murillo. 9 (pagar) Mis amigos nunca . . . la cuenta en el café. 10 (admirar) ¿ . . . ustedes las pinturas de Picasso?

2 Complete these sentences with the appropriate form of the verb in parentheses. (§58 B)

≫ (vender) Mis tíos . . . ropa en esa tienda.
Mis tíos **venden** ropa en esa tienda.

1 (creer) La señora Muñoz . . . que su hija está enferma hoy. 2 (ver) (yo) . . . la Iglesia de San Pedro en la distancia. 3 (prometer) Nosotros . . . volver mañana. 4 (correr) Los chicos . . . por el patio. 5 (aprender) (tú) Julio, ¿ . . . a tocar la guitarra? 6 (comer) ¿Siempre . . . ustedes a las siete de la mañana? 7 (leer) La señora Losa . . . a sus dos hijas. 8 (responder) Nosotros siempre . . . a las cartas de nuestra abuela.

3 Complete these sentences with the appropriate form of the verb in parentheses. (§58 C)

≫ (vivir) Nosotros . . . en la Calle Acevedo.
Nosotros **vivimos** en la Calle Acevedo.

1 (asistir) ¡Muchas personas . . . a los partidos de fútbol! 2 (recibir) (yo[1]) Siempre . . . unas tarjetas para mi cumpleaños. 3 (permitir) La criada no nos . . . jugar en la cocina. 4 (escribir) (tú) Isabel, ¿ . . . otra carta a tu novio? 5 (insistir) Don Gabriel . . . en pagarme cada semana. 6 (abrir) (yo) . . . las ventanas de mi cuarto cuando hace sol. 7 (dividir) Nosotros . . . el trabajo entre toda la familia. 8 (describir) La novela . . . la vida de un detective que vive en Madrid. 9 (decidir) Los médicos . . . que su enfermedad no es muy seria. 10 (vivir) Adela, ¿tú . . . cerca del mercado?

4 Translate these sentences into Spanish. Use the appropriate form of the simple present tense for the indicated verbs. (§58 A, B, C)

1 My children (m.) **are learning** French. 2 Louise **pronounces** very well! 3 Many Indian customs still **exist** in Mexico. 4 Many Americans **speak** Spanish. 5 **I am looking** for[2] a room. 6 Does John **study** in the university? 7 **I live** in the United States but my parents **live** in Bogotá. 8 Robert and I **study** medicine. 9 My cousins (m.) **play** the guitar and **sing.** 10 (tú) Alice, what book **are you reading**?

[1] Omit the subject pronoun "I" in Spanish here and in all subsequent sentences unless you wish to emphasize it.
[2] Omit in translation.

5 Answer the following personal questions affirmatively or negatively (as you wish) with the *yo* form of the verb. All of the indicated verbs are irregular in the first person. (§58 D)

≫ **¿Sale** usted de la casa temprano?
Sí, **salgo** de la casa temprano.

1 **¿Tiene** usted hermanas?   2 **¿Quiere** usted tomar una taza de café?   3 **¿Viene** usted a la fiesta?   4 **¿Dice** usted la verdad?   5 **¿Ve** usted el lago?   6 **¿Da** usted dinero a sus amigos?   7 **¿Es** usted estudiante?   8 **¿Oye** usted mucho ruido? 9 **¿Pone** usted los libros en la mesa?   10 **¿Va** usted a la playa hoy?   11 **¿Hace** usted la cena?   12 **¿Trae** usted los libros a clase?   13 **¿Sabe** usted hablar italiano? 14 **¿Puede** usted tocar la guitarra?

59 / Uses of the Present Tense — Modo de usar el presente

1 Translate these sentences into Spanish. Use the simple present tense for the indicated verbs. (§59 A)

1 **We have** two cars.   2 Carmen **is coming** at three o'clock.   3 Jim **is leaving** tomorrow.   4 (*tú*) Mary, **are you going** to the market?   **We need** milk.   5 Rose **is making** bread.   6 **Shall we talk** tomorrow?   7 **We are giving** a party for[1] Tony. 8 The dog **hears**[2] a noise!   (*Ud.*) **Do you hear** something?

2 Answer the following questions. Include *desde* plus the words in parentheses in your response. (§59 B2)

≫ ¿Desde cuándo viven sus vecinos aquí?   (el verano pasado)
Mis vecinos viven aquí **desde el verano pasado.**

1 Carlos, ¿desde cuándo hablas francés?   (mi primer día en París)   2 ¿Desde cuándo venden ropa en esta tienda?   (el año pasado)   3 ¿Desde cuándo están casados Carmen y Felipe?   (1972)   4 Josefa, ¿desde cuándo están tus tíos aquí?   (el martes) 5 ¿Desde cuándo viven ustedes en los Estados Unidos?   (la guerra civil)   6 ¿Desde cuándo espera usted en la oficina?   (las diez y media)   7 ¿Desde cuándo debes el dinero a Mario?   (el 14 de agosto)

[1]*para*
[2]to hear = *oír*

3 Answer the following questions using *desde hace* plus the words in parentheses in your response. (§59 B3)

≫ ¿Desde cuándo tocas la guitarra? (dos años)
Toco la guitarra **desde hace dos años.**

1 ¿Desde cuándo habla Concha por teléfono? (¡Una hora!) 2 ¿Desde cuándo juegan los niños en el patio? (media hora) 3 ¿Desde cuándo tienen ustedes este coche azul? (tres meses) 4 ¿Desde cuándo está enfermo Guillermo? (unos días) 5 ¿Desde cuándo escribes a tu amigo en español? (seis meses) 6 ¿Desde cuándo están los jóvenes en la playa? (tres horas) 7 ¿Desde cuándo esperas? (poco tiempo)

4 Answer the following questions using the expression *hace . . . que* plus the words in parentheses in your response. (§59 B3)

≫ ¿Desde cuándo está Antonio en Monterrey? (un mes)
Hace un mes que Antonio está en Monterrey.

1 ¿Desde cuándo estudia Felipe en la universidad? (dos años) 2 ¿Desde cuándo está usted aquí en el parque? (unos pocos minutos) 3 ¿Desde cuándo viven ustedes en este apartamento? (unos meses) 4 ¿Desde cuándo se interesa Elisa en la música? (mucho tiempo) 5 ¿Desde cuándo juega Jorge al fútbol? (tres años) 6 ¿Desde cuándo conoces a Roberto? (tres meses)

5 Translate these sentences into Spanish using the expression *desde, desde hace,* or *hace . . . que* and the proper tense. (§59 B1, 2, 3)

1 The children (m.) have been sleeping **since** three o'clock. 2 We have been talking **for** two hours. 3 **For** five days we have been traveling by car. 4 (*tú*) **Since** when have you been waiting? 5 I have been waiting **since** nine o'clock. 6 Mr. Perez has been working here **for** ten years. 7 (*Uds.*) You have been playing cards **for** an hour. 8 I have been reading **for** ten minutes.

60 / *Formation of the Imperfect Tense — Formación del imperfecto*

1 Complete these sentences with the appropriate form of the verb in the imperfect tense. (§60 A)

≫ (trabajar) Mi padre . . . para la compañía de petróleo.
Mi padre **trabajaba** para la compañía de petróleo.

1 (tomar) Nosotros . . . el autobús para ir a la universidad. 2 (preparar) ¡La señora Macías . . . unos postres estupendos! 3 (ganar) (yo) . . . muy poco dinero en la fábrica. 4 (estudiar) Pepe y Alberto . . . hasta las doce. 5 (buscar) Francisco . . . a sus amigos. 6 (pagar) ¿Siempre . . . usted las cuentas? 7 (esperar) Nosotros . . . unas noticias de la guerra. 8 (enseñar) (tú) ¿ . . . las matemáticas en la escuela, Margarita? 9 (hablar) ¿ . . . usted con don Fernando Muñoz? 10 (jugar) El verano pasado (yo) . . . al tenis cada día.

2 Complete these sentences with the appropriate form of the verb in the imperfect tense. (§60 B)

≫ (querer) Yo siempre . . . visitar Inglaterra.
Yo siempre **quería** visitar Inglaterra.

1 (leer) Al llegar a casa, mi padre siempre . . . el periódico. 2 (saber) Mis abuelos . . . mucho acerca de la cultura francesa. 3 (aprender) Cada día (yo) . . . más italiano en la escuela. 4 (comer) Muchas veces nosotros . . . en el restaurante "Miguelito". 5 (creer / poder) ¿ . . . ustedes que nosotros . . . ganar el partido de béisbol? 6 (correr) Todos los días el perro . . . trás los niños. 7 (caer) La lluvia . . . cuando salimos de clase.

3 Complete these sentences with the appropriate imperfect tense form of the verb. These three are the only irregular verbs in the imperfect tense. (§60 C)

≫ (ser) El Coronel Miranda . . . muy famoso cuando murió.
El Coronel Miranda **era** muy famoso cuando murió.

1 (ver) Antes yo . . . muchas películas en el televisor. 2 (ser) Sus vecinos siempre . . . muy buenos. 3 (ir) Nosotros . . . a la iglesia todos los domingos. 4 (ver) María . . . que su novio estaba enojado. 5 (ir) (yo) . . . a clase cuando empezó a llover. 6 (ser) Nosotros . . . estudiantes cuando Diego fue a los Estados Unidos.

61 / Uses of the Imperfect Tense — *Modo de usar el imperfecto*

1 Rewrite the following passage in the descriptive past by changing the verbs in parentheses to the imperfect tense. The English translation of the desired verb form is given after each verb. (§61 A, B, 1)

Cuando salí de casa para esperar a mi amigo, (ser 1) (*it was*) las siete de la mañana. No (haber 2) (*there weren't*) muchos coches a esa hora y algunos chicos (jugar 3) (*were playing*) en la calle. Mientras (esperar 4) (*I was waiting*) a mi amigo, caminé despacio por delante de[1] mi casa. (Ser 5) (*it was*) un día estupendo. (Hacer 6) (*it was*) mucho sol y los pájaros (cantar 7) (*were singing*) en los árboles.

2 Write this descriptive passage in the past. The English translation of the desired verb form is given after each verb. (§61 A, B 1)

Desde el segundo piso de su casa, Javier **ve** 1 (*could see*) que muchas personas **llegan** 2 (*were arriving*) al mercado. Algunos **traen** 3 (*were bringing*) sus productos del campo, otros **quieren** 4 (*wanted*) comprar carne, legumbres, una docena de huevos o artículos de ropa. Varias personas **gritan** 5 (*were shouting*) los precios de sus

[1]*por delante de* = in front of

productos y unos chicos **juegan** 6 (*were playing*) debajo de las mesas. **Hay** 7 (*there was*) mucho ruido. De vez en cuando se **oye** 8 (*one could hear*) una radio portátil tocando música. Algunos camiones grandes **tratan** 9 (*were trying*) de pasar por una calle estrecha del mercado.

3 Complete these sentences with the appropriate form of the verb in parentheses to express a continued past action which is interrupted by some other action. The English equivalent of the desired verb form is given for each verb. (§61 B 2)

≫ (jugar) Pablo y yo . . . (*were playing*) al tenis cuando empezó a llover.
Pably y yo **jugábamos** al tenis cuando empezó a llover.

1 (leer) Ana . . . (*was reading*) una novela cuando llamó Lorenzo. 2 (ir) . . . (*I was going*) al cine cuando vi a una amiga. 3 (escribir) Amalia . . . (*was writing*) una carta cuando volvimos del parque. 4 (trabajar) Nosotros . . . (*were working*) cuando llegó el jefe de la compañía. 5 (estar) (tú) Rafael, ¿ . . . (*were*) en casa cuando ocurrió el accidente?

4 Complete these sentences with the correct form of the verb in parentheses in order to express a customary, habitual, or repeated action in past time. (§61 A, B 3)

1 (comer) Nosotros siempre . . . (*would eat*) en el patio cuando hacía buen tiempo. 2 (ir / jugar) Durante el verano mis hijos . . . (*would go*) a la playa o . . . (*would play*) al tenis todos los días. 3 (ver) Cada semana (yo) . . . (*used to see*) una película nueva en el cine. 4 (volver) Todos los días mi padre . . . (*would return*) a casa a las seis. 5 (escuchar / pasear) Por las noches nosotros siempre . . . (*would listen*) los discos o . . . (*would walk*) por la plaza del pueblo.

5 Translate the following sentences into Spanish, paying special attention to the indicated portions. (§61 A, B, 1,2,3)

1 **I was leaving** the house when I saw the accident. 2 Robert **used to visit** France every[1] summer. 3 Ellen and I **were studying** when Mary arrived.[2] 4 **I used to take** the bus every[1] day. 5 The boys **were watching** television when their mother called[3]. 6 The mail always **used to arrive** in the morning[4]. 7 My father **used to drink** ten cups of coffee every[1] day! 8 **We used to live** in Venezuela.

[1] every = *todos los*
[2] *llegó María*
[3] *llamó su mamá*
[4] *por la mañana*

EXERCISES § 61

6 Complete the following sentences, with the appropriate form of the verb in parentheses. (§61 C)

≫ Hacía tres semanas que (nosotros) . . . (estar) en Caracas.
  Hacía tres semanas que **estábamos** en Caracas.

1 Hacía muchos años que los escritores se . . . (conocer). 2 Felipe . . . (estudiar) desde hacía una hora cuando llamé. 3 Mis padres . . . (estar) casados desde hacía treinta años cuando mi padre murió. 4 Hacía tres días que Enrique . . . (esperar) un billete para Madrid. 5 Don Manuel . . . (vivir) en Hidalgo desde hacía doce años cuando empezó la revolución.

7 Translate these sentences into Spanish, paying special attention to the indicated portions. (§61 C)

1 Mr. Jiménez had been talking **for** an hour when I left. 2 Our neighbors had been living in that house **for** many years when it burned down[1]. 3 Alice had been here **for** a month when she met Tom[2]. 4 It had been raining **for** an hour when my uncle arrived.

62 / Formation of the Preterite — *Formación del pretérito*

1 Rewrite each sentence below, changing the indicated verb from the present to the preterite tense. Also replace the word *hoy* (today) with *ayer* (yesterday), to show that the action took place in the past. (§62 A)

≫ **Trabajo hoy** en casa.
  Trabajé ayer en casa.

1 María **canta hoy** por la radio nacional. 2 ¿**Terminan** la construcción del hospital **hoy**? 3 Víctor, ¿**viajas hoy** a la finca? 4 Mis abuelos **llegan hoy** a Lima. 5 Mi abogado y yo **hablamos**[3] **hoy** sobre el nuevo contrato. 6 Los jóvenes **empiezan** su viaje a Francia **hoy**. 7 Alicia y yo **jugamos**[3] al tenis **hoy**. 8 **Me levanto** temprano **hoy**. 9 La criada **lava** la ropa **hoy**.

2 Rewrite each sentence below, changing the indicated verb from the present to the preterite tense. Also write the English translation of the preterite form after each sentence. (§62 B)

≫ Los chicos **corren** a la escuela.
  Los chicos **corrieron** a la escuela. *ran*

1 El señor López **escribe** su número de teléfono. 2 Mi esposa y yo **comemos**

[1] to burn down = *quemarse*
[2] Remember to use the personal *a*. See §44.
[3] Notice the first person plural *nosotros* form of *-ar* verbs is identical in the present and preterite tenses.

en el restaurante. 3 Aquellos turistas **entienden** italiano. 4 ¿**Abres** la puerta, Concha? 5 **Salgo** de la oficina a las siete. 6 Jorge, ¿**aprendes** mucho en la clase de química? 7 El señor García **promete** contestar por telegrama. 8 Nosotros **volvemos** a casa a las tres.

3 Write the appropriate form of the verb in parentheses in the preterite tense. Remember these three verbs (*dar, ir* and *ser*) are completely irregular in the preterite tense. (§62 C 1)

1 (tú) María, ¿ . . . (dar) una fiesta para Catalina anoche? 2 Nosotros . . . (ir) al museo nacional ayer. 3 Yo . . . (ser) soldado durante tres años. 4 ¿Adónde . . . (ir) los muchachos? 5 Yo . . . (ir) al mercado con Carmen. 6 El señor Blanco . . . (ser) mi profesor de historia el año pasado. 7 La iglesia . . . (dar) mucho dinero a las familias pobres durante la crisis. 8 Yo le . . . (dar) 150 pesos a Patricia para comprar ropa. 9 ¿ . . . (ir) ustedes al cine anoche?

4 Write the appropriate form of the preterite tense of the irregular verbs below. (§62 C 2)

1 (poder) Concha y yo no . . . ir al baile anoche. 2 (decir) (yo) Le . . . a don Alberto que Paco está enfermo hoy. 3 (saber) Esta mañana los padres del muchacho . . . del accidente. 4 (venir) Jaime . . . a las tres. 5 (hacer) (*tú*) Pepe, ¿qué . . . con los discos nuevos? 6 (poner) La criada . . . el plato de fruta en la mesa. 7 (traer) El mozo nos . . . el menú. 8 (querer / poder) Los González . . . venir a la fiesta pero no . . . . 9 (tener) Mariana . . . un examen hoy en la clase de biología. 10 (estar) El señor Robles . . . aquí dos horas. 11 (conducir) Me parece que el chofer . . . el taxi muy rápido. 12 (hacer) Mi hermana mayor . . . la cena. ¿Te gusta la paella? 13 (estar) Agustín, ¿quiénes . . . en el café contigo ayer? 14 (decir) Ricardo me . . . que su hermana está casada.

5 Translate the following sentences into Spanish, paying special attention to the indicated verbs. (§62 A, B, C 1, 2)

1 John **bought** a new watch yesterday. 2 (*tú*) Carmen, **did you read** the paper? 3 **We saw** the accident last night. 4 Richard **sold** his motorcycle. 5 **I wrote** three letters last night. 6 The mechanic **came** this afternoon. 7 Tom **went** with his brother. 8 My son **ate** five eggs this morning! 9 (*Ud.*) Mr. Campos, **did you arrive** by plane?

63 / Uses of the Preterite — Modos de usar el pretérito

1 Rewrite the following paragraph, changing each infinitive in parentheses to the appropriate form of the preterite tense. (§63 A)

Ayer yo (ir 1) al cine a ver una película mexicana. Me (decir 2) mi hermano mayor que las películas mexicanas son buenas. Mis amigos no (querer 3) ir porque ellos no entienden español. Al llegar al cine, (comprar 4) un boleto, se lo (dar 5) a un empleado y (sentarse 6). (Ver 7) una película muy interesante y (entender 8) casi todo en español. (Estar 9) en el cine casi dos horas. Después, (volver 10) a casa inmediatamente porque tenía que estudiar para un examen de química.

2 Rewrite the following paragraph, changing the indicated verbs to the appropriate form of the preterite tense. (§63 A)

Vicente y Carlos **entran** 1 en el restaurante "Victoria". El mozo les **da** 2 el menú. Ellos lo **miran** 3 y luego **piden** 4 arroz con biftec. El mozo no **tarda** 5 mucho en traerles la comida. Después, **vuelve** 6 a servirles a los otros. **Llego** 7 a ese restaurante a las ocho e inmediatamente **veo** 8 a mis dos compañeros allí. **Como** 9 con ellos y luego **pagamos** 10 la comida y **salimos** 11 del restaurante para pasear por las calles de la ciudad.

64 / Combined Uses of the Preterite and the Imperfect — Modo de usar combinados el pretérito y el imperfecto

1 Rewrite the following paragraph, changing the verbs in parentheses to either the preterite or the imperfect tense. Before writing, analyze each sentence to determine whether to use the preterite or the imperfect. (§64)

El viernes yo (ir 1) a la fiesta de Paco a las diez de la noche. Cuando (llegar 2) a su apartamento, Paco (hablar 3) con dos muchachas. En la sala, algunas personas (bailar 4) y en el patio dos muchachos (tocar 5) la guitarra mientras (cantar 6). (Saludar 7) a Paco y lo (felicitar 8) por su cumpleaños. Luego yo (entrar 9) en el patio porque (querer 10) escuchar mejor las canciones. Allí (conocer 11) a varios amigos de Paco que (saber 12) cantar muy bien. (Salir 13) de la fiesta a las doce y (volver 14) a mi casa y (acostarse 15) inmediatamente.

2 Rewrite the paragraph below in the past, changing the indicated verbs to either the preterite or imperfect tense. Before writing, analyze each sentence to determine whether to use the preterite or the imperfect. (§64)

Después de la clase de historia, Arturo y yo **salimos** 1 de la universidad. **Subimos** 2 al coche de Fernando y **vamos** 3 al Café Mirador donde nos **esperan** 4 siempre nuestros compañeros. **Hay** 5 mucho tráfico en las calles porque **son** 6 las cinco de la tarde y muchas personas **regresan** 7 a sus casas. Al llegar al café, Arturo y yo **nos sentamos** 8 con nuestros amigos. Allí **tomamos** 9 unas cervezas y **hablamos** 10 de los deportes, la política, y de muchas otras cosas interesantes.

3 Translate the following paragraph into Spanish. Use either the preterite or the imperfect tense for the indicated verbs. Before writing, analyze each sentence to determine whether to use the preterite or the imperfect. (§64)

When **I woke up it was raining. I washed myself** and **went downstairs**[1]. **There were** many people in the dining room of the hotel. My friends (m) **were eating breakfast**[2]. **I greeted** them[3] and **sat down** with them. While **we were eating,** Robert, our chauffeur, **came in**[4] and **asked for** a cup of coffee.

65 / *Formation of the Future — Formación del futuro*

1 Write the appropriate form of the future tense of the verbs in parentheses. All of the verbs in this exercise are regular in the future tense. (§65 A)

≫ (empezar) El baile . . . a las ocho de la noche.
  El baile **empezará** a las ocho de la noche.

1 (llamar) Carlos dice que . . . esta noche. 2 (ir) (nosotros) . . . a Europa en setiembre. 3 (levantarse) Mañana (yo) . . . a las seis. 4 (volver) (*tú*) Teresa, ¿ . . . aquí mañana? 5 (preparar) Doña Julieta . . . la comida para ustedes esta noche. 6 (estar) ¿ . . . el doctor Valdez en su oficina mañana? 7 (hablar) Miguel y yo . . . mañana en el café. 8 (abrir) Los dueños . . . la tienda a las nueve. 9 (comer) (yo) . . . con unos amigos esta noche. 10 (ver) Ustedes . . . muchos cuadros interesantes en el Prado.

2 Write the first person form of the following infinitives in the future tense. All the verbs in this exercise are irregular in the future tense. (§65 B 1,2,3)

≫ poner   **pondré**

1 saber 2 decir 3 tener 4 salir 5 hacer 6 poder 7 venir 8 valer
9 querer 10 haber

3 Answer the following questions, using the future tense of the indicated verb. In your answer, replace the word *hoy* (today) with *mañana* (tomorrow). (§65 B 1,2,3)

≫ ¿**Viene** Enrique **hoy?**   No, Enrique **vendrá mañana.**
≫ ¿**Sale** usted a las siete **hoy?**   No, **saldré** a las siete **mañana.**

1 ¿**Quieren** los niños ir al parque **hoy?** 2 **Hacen** la cena Raquel y su hermana **hoy**? 3 ¿**Puede** venir la señora Gutiérrez **hoy?** 4 ¿**Hay** muchas personas en el mercado **hoy?** 5 ¿**Vale** este boleto mucho dinero **hoy**? 6 ¿**Saben** los muchachos la lección **hoy?** 7 ¿**Tiene** Orlando que estudiar **hoy**? 8 ¿**Dice** el periódico quién ganó el partido de básquetbol **hoy**?

---

[1] to go downstairs = *bajar*
[2] to eat breakfast = *desayunar*
[3] *los*
[4] *entrar*

1 Translate these sentences into Spanish, paying special attention to the indicated portion. (§66 A)

1 The plane **will leave** at ten o'clock. 2 **We will eat** with Susan and John. 3 (*tú*) Caroline, what **will you do** tomorrow? 4 The child **will sleep** for[1] ten hours. 5 **I will write** the letter tomorrow. 6 Perhaps **there will be** a party tonight. 7 John and Victor **will arrive** on Monday[2]. 8 Who **will buy** the tickets?

2 Translate these sentences into Spanish, using the future tense for the indicated portions to express the idea of probability. (§66 B)

≫ That house **(probably) costs** a lot of money.
  Esa casa **costará** mucho dinero.

1 Mr. Cruz **(probably) lives** alone. 2 They (m.) **(probably) know** that we're not at home[3]. 3 Mary **(probably) thinks** that we're not at home[3]. 4 (*tú*) Charles, you **(probably) read** a lot. 5 Ann cannot come. She **is**[4] **(probably)** sick.

3 Translate these interrogative sentences into English, expressing the idea of conjecture or supposition. (§66 C)

≫ ¿Dónde estarán mis zapatos?
  Where can my shoes be? (*I wonder where my shoes are.*)

1 Alguien llama a la puerta. **¿Quién será?** 2 Son las diez. **¿Dónde estará Vicente?** 3 **¿Cuándo llamará Fernando?** 4 Son las once de la noche. **¿Tendrá hambre Diego?** 5 Paco trabajó mucho hoy. **¿Estará cansado?**

4 Translate the following sentences into Spanish, using the future tense to indicate conjecture or supposition. (§66 C)

1 Where can Joe be[4]? 2 What time can it be[5]? Can it be[5] four o'clock? 3 Can Fernando be[4] here? 4 Will the letter come today?

[1]Omit in translation.
[2]*el lunes*
[3]*en casa*
[4]*estar*
[5]*ser*

67 / *Formation of the Conditional — Formación del condicional*

1 Each of the following verbs is in the present tense. Rewrite them in the conditional tense. (§67 A)

≫ canto   **cantaría**

1 escribo   2 recibes   3 cierro   4 se levanta   5 hablamos   6 encontramos   7 me caso   8 nos acostamos   9 decidimos   10 mandan   11 piden   12 preguntan   13 estoy   14 muere   15 doy   16 vamos   17 somos   18 venden   19 comes   20 aprendo

2 Write the first person plural form of the conditional tense of the following infinitives. (§67 B)

≫ saber   **sabríamos**

1 venir   2 querer   3 tener   4 decir   5 poner   6 valer   7 poder   8 haber   9 salir   10 hacer

68 / *Uses of the Conditional — Modo de usar el condicional*

1 Write the appropriate form of the verb in the conditional tense. All verbs in this exercise are regular in the conditional tense. (§68 A)

≫ (llamar) Alonso prometió que . . . a las seis.
Alonso prometió que **llamaría** a las seis.

1 (esperar) Roberto y Felipe dijeron que nos . . . en el café.   2 (enseñar) Carlos prometió que me . . . a tocar la guitarra.   3 (comer) (tú) Consuelo, ¿no dijiste que . . . con los Gutiérrez esta noche?   4 (levantarse / estar) Alberto dijo que . . . más temprano. También dijo que . . . aquí a las siete.   5 (leer) Prometí que . . . ese artículo sobre la revolución mexicana.   6 (permitir) Mis padres dijeron por qué no nos . . . ir a México.   7 (gustar) Antonio contestó que le . . . ir al teatro con nosotros.   8 (escribir) (*tú*) Amalia, ¿no prometiste que me . . . muy pronto?

2 Rewrite these sentences, changing the first indicated verb to the preterite and the second indicated verb to the conditional tense. (§68 A)

≫ Ana **dice** que **vendrá** a las cinco.
Ana **dijo** que **vendría** a las cinco.

1 Felipe **dice** que mañana **sabrá** la fecha del baile.   2 Nosotros **prometemos** que **podremos** ayudar a Beatriz el martes.   3 Mario **explica** que no **tendrá** tiempo para comer con nosotros.   4 Las muchachas **contestan** que **saldrán** el sábado.   5 Pepe **dice** que **pondrá** los libros en la mesa.   6 El dueño del hotel **promete** que **habrá** una habitación para nosotros.   7 Mi padre **dice** que **hará** el trabajo mañana.

3 Translate these sentences into Spanish, paying special attention to the indicated portion. (§68 A)

1 John said that **he would go.** 2 (*Ud.*) The doctor said that **he would talk** with you. 3 We thought[1] that **they would see** the letter. 4 (*tú*) You promised that **you would come** soon. 5 I thought[2] that the movie **would be** very interesting.

4 Translate these sentences into Spanish, using the conditional tense for the indicated portions in order to express the idea of conjecture or probability in the past. (§68 B)

≫ (*tú*) Alice, **you were (probably)** tired.
   Alicia, **estarías** cansada.

1 **It was (probably)** ten o'clock. 2 Why **did Charles call (I wonder)**? 3 I saw something in the patio! What **was it (I wonder)**? 4 Susan and Mary returned. When **did they arrive (I wonder)**? 5 It's twelve o'clock. (*tú*) I thought[2] that **you were (probably)** hungry, Paco.

5 Translate these sentences into English, expressing the idea of probability or conjecture in the past. (§68 B)

≫ Tengo que salir. **¿Dónde pondría mi abrigo?**
   (*I wonder*) *Where could I have put my coat?*

1 Mis padres no contestaron el teléfono. **¿Dónde estarían?** 2 Tengo sueño. **¿Sería muy tarde cuando me acosté anoche?** 3 Jaime no quiso venir con nosotros. **Estaría ocupado.** 4 **¿Qué diría Agustín? ¿Estaría de acuerdo?**

6 Complete these sentences with the proper conditional tense form of the verb in parentheses. Notice these sentences are all contrary-to-fact as shown by the example. (§68 C)

≫ (comprar) Si (yo) tuviera el dinero, . . . ese coche nuevo.
   Si tuviera el dinero, **compraría** ese coche nuevo.
   (*If I had the money, I would buy that new car.*)

1 (ir) Si Marcos y yo tuviéramos boletos, . . . al teatro esta noche. 2 (poder) Si llegaras más temprano, . . . terminar el trabajo a las cuatro. 3 (estar) ¡Si Alberto comiera menos, no . . . tan gordo! 4 (tener) Si yo trabajara todos los días, . . . el dinero para ir a la capital. 5 (saber) Si mi amiga Carmen estuviera aquí, . . . qué hacer. 6 (ser) ¡Si nosotros viviéramos en España, estos ejercicios . . . muy fáciles!

[1]*creíamos*
[2]*creía*

1 Copy the following sentences and underline the form of the auxiliary verb (*haber*) once, and the main verb twice. Also identify the compound tense. (§69)

≫ Fernando habrá llegado a París ahora.
  Fernando <u>habrá</u> <u><u>llegado</u></u> a París ahora. *future perfect*

1 Los turistas han esperado el tren por media hora. 2 Ana, si hubiéramos sabido[1] tu número de teléfono, habríamos llamado. 3 Guillermo, ¿habías visitado Segovia el año pasado? 4 ¡Dios mío! ¡He perdido los boletos! 5 Juan, cuando leas esta carta, yo habré salido para Madrid.

70 / *Formation of the Perfect — Formación del perfecto*

1 Complete these sentences with the proper form of the auxiliary verb *haber* to form the perfect tense. The past participle of the main verb is already given. (§70)

≫ Mi hermano . . . vendido su coche.
  Mi hermano **ha** vendido su coche.

1 Nosotros . . . ido al museo dos veces. 2 ¿Quién . . . escrito este artículo sobre el teatro? 3 (tú) Rosa, ¿por qué . . . abierto la ventana? 4 Yo . . . jugado a las cartas con Alberto muchas veces. 5 ¿No . . . vuelto ustedes a Francia? 6 Felipe, tú no . . . comido tu almuerzo.

2 Write the following sentences in the perfect tense, using the infinitive in parentheses as the main verb. (§70)

≫ ¡Los chicos (comer) todo el postre!
  ¡Los chicos **han comido** todo el postre!

1 Antonio dice que (recibir) dos cartas de su hermana. 2 Yo (leer) esta novela. Es muy interesante. 3 (tú) Marta, ¿(ver) la casa del señor Flores? 4 Nosotros no (visitar) México. 5 Muchos europeos (venir) a los Estados Unidos. 6 Creo que (yo) (pagar) mucho por mi motocicleta. 7 Don Manuel, ¿(llegar) usted esta mañana? 8 Nosotros no (tener) el tiempo para descansar. 9 ¿(vivir) ustedes en Italia? 10 (tú) Alicia, ¿por qué no (decir) nada?

---

[1]*si hubiéramos sabido* = if we had known (See §96 B.)

71 / *Uses of the Perfect — Modo de usar el perfecto*

1 Rewrite these sentences, changing the indicated verbs to the perfect tense. (§71 A)

≫ Mario **sale** temprano muchas veces.
Mario **ha salido** temprano muchas veces.

1 **Trabajamos** mucho hoy. 2 Amalia, ¿**ves** a Eduardo en la oficina? 3 Mi hermano **va** a ver al dentista muchas veces. 4 Los chicos **juegan** en el patio todo el día. 5 Le **escribo** a Manuel muchas veces.

2 Translate these sentences into Spanish, paying special attention to the indicated portions. (§71 A)

1 (*tú*) Pepe, **have you seen** my hat? 2 In one day **we sold** thirty books! 3 This week **I worked** fifty hours. 4 The president **has announced** a new economic program.
5 **I have eaten** too much!

72 / *Formation of the Pluperfect — Formación del pluscuamperfecto*

1 Complete these sentences with the appropriate form of the auxiliary verb *haber* to form the pluperfect tense. (§72)

≫ José . . . llamado dos veces por teléfono.
José **había** llamado dos veces por teléfono.

1 Elena y yo . . . llegado tarde a la conferencia. 2 Una criada . . . puesto flores en mi habitación. 3 (yo) . . . recibido varios cheques de la compañía. 4 Nuestros amigos . . . venido para despedirse de nosotros. 5 (tú) César, ¿ . . . dormido mucho tiempo cuando llamé a las doce?

2 The following verbs are in the perfect tense. Rewrite them in the pluperfect tense. (§72)

≫ hemos comido   **habíamos comido**

1 han comprado 2 he visto 3 hemos abierto 4 has tenido 5 han hecho
6 me he despertado 7 han traído 8 te has acostado 9 hemos puesto 10 ha muerto

73 / *Use of the Pluperfect — Modo de usar el pluscuamperfecto*

1 Rewrite the following sentences, changing the indicated verb to the pluperfect tense. (§73)

≫ Mi hermana **vive** en Colombia.
Mi hermana **había vivido** en Colombia.

1 El gobierno federal **construye** muchas carreteras en esta región. 2 Los padres

de Arturo le **mandan** el dinero.   3 ¡Emilia **prepara** un postre estupendo para nosotros!
4 ¡Pepito **abre** todos los regalos de Navidad!   5 **Tenemos** la oportunidad de ver las
Pirámides de Teotihuacán.   6 Mis abuelos **vienen** desde Córdoba.   7 **Viajamos** desde
las seis de la mañana hasta las diez de la noche.

2 Translate the following sentences into Spanish, paying special attention to the
indicated portions. (§73)

   1 **I had lost** their address.   2 John came to our house but **we had** already[1] **left.**
3 **It had rained** a lot that night.   4 (*tú*) Teresa, **had you heard** the story[2] before?
5 A man called Perez **had won** the lottery.   6 Someone **had stolen** my watch.   7 **We
had gone** to the bullfight early that afternoon.   8 Mrs. Cruz **had answered** the telephone
and **had said** that her husband wasn't[3] at home.

74 / *Formation of the Preterite Perfect — Formación del pretérito perfecto*
75 / *Use of the Preterite Perfect — Modo de usar el pretérito perfecto*

   Since the Preterite Perfect is not used in conversation and rarely in present-day literature, no exercises are being given.

76 / *Formation of the Future Perfect — Formación del futuro perfecto*

   1 Complete these sentences with the appropriate form of the auxiliary verb *haber* to
form the future perfect tense. The past participle of the main verb is already given.
(§76)

≫ Nosotros . . . regresado a la una.
   Nosotros **habremos** regresado a la una.

   1 (tú) Carlos, ¿. . . leído este libro antes del jueves?   2 Mañana los Salazar . . .
llegado a Monterrey.   3 (yo) . . . decidido qué hacer antes del lunes.   4 El señor
Delgado . . . recibido mi carta pasado mañana.   5 (nosotros) . . . terminado el trabajo
antes de esta noche.   6 Señor Flores, ¡esta noche usted . . . visto La Alhambra!

77 / *Uses of the Future Perfect — Modo de usar el futuro perfecto*

   1 Rewrite the following sentences, changing the indicated verbs to the future perfect
tense. (§77 A and B)

≫ El doctor Gómez **llama** a las diez.
   El doctor Gómez **habrá llamado** a las diez.

   1 La fiesta **comienza** a las nueve de la noche.   2 Ese autobús **pasa** a las cinco.

[1]already = *ya* Place before the auxiliary verb *haber.*
[2]the story = *el cuento*
[3]*no estaba*

3 Marta dice que sus padres **comen** a las nueve. 4 Creo que la criada **empieza** la cena ahora. 5 Son las diez de la noche. **Cierran** las tiendas. 6 Estamos en el mes de diciembre. Estoy seguro que **nieva** en las montañas.

2 Translate these sentences into Spanish, paying special attention to the indicated portions. (§77 A, B)

1 It's ten o'clock. Peter **will have gone** to the university. 2 **I will have eaten** before eight o'clock. 3 By tomorrow[1] Steve **will have talked** with Mr. Morales. 4 Upon arriving[2] at Santiago, **we will have traveled** five hundred kilometers. 5 I'm sure that **they will have opened** the restaurant before six o'clock.

3 Translate these sentences into Spanish, using the future perfect to express probability. (§77 B)

≫ (tú) Johnny, I think that **you must have (probably have) eaten** too much. Juanito, creo que **habrás comido** demasiado.

1 **We must have (probably have) taken**[3] a wrong street[4]. 2 **It must have (probably has) rained** a lot here. 3 **We must have (probably have) talked** for[5] many hours. 4 **I must have (probably have) lost** my keys! 5 The child **must have (probably has) fallen asleep.**

78 / Formation of the Conditional Perfect — Formación del condicional perfecto

1 The following verbs are in the future perfect tense. Write them in the conditional perfect tense. (§78)

≫ habré escrito   **habría escrito**

1 habremos venido 2 habrás sabido 3 habrá regresado 4 habrán sido 5 habremos hecho 6 me habré acostado 7 habrán visto 8 habrá gustado 9 habremos traído   10 habrá construido

---

[1]by tomorrow = *para mañana*
[2]upon arriving = *al llegar*
[3]*tomar*
[4]Frequently the idea of probability illustrated by these examples is expressed by a form of *deber* + *haber* + past participle. Ex. *Debemos haber tomado una calle equivocada.*
[5]*por*

2 Complete these sentences with the appropriate form of the auxiliary verb *haber* to form the conditional perfect tense. The past participle of the main verb is already given. (§78)

≫ Creía que ustedes . . . llegado más temprano.
  Creía que ustedes **habrían** llegado más temprano.

1 Creíamos que Pablo . . . ganado el partido de tenis. 2 Alicia creía que su hermano . . . salido. 3 Yo nunca . . . pagado tanto dinero por el abrigo. 4 Si hubiéramos sabido su dirección, . . . invitado a Víctor. 5 Esos chicos te . . . dado el nombre equivocado.

79 / Uses of the Conditional Perfect — Modo de usar el condicional perfecto

1 The following sentences are in the future perfect tense. Write them in the conditional perfect tense. Write the English equivalent after each sentence. (§79 A)

≫ ¿Habrán terminado el juego los muchachos?
  ¿Habrían terminado el juego los muchachos? *Could the boys have finished the game?*

1 ¿Habrá olvidado estos libros Antonio? 2 ¿Habrá ido María con Felipe? 3 Ana, ¿habrás pagado mucho dinero por este cuadro? 4 ¿Nos habrán esperado Carolina y Susana desde las tres? 5 ¿Habremos estado equivocados?

80 / The Infinitive — El infinitivo

1 Complete these sentences with the Spanish equivalent of the English in parentheses. The infinitive will be used throughout this exercise. (§80 A, B)

≫ Quiero . . . (*to see*) los países de Europa.
  Quiero **ver** los países de Europa.

1 Es importante . . . (*to eat*) y . . . (*to sleep*) bien, ¿verdad? 2 Tomás, ¿puedes . . . (*to come*) con nosotros al cine? 3 Queremos . . . (*to know*) dónde está Víctor. 4 Tengo que . . . (*to go*) a trabajar. 5 ¿Es difícil . . . (*to learn*) a . . . (*to speak*) el español? 6 Vamos a . . . (*to talk*) con el profesor García. 7 Luisa sabe . . . (*to play*) la guitarra muy bien.

2 Translate these sentences into Spanish, using a Spanish infinitive for the indicated portions. (§80 C)

1 **Living** in this city is expensive. 2 **Playing** the violin is very difficult. 3 **Swimming** and **skiing** are my favorite sports. 4 **Seeing** is[1] **believing.** 5 **Watching** television is boring. 6 **Smoking** is bad for your[2] health.

[1]*para*
[2]*la*

3 Complete these sentences, with the Spanish equivalent of the English in parentheses. (§80 D)

≫ Antes de . . . (*entering*) en el cine, pagamos los boletos.
   Antes de **entrar** en el cine, pagamos los boletos.

1 Después de . . . (*leaving*) del café, regresamos inmediatamente a casa. 2 Además de . . . (*working*), estudio en la universidad. 3 Tomamos el tren en vez de . . . (*going*) por avión. 4 ¿Consiguió usted un pasaporte antes de . . . (*visiting*) México? 5 Antes de . . . (*arriving*) a Vera Cruz, pasamos por Jalapa. 6 En lugar de . . . (*reading*), Javier escucha música. 7 Además de . . . (*eating*) mucho, ese perro duerme todo el día. 8 Mis abuelos nos visitaron sin . . . (*calling*) por teléfono.

4 Complete these sentences, with the Spanish equivalent of the English in parentheses. (§80 E)

≫ . . . (*upon sitting down*), el médico empezó a escribir.
   Al sentarse, el médico empezó a escribir.

1 Manuel se puso muy contento . . . (*upon finding*) su cartera. 2 . . . (*upon seeing*) la foto, reconocí a mi amiga Amalia. 3 . . . (*upon entering*) en el apartamento, encontramos muchos defectos. 4 . . . (*upon opening*) la puerta, vimos a un hombre alto y guapo. 5 . . . (*upon awakening*), Carlos bajó a la cocina.

81 / Formation of the Present Participle — *Formación del gerundio*

1 Rewrite these phrases, changing the infinitive to the present participle. (§81 A)

≫ comprar ropa   **comprando ropa**

1 bailar en la fiesta 2 bajar del autobús 3 trabajar todo el día 4 mirar la televisión 5 tomar café 6 jugar al dominó 7 escribir una carta 8 beber vino 9 sufrir mucho 10 abrir las ventanas

2 Rewrite these phrases, changing the infinitive to the present participle. All of the verbs in this exercise have irregular present participles[1]. (§81 B)

≫ repetir los números   **repitiendo los números**

1 dormir tarde 2 morir de hambre 3 leer una revista 4 traer los libros 5 servir la comida 6 pedir más pan 7 decir la verdad 8 venir a tiempo 9 levantarse a las ocho

[1]See footnote regarding the formation of irregular present participles under §81 of the Grammar.

82 / Uses of the Present Participle — Modo de usar el gerundio

1 Rewrite these sentences, changing the infinitive in parentheses to the present participle. (§82 A, B)

≫ María, (pensar) en su hijo, compró el juguete.
María, **pensando** en su hijo, compró el juguete.

1 Carlos, (abrir) el regalo, se puso muy nervioso.   2 (ver) a nuestros amigos en la distancia, empezamos a correr hacia ellos.   3 Mi tía siempre comía muy despacio, (cortar) cada pedazo de carne con cuidado.   4 El chico leía despacio, (pronunciar) las palabras muy claramente.   5 (hablar) de deportes, ¿vas al partido de fútbol, Víctor?   6 (mirar) a su novio, Alicia le dijo algo en secreto.

2 Translate these sentences into Spanish. The indicated portion should be expressed by a *que* clause. (§82 C)

≫ That man *talking* is the boss.
Ese hombre **que habla** es el jefe.

1 The boys **playing** basketball are my cousins.   2 Those women **walking by**[1] are going to the market.   3 That man **approaching**[2] the house is my neighbor.   4 That boy **running** is called Joe.

83 / Progressive Forms -- Formas de estar con el gerundio

1 Rewrite these sentences, changing the indicated verb to the present progressive tense. (§83 A, B)

≫ Carlos **lee** el periódico.
Carlos **está leyendo** el periódico.

1 Estela **habla** con su mamá.   2 Los hermanos **trabajan** en la fábrica.   3 ¿**Duermen** los niños?   4 **Hago** la cena.   5 Alicia, ¿**esperas** a tus compañeras?   6 **Como** en casa de Roberto.   7 Jaime **se baña**[3].

2 Rewrite these sentences, changing the indicated verb to the imperfect progressive tense. (§83 A, B)

≫ Luisa **lloraba** en su cuarto.
Luisa **estaba llorando** en su cuarto.

1 Los chicos **corrían** en la calle.   2 Toda la familia **miraba** la televisión.   3 **Jugábamos** al béisbol en el parque.   4 **Abrían** las tiendas del pueblo.   5 **Tomábamos** café en el

---

[1] to walk by = *pasar*
[2] to approach = *acercarse a*
[3] See §30 E for the optional placement of the reflexive *se*.

restaurante. 6 Dos mujeres **lavaban** ropa en el río. 7 Mi abuela **vivía** con nosotros. 8 El mozo **servía** la sopa.

3 Complete these sentences with the Spanish equivalent of the English in parentheses. Use a form of *seguir, ir, venir* or *andar* plus the present participle to indicate continued action. (§83 C)

≫ El perro . . . (*kept on barking*).
El perro **siguió ladrando.**

1 Los empleados . . . (*continued working*). 2 . . . (*I kept on waiting for*[1]) la carta de Luis. 3 . . . (*We gradually arrived*[2]) a la frontera. 4 . . . (*I was beginning to accustom myself*[2]) a la vida francesa. 5 La niña . . . (*came crying*[1]) hacia nosotros. 6 Los muchachos . . . (*came running*[1]) desde la calle. 7 Ese pobre hombre . . . (*goes around asking for*) trabajo.

4 Translate these sentences into Spanish, paying special attention to the indicated portion. (§83 A, B, C)

1 **I'm looking for** a good restaurant. 2 (*tú*) Ann, **are you eating?** 3 The train **was arriving** in[3] Barcelona. 4 **We were watching** the planes at[4] the airport. 5 My father **kept on talking.**

84 / Formation of the Past Participle — *Formación del participio pasado*

1 Write the past participle forms of the following verbs. (§84 A, B)

≫ comprar   **comprado**

1 aprender 2 llegar 3 salir 4 trabajar 5 leer[5] 6 comer 7 ver 8 decir 9 morir 10 volver 11 abrir 12 hacer 13 descubrir 14 escribir

85 / Uses of the Past Participle — *Modo de usar el participio pasado*

1 Rewrite these sentences, changing the verb in parentheses to the past participle. Remember the past participle must agree with the noun. (§85 A)

≫ La lluvia entró por la ventana (abrir).
La lluvia entró por la ventana **abierta.**

1 La policía encontró a los niños (perder). 2 Ese hombre dice que el coche verde está (vender). 3 Nosotros estamos muy (ocupar) hoy. 4 Encontré una carta

[1]Use the preterite for the first verb.
[2]Use the imperfect tense for the first verb.
[3]*a*
[4]*en*
[5]Remember the written accent over the *i*. Other verbs taking a written accent are *creer, caer, traer,* and *oír.*

(escribir) en italiano.   5 Veo a Gabriela (sentar) en el patio.   6 Todas las tiendas del pueblo están (cerrar).   7 Jorge está muy (preocupar) por su novia.   8 ¿Cuál es su color (preferir)?   9 Este abrigo dice "(hacer) en México."   10 ¡Este ejercicio está (terminar)!

2 Write the past participle of the following verbs. These past participle forms are frequently used as nouns in Spanish. The English equivalent is given in parentheses. (§85 B)

Verb	Past Participle Used as Noun
≫ entrar	la **entrada** (*the entrance*)
1 salir	la . . . (*the exit*)
2 emplear	el . . . (*the employee*)
3 responder	la . . . (*the answer*)
4 vestir	el . . . (*the dress*)
5 morir	el . . . (*the dead person*)
6 parar(se)	la . . . (*the stop*)
7 herir	el . . . (*the wounded person*)
	la . . . (*the wound*)
8 casarse	los . . . (*the married couple*)
9 invitar	los . . . (*the guests*)

3 Translate these sentences into Spanish, paying particular attention to the indicated portions. (§85 A, B, C)

1 We are[1] (m.) **invited** to a party!   2 The door is[1] **open**.   3 How many **employees** (m.) work here?   4 (*tú*) John, **have you seen** my pen?   5 **We had celebrated** my birthday.   6 **The entrance** was[1] closed.

86 / Formation of the Passive Voice — *Formación de la voz pasiva*

1 Change the following sentences from the active to the passive voice. The tense of the verb *ser* in the passive voice should be the same as that of the active voice. (§86 A, B, C)

≫ Muchas personas ven los cuadros de Picasso.
  Los cuadros de Picasso son vistos por muchas personas.

1 Dos ladrones han robado el Banco Nacional.   2 Los turistas habían tomado todas las habitaciones del hotel.   3 Mi amigo Fernando arregló mi coche.   4 El gobierno controlaba el sistema de ferrocarriles.   5 Nuestros abogados escribirán el nuevo contrato.

[1] *estar*

1 Change these sentences from the active to the passive voice. (§87 A)

≫ Mi esposa preparó esta cena.
Esta cena fue preparada por mi esposa.

1 Los tíos de Paco recibieron el telegrama. 2 El gobernador Juárez inauguró el nuevo edificio. 3 Dos policías vieron el accidente. 4 El señor Miró escribió estos artículos. 5 Muchas personas oyeron la explosión de la bomba. 6 Los alemanes ganaron el campeonato de fútbol. 7 El gobierno federal construyó este puente.

2 Complete these sentences with the Spanish equivalent of the English words in parentheses. (§87 B 1)

≫ (*is spoken*) . . . portugués en el Brasil.
Se habla portugués en el Brasil.

1 (*it is known*) . . . que hay mucho petróleo debajo del océano. 2 La influencia de la cultura africana (*is seen*) . . . en los países del Caribe. 3 El español (*is heard*) . . . mucho en las calles de Nueva York. 4 (*it is believed*) . . . que todos los pasajeros sobrevivieron el accidente. 5 (*it is said*) . . . que el señor Murillo vendrá mañana.

3 Complete these sentences with the Spanish equivalent of the English words in parentheses. (§87 B 2)

≫ (*they say*) . . . que el señor Pérez es de Bogotá.
Dicen que el señor Pérez es de Bogotá.

1 (*they sell*) . . . aspirinas en esta farmacia. 2 (*they pay*) . . . muy bien a los empleados que trabajan aquí. 3 (*they serve*) . . . la cena entre las seis y las diez de la noche. 4 ¿A qué hora (*do they open*) . . . las tiendas aquí?

4 Complete the following sentences with *por* or *de*, according to the context of the sentence. (§87 C 1, 2)

≫ Nuestra casa está rodeada . . . muchos árboles.
Nuestra casa está rodeada **de** muchos árboles.

1 El asesino fue arrestado . . . la policía. 2 En la foto vimos a mi padre rodeado . . . sus hijos. 3 El presidente fue recibido . . . varios oficiales del gobierno. 4 Este paquete llegó acompañado . . . una carta. 5 Este periódico es leído . . . todos los habitantes de la capital.

5 Translate the following sentences into Spanish, paying special attention to the indicated portions. (§87 A, B, C)

1 The actress **was surrounded by** the police. 2 We watched a movie **followed by** the news. 3 The money **was found by** Mary. 4 **They closed** the cinema last week. 5 *Don Quijote* **was written by** Cervantes.

88 / *Formation of the Present Subjunctive — Formación del presente de subjuntivo*

1 Write the first person singular present indicative form of each of the following infinitives. Also write the appropriate present subjunctive form according to the pronoun given. (§88 A, B)

Infinitive	Present Indicative (first person singular)		Present Subjunctive
≫ llorar	**lloro**	(tú)	**llores**
≫ volver	**vuelvo**	(ellos)	**vuelvan**
1 vender	. . .	(él)	. . .
2 vivir	. . .	(Ud.)	. . .
3 encontrar	. . .	(yo)	. . .
4 decir	. . .	(nosotros)	. . .
5 poder	. . .	(tú)	. . .
6 pensar	. . .	(ella)	. . .
7 hacer	. . .	(nosotros)	. . .
8 tener	. . .	(yo)	. . .
9 venir	. . .	(Uds.)	. . .
10 ver	. . .	(tú)	. . .
11 poner	. . .	(él)	. . .
12 salir	. . .	(Ud.)	. . .

2 Supply the missing present subjunctive forms of the infinitives indicated. All verbs in this exercise are irregular in the present subjunctive. (§88 C)

	dar	saber	estar	ir	haber	ser
1 (yo)	dé	. . .	. . .	. . .	. . .	sea
2 (tú)	. . .	sepas	. . .	. . .	. . .	. . .
3 (él)	. . .	. . .	esté	. . .	. . .	. . .
4 (nosotros)	. . .	. . .	. . .	·vayamos	. . .	. . .
5 (Uds.)	. . .	. . .	. . .	. . .	hayan	. . .

1 Supply the missing verb forms. Use the *-ra* set of endings for the imperfect subjunctive. (§89 A, B)

Infinitive	Third Person Plural Preterite	Imperfect Subjunctive
≫ comprar	**compraron**	(él) **comprara**
1 beber	. . .	(nosotros) . . .
2 decir	. . .	(yo) . . .
3 ser	. . .	(María) . . .
4 comer	. . .	(tú) . . .
5 . . .	llegaron	(Uds.) . . .
6 . . .	vivieron	(yo) . . .
7 . . .	encontraron	(Ud.) . . .
8 . . .	dieron	(ella) . . .
9 . . .	siguieron	(tú) . . .
10 . . .	. . .	(Uds.) pusieran
11 . . .	. . .	(ella) pudiera
12 . . .	. . .	(Ana y yo) sintiéramos
13 . . .	. . .	(tú) vinieras
14 . . .	. . .	(nosotros) tuviéramos

2 Rewrite these sentences, changing the imperfect subjunctive *-se* endings to the *-ra* form. (§89 C)

≫ Era posible que Julia **viniese** con ellos.
Era posible que Julia **viniera** con ellos.

1 Era natural que Pepito **quisiese** ir con su padre. 2 Tomás no creía que **pudieses** venir. 3 No creíamos que nuestros padres nos **diesen** el dinero. 4 ¿No creías que el señor Cruz me **escuchase?** 5 Dudaban que nosotros **hablásemos** con el director. 6 Rafael no creía que (yo) **recordase** su cumpleaños.

90 / *Formation of the Perfect Subjunctive — Formación del perfecto de subjuntivo*

1 Complete these sentences with the appropriate form of the auxiliary verb *haber* to form the perfect subjunctive. The past participle of the main verb is already given. (§90)

≫ Me alegro que ustedes . . . llegado.
Me alegro que ustedes **hayan** llegado.

1 Juan se alegra que su padre . . . comprado un coche nuevo. 2 Tengo miedo que los chicos no . . . ido a casa. 3 Carmen tiene miedo que (tú) no . . . recibido su carta. 4 Siento que usted no . . . podido ver a don Alberto. 5 Mis amigos se alegran que (yo) . . . encontrado trabajo. 6 Tengo miedo que nosotros . . . perdido el campeonato de fútbol. 7 ¡Me alegro que nosotros . . . terminado este ejercicio!

91 / Formation of the Pluperfect Subjunctive — *Formación del pluscuamperfecto de subjuntivo*

1 Rewrite these sentences, changing the infinitive in parentheses to the appropriate form of the pluperfect subjunctive. Use the *-ra* subjunctive endings for the auxiliary verb *haber*. (§91)

≫ Si Juan (saber) la verdad, nos habría dicho.
Si Juan **hubiera sabido** la verdad, nos habría dicho.

1 Si (tú) (hablar) francés, habrías conocido mejor a Mónica. 2 Si (yo) (hacer) la cena, habría preparado arroz con pollo. 3 Si las muchachas (escribir), habríamos contestado. 4 Si (tú) (traer) los discos, habríamos bailado. 5 Si ellos (ver) esa película, les habría gustado mucho. 6 Si nosotros (poner) la bicicleta en el garaje, no la habrían robado. 7 Si (yo) (vender) el coche, me habrían pagado tres mil dólares. 8 Si nosotros (quedarse) con Amalia, habríamos visto la feria.

92 / Uses of the Subjunctive — *Modo de usar el subjuntivo*

1 Rewrite the sentences below, beginning each with the impersonal expression in parentheses. Make any necessary changes in the indicated verb. (§92 B)

≫ (es importante que) Rosa **limpia** la casa hoy.
Es importante que Rosa **limpie** la casa hoy.

1 (es necesario que) Juan **viene** esta noche. 2 (puede ser que) Paco **llamará** por teléfono. 3 (es posible que) Arturo **vuelve** antes de las seis. 4 (es natural que) **Buscamos**[1] una casa más cómoda. 5 (es preciso que) ¿Te **levantas** a las siete, Carlos? 6 (es raro que) **Vemos** tantos camiones en este barrio. 7 (es probable que) No **tengo** que trabajar mañana.

2 Rewrite the sentences below, beginning each with the phrase in parentheses. Make any necessary changes in the indicated verb. (§92 C)

≫ (tenemos miedo que) Juan y Pepe **llegan** tarde a la misa.
Tenemos miedo que Juan y Pepe **lleguen** tarde a la misa.

1 (siento mucho que) Carmen no **puede** acompañarme al cine. 2 (es lástima que) No **conocemos**[2] esta ciudad. 3 (los padres se alegran que) Los hijos se **divierten** en la finca. 4 (los oficiales temen que) **Entra** demasiada gente en el estadio de fútbol. 5 (tengo miedo que) Susana **pierde** los discos. 6 (sentimos mucho que) El coche de Paco no **funciona**.

---

[1]There is a spelling change. See §107 C.
[2]There is a spelling change. See §107 E.

3 Rewrite the sentences below, beginning each with the phrase in parentheses. Make any necessary changes in the indicated verb. (§92 D)

≫ (no creo que) Alicia **está** enferma.
 No creo que Alicia **esté** enferma.

1 (mis amigos dudan que) Pedro **se casa** con Luisa. 2 (no crees que) ¿Juan **quiere** estos libros? 3 (dudamos que) Nuestro tren **llega**[1] a tiempo. 4 (no creemos que) **Lloverá** esta noche. 5 (Felipe duda que) Carlos siempre **paga**[1] sus cuentas. 6 (no creo que) **Esperamos** a Catalina.

4 Rewrite each sentence, substituting the indicated portions with the words in parentheses. Change the relative clause to show doubt or denial of the existence or attainability of the antecedent. (§92 E)

≫ **Conozco** a una persona que habla varios idiomas. (Busco)
 Busco a una persona **que hable** varios idiomas.

1 **Mis tíos conocen** un restaurante donde sirven paella. (Mis tíos buscan) 2 **Tengo un amigo** que me ayuda. (No hay nadie) 3 **Vivimos en** una casa que tiene dos pisos. (Buscamos) 4 **Alberto** sabe la dirección del señor Pacheco. (No hay nadie que) 5 **Hay muchas personas** que son ricas. (No hay nadie) 6 **Mi hermano** trabaja doce horas por día. (No hay nadie que) 7 **Conozco** a un estudiante que es de Chile. (Busco) 8 **Tengo** un reloj que funciona bien. (Busco)

5 Rewrite the sentences below, beginning each with the phrase in parentheses. Make any necessary changes in the indicated verb. (§92 F)

≫ (quiero que) Arturo me **vende** su tocadiscos.
 Quiero que Arturo me **venda** su tocadiscos.

1 (el banco prefiere que) Ustedes **pagan**[1] sus cuentas. 2 (quiere usted que) ¿La **ayudo**, señora Martínez? 3 (exigen que) **Tenemos** los pasaportes en la frontera. 4 (Ana nos ruega que) Le **escribimos** mucho. 5 (mis padres sugieren que) **Busco**[2] trabajo para el verano. 6 (Susana insiste en que) **Vengo** a las ocho a comer. 7 (Carlos me pide que) Lo **llamo** por teléfono. 8 (Fernando desea que) **Traemos** unos discos populares. 9 (el oficial permite que) ¿**Entramos** por esa puerta? 10 (los niños prefieren que) **Vamos** a la piscina. 11 (Los Salazar quieren que) **Nos quedamos** en Caracas dos días más.

[1]There is a spelling change. See § 107 B.
[2]There is a spelling change. See § 107 C.

6 Rewrite these sentences, substituting the indicated conjunction with the one in parentheses. Make any other necessary changes. (§92 G)

≫ Vendrán a nuestra casa **y** veremos sus fotos de España. (para que)
Vendrán a nuestra casa **para que veamos** sus fotos de España.

1 Pedro nos abrirá la puerta **y** entraremos a trabajar temprano. (para que) 2 Paco vendrá a Bogotá **y** lo encontraremos allí. (a fin de que) 3 Compraré este abrigo **y** mi madre lo pagará[1]. (con tal que) 4 Iré a México en coche **y** el viaje costará menos dinero. (a fin de que) 5 Enrique se acostará **y** regresará su padre a las doce. (antes de que) 6 Voy a visitar Europa **si** mis padres me lo permiten. (con tal que)
7 Leeremos el menú **y luego** vendrá el mozo. (antes de que)

7 Rewrite these sentences, changing the infinitive in parentheses to the appropriate form of the subjunctive or indicative as needed. (§92 H)

≫ Llamaré a Enrique tan pronto como (llegar) a casa.
Llamaré a Enrique tan pronto como **llegue** a casa.

1 Comeremos cuando tus tíos (estar) aquí. 2 Esperé a Luisa hasta que (volver) del mercado. 3 Después que toda la familia (comer), los niños salieron para jugar.
4 Jaime se acostó después que (leer) el periódico. 5 Vamos a salir cuando (venir) Sara y Víctor. 6 En cuanto nosotros (llegar[1]) a la estación, compraremos los boletos.
7 Mi padre venderá su coche tan pronto como (encontrar) otro mejor. 8 Pienso practicar la guitarra hasta que la (tocar[2]) bien. 9 Los equipos siguieron jugando al fútbol hasta que (empezar) a llover. 10 Hablaremos con el director tan pronto como lo (ver).

8 Rewrite the following sentences, changing the indicated verb to the corresponding subjunctive form, in order to show that the truth of the clause is not conceded. The second verb in each sentence will be in the future tense. The English translation of the desired sentence is given in parentheses. (§92 I)

≫ Aunque Manuel **está** en Acapulco, no es feliz.
Aunque Manuel **esté** en Acapulco, no **será** feliz. (*Although Manuel **may be** in Acapulco, he **won't be** happy.*)

1 Aunque mis amigos **son** pobres, están contentos. (*Although my friends **may be** poor, they **will be** happy.*) 2 Aunque Pepe no **paga**[1] sus cuentas, somos buenos amigos. (*Although Pepe **may not pay** his bills, we **will be** good friends.*) 3 Aunque **llegas**[1] temprano, no encuentras asientos. (*Although **you may arrive** early, **you won't find** seats.*) 4 Aunque **me siento** bien, no voy a la reunión. (*Although **I may feel** well, I **won't go** to the meeting.*)

---

[1]There is a spelling change. See § 107 B.
[2]There is a spelling change. See § 107 C.

9 Rewrite these sentences, changing the indicated verb to the appropriate form of the subjunctive to show that the conjunctions *de manera que* and *de modo que* indicate purpose, rather than fact. The English translation of the desired sentence is given in parentheses. (§92 I)

≫ Vivimos en una casa grande, de modo que los niños **tienen** espacio para jugar.
Vivimos en una casa grande de modo que los niños **tengan** espacio para jugar.
(*We live in a large house so that the children **have** room to play.*)

1 Esperaremos hasta las seis, de modo que Carlos **puede** ir también. (*We will wait until six so that Carlos **may go** too.*)   2 Vivimos cerca de la oficina, de modo que mi esposo no **necesita** tomar el coche. (*We live near the office so that my husband doesn't **need** to take the car.*)   3 Toda la familia se quedó en la capital una semana más, de manera que los niños **vieron** el Carnaval. (*The entire family stayed in the capital a week longer in order that the children **might see** the Carnival.*)   4 Mi jefe me dio tres semanas de vacaciones, de manera que **voy** a visitar Europa. (*My boss gave me three weeks of vacation so that I **may visit** Europe.*)

10 Rewrite these sentences, changing the infinitive in parentheses to the appropriate form of the present subjunctive. (§92 J, K)

≫ Tal vez María me (escribir) hoy.
Tal vez María me **escriba** hoy.

1 Quizás no (llover) hoy.   2 Por mucho que (querer) ir a España, no tengo el dinero suficiente.   3 Ojalá que nosotros no (pagar[1]) tanto por la gasolina aquí.
4 Por mucho que Alfredo (practicar[2]), no baila bien.   5 Tal vez Vicente y Mario (ir) a la playa con nosotros.   6 Ojalá el mozo nos (servir) pronto en el restaurante.

11 Rewrite the following sentences, changing the infinitive in parentheses to the appropriate form of either the indicative or the subjunctive. In some cases the infinitive may be kept. (§92 B, C, D, E, F, G, H, J, K)

1 Me alegro que ustedes (tener) buenos vecinos.   2 Trabajaré aquí hasta (terminar) este proyecto.   3 Es posible (romper) esta lámpara fácilmente.   4 La policía tiene miedo que el ladrón (llevar) una pistola.   5 Creo que los González (vivir) en la Calle Florida.   6 Siento que Beatriz (estar) enferma hoy.   7 Buscamos a un empleado que (saber) escribir a máquina.   8 Dudo que ese mecánico (poder) arreglar mi coche.
9 Ojalá Carlos me (pagar[1]) mañana.   10 Es seguro que ustedes (encontrar) un restaurante en esa calle.   11 No creemos que ese televisor (valer) tanto dinero.

[1]There is a spelling change. See § 107 B.
[2]There is a spelling change. See § 107 C.

12 Rewrite the following sentences, changing the infinitive in parentheses to the appropriate form of either the indicative or the subjunctive. In some cases the infinitive may be kept. (§92 B, C, D, E, F, G, H, J, K)

1 Los hermanos querían (comprar) la finca. 2 (tú) Elena, era necesario que (esperar) unos minutos más para nosotras. 3 No había nadie que (conocer) al señor Campos. 4 Empecé a trabajar antes de que Felipe (llamar). 5 Después de (comer), fui al cine. 6 Era importante (recordar) las fechas para el examen. 7 Entramos en el museo para (ver) los cuadros famosos. 8 Preferí que el empleado me (vender) un boleto de primera clase. 9 Marta pidió que (yo) (jugar) con los niños. 10 (yo) Temía que su carta no (llegar).

13 See §96 for exercises illustrating contrary-to-fact conditions. (§92 L)

93 / Sequence of Tenses — Concordancia de los tiempos

1 Rewrite the following sentences, changing them to the past. Use the imperfect tense in the main clause and the *-ra* form of the imperfect subjunctive in the subordinate clause. (§93 A, C)

≫ Marta **quiere** que **volvamos** a las tres.
Marta **quería** que **volviéramos** a las tres.

1 Rosa, **quiero** que **limpies** tu cuarto hoy. 2 Los hijos **prefieren** que **comamos** en un restaurante. 3 Mis padres **temen** que **volvamos** muy tarde de la fiesta. 4 No **creo** que ese traje azul **cueste** tanto. 5 ¿**Es** importante que **vayamos** a la reunión? 6 El jefe **desea** que **trabajemos** los sábados. 7 **Es** posible que esta radio no **funcione**. 8 Los agricultores **esperan** que **llueva** pronto.

2 Rewrite the following sentences changing them to the past. Use the imperfect tense in the main clause and the *-ra* form of the pluperfect subjunctive in the subordinate clause. (§93 B, D)

≫ **Me alegro** de que su esposo **haya regresado** de Francia.
Me alegraba de que su esposo **hubiera regresado** de Francia.

1 **Es** posible que Juana no **haya recibido** el telegrama. 2 No **creo** que Fernando y Paco **hayan estudiado** suficiente. 3 **Sentimos** que ustedes **hayan olvidado** los documentos. 4 **Nos alegramos** de que nuestro equipo **haya ganado** el campeonato. 5 Ernesto **duda** que **hayamos jugado** tan bien al tenis. 6 **Es** natural que los chicos **hayan querido** ir a la feria. 7 **Temo** que Alicia y María no **hayan venido**. 8 **Tenemos** miedo de que **hayamos perdido** nuestras bicicletas.

3 Translate the following sentences into Spanish, using a form of the subjunctive for the indicated portion. (§93 A, B, C, D, E)

1 John wants us **to come** tomorrow[1]. 2 My parents wanted me **to work** this summer[2]. 3 (*Ud.*) We were very sorry[3] that **you had not talked** with Mrs. García. 4 I didn't think[4] that Susan **was** so young. 5 (*tú*) I'm glad that **you are selling** your motorcycle. 6 (*tú*) I'm glad that **you have sold** your motorcycle. 7 It was rare that Richard **came** here. 8 It is rare that Richard **comes** here. 9 (*Ud.*) Do you know[5] a writer who **speaks** German? 10 (*Ud.*) Did you know[5] a writer who **spoke** German?

94 / The Infinitive Instead of the Subjunctive — El infinitivo en lugar del subjuntivo

1 Rewrite these sentences making the subject of the subordinate clause the same as the subject of the main clause. Use an infinitive construction instead of the subjunctive clause. The English translation of the desired sentence is given in parentheses. (§94 A)

≫ Orlando se alegra de **que Elena vaya** a la fiesta.
Orlando se alegra de **ir** a la fiesta. (*Orlando is happy to go to the party.*)

1 Los niños prefieren **que vayamos** a la piscina. (*The children prefer to go to the swimming pool.*) 2 Lucia, ¿quieres **que yo sirva** el café? (*Lucia, do you want to serve the coffee?*) 3 Quiero **que leas** este artículo. (*I want to read this article.*) 4 Prefiero **que mis vecinos no hagan** tanto ruido. (*I prefer not to make so much noise.*) 5 Don Antonio esperaba **que viéramos** los documentos. (*Don Antonio hoped to see the documents.*) 6 Mis abuelos pidieron **que (yo) viniera** a Santa Cruz. (*My grandparents asked to come to Santa Cruz.*)

2 Rewrite these sentences, changing the indicated conjunctions to their corresponding prepositions. Make any other changes necessary. (§94 B)

≫ Pedro nos mandará un telegrama **antes de que** lleguen aquí.
Pedro nos mandará un telegrama **antes de llegar** aquí.

1 Mariana, siéntate un rato **para que** podamos hablar. 2 Javier compró los boletos **para que** fueran al teatro. 3 Discutimos el precio del taxi **antes de que** saliera de la estación. 4 **Después que** comamos, Fernando saldrá para la universidad. 5 Los amigos vinieron **a fin de que** habláramos juntos. 6 Víctor se quedará en la oficina **hasta que** (yo) termine el trabajo.

---

[1]Reword: John wants that we may come tomorrow.
[2]Reword: My parents wanted that I work this summer.
[3]We were very sorry = *Sentimos mucho*
[4]I didn't think = *No creía*
[5]to know (a person) = *conocer a*

3 Rewrite the following sentences, using a subjunctive clause instead of the infinitive construction. (§94 C, D)

≫ Los oficiales **nos prohiben fumar** en el autobús.
  Los oficiales **prohiben que fumemos** en el autobús.

1 Juan, ¿tus padres **te aconsejan ir** a la universidad? 2 El gobierno **nos permite manejar** hasta 90 kilómetros por hora. 3 El juez municipal **me manda pagar** la multa. 4 **Nos importa vender** la casa pronto. 5 La lluvia **nos impide seguir** adelante. 6 Mis padres **me dejan vivir** en un apartamento.

95 / The Imperative — El imperativo

1 Write the first person singular, present indicative form of each of the following infinitives. Also write the *usted* and *ustedes* imperatives. (§95 A, B, C)

Infinitive	Present Indicative (first person singular)	*Usted* Command	*Ustedes* Command
≫ esperar	**espero**	**espere Ud.**	**esperen Uds.**
≫ escribir	**escribo**	**escriba Ud.**	**escriban Uds.**
1 hacer	. . .	. . .	. . .
2 salir	. . .	. . .	. . .
3 cerrar	. . .	. . .	. . .
4 poner	. . .	. . .	. . .
5 ver	. . .	. . .	. . .
6 tener	. . .	. . .	. . .
7 venir	. . .	. . .	. . .
8 decir	. . .	. . .	. . .
9 comprar	. . .	. . .	. . .
10 oír	. . .	. . .	. . .
11 saber	. . .	. . .	. . .
12 traer	. . .	. . .	. . .
13 recordar	. . .	. . .	. . .

2 Rewrite the following sentences, omitting the indicated portion and changing the remainder to the *ustedes* command. (§95 A, B, C)

≫ **Los amigos** miran las fotos.
  Miren ustedes las fotos.

1 **Los invitados** pasan al comedor. 2 **Los señores Menéndez** salen temprano. 3 **Los muchachos** vuelven a las once. 4 **Los niños** duermen bien. 5 **Los turistas** suben al avión. 6 **Los empleados** lavan los pisos.

3 Complete these phrases with the imperative form of the verb in parentheses. All verbs in this exercise are irregular in the imperative. (§95 D)

> (ir) . . . Ud. con el señor Rodríguez.
Vaya Ud. con el señor Rodríguez.

1 (dar) . . . Ud. el boleto al empleado. 2 (ser . . . Uds. honrados. 3 (ir) . . . Uds. a la embajada para conseguir los pasaportes. 4 (estar) . . . Uds. aquí a las siete y media.

4 Complete the following sentences, changing the infinitive in parentheses to the *nosotros* imperative. (§95 E 1)

> (subir) . . . al autobús.
Subamos al autobús.

1 (buscar[1]) . . . un buen hotel. 2 (dar) . . . esta ropa vieja a los pobres. 3 (empezar[2]) . . . el trabajo, señor Martínez. 4 (abrir) Hace calor. . . . las ventanas 5 (jugar[3]) Felipe, . . . al tenis. 6 (volver) Estoy cansado. . . . a casa.

5 Rewrite these sentences, changing the *nosotros* imperative to the *vamos a* + <u>infinitive</u> construction. (§95 E 1, 2)

> **Escuchemos** música ahora.
Vamos a escuchar música ahora.

1 **Traigamos** unos discos a la fiesta. 2 No nos gusta ese programa. **Apaguemos** la radio. 3 Alicia, **hagamos** otra cosa ahora. 4 **Pasemos** al patio para conversar. 5 **Vayamos** al cine esta noche. 6 **Tomemos** café en ese restaurante. 7 **Comamos** a las diez.

6 Rewrite these sentences, changing the *usted* imperative to a *tú* imperative. Change the name of the person to whom you are speaking to that of a good friend of yours. (§95 F)

> **Tome Ud.** el dinero, señor Muñoz.
Toma el dinero, [Paco].

1 **Mire Ud.** esos edificios nuevos, señor Murillo. 2 **Escriba Ud.** la carta por favor, señorita Campos. 3 **Lea Ud.** el documento, Sargento. 4 **Pague Ud.** la cuenta, señor. 5 **Traiga Ud.** unos lápices, señorita Martínez. 6 **Vuelva Ud.** pronto, señora Delgado. 7 **Responda Ud.** para el lunes, señor Galdós.

---

[1]There is a spelling change. See § 107 C.
[2]There is a spelling change. See § 107 A.
[3]There is a spelling change. See § 107 B.

7 Rewrite the following sentences, changing the indicated verb to the *usted* imperative. Omit the first name. (§95 A, B, C, D, F)

≫ Ana, **cierra** la puerta, por favor
   Cierre Ud. la puerta, por favor.

1 Enrique, **pide** la lista de nombres. 2 Fernando, **vive** con nosotros. 3 Luisa, **entra**, por favor. 4 Pepito, **escucha** el programa. 5 Susana, **busca** el número en este libro. 6 Rosa, **lava** los platos y las tazas. 7 Chico, **describe** al ladrón.

8 Change these affirmative *tú* commands to the negative. Write the infinitive of each indicated verb before each sentence. (§95 F, G)

≫ Elena, **trae** la medicina para don Julio.
   (traer) Elena, **no traigas** la medicina para don Julio.

1 Pepe, **toma** el dinero. 2 Juanito, **sal** de la casa. 3 Sara, **ve** a la puerta. 4 Manuel, **pon** el televisor. 5 Chico, **haz** el favor. 6 Pablo, **lee** los primeros capítulos. 7 Elisa, **describe** la película, por favor. 8 Hijo, **ven** ahora. 9 Luis, **sé** justo. 10 María, **ten** miedo a los extranjeros.

9 Rewrite the sentences in the previous exercise, changing the indicated verbs to the negative *usted* command form. Use *señor, señora* and *señorita* instead of the first name. (§95 A, B, C, F)

≫ Elena, **trae** la medicina para don Julio.
   Señora, **no traiga Ud.** la medicina para don Julio.

10 Translate the following sentences into Spanish, paying special attention to the indicated imperative verb form. (§95 A, B, C, D, E, F, G)

1 (*tú*) Amalia, **bring** my coat. 2 (*tú*) **Tell** the truth. 3 (*Ud.*) **Don't forget**[1] your passport. 4 (*Uds.*) **Don't go**[2]. 5 (*tú*) Ellen, **come** here. **Eat**[3] your supper. 6 **Let's leave** now. 7 (*tú*) **Be** sincere. 8 (*Ud.*) **Put** the books there. 9 **Let's call**[4] the train station. 10 (*Uds.*) **Sit down**, please.

96 / Conditions — Condiciones

1 Rewrite these sentences, changing them to contrary-to-fact conditions. Use the *-ra* form of the imperfect subjunctive in the *si* clause, and the conditional tense in the conclusion. (§96 A, B)

[1] to forget = *olvidar*
[2] to go = *ir* or *irse* (*Irse* is more emphatic.)
[3] to eat = *tomar* or *comer*
[4] to call = *llamar a*

≫ Si **tengo** dinero, **iré** al cine.
Si **tuviera** dinero **iría** al cine.
≫ Te **daré** el dinero, si me lo **pides**.
Te **daría** el dinero, si me lo **pidieras**.

1 Si **buscamos** por aquí, **encontraremos** una farmacia. 2 Si **leen** el periódico, **sabrán** estas noticias. 3 María, si **vienes** ahora, **verás** a tus primos. 4 Si Carlos **necesita** más tiempo, me lo **pedirá**. 5 Arturo nos **llamará** si **está** en casa. 6 Los niños **comerán** si **tienen** hambre. 7 No **entraremos** si **llegamos** tarde. 8 **Verás** la estatua de Carlos V si **vas** a la plaza. 9 No **oirán** tanto ruido si **cierran** las ventanas.

2 Complete the result clause of these contrary-to-fact sentences by changing the infinitives in parentheses to the appropriate form of the conditional perfect tense. (§96 A, B)

≫ Si (yo) hubiera sabido la verdad, no le (prestar) el dinero a Paco.
Si hubiera sabido la verdad, no le **habría prestado** el dinero a Paco.

1 Si no hubiera llovido, (yo) (salir) anoche. 2 Si nuestro coche hubiera funcionado, nosotros (llegar) a tiempo. 3 Si esa tienda hubiera tenido un par de zapatos más grandes, (yo) los (comprar). 4 Si yo hubiera ido a la universidad, (estudiar) arquitectura. 5 Si hubiera hecho buen tiempo, Jaime y yo (ir) a la playa. 6 Si Rosa no se hubiera casado, (ser) actriz.

3 Change these sentences to contrary-to-fact conditions using the pluperfect subjunctive in the *si* clause and the conditional perfect in the conclusion. (§96 A, B)

≫ Si César **es** actor, **gana** mucho dinero.
Si César **hubiera sido** actor, **habría ganado** mucho dinero.
≫ Los chicos **estarán** cansados, si **se acuestan** tarde.
Los chicos **habrían estado** cansados, si **se hubieran acostado** tarde.

1 Si Roberto **maneja** su coche más rápido, **tendrá** un accidente. 2 Si la casa **es** grande, la **compraremos**. 3 Si Rafael **llega** tarde, **empezaremos** sin él. 4 **Iré** a la fiesta si no **estoy** enfermo. 5 **Comeremos** en un restaurante si los precios no **son** tan altos. 6 Doña Amalia nos **visitará** si **tiene** la oportunidad.

4 Complete these sentences with the appropriate form of the verb in parentheses. You must first decide whether the verb is in the condition or the conclusion of the sentence. Note that some of these sentences are contrary-to-fact and others are not. (§96 A, B)

≫ Escribiríamos a Fernando si (saber) su dirección.
Escribiríamos a Fernando si **supiéramos** su dirección.
≫ Si (hacer) buen tiempo, (yo) iba al parque.
Si **hacía** buen tiempo, iba al parque.

1 Yo iría a la fiesta si no (estar) tan ocupado. 2 Si Arturo tiene mucho trabajo, (salir) temprano para la oficina. 3 Si Carlos (prometer) manejar el coche despacio, iremos con él. 4 Si la casa fuera más grande, mis vecinos la (comprar). 5 (vender) el cuadro si don Mario me lo dijera. 6 Me (gustar) ayudarlo si me permitiera. 7 (yo) No habría estado tan cansado si (acostarse) más temprano. 8 Habríamos visto al presidente si (quedarse) en la capital.

5 Translate these sentences into Spanish, paying particular attention to the indicated portions. (§96 A, B)

1 If Javier **finishes** at six, **he'll come** with us. 2 If Javier **were to finish** at six, **he would come** with us. 3 If Javier **had finished** at six, **he would have come** with us. 4 **I'll buy** the tickets if **we go** by plane[1]. 5 **I would buy** the tickets if **we went** by plane. 6 **I would have bought** the tickets if **we had gone** by plane.

6 Translate these sentences into Spanish, paying special attention to the indicated portions. (§96 B, C, D)

1 (*Ud.*) If **you would give** me your address, **I would send** you the package. 2 Mr. Perez talks **as if** he were my father. 3 Paul lives **as if** he were rich!   4 If **they will buy** the food, **we will bring** the wine. 5 Miss Martínez sings **as if** she were a professional.

97 / Uses of the Verb ser — *Modo de usar el verbo* ser

1 Complete each sentence below with the appropriate form of the present tense of the verb *ser*. Also indicate the division of §97 which explains the particular use of *ser*. (§97 A, B, C, D, E)

≫ Las primas de Ernesto . . . muy lindas, ¿no?
   Las primas de Ernesto **son** muy lindas, ¿no?   (97E)

1 El señor Galván y su esposa . . . mis tíos. 2 ¿Cuándo . . . el cumpleaños de Manuel? 3 El señor Gómez . . . amado por toda su familia. 4 El Hotel Dorado . . . muy moderno, ¿verdad?   5 ¿Conoces a Paco y Rafael? . . . de Costa Rica. 6 La comida en este restaurante . . . muy rica, ¿verdad? 7 (yo) . . . estudiante de química. 8 Estos libros . . . de Juanita.

---

[1]by plane = *por avión*

1 Complete each sentence below with the appropriate form of the present tense of the verb *estar.* Also indicate the division of §98 which explains the particular use of *estar.* (§98 A, B, C, D)

≫ Mariana . . . en el patio con David.
  Mariana **está** en el patio con David. (98A)

1 (nosotros) . . . mirando un programa de televisión. 2 Sara, ¿dónde . . . Víctor y Daniel? 3 Doña Amalia dice que la cena . . . preparada. 4 Jorge y Antonio . . . hablando sobre la política. 5 Nuestra maletas . . . encima del coche. 6 (yo) . . . enojada porque Carlos no me llamó anoche. 7 (tú) Carmen, ¿por qué . . . triste hoy?

2 Complete these sentences with the appropriate form of the present tense of either *ser* or *estar,* according to the context. Also, indicate the division of §§97 & 98 which explains the particular use of *ser* or *estar.* (§§97, 98 A, B, C, D, E)

≫ Los chicos . . . muy contentos.
  Los chicos **están** muy contentos. (98D)

1 ¡Esas casas . . . grandes! 2 El padre . . . abogado. 3 ¡(yo) . . . cansado! 4 Los niños . . . enfermos. 5 El parque . . . en la Avenida Murillo. 6 Los padres . . . franceses. 7 Aquellos países . . . muy poderosos. 8 Nuestro coche . . . aquí. 9 Mi amiga . . . de España. 10 ¡El agua . . . caliente! 11 Los muchachos . . . jugando. 12 El cumpleaños . . . mañana.

3 Translate these sentences into Spanish, using *ser* or *estar* for the indicated portion. (§§97, 98 A, B, C, D, E)

1 **I am** from San Francisco. (*Ud.*) Where **are** you from? 2 The bank **is** closed. 3 **We are listening to** the music. 4 The book **is written** by Enrique Lamadrid. 5 Alice **is** from Venezuela but now **she is** in Spain. 6 (*tú*) Pete, **are you** ready? **It's** six o'clock. 7 This town **is** boring. 8 John **is** very smart (clever). 9 (m.) **I am** very happy[1] today! 10 Today **is** Monday. Where **is** the meeting? 11 (*Ud.*) --**Are you** a[2] student? --Yes, **I'm** a[2] student. 12 My car **is** new. **It's** in the street.

99 / *Meanings of the Verb* deber — *Diversos significados del verbo* deber

1 Translate these sentences into English, paying special attention to the indicated portions. (§99 A, B, C, D, E)

1 Rosa, **debieras escribirles** a tus abuelos. 2 **Debo estudiar** esta noche. 3 Cuando murió, mi padre **debía** mucho dinero. 4 Ustedes **deben de viajar** mucho, ¿verdad? 5 Felipe **debe haber llegado** a París hoy.

[1]happy = *contento*
[2]Omit in translation.

2 Translate these sentences into Spanish, using a form of *deber* for the indicated portions. (§99 A, B, C, D, E)

1 **I should (ought to)** visit my aunt in Lima.   2 Mr. García **must earn (probably earns)** a lot of[1] money.   3 **I must have (probably) slept** ten hours last night[2]. 4 Paul and Michael **must have (probably have) left.**   5 George **owes** thirty pesos for[3] the tickets.   6 (*tú*) Richard, **you ought to go** to the meeting.   7 **I must (ought to)** call the[4] airport.

100 / *Constructions with* gustar *(like),* faltar *(lack),* quedar *(remain)*
Modo de usar gustar, faltar, quedar

1 Answer these questions affirmatively or negatively (as you like) in complete sentences in Spanish. (§100 A, B)

≫ ¿Le gusta mirar la televisión?
Sí, (No, no) me gusta mirar la televisión.
≫ ¿Le gustan los coches europeos?
No, no (Sí,) me gustan los coches europeos.

1 ¿Le gusta la comida italiana?   2 ¿Le gusta el clima de esta región?   3 ¿Les gusta a sus amigos hablar español?   4 ¿Les gustan a sus amigos las películas extranjeras?   5 ¿Le gustan los vinos de California?   6 ¿Le gusta a usted levantarse temprano?   7 ¿Te gusta viajar?   8 ¿Te gusta el español?   9 ¿Te gustó la cena anoche?   10 ¿Te gustaron las noticias del periódico ayer?   11 ¿Les gustó a sus amigos la fiesta?   12 ¿Te gustaría visitar Europa?   13 ¿Te gustarían las playas de Acapulco?   14 ¿Te falta dinero?   15 ¿Te falta un coche?   16 ¿Le faltan amigos?   17 ¿Le queda mucho tiempo libre?   18 ¿Le quedan muchos pesos?   19 ¿Les quedan a sus amigos muchos discos populares?

2 Translate these sentences into Spanish, using *gustar, faltar,* or *quedar.* (§100 A, B)

1 I have ten dollars **left.**   2 (*Ud.*) **Do you like** grapes?   3 **We like** to swim.
4 Ernest[5] **lacks** the money to buy[6] a record player.   5 **I would like** a car.   6 Mark[7] has five dollars **left.**

[1]a lot of = *mucho*
[2]last night = *anoche*
[3]*por*
[4]*al*
[5]*A Ernesto*
[6]to buy = *para comprar*
[7]*A Marcos*

101 / *Uses of the Verb* haber — *Modo de usar el verbo* haber

1 Translate the following sentences into Spanish, using *hay, había, hubo, hay que* or *haber* + *de* + <u>infinitive</u> to express the indicated portion. (§101 A, B, C, D)

1 **There are** many students here. 2 **It's necessary to know** how[1] to read and write. 3 **Are there** any restaurants on this street? 4 **It is necessary to work** in order to[2] live. 5 **There is** a party tonight! 6 **We are to leave** immediately for[3] Spain. 7 **There is** a lot of noise on this street. 8 (*Ud.*) **You are to call** the[4] hospital immediately. 9 **There were** ten children in my family. 10 **There was** (took place) a meeting last night.

102 / *Uses of the Verb* hacer — *Modo de usar el verbo* hacer

1 Answer the following questions as you wish, in complete sentences in Spanish. (§102 A)

≫ ¿Hace fresco hoy?
No, no (Sí,) hace fresco hoy.

1 ¿Hace buen tiempo hoy? 2 ¿Hizo buen tiempo ayer? 3 ¿Hará buen tiempo este fin de semana? 4 ¿Qué tiempo hace? 5 ¿Qué tiempo hace aquí en verano? 6 ¿Qué tiempo hace aquí en invierno? 7 ¿Dónde hace más calor, en Alaska o en Arizona? 8 ¿Hace mucho frío aquí?

2 Answer the following questions, using *hace* plus the period of time indicated in parentheses. The word order in your answer should be: subject + verb + *hacer* + period of time. (§102 B)

≫ ¿Cuándo llegó Felipe? (una hora)
Felipe llegó **hace una hora.** (*Philip arrived an hour ago.*)

1 ¿Cuándo llamó el señor Rodríguez? (media hora) 2 ¿Cuándo ganó Marta al tenis? (unos días) 3 ¿Cuándo era popular ese baile? (unos años) 4 ¿Cuándo inventaron la radio? (unos cincuenta años) 5 ¿Cuándo estuvo aquí el presidente? (tres meses)

3 Translate these sentences into Spanish, paying special attention to the indicated portion. (§102 A, B, D)

1 **What's the weather like?** 2 **It's hot!** 3 They sold the car three months **ago.** 4 **I had** a garage **built.** 5 (*Ud.*) **Did you have** that dress **sewn?** 6 It

[1]Omit in translation.
[2]in order to = *para*
[3]*para*
[4]*al*

rained two days **ago**.   7 **We had** the package **sent** by mail[1].   8 **It's nice weather** today.

103 / Uses of the Verb tener — Modo de usar el verbo tener

1 Complete these sentences with the most appropriate idiomatic expression with *tener.* (§ 103 B)

≫ Pablo dice que la farmacia está en la Avenida Juárez. Creo que . . . .
   Creo que **tiene razón.**

   1 Susana olvidó su abrigo. Por eso . . . . 2 Mis hijos siempre piden algo para comer. Parece que ellos siempre . . . . 3 Mi abuela nació en 1900. Por eso . . . . 4 Manuel está trabajando al sol. Por eso . . . . 5 Anoche Jorge estudió toda la noche para un examen. Hoy . . . . 6 Mi padre sabe manejar su coche muy bien. Cuando maneja siempre . . . . 7 No bebimos nada en el restaurante. Ahora . . . . 8 Don Fernando está muy ocupado. No tiene tiempo para hablar con nadie. Parece que siempre . . . . 9 Mi esposa prefiere viajar por coche porque . . . de viajar por avión. 10 La conferencia . . . en el salón del Hotel Plaza a las ocho. 11 Mi tío es dueño de varios hoteles. También es senador del estado. Sus amigos dicen que . . . . 12 La criada rompió las tazas y los platos en la cocina. Ella . . . del accidente.

2 Translate these sentences into Spanish, paying special attention to the indicated portion. (§ 103 A, B)

≫ The novel **takes place** in Colombia.
   La novela **tiene lugar** en Colombia.

   1 Alice says that **she's thirsty.** (*tú*) **Are you thirsty,** Juana? 2 John **has to work** tomorrow. 3 **We are cold** and **we are hungry.** 4 (*tú*) Martha, **do you feel like** going[2] to the beach today? 5 (*tú*) **I am eighteen years old. How old are you?** 6 **I had to leave** early. 7 (*tú*) Jack, **you're right.** Tomorrow is Friday. 8 I can't talk now. **I'm in a hurry.**

104 / Ways of Expressing the English Verb become in Spanish
Modo de expresar el verbo inglés become en español

1 Complete these sentences with the appropriate form of *hacerse, llegar a ser, ponerse,* or *volverse,* according to the context. (§ 104 A, B, C, D)

≫ Después del accidente, mi tía . . . enferma.
   Después del accidente, mi tía **se puso** enferma.

   1 Al ver los juguetes, la niña . . . muy contenta. 2 Después de estudiar en la

[1]by mail = *por correo*
[2]going = *de ir*

Facultad de Leyes, Carlos . . . abogado. Más tarde . . . juez. 3 El niño siempre . . . nervioso cuando ve a los extranjeros. 4 Felipe Gómez . . . presidente del país en 1973. 5 Nuestro equipo de fútbol . . . campeón del Estado de Manejas. 6 Su mamá dice que Juanito . . . malo en la escuela ayer. 7 Ayer los hermanos . . . dueños del restaurante "Nopalito". 8 Cuando murió el señor Martínez, su hijo . . . dueño de la compañía.

2 Translate these sentences, paying special attention to the verb "become." (§104 A, B, C, D)

1 John wants **to become** an engineer. 2 (*Ud.*) Do you want **to become** president of the United States? 3 Charles **became** very nervous at[1] the wedding. 4 I think that my uncle **became** crazy. 5 My father **would become**[2] very angry with me[3]. 6 The Hidalgo family **became** very rich.

105 / *Reflexive Verbs — Verbos reflexivos*

1 Rewrite these sentences, replacing the indicated direct object with a reflexive object. (§105 A)

≫ María acuesta **a su hijo.**
María **se** acuesta.

1 Mi padre cortó **la carne.** 2 Despierto **a mi hermano** a las siete. 3 El soldado mató **al enemigo.** 4 El señor Ramírez **me** enoja. 5 Juana peina **a su hermana.**

2 Rewrite these sentences, giving the proper form of the reflexive verb in parentheses. (§105 B)

≫ Antes de comer, (yo) (lavarse) las manos.
Antes de comer, **me lavo** las manos.

1 Agustín (sentarse) para leer el periódico. 2 (yo) (acostarse) a las once y (levantarse) a las siete. 3 Rosa dice que (sentirse) enferma. 4 El avión (acercarse) al aeropuerto. 5 Nosotros siempre (divertirse) en las fiestas de Navidad. 6 Los hijos de Carmen (despertarse) a las ocho.

3 Translate these sentences into Spanish using a reflexive verb for the indicated portions. (§105 C 1)

1 **They go to bed** late and **they fall asleep** immediately. 2 (*tú*) Joe, why **do you sit** in my chair? 3 (*Ud.*) **Do you have a good time** at the beach? 4 Generally **I wake up** early. 5 John always **complains** about[4] the food.

[1]at = *en*
[2]Use the imperfect tense.
[3]with me = *conmigo*
[4]about = *de*

4 Change these sentences, to affirmative commands. Give special attention to the position of the reflexive pronoun, as well as to the placement of the written accent. (§105 D 1 a, b, c)

≫ **Nos levantamos** a las seis.
Levantémonos a las seis.
≫ **Se lavan** las manos.
Lávense Uds. las manos.

1 **Se despiertan** y **se levantan.**   2 ¡**Te imaginas** los hoteles en Acapulco!   3 ¡**Te atreves** a preguntarle su nombre!   4 **Se acerca** al capitán.   5 **Se fijan** en el acueducto romano.   6 **Nos acostamos** pronto.   7 ¿**Te sientas** ahí en una silla?

5 Change these affirmative commands, to negative commands. Pay special attention to the position of the reflexive pronoun.   (§105 D 2 a, b, c)

≫ **Levántense** ustedes.
No se levanten ustedes.

1 **Fíjense** ustedes en los detalles del cuadro.   2 Pepito, **lávate** en la cocina.
3 **Acostémonos** temprano.   4 **Siéntese** allí.   5 **Despiértense** temprano, por favor.
6 **Duérmete,** hijo mío.   7 **Acuérdense** ustedes de la guerra civil.

6 Translate these commands into Spanish, paying special attention to the position of the reflexive pronoun and, when necessary, to the placement of the written accent. (§105 D 1 a, b, c / 2 a, b, c)

1 (*Uds.*) **Go to bed** right now!   2 (*tú*) **Wake up** and **get up!**   3 (*Uds.*) Please, **don't sit down.**   4 (*tú*) Johnny, **introduce yourself** to the lady.   5 (*Ud.*) **Don't forget**[1] the tickets.

---

[1] to forget = *olvidarse*

ANSWERS

1 / **1** 1 un
2 unos
3 unas
4 una
5 un
6 unas
7 una
8 unos
9 un
10 un

2 1 ¿Hay un restaurante aquí?
2 Hay una farmacia en la esquina.
3 ¿Tienes unos libros interesantes?
4 ¿Dónde puedo comprar unas estampillas (unos sellos)?
5 Hay un café allí.
6 ¿Encontró unas sillas?

2 / **1** 1 el
2 el
3 el
4 la
5 la
6 el
7 las
8 los
9 las
10 los

2 1 ¿Vas a comprar la casa?
2 El médico no está aquí.
3 ¿Dónde están los discos?
4 Aquí está la carta.
5 ¿Prefieren el teatro o el cine?
6 ¿Dónde están las muchachas?

3 / **1** (a) 1 del hotel
2 del aeropuerto
3 de la capital
4 del parque
5 del baile
6 de la conferencia

(b) 1 de la escuela
2 del apartamento
3 de la casa
4 del coche
5 del cine
6 de la fábrica

(c) 1 al centro
2 a la estación
3 al mercado
4 al cuarto
5 a la cocina
6 al patio

(d) 1 al chico
2 al alumno
3 al señor
4 al profesor
5 a la señorita
6 a la secretaria

4 / **1** 1 —
2 —, el
3 —, —
4 —

2 1 El béisbol es popular en México.
2 Los niños siempre son curiosos.
3 ¿Prefiere los gatos o los perros?
4 El café y el té son bebidas favoritas en los Estados Unidos.

3 1 el, —
2 —, la
3 —, la

4 1 —
2 —
3 un, —
4 —
5 —, —

5 1 la, —
2 —, —, el, el
3 —, los
4 —, —

6 1 Los coches europeos son económicos pero los coches americanos son más cómodos.
2 --Buenos días, Sr. Torres. ¿Está en casa la Sra. Torres?
3 No tiene que saber inglés. Yo hablo francés.

4 Adiós, don Pablo.

5 El vino blanco es muy barato en España. ¿Te gusta el vino blanco?

6 Mi padre es abogado. Yo quiero ser abogado también.

7 Me gusta el francés, pero prefiero estudiar español.

8 ¿Quién es el Sr. Carrera? ¿Es español o cubano?

9 El Sr. García es americano. Habla inglés y español.

10 Juan es estudiante. Quiere ser ingeniero.

7 1 Hoy es . . . .

2 Mañana es . . . .

3 El domingo es el primer día de la semana en los Estados Unidos.

4 Tengo clases los . . . y los . . . .

5 No tengo clases los . . . y los . . . .

6 La gente va a la iglesia (todos) los domingos.

8 1 ¿Hoy es lunes o martes?

2 Vamos al parque (todos) los domingos.

3 ¿Viene Roberto el viernes o el sábado?

4 ¿Qué día es tu cumpleaños, el miércoles o el jueves?

5 El Sr. Romero me paga todos los viernes.

9	**10**	**11**
1 la	1 la cabeza	1 la
2 el	2 el pelo	2 los
3 el, los	3 el ojo	3 la
4 la	4 la nariz	4 el, los
5 la	5 la boca	5 el, los
6 el, los	6 la oreja	6 la, las
7 la, las	7 la cara	7 el
8 el, los	8 el corazón	8 la
9 la, las	9 el dedo	9 la
10 la, las	10 el estómago	10 el
11 la	11 las piernas	11 el
12 el, los	12 los pies	12 el, los
13 la	13 la mano	13 el
14 el, los	14 el brazo	
15 el, los		
16 el		
17 el		

12 1 Carlos se está poniendo (se pone) la camisa.

2 Me pongo los zapatos y los calcetines.

3 Alberto dijo que se rompió el brazo y la nariz en el accidente.

4 Cuando Domingo no tiene nada que hacer mete las manos en los bolsillos.

5 Juan se está quitando (se quita) el sombrero y los guantes.

6 Pepito siempre come con las manos.

13	**14**
1 la	1 Los, —
2 —	2 El, —, —
3 —	3 —, —
4 el, el	4 —, —, —
	5 la, —
	6 —, —

15 1 Mi amiga Alicia va a Chile. Otra amiga fue allá el verano pasado.

2 Cervantes, el famoso escritor español, murió en 1616.

3 El científico va al Brasil para buscar cierto tipo de mineral. Otro científico va también.

4 Saltillo, ciudad en el norte de México, es famosa por sus sarapes.
5 Cierto grupo de estudiantes siempre va allí los viernes.

5 /
1 1 Lo importante es recordar los boletos.
2 Lo difícil es llegar temprano.
3 Lo malo es que no tenemos coche.
4 El clima es lo mejor de esta región.
5 Lo principal es encontrar la calle.

2 1 Lo de encontrar su casa era difícil.
2 ¿Puedes contarme lo de tu tía?
3 Lo de la rebelión es interesante.
4 ¿Sabe lo del Sr. Arango?

3 1 Carlos dijo que los precios son altos, lo cual es verdad.
2 El Sr. Fernández habla bien el inglés, lo que me sorprende.
3 Domingo tiene ideas muy serias, lo cual es raro para un niño de su edad.
4 No puedo ir, lo que quiere decir que Pepe tiene que ir solo.

4 1 Quiero saber lo que estás haciendo.
2 Ella explicó lo que dijo Juan en la carta.
3 ¿Sabes lo que prefieres hacer?
4 ¿Recuerda lo que dijo el doctor?

5 1 lo de, lo
2 lo
3 Lo de, lo, lo
4 lo que
5 lo que, lo que
6 lo

6 /
1 1 la
2 los
3 la
4 las
5 los

2 1 una
2 un
3 una
4 una
5 un
6 una
7 una

8 un
9 una
10 una
11 un
12 una
13 una
14 una

3 1 La ciudad tiene un problema con la contaminación (del aire).
2 La inauguración tuvo lugar durante el mes de junio.
3 ¿Tienen un mapa de la universidad?
4 La siesta todavía es una costumbre en muchas partes de México.

7 /
1 1 las economías
2 los atletas
3 los tocadiscos
4 los aviones
5 los jóvenes
6 las leyes
7 las paredes
8 los papeles
9 los trenes
10 las flores

2 1 la voz, *the voice*
2 la vez, *the time*
3 la actriz, *the actress*
4 la luz, *the light*
5 un lápiz, *a pencil*
6 un juez, *a judge*
7 una cruz, *the cross*
8 un pez, *a fish*

3 1 ¿Perdiste un lápiz?
2 Vimos las luces del avión en la noche.
3 La actriz habló en una voz clara.
4 Muchas veces tomamos el tren a Madrid.
5 Un juez tiene que saber muy bien las leyes.

8 /
1 1 amarilla
2 alto
3 bonitas
4 famosos
5 limpios

6 blanco, blancos, negros
7 enteros
8 buenos
9 rubias
10 enfermos

9 /

1
1 la chica contenta
2 una historia larga
3 la estatua moderna
4 una obra magnífica
5 una camisa roja
6 la avenida ancha

2
1 las montañas hermosas
2 unos relojes viejos
3 unos días especiales
4 unas preguntas fáciles
5 las hijas menores
6 los bailes alegres
7 unos trabajos útiles
8 unas muchachas inteligentes

3
1 Las chicas morenas son bonitas.
2 Unos amigos de Tomás son españoles.
3 ¿Los hijos mayores van a la universidad?
4 Unas jóvenes inglesas buscan trabajo aquí.
5 Los problemas de Enrique son difíciles.
6 Las voces de los niños eran muy altas.

4 (a) nueva, oscuros, pasada, mucha, fina, pequeña
(b) española, morena, español, francesa, amables

5
1 El Retiro es un parque famoso en Madrid.
2 Las calles de Lima son anchas y hermosas.
3 ¿Tiene Lima muchos edificios modernos?
4 Tengo un tío y dos tías en California. Son americanos.
5 Prefiero las novelas cortas. ¿Lees muchos libros interesantes?
6 En Sevilla vivimos en una casa típica con paredes blancas y tejado rojo.

10 /

1 (a) 1 un abuelo
2 unas primas
3 unos primos
4 un tío

(b) 1 el primer día
2 el primer mes
3 la primera hora

(c) 1 algunos restaurantes
2 algún banco
3 alguna peluquería
4 algunas fábricas

(d) 1 buen muchacho
2 Son buenas profesoras.
3 Son buenos compañeros.
4 buen jefe

2 1 un, pequeño
2 gran
3 algunas
4 enferma, mala

5 grande
6 algún
7 ningún
8 último

3 (a) cien, ciento cincuenta, doscientos, ciento cinco
(b) San Juan, San Francisco, Santo Tomás, San Sebastián

4
1 Mi hermano vive en San Agustín. Es el tercer hijo de la familia.
2 Ramón Jiménez es un gran poeta. Algunos poemas están en inglés.
3 Pablo pide cien dólares por su bicicleta. Creo que es una bicicleta buena.

11 /

1
1 ¿Prefieres el vino francés?
2 ¡Creo que es una muchacha bonita!
3 Comimos en un restaurante italiano.
4 La Sra. Macías preparó chocolate caliente.
5 Compré una camisa azul ayer.

2
1 dirección exacta
2 ideas interesantes
3 última silla
4 arte cruel
5 calle comercial
6 barrio antiguo
7 música clásica
8 primera casa blanca
9 muchos apartamentos nuevos

3 1 ¿Cuántos amigos vienen?

2 Estas fotos son viejas.

3 ¿Qué día es mañana?

4 Su hija trabaja aquí.

5 Hablé con un amigo suyo.

6 Los dos hermanos son ingenieros.

7 El día catorce salimos de Quito.

8 Vivo en la segunda casa de la esquina.

9 ¿Cuánto dinero tienes?

10 ¡Este abrigo es mío!

11 El policía me hizo algunas preguntas.

4 (a) 1 Eduardo fue un gran hombre.

2 Eduardo fue un hombre grande.

(b) 1 ¡Compré un coche nuevo!

2 Compré un nuevo coche.

(c) 1 Este pobre niño, está cansado.

2 El niño pobre necesita ropa.

(d) 1 ¡Es pura mentira!

2 Es agua pura.

12 /

1 1 más difícil que la biología

2 más agradable que el clima de aquí

3 más delgada que Susana

4 más grande que San Francisco

5 más aplicado que Manuel

6 más ocupado que ayer

2 1 Roberto es más ambicioso que yo.

2 El actor parece menos nervioso que antes.

3 Ese vestido es menos típico que otros muchos.

4 Inés es menos práctica que su hermana.

5 Este café está más fuerte que ayer.

3 1 la iglesia más antigua

2 el coche más económico

3 el deporte más popular

4 el caballo más fino

5 el programa más divertido

6 el plato más famoso

4 1 Santiago es la ciudad más grande de Chile.

2 Hoy es el día más largo del año.

3 ¿Cuál es lo menos interesante de su trabajo?

4 ¿Cuál fue el momento más horrible de tú vida?

5 ¿Cuál fue la parte más interesante de tú viaje?

5 1 peor

2 mejor

3 mayor

4 peor

5 menor

6 mejor

6 1 Es un abrigo muy bueno. Es el mejor abrigo que tengo.

2 Esteban es un muchacho grande. Es el muchacho mayor de la familia.

3 Este vino es muy bueno. ¿Crees que es el mejor vino de España?

4 Hoy fue un día muy malo. Creo que fue el peor día de mi vida.

5 ¿Es Adelita la hija menor de la familia?

6 Fue un viaje muy malo. Fue el peor viaje a Europa en diez años.

7 1 Este color es feísimo.

2 Los Andes son montañas altísimas.

3 Esta canción es bellísima.

4 Su perro es gordísimo.

8 1 Susana tiene más de veinte discos. Yo no tengo más que doce.

2 Juan leyó más de cinco libros esta semana.

3 María y Julia tienen menos tiempo que nosotros.

4 No tengo más que diez minutos.

5 Carlos vendió más de cincuenta boletos. Yo no vendí más que treinta y cinco.

9 1 El café de Colombia es tan bueno como el café del Brasil.

2 México es una ciudad tan moderna como Lima.

3 La ropa allá cuesta tan poco dinero como la ropa aquí.

4 La novela fue tan divertida como la película.
5 ¿Está usted tan cansada como yo?
6 Mi tío es un hombre tan generoso como mi padre.

10 1 Mi hijo quiere ser tan grande como yo.
2 Don Fernando es tan viejo como mi abuelo.
3 Estas sillas son tan duras como las otras.
4 Alberto es tan guapo como su padre.
5 Este libro es tan interesante como dijeron.

11 1 de lo que
2 de la que
3 del que
4 de lo que
5 de lo que
6 de las que
7 de los que

13 / **1** 1 la primera
2 los ricos
3 la morena
4 los mayores

14 / **1** 1 mis
2 nuestros
3 sus
4 tus
5 nuestro
6 su
7 su
8 tu

2 1 los tíos de ella
2 la dirección de ellos
3 la carta de ellas
4 el primo de él
5 los invitados de ustedes

3 1 los documentos suyos
2 las maletas nuestras
3 la amiga suya
4 el coche tuyo
5 los problemas míos
6 los productos nuestros
7 el abrigo suyo
8 la pregunta tuya

4 1 Estos libros son míos.
2 ¿Los discos sobre la mesa son tuyos?
3 Un primo nuestro es dentista.
4 ¿Este café es suyo o mío?
5 Algunos amigos suyos van a tener una fiesta.
6 Una amiga nuestra va con nosotros.
7 ¿Este dinero es suyo? No, no es mío.
8 ¿Estas cartas son suyas?

15 / **1** (a) 1 Estas canciones son bonitas.
2 Esta pintura es bonita.
3 Este sombrero es bonito.
4 Estos animales son bonitos.

(b) 1 esas camisas blancas
2 ese color blanco
3 esas flores blancas
4 esos papeles blancos

(c) 1 aquellos edificios famosos
2 aquella playa famosa
3 aquella iglesia famosa
4 aquella hacienda famosa

2 1 ese
2 estas
3 aquellas
4 esta
5 esos
6 aquellos

3 1 Ese hombre a la izquierda se llama Sr. Cruz.
2 Estos zapatos son muy baratos.
3 Este cuadro es muy moderno.
4 Esa ciudad es la más grande de México.
5 Esos niños tienen hambre.
6 Discutiremos esas preguntas mañana.
7 Esa muchacha nunca viene aquí.
8 ¿Vio Macchu Picchu? Visité aquel sitio el año pasado.

16 /

1
1. qué
2. cuántos
3. qué
4. cuántas
5. cuánto
6. cuánta
7. cuántas
8. cuántos

2
1. ¿Cuánto dinero gana usted aquí?
2. ¿Cuántos nombres hay en la lista?
3. ¿Qué deporte prefieres, Alicia?
4. ¿Qué libro necesita?
5. ¿Cuánta ropa vendiste?
6. ¿Cuántas veces llamó Felipe?

3
1. ¡Qué sorpresa!
2. ¡Qué bonita estás, Ana!
3. ¡Qué hombre!
4. ¡Qué nervioso estoy!
5. ¡Qué frío está!
6. ¡Qué horrible!
7. ¡Qué película!
8. ¡Qué cansado estoy!

17 /

1

(a)
uno	once
dos	doce
tres	trece
cuatro	catorce
cinco	quince
seis	dieciséis
siete	diecisiete
ocho	dieciocho
nueve	diecinueve
diez	veinte

(b)
diez
veinte
treinta
cuarenta
cincuenta
sesenta
setenta
ochenta
noventa
cien, ciento

(c)
cien, ciento
doscientos
trescientos
cuatrocientos
quinientos
seiscientos
setecientos
ochocientos
novecientos
mil

(d)
dieciséis
veintidós
treinta y cuatro
cuarenta
setenta y tres
noventa y seis
ciento uno
mil novecientos setenta y seis

(e)
11
15
27
69
105
500
1713

2
1. Mi tía vive aproximadamente a cien kilómetros de aquí.
2. Necesitamos una docena de huevos y unos cinco kilos de azúcar.
3. Esta ciudad tiene cinco millones de habitantes.
4. Tres americanos llegaron a la luna en mil novecientos sesenta y nueve.

18 /

1
primero	sexto
segundo	séptimo
tercero	octavo
cuarto	noveno
quinto	décimo

2
1. Mis abuelos vinieron de España el 1° de septiembre de 1965.
2. El último capítulo es el quince.
3. ¿Has leído mucha literatura francesa del siglo veinte?
4. La Reina Isabel Segunda tiene tres niños.
5. Es mi segundo viaje a México.

19 /

1
1. probablemente
2. generalmente
3. ansiosamente
4. rápida y fácilmente

2
1. Estoy completamente perdido.
2. Carlos trabaja rápida y profesionalmente.
3. Hablamos muy brevemente con el doctor.
4. Desafortunadamente no puedo ir mañana.
5. Afortunadamente nadie está enfermo hoy.
6. Mi padre siempre llega exactamente a tiempo.

3 (a) 1 ahora
2 temprano
3 después

(b) 1 tarde
2 despacio
3 rápido

20

1 1 más puntualmente que sus hermanos
2 más rápidamente que los otros
3 más libremente que nosotros
4 más claramente que los niños
5 más sinceramente que los otros políticos

2 1 La Sra. García nos saludó más cortésmente hoy que ayer.
2 Veo a Víctor ahora menos frecuentemente que el año pasado.
3 El Gobernador Sánchez habla más sinceramente que los otros oficiales.
4 Alicia canta más clara y perfectamente que las otras muchachas.

3 1 peor
2 mejor
3 peor
4 mejor

4 1 Roberto escribe mal. Escribe peor que yo.
2 Este coche funciona bien. Funciona mejor que el otro.
3 Miguel no juega bien al tenis. Jugará mejor el año que viene.

1 1 dónde, donde
2 donde
3 dónde
4 adónde
5 donde
6 dónde
7 de dónde
8 por dónde
9 por dónde
10 donde
11 de donde

2 1 Carlos, ¿adónde vas?
2 ¿Va a París? ¿De dónde sale?
3 ¿Dónde está el teléfono?
4 ¿Recuerdan la tienda donde vimos las pinturas francesas?
5 ¿Saben los niños adónde ir?
6 Encontré un lugar donde venden libros viejos.
7 ¿Dónde tiene lugar la novela?
8 ¿Por dónde entró el ladrón?
9 ¿Dónde trabajó el año pasado?
10 ¿Vas a salir? ¿Adónde?
11 ¿Por dónde salieron de la ciudad?
12 Juan viene de donde hablan catalán.

22

1 1 no se llama
2 no le escribo
3 no le gusta
4 no sabe tocar
5 no está preparada
6 no he visto

2 1 nadie
2 nada
3 nunca
4 tampoco
5 ni . . . ni
6 ninguno

3 1 tampoco
2 nunca
3 nadie
4 nunca
5 tampoco
6 ni . . . ni

4 1 no trabajamos nunca
2 no voy tampoco
3 no sabemos nada
4 no estuvo nadie
5 no hizo nunca

5 1 Nunca recibí tu carta.

2 Ni mi hermana ni yo oímos el teléfono.

3 Nadie viene aquí.

4 Juan no sabe nada de música.

5 --¿Tienes algunas primas? --No, no tengo ninguna prima.

6 Enrique no va al cine. Nosotros no vamos tampoco.

7 En mi familia ningún niño es perezoso.

6 1 no estaba hablando   4 no hubieran llegado, no me habrían visto

2 no me ha pedido   5 no ha sido firmado

3 no hemos visto

23 /

1
1 yo	6 ellos	
2 ellos	7 ellas	
3 nosotros	8 tú	
4 yo	9 él	
5 ella	10 nosotros	

2
1 ellos	5 ella
2 nosotros	6 ustedes
3 él	7 nosotros
4 ustedes	8 ellas

3 1 ¿Cómo está usted, Sr. Díaz?

2 --¿Es usted mexicano? --No, yo soy colombiano.

3 El Sr. Giménez y la Srta. Guzmán son españoles. Él es de Madrid, y ella es de Sevilla.

4 Carlos quiere ir a la fiesta. Yo no quiero ir.

5 Roberto lee más que nosotros.

6 Yo vivo en un apartamento pero ellos viven con sus padres.

7 Susana y Pablo son primos. Ella va a la universidad y él trabaja.

4 1 --¿Eres tú Carlos? --Sí, soy yo.

2 Son ellos que quieren visitar Lima.

3 ¿Quién llamó? ¿Fue usted o María?

4 --¿Quién es? --Somos nosotros.

24 /

1
1 los visita	7 lo (le) invitamos
2 los llevas	8 la vemos
3 la compro	9 lo dejamos
4 la llamo	10 la preparo
5 las admiramos	11 lo vi
6 la escribió	12 lo (le) veo

2
1 nos	6 nos
2 me	7 me
3 te	8 nos
4 me	9 me
5 te	10 nos

3 1 Juan quiere usar mi coche. Lo necesita mañana.

2 Carlos prefiere la música clásica. La escucha todo el tiempo.

3 El señor García me felicitó ayer.

4 Las dejamos en el aeropuerto.

5 Alicia le (lo) entiende perfectamente en español.

6 Ese policía nos saluda todos los días.

7 No te creo. Es imposible.

8 Mis abuelos viven en Laredo. Los visito cada año.

9 Veo a Andrés todos los días. Lo (le) conozco bien.

25 /

1
1 le	4 les
2 les	5 les
3 le	6 le

2
1 nos	5 te
2 me	6 nos
3 te	7 me
4 me	8 nos

3 1 ¿Le paga la compañía cada semana?

2 Les mandamos una lista de libros.

3 Carmen siempre me pide dinero.

4 Te escribiré pronto.
5 Jaime nos dice que tienes que salir a las diez.
6 Pablo me enseña su coche nuevo (su nuevo coche).
7 Luisa llamó. Le hablé de los boletos.
8 Nuestros amigos vinieron a las ocho. Les preparamos una comida.

4 1 a Ud.
2 a ella
3 a Ud.
4 a ellos
5 a Uds.

5 1 El señor Moreno le corta el pelo a mi hijo.
2 La madre le pone el abrigo a su hijo.
3 La señora González le quita los zapatos a Juanito.

26 / **1** 1 me
2 te
3 se
4 se
5 nos
6 se

2 1 Lorenzo siempre se lava antes de comer.
2 ¿Los niños se sienten mejor hoy?
3 Me llamo Mariana.
4 Nos preocupamos por el mal tiempo.
5 Las secretarias se quejan mucho de su trabajo.
6 ¿Te despiertas cuando se levanta el sol?

3 1 se levantan
2 se preocupan
3 nos sentamos
4 se divierten
5 se interesa

27 / **1** 1 me lavo
2 se divirtió
3 te bañas
4 nos acostamos
5 me preparé
6 te levantaste

2 1 Mi hermano siempre se acuesta a las diez.
2 ¿Se queja Juan de los vecinos?
3 ¿Se casa tu hermana en agosto?
4 ¿Se comieron todo el pan?
5 ¿Quién se llevó mi abrigo?
6 María se parece a su madre.
7 La Sra. Guzmán se cayó en la calle.
8 ¿Te atreves a pedir más postre?

3 1 Alicia y Tomás se escriben mucho.
2 ¿Se conocen Esteban y Antonio?
3 ¿Se ven los primos mucho?
4 Esos gatos se odian.
5 Los vecinos se visitan mucho.
6 Los niños se ayudan en la escuela.
7 Mi esposa y mi suegra se hablan todos los días.

4 1 Alfredo y Vicente se ayudan mucho uno a otro.
2 Los jóvenes no se entienden unos a otros.
3 Esos dos atletas se estiman uno a otro.
4 Esos dos enemigos se engañan mucho uno a otro.

28 / **1** 1 se oye
2 se venden
3 se escribe
4 se observan
5 se examinan
6 se prepara
7 se discutieron
8 se inauguró

2 1 Se ve a muchos turistas americanos en España.
2 Se conoce a la gente bien en los pueblos pequeños.
3 Se emplea a una criada si la familia es grande.
4 Se invita a todos los amigos a una boda.

3 1 se dice
2 se cierra
3 se solicita
4 se celebra

5 se usa
6 se vende
7 se come
8 se empieza

29 / **1** 1 ellos
2 ustedes
3 él
4 ella
5 ellas
6 nosotros

2 1 Rosa, no puedo ir sin tí.
2 ¿Come Fernando con usted?
3 ¿Hablan de mí?
4 Un perro estaba corriendo (corría) tras ellos.
5 Un hombre alto se sentó delante de nosotros.
6 ¿Esta carta es para mí?
7 Vengo a ti porque necesito ayuda.

3 1 conmigo
2 contigo
3 consigo

4 conmigo
5 contigo
6 consigo

30 / **1** 1 Pilar no los recuerda.
2 No lo entiendo.
3 Doña Elisa los mira.
4 ¿Lo (le) buscas?
5 Siempre la veo en el colegio.

2 (a) 1 Espérenlas, por favor.
2 Ábrala.
3 Escúchenlos.
4 Tráigala.
5 Pídala.

(b) 1 ¿Piensas avisarlo (avisarle) de las noticias?
2 Alonso dice que va a venderlos.
3 Ana desea empezarlo el lunes.
4 Vamos a buscarla en la oficina.
5 Jaime prefiere verla.

(c) 1 ¿Estás preparándola?
2 Estoy esperándolos.
3 Estamos escuchándolo.
4 Mi hermana está leyéndolas.
5 María está explicándola.

3 1 No nos esperen en casa.
2 No me diga lo que pasó en la reunión.
3 El señor Oviedo no tiene el documento. No se lo pida.
4 Doña Claudia no quiere ver las fotos. No se las dé.

4 (a) 1 Le quiero presentar a mi esposa.
2 ¿Las piensas devolver mañana, Carlos?
3 El jefe le va a contestar por carta.
4 Las secretarias se los pueden mandar inmediatamente.

(b) 1 Lo estamos terminando ahora mismo.
2 Alicia se lo está escribiendo.
3 Se los estoy comprando.
4 Lo están arreglando.

5 1 Nuestros padres viven en Santiago. Vamos a visitarlos en junio.
2 Señora Macías, espéreme aquí.
3 ¿Dónde están los libros? No puedo encontrarlos.
4 Es demasiado dinero. No puedo aceptarlo.
5 Un policía nos ayudó a encontrar el museo.
6 El Sr. Robles es el guía. Síganlo (Síganle), por favor.
7 ¿Perdiste la bolsa? ¿Puedes describirla?

8 ¡Mi esposa está preparando una comida especial para nosotros!

9 Este capítulo es importante. ¡Estúdienlo con cuidado!

10 La casa es muy moderna. Están construyéndola ahora.

31 /

1 1 nos lo prepara
2 te lo dio .
3 me los mandan
4 te la enseñó

2 1 se la escribió
2 se las explicó
3 no se lo pediste
4 se la preparó
5 se las compró
6 se los mandó

3 1 Se la mandé.
2 Felipe nos las pidió.
3 ¿Cuándo se lo diste?
4 Te la enseñaré mañana.

32 /

1 1 los míos
2 la suya
3 el suyo
4 la nuestra
5 los suyos
6 las mías

2 1 el nuestro
2 los suyos
3 la suya
4 el mío
5 el tuyo
6 los nuestros
7 la tuya
8 las mías

3 1 los suyos
2 la suya
3 las nuestras
4 los míos
5 el tuyo

4 1 Son míos.
2 Son suyos.
3 Son suyos.
4 Es nuestra.

5 1 la mía
2 la nuestra
3 el tuyo
4 el mío
5 los nuestros
6 las tuyas

6 1 la de ella
2 las de ellos
3 los de usted
4 la de ellos
5 los de él
6 los de ella

33 /

1 1 ése
2 ésos
3 ésa
4 éstos
5 aquéllos

2 1 ésta
2 éste
3 ésta
4 ésas
5 éstos
6 ése

3 1 Víctor, ¿dónde están tus corbatas nuevas? Éstas son viejas.
2 --Doctor Flores, ¿es ésta su oficina o (es) aquélla?
3 Ésos son mis hijos.
4 De todas las ciudades de España, me gusta ésa.
5 ¿Es éste tu número de teléfono?

4 1 éste, aquél
2 ésta, aquélla
3 ésta, aquéllos

5 1 Roberto, esto es un regalo.
2 María quiere ser una actriz famosa. ¡Esto es muy difícil!
3 Susana, ¿qué es eso?
4 ¡Esto es muy bueno!

6 1 Estas calles son más anchas que las del centro.
2 El coche nuevo (nuevo coche) de Felipe es más económico que el que vendió.
3 Los que llegaron tarde esperaron mucho tiempo.
4 Las ideas de María son mejores que las de sus novios.
5 El que pierde su pasaporte tiene que obtener otro.

34 /

1 1 a quién
2 cuál
3 qué
4 cuánto
5 quiénes

2 1 ¿Cuál de los vestidos prefieres?
2 ¿Quién llamó por teléfono?
3 ¿Cuántos hay en la universidad?
4 ¿Qué podemos hacer?
5 ¿Cuánto pagó por el libro?

6 de quiénes
7 cuáles
8 cuántos

3 1 cuál
2 cuáles
3 qué
4 cuál
5 cuáles
6 qué

6 ¿De quién es este perro?
7 ¿Cuántas viven en Mendoza?
8 ¿Quiénes vienen a la fiesta?

4 1 ¿Cuál es su dirección?
2 ¿Qué es un criollo?
3 ¿Cuáles son los mejores restaurantes de Málaga?
4 ¿Qué es Barcelona?

35 / **1** 1 Elena es mi tía que vive en Monterrey.
2 El señor Castillo es el juez que vimos anoche.
3 ¿Has leído esta novela que ganó el premio literario?
4 Ésos son paquetes de ropa que llegaron hoy.
5 Ésta es la carretera que va hasta Santa Cruz.
6 Hay más de treinta mil jóvenes aquí que van a la universidad.

2 1 María es la muchacha que toca el piano.
2 Compré un coche que es económico.
3 Éste es el mismo programa que vimos antes.
4 Hay un autobús que va a la playa.

36 / **1** 1 que
2 quien
3 que
4 quienes

5 que
6 quienes
7 que

2 1 Mi padre, quien nació en Toledo, es doctor.
2 El señor Silva, quien llamó ayer, es el alcalde de la ciudad.
3 Mi hija, quien habla español y francés, viaja mucho.
4 Sus padres, quienes viven en Monterrey, vienen aquí.

3 1 Quien . . . *He who laughs last, laughs most.*
2 Quien . . . *Great talkers make great mistakes.*
3 Quien . . . *He who lives ill, dies ill.*
4 Quien . . . *He who sings frightens away his woes.*
5 Quien . . . *Grasp all, lose all.*

37 / **1** 1 la cual
2 los cuales
3 las cuales
4 la cual
5 lo cual

2 1 los cuales
2 las cuales
3 del cual
4 la cual

3 1 los que
2 las que
3 el que
4 los que
5 el que
6 la que

4 1 quien
2 el que
3 la cual / la que
4 las cuales
5 que
6 el que
7 la cual
8 que

5 1 ¿Dónde está el disco que compró Gregorio?
2 Carlos es el hombre con quien trabajo.
3 El Café Victoria es un restaurante viejo en el cual se reunen muchos estudiantes para comer y hablar.

4 Visitamos la iglesia de Santa María cerca de la cual encontramos un buen hotel.

5 Mi tío, quien es capitán en el ejército, habla tres idiomas.

38 /

1
1 cuyo
2 cuyos
3 cuyo
4 cuyos
5 cuya
6 cuyas
7 cuyo

2
1 Concha es la mujer cuyos hijos murieron en la guerra.
2 ¿Dónde está el hotel cuyo restaurante sirve comida italiana?
3 ¿Cómo está el muchacho cuya pierna se rompió?
4 ¿Quién es el doctor cuya casa compramos?
5 Juan Ramón Jiménez es el escritor cuya poesía es muy famosa.
6 El señor Durán es el hombre cuya hija se casó con Carlos.
7 Juan es el muchacho cuyos cuentos son siempre divertidos.

39 /

1
1 algo
2 alguno
3 alguien

2
1 ¿Me puede decir algo de su familia?
2 Alguien olvidó sus libros.
3 José está algo curioso acerca de sus nuevos vecinos.
4 Algunos de mis amigos son franceses.
5 Alguien dijo que María está enferma.
6 Algunas ciudades americanas tienen nombres españoles.
7 Veo algo en el tejado.
8 --Pedro, ¿has visto los coches nuevos? --Sí, he visto algunos.

3
1 abren
2 importan
3 piden
4 hablan
5 cierran

4
1 Uno tiene que llegar temprano para comprar un boleto.
2 Dicen que los coches nuevos son más caros.
3 Cierran la oficina a las seis.
4 Se necesita cambiar dólares por pesos en México.
5 Uno tiene que practicar mucho para ser músico.
6 Producen plata fina en Taxco.

40 /

1
(a) con, hasta
(b) desde/de, entre, debajo de, en
(c) menos, según, excepto

2
1 en
2 sobre/en
3 para
4 contra
5 de/desde
6 por
7 según, de/sobre
8 bajo
9 desde
10 durante/hasta

41 /

1
1 alrededor de
2 en lugar de / en vez de
3 delante de, al lado de
4 a causa de
5 cerca de
6 fuera de
7 después de
8 encima de
9 debajo de
10 dentro del

2 1 delante de
2 cerca de
3 después de
4 fuera de

3 1 en cuanto a
2 frente a
3 tocante a / respecto a
4 junto a

4 1 Roberto, ¿vives cerca de la escuela?
2 A pesar de su edad, ¡mi abuela se casó otra vez!
3 Mi coche está delante de la tienda.
4 En cuanto a Susana y Carlos, vendrán a las siete.
5 El garaje está detrás de la casa.
6 Felipe, ¿puedes trabajar hoy en vez de / en lugar de mañana?
7 Además de lavar la ropa, tengo que preparar la cena.
8 Respecto a / Tocante a la carta, está en la mesa.
9 Dos niños se sentaron frente a la estatua.

42 /   **1** 1 Aquí está la casa del Sr. Castillo.
2 Hoy es el cumpleaños de Alicia.
3 Aquí está el reloj de Carlos.
4 ¡La hermana de José es muy bonita!
5 El ascensor del hotel no funciona.

43 /   **1** 1 Esta máquina de escribir funciona bien.
2 María trabaja en un salón de belleza.
3 La estación de gasolina está en la esquina.
4 Necesito comprar el libro de inglés.
5 Mi padre trabaja para la compañía de seguros.

44 /   **1** (a) 1 al señor Blanco
2 a la señorita Muñoz
3 el parque
4 el hotel
5 a Ricardo
6 al niño

             (b) 1 a mis compañeras
2 los periódicos
3 a los chicos
4 a los soldados
5 la casa
6 a las muchachas

2 1 a
2 a
3 —
4 —
5 a
6 a
7 —

3 1 Antonio admira a Carmen.
2 Carlos admira el coche nuevo.
3 Veo a mi jefe todos los días.
4 No conozco al señor González.
5 Ana, ¿ves el autobús?
6 Pepe tiene dos tíos.

45 /   **1** 1 Taxco es célebre por sus artículos de plata.
2 Podemos salir por esa puerta.
3 El correo llega por la mañana.
4 Este edificio fue construido por la Compañía Hércules.
5 Roberto va a estar aquí por unos cinco días.
6 Los amantes pasean por el río los domingos.

       2 1 Tienen que terminar la construcción de la casa para el primero de agosto.
2 Mario trabaja para el Banco Central.
3 Paco necesita estas herramientas para arreglar su coche.
4 Necesitan la ropa lavada para mañana.
5 Estos paquetes son para Alicia y Mariana.
6 Jorge estudia para ser médico.
7 Este vaso es para vino.

3
1 para (3)
2 por (6)
3 para (1)
4 por (12); para (1)
5 para (1); por (8)
6 por (1)
7 por (2)
8 para (4)
9 por (1)
10 por (4)
11 para (5)
12 por (6 or 12); por (6 or 12)
13 por (5)
14 para (1)
15 por (10)
16 por (5)

4
1 El recado es para María.
2 Para llegar a las 8:00, Juan sale temprano.
3 Gracias por todo, Carlos.
4 Vámonos por la Calle Miraflores.
5 Para un francés, Pablo habla inglés muy bien.
6 Mis padres saldrán para Europa mañana. Van por avión.
7 Julia, ¿puedes terminar para las nueve?
8 Jaime pagó sesenta pesos por los boletos.
9 Pepe tiene que estudiar por la tarde.
10 Llamaré por la mañana.

46 /

1
1 de
2 al
3 de
4 de
5 en
6 a
7 con
8 en
9 a
10 de

2
1 se parece a
2 salgo de
3 llegamos a
4 consiste en
5 entró en
6 sonríe a
7 se asusta de
8 pertenece a
9 se casó con
10 confía en

3
1 Ramón cuenta con sus padres para dinero.
2 El Dr. Campos sale de su oficina a las seis.
3 Tomás piensa en su trabajo.
4 Susana sueña con su novio.
5 Este cuadro pertenece a Margarita.
6 Los dos niños entraron en mi cuarto.
7 Nuestro viaje depende de la huelga de aviones.
8 Juan, ¿quieres jugar a las cartas?

47 /

1
1 a
2 a
3 —
4 a
5 —
6 —
7 —
8 a
9 —
10 a
11 —
12 —

2
1 insisten en
2 se alegra de
3 tratamos de
4 dejé de
5 se ocupa en
6 piensan en
7 quedamos en
8 tardó tres días en

3
1 Rosa ayuda a preparar la cena.
2 Voy a comprar una camisa nueva.

3 Carlos quiere dedicarse a estudiar.
4 Alicia y Esteban trataron de llamar ayer.
5 Juan, ¿por qué insistes en pagar la cuenta?
6 ¡María se olvidó de darme su dirección!
7 Pedro aprendió a nadar el verano pasado.

48 /

1 1 e historia
    2 e inmensa en Sud América
    3 y moreno
    4 y Carlos irá también
    5 e idealista

2 1 u ocupada
    2 o té
    3 u oro
    4 u hombre
    5 o mañana

49 /

1 1 pero
    2 sino
    3 sino
    4 pero
    5 sino
    6 pero

2 1 sino
    2 sino que
    3 sino que
    4 sino que
    5 sino

3 1 Antonio no es de España sino de Italia.
    2 Ana quiere ir pero está enferma.
    3 ¡No solo escribí una carta, sino que llamé por teléfono también!
    4 María y yo estamos cansadas, pero contentas.
    5 El telegrama no es para Pablo, sino para Roberto.

50 /

1 1 si
    2 si
    3 si
    4 si
    5 si

2 1 Si vienes, ¿puedes venir temprano?
    2 Quiero ver el libro mañana si es posible.
    3 No sabemos si ganamos o perdimos el juego.
    4 Si María va, Alicia irá con ella.

51 /

1 1 El cinco de junio es miércoles.
    2 El veintiuno de junio es viernes.
    3 El diecisiete de junio es lunes.
    4 El primero de junio es sábado.
    5 El treinta de junio es domingo.
    6 El doce de junio es miércoles.
    7 El seis de junio es jueves.

2 1 Celebramos la independencia de los Estados Unidos en julio.
    2 Celebramos la Navidad en diciembre.
    3 Los tres meses del verano son junio, julio, y agosto.
    4 Los tres meses del otoño son septiembre, octubre, y noviembre.
    5 Los tres meses del invierno son diciembre, enero, y febrero.
    6 Los tres meses de la primavera son marzo, abril, y mayo.
    7 Celebramos los cumpleaños de Jorge Washington y Abrahán Lincoln en febrero.
    8 El primer mes del año es enero.
    9 El último mes del año es diciembre.
   10 Febrero tiene ventiocho días.

3 1 Juan y yo iremos a Europa por el verano. Volveremos en agosto.
    2 Susana, ¿qué estación prefieres, la primavera o el otoño?
    3 Mis padres irán a Miami por el invierno. Saldrán en enero o febrero.
    4 Generalmente hay nieve aquí en octubre o noviembre.
    5 Mi cumpleaños es en abril y nuestro aniversario es en mayo.

4 1 Son las seis de la mañana.

2 Son las tres de la tarde.

3 Son las dos y media de la mañana.

4 Es la una de la mañana.

5 Es la una y media.

6 Son las tres y diez.

7 Son las siete menos cuarto.

8 Son las tres menos cinco.

5 1 Rosa, ¿qué hora es?

2 Son las cinco de la tarde.

3 Es la una y cuarto.

4 ¿Son las ocho o las nueve?

5 ¡Es la una y media de la mañana! Tengo que ir a casa.

52 / **1** 1 un librito

2 un viejito

3 mi abuelita

4 Juanito

5 un momentito

6 un perrito

53 / **1** 1 ya

2 ya

3 ya que

4 ya

5 ya no

6 ya

7 ya

8 ya que

9 ya

2 1 Carmen ya comió. Está en su cuarto.

2 Ya no hablamos de la guerra.

3 Ya escribiré la carta.

4 ¡Mi hijo ya sabe leer!

5 Susana ya no toma el autobús a las ocho.

54 / **1** 1 Los invitados llegarán a las ocho a comer.

2 La familia Salazar vive enfrente del parque.

3 El Lago de Junín se encuentra cerca del pueblo.

4 María llamó para hablar con su mamá.

5 Dos policías llegaron para hacerme preguntas sobre el accidente.

6 Fuimos a pasear por el río, fuera de la ciudad, donde cultivan olivos.

2 1 Nunca he leído ese libro.

2 Carlos siempre ha vivido con nosotros.

3 Nunca habíamos visto esa película.

4 Mi abuelo siempre había deseado visitar España.

5 --Pepita, ¡apenas has comido la cena!

6 Generalmente hemos empezado nuestro trabajo a las ocho.

3 1 Había otros tres pasajeros en el coche de Antonio.

2 Federico nos dio unos muebles y otras pocas cosas.

3 El barrio de San Isidro tiene otras cuatro escuelas.

55 / **1** 1 ¿Llega Jaime a las once y media?

2 ¿Come Pepe con sus padres?

3 ¿Trabaja Pablo los sábados?

4 ¿Gana Fernando mucho dinero en la fábrica?

5 ¿Espera Carolina a su novio?

6 ¿Están casadas sus dos hijas?

7 ¿Es Rafael estudiante en la universidad?

8 ¿Llega el correo por la tarde?

2 1 ¿Juega mal al tenis Antonio?

2 ¿Habla bien el inglés Consuelo?

3 ¿Necesitan más tiempo los obreros?

4 ¿Toman café y pan para el desayuno muchas familias?

5 ¿Es muy moderna esta iglesia?

6 ¿Habla varias lenguas la secretaria inglesa?

7 ¿Salen al centro todos los días los muchachos?
8 ¿Tienen un coche muchas familias norteamericanas?
9 ¿Vende gasolina y otros productos la compañía de petróleo?

3 1 Ésta es una novela aburrida, ¿verdad?
2 Josefa tiene dos hermanos, ¿verdad?
3 Amalia sabe la dirección, ¿verdad?
4 Mañana es viernes, ¿verdad?
5 Jaime compró la radio nueva, ¿verdad?
6 Esta silla es muy cómoda, ¿verdad?

4 1 ¿Tiene Mendoza un aeropuerto?
2 ¿Trabaja Roberto en la farmacia?
3 ¿Es muy tradicional la música flamenca?
4 ¿Son muy violentas las películas americanas?
5 ¿Está muy enojado el señor Murillo?
6 El juego empieza a las dos, ¿verdad?
7 ¿Tiene tu hermano dos coches?
8 ¿Vienen turistas aquí durante el verano?
9 ¿Baila bien Susana?
10 María, ¿ves sus flores?

56 / **1** *-ar* verbs: hablar, habl-; comprar, compr-; llegar, lleg-; estudiar, estudi-; trabajar, trabaj-; necesitar, necesit-; pasear, pase-; entrar, entr-; escuchar, escuch-.
-er verbs: comer, com-; vender, vend-; leer, le-; creer, cre-; responder, respond-; ver, v-; correr, corr-; prometer, promet-.
-ir verbs: vivir, viv-; escribir, escrib-; insistir, insist-; abrir, abr-; recibir, recib-.

57 / **1** 1 will call, future
2 would come, conditional
3 will return, future
4 was listening, imperfect
5 arrived, preterit
6 was reading, imperfect
7 we saw, preterit
8 are you, present

2 1 have you sent, perfect
2 would have left, conditional perfect
3 we would have arrived, conditional perfect
4 has brought, perfect
5 had waited, pluperfect

3 1 Carlos ha vendido su coche.
2 Habría insistido pero habían comprado los boletos.
3 Elena abrió el regalo.
4 Los muchachos estudiaban historia.
5 La criada siempre prepara el desayuno.
6 Nuestro avión saldrá a las dos.
7 He escrito la carta.
8 Jorge, ¿leíste este capítulo?

58 / **1** 1 busco
2 trabaja
3 necesitas
4 habla
5 enseña
6 entran
7 espero
8 pasean
9 pagan
10 admiran

2 1 cree
2 veo
3 prometemos
4 corren
5 aprendes
6 comen
7 lee
8 respondemos

3 1 asisten
2 recibo
3 permite
4 escribes
5 insiste
6 abro
7 dividimos
8 describe
9 deciden
10 vives

4 1 Mis hijos aprenden francés.
2 ¡Luisa pronuncia muy bien!
3 Muchas costumbres indias aún existen en México.
4 Muchos americanos hablan español.
5 Busco un cuarto.
6 ¿Estudia Juan en la universidad?
7 Yo vivo en los Estados Unidos, pero mis padres viven en Bogotá.
8 Roberto y yo estudiamos medicina.
9 Mis primos tocan la guitarra y cantan.
10 Alicia, ¿qué libro lees?

5 1 Sí, (No, no) tengo hermanas.
2 Sí, (No, no) quiero tomar una taza de café.
3 Sí, (No, no) vengo a la fiesta.
4 Sí, (No, no) digo la verdad.
5 Sí, (No, no) veo el lago.
6 Sí, (No, no) doy dinero a mis amigos.

7 Sí, (No, no) soy estudiante.
8 Sí, (No, no) oigo mucho ruido.
9 Sí, (No, no) pongo los libros en la mesa.
10 Sí, (No, no) voy a la playa hoy.
11 Sí, (No, no) hago la cena.
12 Sí, (No, no) traigo los libros a clase.
13 Sí, (No, no) sé hablar italiano.
14 Sí, (No, no) puedo tocar la guitarra.

59 / **1** 1 Tenemos dos coches.
2 Carmen viene a las tres.
3 Jaime sale mañana.
4 María, ¿vas al mercado? Necesitamos leche.
5 Rosa hace pan.
6 ¿Hablamos mañana?
7 Damos una fiesta para Antonio.
8 ¡El perro oye un ruido! ¿Oye Ud. algo?

2 1 Hablo francés desde mi primer día en París.
2 Venden ropa en esta tienda desde el año pasado.
3 Carmen y Felipe están casados desde 1972.
4 Mis tíos están aquí desde el martes.
5 Vivimos en los Estados Unidos desde la guerra civil.
6 Espero en la oficina desde las diez y media.
7 Debo el dinero a Mario desde el 14 de agosto.

3 1 ¡Concha habla por teléfono desde hace una hora!
2 Los niños juegan en el patio desde hace media hora.
3 Tenemos este coche azul desde hace tres meses.
4 Guillermo está enfermo desde hace unos días.
5 Escribo a mi amigo en español desde hace seis meses.
6 Los jóvenes están en la playa desde hace tres horas.
7 Espero desde hace poco tiempo.

4 1 Hace dos años que Felipe estudia en la universidad.
2 Hace unos pocos minutos que estoy aquí en el parque.
3 Hace unos meses que vivimos en este apartamento.
4 Hace mucho tiempo que Elisa se interesa en la música.
5 Hace tres años que Jorge juega al fútbol.
6 Hace tres meses que conozco a Roberto.

5 1 Los niños duermen desde las tres.
2 Hace dos horas que hablamos. (Hablamos desde hace dos horas.)
3 Hace cinco días que viajamos por coche. (Viajamos por coche desde hace cinco días.)
4 ¿Desde cuándo esperas?
5 Espero desde las nueve.
6 Hace diez años que el señor Pérez trabaja aquí. (El señor Pérez trabaja aquí desde hace diez años.)
7 Hace una hora que juegan a las cartas. (Juegan a las cartas desde hace una hora.)
8 Hace diez minutos que leo. (Leo desde hace diez minutos.)

60 / **1** 1 tomábamos
2 preparaba
3 ganaba
4 estudiaban
5 buscaba
6 pagaba
7 esperábamos
8 enseñabas
9 hablaba
10 jugaba

2 1 leía
2 sabían
3 aprendía
4 comíamos
5 creían / podíamos
6 corría
7 caía

3 1 veía
2 eran
3 íbamos
4 veía
5 iba
6 éramos

61 /

1
1 eran
2 había
3 jugaban
4 esperaba
5 era
6 hacía
7 cantaban

2
1 veía
2 llegaban
3 traían
4 querían
5 gritaban
6 jugaban
7 había
8 oía
9 trataban

3
1 leía
2 iba
3 escribía
4 trabajábamos
5 estabas

4
1 comíamos
2 iban, jugaban
3 veía
4 volvía
5 escuchábamos, paseábamos

5
1 Salía de la casa cuando vi el accidente.
2 Roberto visitaba Francia todos los veranos.
3 Elena y yo estudiábamos cuando llegó María.
4 Tomaba el autobús todos los días.
5 Los muchachos miraban la televisión cuando llamó su mamá.
6 El correo siempre llegaba por la mañana.
7 ¡Mi padre tomaba diez tazas de café todos los días!
8 Vivíamos en Venezuela.

6
1 conocían
2 estudiaba
3 estaban
4 esperaba
5 vivía

7
1 El señor Jiménez hablaba desde hacía una hora cuando salí.
2 Nuestros vecinos vivían en esa casa desde hacía muchos años cuando se quemó.
3 Hacía un mes que Alicia estaba aquí cuando conoció a Tomás.
4 Llovía desde hacía una hora cuando llegó mi tío.

62 /

1
1 María cantó ayer por la radio nacional.
2 ¿Terminaron la construcción del hospital ayer?
3 Víctor, ¿viajaste ayer a la finca?
4 Mis abuelos llegaron ayer a Lima.
5 Mi abogado y yo hablamos ayer sobre el nuevo contrato.
6 Los jóvenes empezaron su viaje a Francia ayer.
7 Alicia y yo jugamos al tenis ayer.
8 Me levanté temprano ayer.
9 La criada lavó la ropa ayer.

2
1 escribió, *wrote*
2 comimos, *ate*
3 entendieron, *understood*
4 abriste, *did you open*
5 salí, *I left*
6 aprendiste, *did you learn*
7 prometió, *promised*
8 volvimos, *returned*

3
1 diste
2 fuimos
3 fui
4 fueron
5 fui
6 fue
7 dio
8 di
9 fueron

4
1 pudimos
2 dije
3 supieron
4 vino
5 hiciste
6 puso
7 trajo

8 quisieron, pudieron
9 tuvo
10 estuvo
11 condujo
12 hizo
13 estuvieron
14 dijo

5
1 Juan compró un reloj nuevo ayer.
2 Carmen, ¿leíste el periódico?
3 Vimos el accidente anoche.
4 Ricardo vendió su motocicleta.
5 Escribí tres cartas anoche.
6 El mecánico vino esta tarde.
7 Tomás fue con su hermano.
8 ¡Mi hijo comió cinco huevos esta mañana!
9 Señor Campos, ¿llegó Ud. por avión?

63 /

1
1 fui
2 dijo
3 quisieron
4 compré
5 di
6 me senté
7 vi
8 entendí
9 estuve
10 volví

2
1 entraron
2 dio
3 miraron
4 pidieron
5 tardó
6 volvió
7 llegué
8 ví
9 comí
10 pagamos
11 salimos

64 /

1
1 fui
2 llegué
3 hablaba
4 bailaban
5 tocaban
6 cantaban
7 saludé
8 felicité
9 entré
10 quería
11 conocí
12 sabían
13 salí
14 volví
15 me acosté

2
1 salimos
2 subimos
3 fuimos
4 esperaban
5 había
6 eran
7 regresaban
8 nos sentamos
9 tomamos
10 hablamos

3 Cuando me desperté llovía. Me lavé y bajé. Había mucha gente en el comedor del hotel. Mis amigos desayunaban. Los saludé y me senté con ellos. Mientras comíamos, Roberto, nuestro chófer, entró y pidió una taza de café.

65 /

1
1 llamará
2 iremos
3 me levantaré
4 volverás
5 preparará
6 estará
7 hablaremos
8 abrirán
9 comeré
10 verán

2
1 sabré
2 diré
3 tendré
4 saldré
5 haré
6 podré
7 vendré
8 valdré
9 querré
10 habré

3
1 No, querrán ir mañana.
2 No, harán la cena mañana.
3 No, la señora Gutiérrez podrá venir mañana.
4 No, habrá muchas personas en el mercado mañana.
5 No, este boleto valdrá mucho dinero mañana.
6 No, los muchachos sabrán la lección mañana.
7 No, Orlando tendrá que estudiar mañana.
8 No, el periódico dirá quién ganó el partido de básquetbol mañana.

66 /

1
1 El avión saldrá a las diez.
2 Comeremos con Susana y Juan.
3 Carolina, ¿qué harás mañana?
4 El niño dormirá diez horas.
5 Escribiré la carta mañana.
6 Quizás habrá una fiesta esta noche.
7 Juan y Víctor llegarán el lunes.
8 ¿Quién comprará los boletos?

2
1 El señor Cruz vivirá solo.
2 Ellos sabrán que no estamos en casa.
3 María pensará que no estamos en casa.
4 Carlos, tú leerás mucho.
5 Ana no puede venir. Estará enferma.

3
1 Someone is at the door. Who can it be?
2 It's ten o'clock. Where can Vincent be?
3 When will Fernando call? (I wonder when Fernando will call.)
4 It's 11:00 p.m. I wonder whether Diego is hungry.
5 Paco worked a lot today. I wonder whether he's tired.

4
1 ¿Dónde estará José?
2 ¿Qué hora será? ¿Serán las cuatro?
3 ¿Estará aquí Fernando?
4 ¿Llegará la carta hoy?

67 /

1
1 escribiría
2 recibirías
3 cerraría
4 se levantaría
5 hablaríamos
6 encontraríamos
7 me casaría
8 nos acostaríamos
9 decidiríamos
10 mandarían
11 pedirían
12 preguntarían
13 estaría
14 moriría
15 daría
16 iríamos
17 seríamos
18 venderían
19 comerías
20 aprendería

2
1 vendríamos
2 querríamos
3 tendríamos
4 diríamos
5 pondríamos
6 valdríamos
7 podríamos
8 habríamos
9 saldríamos
10 haríamos

68 /

1
1 esperarían
2 enseñaría
3 comerías
4 se levantaría, estaría
5 leería
6 permitirían
7 gustaría
8 escribirías

2
1 dijo, sabría
2 prometimos, podríamos
3 explicó, tendría
4 contestaron, saldrían
5 dijo, pondría
6 prometió, habría
7 dijo, haría

3
1 Juan dijo que iría.
2 El doctor dijo que hablaría con Ud.
3 Creíamos que verían la carta.
4 Prometiste que vendrías pronto.
5 Creía que la película sería muy interesante.

4
1 Serían las diez.
2 ¿Por qué llamaría Carlos?
3 ¡Vi algo en el patio! ¿Qué sería?
4 Susana y María regresaron. ¿Cuándo llegarían?
5 Son las doce. Creía que tendrías hambre, Paco.

5
1 My parents didn't answer the telephone. (I wonder) Where could they be?
2 I'm sleepy. (I wonder) Could it have been very late when I went to bed last night?
3 Jim didn't want to come with us. He was probably busy.
4 What would Augustine say? Would he be in agreement?

6
1 iríamos
2 podrías
3 estaría
4 tendría
5 sabría
6 serían

69 /

1
1 han esperado, *perfect*
2 habríamos llamado, *conditional perfect*
3 habías visitado, *pluperfect*
4 he perdido, *perfect*
5 habré salido, *future perfect*

70 /

1
1 hemos
2 ha
3 has
4 he
5 han
6 has

2
1 ha recibido
2 he leído
3 has visto
4 hemos visitado
5 han venido
6 he pagado
7 ha llegado
8 hemos tenido
9 han vivido
10 has dicho

71 /

1
1 hemos trabajado
2 has visto
3 ha ido
4 han jugado
5 he escrito

2
1 Pepe, ¿has visto mi sombrero?
2 ¡En un día hemos vendido treinta libros!
3 Esta semana he trabajado cincuenta horas.
4 El presidente ha anunciado un nuevo programa económico.
5 ¡He comido demasiado!

72 /

1
1 habíamos
2 había
3 había
4 habían
5 habías

2
1 habían comprado
2 había visto
3 habíamos abierto
4 habías tenido
5 habían hecho

6 me había despertado
7 habían traído
8 te habías acostado
9 habíamos puesto
10 había muerto

73 /

1
1 había construido
2 habían mandado
3 había preparado
4 había abierto

5 habíamos tenido
6 habían venido
7 habíamos viajado

2
1 Había perdido su dirección.
2 Juan vino a nuestra casa pero ya habíamos salido.
3 Había llovido mucho esa noche.
4 Teresa, ¿habías oído el cuento antes?
5 Un hombre llamado Pérez había ganado la lotería.
6 Alguien había robado mi reloj.
7 Habíamos ido a la corrida de toros temprano esa tarde.
8 La señora Cruz había contestado el teléfono y había dicho que su esposo no estaba en casa.

76 /

1
1 habrás
2 habrán
3 habré

4 habrá
5 habremos
6 habrá

77 /

1
1 habrá comenzado
2 habrá pasado
3 habrán comido

4 habrá empezado
5 habrán cerrado
6 habrá nevado

2
1 Son las diez. Pedro habrá ido a la universidad.
2 Habré comido antes de las ocho.
3 Para mañana Esteban habrá hablado con el señor Morales.
4 Al llegar a Santiago, habremos viajado quinientos kilómetros.
5 Estoy seguro que habrán abierto el restaurante antes de las seis.

3
1 Habremos tomado una calle equivocada.
2 Habrá llovido mucho aquí.
3 Habremos hablado por muchas horas.
4 ¡Habré perdido mis llaves!
5 El niño se habrá dormido.

78 /

1
1 habríamos venido
2 habrías sabido
3 habría regresado
4 habrían sido
5 habríamos hecho

6 me habría acostado
7 habrían visto
8 habría gustado
9 habríamos traído
10 habría construido

2
1 habría
2 habría
3 habría
4 habríamos
5 habrían

79 /

1
1 ¿Habría olvidado estos libros Antonio? *Could Anthony have forgotten these books?*
2 ¿Habría ido María con Felipe? *Could Mary have gone with Philip?*
3 Ana, ¿habrías pagado mucho dinero por este cuadro? *Ann, could you have paid a lot of money for this painting?*
4 ¿Nos habrían esperado Carolina y Susana desde las tres? *Could Caroline and Susan have waited for us since three o'clock?*
5 ¿Habríamos estado equivocados? *Could we have been mistaken?*

80 /

1
1 comer, dormir
2 venir
3 saber
4 ir
5 aprender, hablar
6 hablar
7 tocar

2
1 Vivir en esta ciudad es caro.
2 Tocar el violín es difícil.
3 Nadar y esquiar son mis deportes preferidos.
4 Ver para creer.
5 Mirar la televisión es aburrido.
6 Fumar es malo para la salud.

3
1 salir
2 trabajar
3 ir
4 visitar
5 llegar
6 leer
7 comer
8 llamar

4
1 al encontrar
2 al ver
3 al entrar
4 al abrir
5 al despertarse

81 /

1
1 bailando en la fiesta
2 bajando del autobús
3 trabajando todo el día
4 mirando la televisión
5 tomando café
6 jugando al dominó
7 escribiendo una carta
8 bebiendo vino
9 sufriendo mucho
10 abriendo las ventanas

2
1 durmiendo tarde
2 muriendo de hambre
3 leyendo una revista
4 trayendo los libros
5 sirviendo la comida
6 pidiendo más pan
7 diciendo la verdad
8 viniendo a tiempo
9 levantándose a las ocho

82 /

1
1 abriendo
2 viendo
3 cortando
4 pronunciando
5 hablando
6 mirando

2
1 Los muchachos que juegan al básquetbol son mis primos.
2 Esas mujeres que pasan van al mercado.
3 Ese hombre que se acerca a la casa es mi vecino.
4 Ese muchacho que corre se llama José.

83 /

1
1 está hablando
2 están trabajando
3 están durmiendo
4 estoy haciendo
5 estás esperando
6 estoy comiendo
7 se está bañando / está bañándose

2
1 estaban corriendo
2 estaba mirando
3 estábamos jugando
4 estaban abriendo
5 estábamos tomando
6 estaban lavando
7 estaba viviendo
8 estaba sirviendo

3
1 siguieron trabajando
2 seguí esperando
3 íbamos llegando
4 iba acostumbrándome
5 vino llorando
6 vinieron corriendo
7 anda buscando

4
1 Estoy buscando un buen restaurante.
2 Ana, ¿estás comiendo?
3 El tren iba llegando a Barcelona.
4 Estábamos mirando los aviones en el aeropuerto.
5 Mi padre siguió hablando.

84 /

1
1 aprendido
2 llegado
3 salido
4 trabajado
5 leído
6 comido
7 visto
8 dicho
9 muerto
10 vuelto
11 abierto
12 hecho
13 descubierto
14 escrito

85 /   **1** 1 perdidos
2 vendido
3 ocupados
4 escrita
5 sentada

6 cerradas
7 preocupado
8 preferido
9 hecho
10 terminado

2 1 salida
2 empleado
3 respuesta
4 vestido
5 muerto

6 parada
7 herido, herida
8 casados
9 invitados

3 1 ¡Estamos invitados a una fiesta!
2 La puerta está abierta.
3 ¿Cuántos empleados trabajan aquí?
4 Juan, ¿has visto mi pluma?
5 Habíamos celebrado mi cumpleaños.
6 La entrada estaba cerrada.

86 /   **1** 1 El Banco Nacional ha sido robado por dos ladrones.
2 Todas las habitaciones del hotel habían sido tomadas por los turistas.
3 Mi coche fue arreglado por mi amigo Fernando.
4 El sistema de ferrocarriles era controlado por el gobierno.
5 El nuevo contrato será escrito por nuestros abogados.

87 /   **1** 1 El telegrama fue recibido por los tíos de Paco.
2 El nuevo edificio fue inaugurado por el gobernador Juárez.
3 El accidente fue visto por dos policías.
4 Estos artículos fueron escritos por el señor Miró.
5 La explosión de la bomba fue oída por muchas personas.
6 El campeonato de fútbol fue ganado por los alemanes.
7 Este puente fue construido por el gobierno federal.

2 1 se sabe
2 se ve
3 se oye
4 se cree
5 se dice

3 1 venden
2 pagan
3 sirven
4 abren

4 1 por
2 de
3 por
4 de
5 por

5 1 La actriz fue rodeada por la policía.
2 Vimos una película seguida de las noticias.
3 El dinero fue encontrado por María.
4 Cerraron el cine la semana pasada.
5 *Don Quijote* fue escrito por Cervantes.

88 /   **1** 1 vendo, venda
2 vivo, viva
3 encuentro, encuentre
4 digo, digamos
5 puedo, puedas
6 pienso, piense

7 hago, hagamos
8 tengo, tenga
9 vengo, vengan
10 veo, veas
11 pongo, ponga
12 salgo, salga

2 1 sepa, esté, vaya, haya
2 des, estés, vayas, hayas, seas
3 dé, sepa, vaya, haya, sea
4 demos, sepamos, estemos, hayamos, seamos
5 den, sepan, estén, vayan, sean

269

89 /

1
1 bebieron, bebiéramos
2 dijeron, dijera
3 fueron, fuera
4 comieron, comieras
5 llegar, llegaran
6 vivir, viviera
7 encontrar, encontrara

8 dar, diera
9 seguir, siguieras
10 poner, pusieron
11 poder, pudieron
12 sentir, sintieron
13 venir, vinieron
14 tener, tuvieron

2
1 quisiera
2 pudieras
3 dieran
4 escuchara
5 habláramos
6 recordara

90 /

1
1 haya
2 hayan
3 hayas
4 haya

5 haya
6 hayamos
7 hayamos

91 /

1
1 hubieras hablado
2 hubiera hecho
3 hubieran escrito
4 hubieras traído

5 hubieran visto
6 hubiéramos puesto
7 hubiera vendido
8 nos hubiéramos quedado

92 /

1
1 Es necesario que Juan venga esta noche.
2 Puede ser que Paco llame por teléfono.
3 Es posible que Arturo vuelva antes de las seis.
4 Es natural que busquemos una casa más cómoda.
5 ¿Es preciso que te levantes a las siete, Carlos?
6 Es raro que veamos tantos camiones en este barrio.
7 Es probable que no tenga que trabajar mañana.

2
1 Siento mucho que Carmen no pueda acompañarme al cine.
2 Es lástima que no conozcamos esta ciudad.
3 Los padres se alegran que los hijos se diviertan en la finca.
4 Los oficiales temen que entre demasiada gente en el estadio de fútbol.
5 Tengo miedo que Susana pierda los discos.
6 Sentimos mucho que el coche de Paco no funcione.

3
1 Mis amigos dudan que Pedro se case con Luisa.
2 ¿No crees que Juan quiera estos libros?
3 Dudamos que nuestro tren llegue a tiempo.
4 No creemos que llueva esta noche.
5 Felipe duda que Carlos siempre pague sus cuentas.
6 No creo que esperemos a Catalina.

4
1 Mis tíos buscan un restaurante donde sirvan paella.
2 No hay nadie que me ayude.
3 Buscamos una casa que tenga dos pisos.
4 No hay nadie que sepa la dirección del señor Pacheco.
5 No hay nadie que sea rico.
6 No hay nadie que trabaje doce horas por día.
7 Busco un estudiante que sea de Chile.
8 Busco un reloj que funcione bien.

5
1 El banco prefiere que ustedes paguen sus cuentas.
2 ¿Quiere usted que la ayude, señora Martínez?
3 Exigen que tengamos los pasaportes en la frontera.
4 Ana nos ruega que le escribamos mucho.
5 Mis padres sugieren que busque trabajo para el verano.
6 Susana insiste en que venga a las ocho a comer.
7 Carlos me pide que lo llame por teléfono.
8 Fernando desea que traigamos unos discos populares.
9 ¿El oficial permite que entremos por esa puerta?
10 Los niños prefieren que vayamos a la piscina.
11 Los Salazar quieren que nos quedemos en Caracas dos días más.

6 1 Pedro nos abrirá la puerta para que entremos a trabajar temprano.
2 Paco vendrá a Bogotá a fin de que lo encontremos allí.
3 Compraré este abrigo con tal que mi madre lo pague.
4 Iré a México en coche a fin de que el viaje cueste menos dinero.
5 Enrique se acostará antes de que regrese su padre a las doce.
6 Voy a visitar Europa con tal que mis padres me lo permitan.
7 Leeremos el menú antes de que venga el mozo.

7 1 estén
2 volvió
3 comió
4 leyó
5 vengan
6 lleguemos
7 encuentre
8 toque
9 empezó
10 veamos

8 1 sean, estarán
2 pague, seremos
3 llegues, encontrarás
4 me sienta, iré

9 1 pueda
2 necesite
3 vieran
4 vaya

10 1 llueva
2 quiera
3 paguemos
4 practique
5 vayan
6 sirva

11 1 tengan
2 terminar
3 romper
4 lleve
5 viven
6 esté
7 sepa
8 pueda
9 pague
10 encuentran
11 valga

12 1 comprar
2 esperaras
3 conociera
4 llamara
5 comer
6 recordar
7 ver
8 vendiera
9 jugara
10 llegara

93 /
1 1 quería, limpiaras
2 preferían, comiéramos
3 temían, volviéramos
4 creía, costara
5 era, fuéramos
6 deseaba, trabajáramos
7 era, funcionara
8 esperaban, lloviera

2 1 era, hubiera recibido
2 creía, hubieran estudiado
3 sentíamos, hubieran olvidado
4 nos alegrábamos, hubiera ganado
5 dudaba, hubiéramos jugado
6 era, hubieran querido
7 temía, hubieran venido
8 teníamos, hubiéramos perdido

3 1 Juan quiere que vengamos mañana.
2 Mis padres querían que trabajara este verano.
3 Sentimos mucho que no hubiera hablado con la Sra. García.
4 No creía que Susana fuera tan joven.
5 Me alegro (de) que vendas tu motocicleta.
6 Me alegro (de) que hayas vendido tu motocicleta.
7 Era raro que Ricardo viniera aquí.
8 Es raro que Ricardo venga aquí.
9 ¿Conoce a un escritor que hable alemán?
10 ¿Conocía a un escritor que hablara alemán?

94 /
1 1 ir
2 servir
3 leer
4 no hacer
5 ver
6 venir

2 1 Mariana, siéntate un rato para poder hablar.

2 Javier compró los boletos para ir al teatro.

3 Discutimos el precio del taxi antes de salir de la estación.

4 Después de comer, Fernando saldrá para la universidad.

5 Los amigos vinieron a fin de hablar juntos.

6 Víctor se quedará en la oficina hasta terminar el trabajo.

3 1 aconsejan que vayas

2 permite que manejemos

3 manda que pague

4 es importante que vendamos

5 impide que sigamos

6 dejan que viva

95 / **1** 1 hago, haga, hagan

2 salgo, salga, salgan

3 cierro, cierre, cierren

4 pongo, ponga, pongan

5 veo, vea, vean

6 tengo, tenga, tengan

7 vengo, venga, vengan

8 digo, diga, digan

9 compro, compre, compren

10 oigo, oiga, oigan

11 sé, sepa, sepan

12 traigo, traiga, traigan

13 recuerdo, recuerde, recuerden

2 1 Pasen al comedor.

2 Salgan temprano.

3 Vuelvan a las once.

4 Duerman bien.

5 Suban al avión.

6 Laven los pisos.

3 1 dé

2 sean

3 vayan

4 estén

4 1 busquemos

2 demos

3 empecemos

4 abramos

5 juguemos

6 volvamos

5 1 vamos a traer

2 vamos a apagar

3 vamos a hacer

4 vamos a pasar

5 vamos a ir

6 vamos a tomar

7 vamos a comer

6 1 mira

2 escribe

3 lee

4 paga

5 trae

6 vuelve

7 responde

7 1 pida usted

2 viva usted

3 entre usted

4 escuche usted

5 busque usted

6 lave usted

7 describa usted

8 1 (tomar) no tomes

2 (salir) no salgas

3 (ir) no vayas

4 (poner) no pongas

5 (hacer) no hagas

6 (leer) no leas

7 (describir) no describas

8 (venir) no vengas

9 (ser) no seas

10 (tener) no tengas

9 1 no tome usted

2 no salga usted

3 no vaya usted

4 no ponga usted

5 no haga usted

6 no lea usted

7 no describa usted

8 no venga usted

9 no sea usted

10 no tenga usted

10 1 Amalia, trae mi abrigo.

2 Di la verdad.

3 No olvide usted su pasaporte.

4 ¡No se vayan!

5 Elena, ven aquí (acá). Come la cena.

6 Salgamos ahora.

7 Sé sincero.

8 Ponga los libros ahí.

9 Llamemos a la estación de trenes.

10 Siéntense, por favor.

96 /

1 1 buscáramos, encontraríamos
2 leyeran, sabrían
3 vinieras, verías
4 necesitara, pediría
5 llamaría, estuviera
6 comerían, tuvieran
7 entraríamos, llegáramos
8 verías, fueras
9 oirían, cerraran

2 1 habría salido
2 habríamos llegado
3 habría comprado
4 habría estudiado
5 habríamos ido
6 habría sido

3 1 hubiera manejado, habría tenido
2 hubiera sido, habríamos comprado
3 hubiera llegado, habríamos empezado
4 habría ido, hubiera estado
5 habríamos comido, hubieran sido
6 habría visitado, hubiera tenido

4 1 estuviera
2 sale
3 promete
4 comprarían
5 vendería
6 gustaría
7 me hubiera acostado
8 nos hubiéramos quedado

5 1 Si Javier termina a las seis, vendrá con nosotros.
2 Si Javier terminara a las seis, vendría con nosotros.
3 Si Javier hubiera terminado a las seis, habría venido con nosotros.
4 Compraré los boletos (billetes) si vamos por avión.
5 Compraría los boletos si fuéramos por avión.
6 Habría comprado los boletos si hubiéramos ido por avión.

6 1 Si me diera su dirección, le mandaría el paquete.
2 El Sr. Pérez habla como si fuera mi padre.
3 ¡Pablo vive como si fuera rico!
4 Si ellos compran (comprarán) la comida, traeremos el vino.
5 La Srta. Martínez canta como si fuera profesional.

97 /

1 1 son (A)
2 es (D)
3 es (C)
4 es (E)
5 son (B)
6 es (E)
7 soy (A)
8 son (B)

98 /

1 1 estamos (B)
2 están (A)
3 está (C)
4 están (B)
5 están (A)
6 estoy (D)
7 estás (D)

2 1 son (97E)
2 es (97A)
3 estoy (98D)
4 están (98D)
5 está (98A)
6 son (97B)
7 son (97E)
8 está (98A)
9 es (97B)
10 está (98D)
11 están (98B)
12 es (97D)

3 1 Soy de San Francisco. ¿De dónde es usted?
2 El banco está cerrado.
3 Estamos escuchando la música.
4 El libro es escrito por Enrique Lamadrid.
5 Alicia es de Venezuela pero ahora está en España.
6 Pedro, ¿estás listo? Son las seis.
7 Este pueblo es aburrido.
8 Juan es muy listo.
9 ¡Estoy muy contento hoy!
10 Hoy es lunes. ¿Dónde es la reunión?

11 --¿Es usted estudiante? --Sí, soy estudiante.
12 Mi coche es nuevo. Está en la calle.

99 /   **1** 1 Rose, you should write to your grandparents.
2 I must (ought to) study tonight.
3 When my father died, he owed a lot of money.
4 You must (probably) travel a lot, don't you?
5 Philip must have arrived in Paris today.

2 1 Debo visitar a mi tía en Lima.
2 El Sr. García debe de ganar mucho dinero.
3 Debo haber dormido diez horas anoche.
4 Pablo y Miguel deben haber salido.
5 Jorge debe treinta pesos por los boletos (billetes).
6 Ricardo, debes ir a la reunión.
7 Debo llamar al aeropuerto.

100 /   **1** 1 Sí, (No, no) me gusta la comida italiana.
2 Sí, (No, no) me gusta el clima de esta región.
3 Sí, (No, no) les gusta a mis amigos hablar español.
4 Sí, (No, no) les gustan a mis amigos las películas extranjeras.
5 Sí, (No, no) me gustan los vinos de California.
6 Sí, (No, no) me gusta levantarme temprano.
7 Sí, (No, no) me gusta viajar.
8 Sí, (No, no) me gusta el español.
9 Sí, (No, no) me gustó la cena anoche.
10 Sí, (No, no) me gustaron las noticias del periódico ayer.
11 Sí, (No, no) les gustó a mis amigos la fiesta.
12 Sí, (No, no) me gustaría visitar Europa.
13 Sí, (No, no) me gustarían las playas de Acapulco.
14 Sí, (No, no) me falta dinero.
15 Sí, (No, no) me falta un coche.
16 Sí, (No, no) me faltan amigos.
17 Sí, (No, no) me queda mucho tiempo libre.
18 Sí, (No, no) me quedan muchos pesos.
19 Sí, (No, no) les quedan a mis amigos muchos discos populares.

2 1 Me quedan diez dólares.
2 ¿Le gustan las uvas?
3 Nos gusta nadar.
4 A Ernesto le falta el dinero para comprar un tocadiscos.
5 Me gustaría un coche.
6 A Marcos le quedan cinco dólares.

101 /   **1** 1 Hay muchos estudiantes aquí.
2 Hay que saber leer y escribir.
3 ¿Hay algunos restaurantes en esta calle?
4 Hay que trabajar para vivir.
5 ¡Hay una fiesta esta noche!
6 Hemos de salir inmediatamente para España.
7 Hay mucho ruido en esta calle.
8 Ha de llamar al hospital inmediatamente.
9 Había diez hijos en mi familia.
10 Hubo una reunión anoche.

102 / **1** 1 Sí, (No, no) hace buen tiempo hoy.

2 Sí, (No, no) hizo buen tiempo ayer.

3 Sí, (No, no) hará buen tiempo este fin de semana.

4 Hace . . . .

5 En verano aquí hace . . . .

6 En invierno aquí hace . . . .

7 Hace más calor en Arizona.

8 Sí, (No, no) hace mucho frío aquí.

3 1 ¿Qué tiempo hace?

2 ¡Hace calor!

3 Vendieron el coche hace tres meses.

4 Hice construir un garaje.

5 ¿Hizo coser ese vestido?

6 Llovió hace dos días.

7 Hicimos mandar el paquete por correo.

8 Hace buen tiempo hoy.

2 1 El señor Rodríguez llamó hace media hora.

2 Marta ganó al tenis hace unos días.

3 Ese baile era popular hace unos años.

4 Inventaron la radio hace unos cincuenta años.

5 El presidente estuvo aquí hace tres meses.

103 / **1** 1 tiene frío

2 tienen hambre

3 tiene setenta y cinco años

4 tiene calor

5 tiene sueño

6 tiene cuidado

7 tenemos sed

8 tiene prisa

9 tiene miedo

10 tiene lugar

11 tiene éxito

12 tiene la culpa

2 1 Alicia dice que tiene sed. ¿Tienes sed, Juana?

2 Juan tiene que trabajar mañana.

3 Tenemos frío y tenemos hambre.

4 Marta, ¿tienes ganas de ir a la playa hoy?

5 Tengo diez y ocho años. ¿Cuántos años tienes tú?

6 Tuve que salir temprano.

7 Joaquín, tienes razón, mañana es viernes.

8 No puedo hablar ahora. Tengo prisa.

104 / **1** 1 se puso

2 se hizo, llegó a ser

3 se pone

4 se hizo

5 llegó a ser

6 se puso

7 se hicieron

8 se hizo

2 1 Juan quiere hacerse ingeniero.

2 ¿Quiere llegar a ser presidente de los Estados Unidos?

3 Carlos se puso muy nervioso en la boda.

4 Creo que mi tío se volvió loco.

5 Mi padre se ponía muy enojado conmigo.

6 La familia Hidalgo llegó a ser muy rica.

105 / **1** 1 se cortó

2 me despierto

3 se mató

4 se enoja

5 se peina

2 1 se sienta

2 me acuesto, me levanto

3 se siente

4 se acerca

5 nos divertimos

6 se despiertan

275

3 1 Se acuestan tarde y se duermen
    inmediatamente.
2 José, ¿por qué te sientas en mi silla?
3 ¿Se divierte en la playa?
4 Generalmente me despierto temprano.
5 Juan siempre se queja de la comida.

5 1 no se fijen
2 no te laves
3 no nos acostemos
4 no se siente
5 no se despierten
6 no te duermas
7 no se acuerden

4 1 despiértense, levántense
2 imagínate
3 atrévete
4 acérquese
5 fíjense
6 acostémonos
7 siéntate

6 1 ¡Acuéstense ahora mismo!
2 ¡Despiértate y levántate!
3 Por favor, no se sienten.
4 Juanito, preséntate a la señora.
5 No se olvide los boletos (billetes).

SPANISH-ENGLISH VOCABULARY

abbr.	abbreviation	*indef.* indefinite
adj.	adjective	*indir.* indirect
adv.	adverb	*inf.* infinitive
art.	article	*interr.* interrogative
cond.	conditional	*imp.* imperfect
conj.	conjunction	*m.* masculine
def.	definite	*obj.* object
dem.	demonstrative	*pers.* person
dir.	direct	*pl.* plural
f.	feminine	*p.p.* past participle

prep.	preposition/ prepositional
pret.	preterite
pres.	present
pron.	pronoun
refl.	reflexive
rel.	relative
sing.	singular
subj.	subject

The vocabulary which follows contains all Spanish words used in the exercises. Parts of speech are given when necessary to distinguish meanings of a word which is used in several functions. The gender of all nouns is indicated except that of masculine nouns in *-o* and feminine nouns in *-a*. If a verb is irregular, the principal parts are given, or if slightly irregular, the irregular forms. Reference to § 110 indicates that a verb is irregular and follows the pattern of the verb referred to; reference to § 107 indicates that the verb undergoes a spelling-change explained in the subsection given; radical-changing verbs are indicated by placing the vowel-change in parentheses after the verb. When there is one vowel-change in the present and the same or another in the preterite, both changes are indicated, as *dormir* (*ue, u*). The prepositional construction following a verb is indicated in parentheses wherever possible. Simple verbs that become reflexive with a reflexive meaning are given only in the simple form; when the meaning changes in the reflexive form, both simple and reflexive verbs are listed; when a verb is used simply and reflexively with the same English meaning, *-se* is indicated in parentheses, as *morir*(*se*). Parentheses around words indicate that they are being used as an example and that any other appropriate word might be substituted, as *tiene* (*veinte*) *años*, where any age could have been used. Idiomatic expressions containing verbs are given in the third person singular rather than in the infinitive. In cases where the Spanish adverb is formed by adding *-mente* to the adjective, only the adjectival form is given in this vocabulary. For instance, if the adverb *generalmente* is found in the exercises, only the adjective *general* will be found in this vocabulary.

Since in the Spanish alphabet *ch, ll,* and *ñ* are separate letters, they follow *c, l,* and *n* in alphabetical order; *rr* is not alphabetized as a separate letter.

A

a to; at, in, into, on, by, with, etc; (*after verbs of separation*) from; *not to be translated when* used to indicate the direct object (§44 A)
al sol in the sun; outdoors

a casa (to) home
a causa de because of
a fin de que in order that

a las (ocho) at (eight) o'clock
a lo largo along
a menos que unless
a menudo often
a pesar de in spite of
¿A qué hora? At what time?
a tiempo on time
a veces sometimes; at times
a ver let's see
abarcar grasp; encompass
  "Quien mucho abarca, poco
  aprieta." "Grasp all, lose all."
abierto (p.p. of abrir) opened;
  open
abogado lawyer
abrigo topcoat; overcoat
abril (m.) April
abrir (p.p. abierto) open
abuelita "dear old" grandmother
abuelo grandfather
aburrido (p.p. of aburrir) (§98 E)
  bored; boring
aburrirse be bored; become bored
acá (less precise than aquí) here,
  over here
acabar end, finish
  acaba de (llegar) he has just
  (arrived)
Acapulco tropical Mexican seaport on the Pacific noted for its
  beaches
accidente (m.) accident
aceite (m.) oil; olive oil
aceptar accept
acerca de (prep.) about, concerning
acercarse (a + noun) (§107 C)
  approach
acompañar accompany, go with
aconsejar (+ inf.; + que + subjunctive) (§94 C) advise
acordarse (ue) (de + inf.; de +
  noun) remember
acostarse (ue) go to bed
actividad (f.) activity
actor (m.) actor
actriz (f.) actress
acueducto aqueduct
acuerdo, de in agreement
además (adv.) besides, moreover
además de (prep.) besides
adiós good-by
adjetivo adjective
admirar admire

adonde where, to which
¿Adónde? Where? Where to?
adverbio adverb
aeropuerto airport
África Africa
africano, -a African
agosto August
agricultor (m.) farmer
agua (f. but el) water
Agustín Augustine
¡Ah! Ah! Oh! (interjection expressing surprise)
ahora now
  ahora mismo right now
aire (m.) air
al (a + el) to the
  al extranjero abroad
  al lado de beside
  al (llegar) upon (arriving)
Alaska Alaska
Alberto Albert
alegrarse (de + inf.; (de) que +
  subjunctive) be glad
alegre happy
alejarse (de + noun) go away,
  move away, draw away
alemán, -a German
Alemania Germany
Alfonso boy's name
algo (indef. pron.) something;
  (adv.) somewhat, rather
alguien someone, somebody
algún(o) (§10 A) (adj.) some,
  any; (pron.) someone, anyone,
  some, any
Alhambra famous Moorish palace
  and fortress in Granada
Alicia Alice
almorzar (ue) eat lunch; in some
  parts of the Spanish-speaking
  world it means "eat breakfast,"
  in others it refers to noon meal
almuerzo late morning lunch;
  breakfast
Alonso boy's name
alrededor (adv.) around, about
alrededor de (prep.) around
alto high; tall; (referring to voice)
  loud
alumno, alumna pupil
allá (farther away than allí) there
  más allá farther
allí there
  por allí over there, around there

amable (adj.) kind
amado (p.p. of amar) loved; (p.p.
  as noun) loved one
Amalia girl's name
amante (m. and f.) lover
amar love
amarillo yellow
americano, -a American
América America
  Norte América North America
  Sud América South America
amigo friend
amistad (f.) friendship
amor (m.) love
Ana Ann
ancho wide, broad
Andalucía Andalusia, region of
  southern Spain
andar (pret. anduve) (§110, no. 9)
  go (without definite destination);
  walk
animal (m.) animal
anoche last night
ansioso anxious
antes (adv.) (in time) before,
  sooner
antes de (prep.) before
  antes de (comer) before (eating)
antes (de) que (+ subjunctive)
  (conj.) before
antiguo (of things) old, ancient
Antonio Anthony
año year
  tiene (veinte) años he is
  (twenty) years old
apagar (§107 B) turn off, put out
apartamento apartment
aplicado industrious
aprender (a + inf.) learn
apretar tighten, clutch
  "Quien mucho abarca, poco
  aprieta." "Grasp all, lose all."
aprovechar profit by, take advantage of (an opportunity)
aprovecharse (de + noun) take advantage of
aproximado approximate
aquel, aquella, aquellos, aquellas
  (dem. adj.) that, those
aquél, aquélla, aquéllos, aquéllas
  (dem. pron.) that one; the
  former; that; those; they
aquí here
  por aquí this way

árbol (m.) tree
Argentina, la country in southern part of South America
Arizona state in the United States
arquitectura architecture
arreglar put in order, fix
arrestar arrest
arroz (m.) rice
arte (m. and f. but el) art
artículo article
  artículo determinado definite article
  artículo indeterminado indefinite article
artista (m. and f.) artist
Arturo Arthur
asesinar assassinate; murder
asesino assassin; murderer
así so, thus, in this way
asiento seat
asistir attend, be present at
  asiste a (la clase) he attends (class)
aspecto aspect
aspirina aspirin
asustar frighten, scare
asustarse de be afraid of
Atlántico Atlantic
atleta (m.) athlete
atreverse (a + inf.) dare
aunque although
autobús (m.) bus
automóvil (m.) automobile, car
autor (m.) author
avanzar (§107 A) advance
avenida avenue
avión (m.) airplane
avisar inform, let know
¡Ay! Oh!; Ouch! (expressing pain)
ayer yesterday
ayuda help
ayudar help, aid
azteca (adj. m. and f.) Aztec
azúcar (m.) sugar
azul blue

B

bailar dance
baile (m.) dance
bajar go down; bring down
bajo (adj.) low; (prep.) under

banco bank
bañarse take a bath
bañera bathtub
baño bath; bathroom
Barcelona second largest city of Spain, located in the northeastern part of Spain on the Mediterranean in the region of Catalonia
barrio district (of a city)
básquetbol (m.) basketball
bastante (adj. and pron.) enough; (adv.) enough; rather; rather much
Beatriz Beatrice
bebé (m. or f.) baby
beber drink
béisbol (m.) baseball
bello beautiful
bicicleta bicycle
bien (adv.) well; clearly, perfectly; very
billete (m.) (Spain) ticket; (paper) bill
biología biology
blanco white
blusa blouse
boca mouth
boda wedding
Bogotá Bogota, capital of Colombia
boleto (Mexico) ticket
Bolivia country of South America
bolsillo pocket
bomba bomb
bonito pretty
Brasil, el Brazil
brazo arm
breve short; brief
buen(o) (§10 A) good
  buenos días good morning
  buenas tardes good afternoon
  hace buen tiempo it is good weather
burlar ridicule, mock
  burlarse de to make fun of, poke fun at
buscar (+ noun) (§107 C) seek, look for; get

C

caballo horse
caber fit
cabeza head
cada (adj. m. and f.) each, every
caer (pres. yo caigo) (§110, no. 11) fall
  caerse fall down
café (m.) coffee; popular establishment, often with terrace on sidewalk, where drinks are sold
caída fall
cajón (m.) box
cámara camera; chamber
  cámara de representantes chamber of representatives
camarero waiter
cambiar (de + noun) change
caminar walk; travel
camino road
camión (m.) truck; (Mexico) bus (especially city bus)
camisa shirt
campeonato championship
campesino farmer, peasant
campo field; country (as contrasted with city)
Canadá, el Canada
canción (f.) song
Candia girl's name
cansado tired
cantar sing
cantidad (f.) quantity
capital (f.) capital (city)
capitán (m.) captain
capítulo chapter
cara face
Caracas capital of Venezuela
Cárdenas (Lázaro) (1895–1970) reformist president of Mexico from 1934 to 1940
Caribe, el Caribbean
Carlos Charles
Carmen girl's name
carnaval (m.) carnival
carne (f.) meat
caro dear, expensive
Carolina Caroline
carrera career; running, race
carretera highway
carta letter; (pl.) playing cards
cartera billfold, purse
casa house

a casa (to) home

en casa at home

casado married

los casados married couple

casarse (*con* + person) marry, get married

casi almost

casita little house

catalán, -a Catalan, referring to the region of Catalonia; language of Catalonia; native of Catalonia

Catalina Catherine

Cataluña Catalonia, region of northeastern Spain of which Barcelona is the capital

católico Catholic

catorce fourteen

causa cause

a causa de because of

Cecilia girl's name

celebrar celebrate; hold an event

célebre famous

cena supper

centro downtown; center

Centro América Central America

cerca (adv.) near, near by

cerca de (prep.) near

cerrar (ie) close, shut

Cervantes (Miguel de) (1547–1616) famous Spanish author of *Don Quijote*

cerveza beer

César Caesar

cielo sky

cien(to) (*§10 C*) hundred

cierto (*§4 I*) certain

cigarillo cigarette

cinco five

cincuenta fifty

cine (m.) movie(s), cinema

ciudad (f.) city

civil civil; civilian

guerra civil civil war

civilización (f.) civilization

Clara Claire

claro clear

clase (f.) class; kind, sort

sala de clase classroom

clásico classic; classical

Claudia Claudia

clima (m.) climate

clínica clinic

coche (m.) car

cocina kitchen

colegio private secondary school; boarding school

colina hill

Colombia country in South America

comedor (m.) dining room

comenzar (ie) (*a* + inf.) (*§107 A*) begin

comer eat

comercial commercial

cómico comedian, comic

comida meal; dinner (in Spain the largest meal, which is usually served at about two o'clock in the afternoon)

como as, like, such as; when; since; provided that

¿Cómo? How? Why? What?

¡Cómo no! Of course! Certainly!

¿Cómo se llama . . .? What is the name of . . .?

tan . . . como as . . .as

tanto . . . como as much . . . as

cómodo comfortable, convenient

compañero companion

compañero de escuela classmate

compañía company

completo complete

complicado complicated

compra purchase

comprar buy

con with

con cuidado with care, carefully

con tal que (+ subjunctive) (conj.) provided that

Concha diminutive form of girl's name *Concepción*

condición (f.) condition

condicional (m.) conditional

conducir (*§110, no. 12*) lead, conduct

conferencia conference, lecture

confiar (+ *en*) trust, rely on

conmigo (*con* + *mí*) with me

conocer (pres. *yo conozco*) (*§110, no. 13*) be acquainted with, know; meet

conocido well-known; famous

conseguir (i, i) (+ inf.) (*§107 H*) get, secure, obtain

conservador, -a conservative

conservar preserve, keep

consigo with himself; herself, themselves, yourself, yourselves

consistir (*en* + inf.; *en* + noun) consist

consonante (f.) consonant

Constanza Constance

construcción (f.) construction

construir (*§110, no. 14*) construct

Consuelo girl's name

contaminación (f.) contamination, pollution

contar (ue) tell, relate; count

contento content, happy

contestación (f.) answer

contigo (*con* + *ti*) with you

continente (m.) continent

contra against

contrario contrary

contrato contract

control (m.) control

controlar control

conversar converse, talk

corazón (m.) heart

Córdoba Spanish city in Andalusia

coronel (m.) colonel

correo mail

por correo by mail

correr run

corresponde(n) corresponds (correspond)

corrida bullfight

corrida de toros bullfight

cortar cut

cortés courteous

cosa thing

Costa Rica country in Central America

costar (ue) cost

costumbre (f.) custom

creer (*§110, no. 21*) believe

criado, criada servant

crisis (f.) crisis

cruel cruel

cruz (f., pl. *cruces*) cross

cruzar (*§107 A*) cross

cuadro painting

cual, el (rel. pron.) who, which

¿Cuál? (interr. pron.) Which? Which one? What?

lo cual which

cualquier(a) (adj.) (*§10 E*) any, anyone at all; (pron.) anyone

cuando when

¿Cuándo? When?

cuanto as much as, as many as

  en cuanto as soon as

  en cuanto a as for

¿Cuánto? How much?

¡Cuánto! How much!

cuarenta forty

cuarto room

cuarto fourth

Cuba Cuba

cubierto (p.p. of *cubrir*) covered

cubrir (p.p. *cubierto*) (*de* + noun) cover

cuenta bill

cuento (short) story, tale

cuerpo body

cuidado care

  con cuidado with care, carefully

  tiene cuidado he takes care

cultivar cultivate

cultura culture

cumpleaños (m. sing. and pl.) birthday

cumplir fulfill, keep (a promise)

  cumplir con fulfill, keep

curso course

cuyo whose, of whom

CH

Chapultepec name of wooded park in Mexico City

cheque (m.) check

chica (noun) (*Spain*) girl

chico (noun) (*Spain*) boy

Chile country in South America

chileno Chilean

chocolate (m.) chocolate

chófer (*Spain*), **chofer** (*Mexico*) (m.) chauffeur, driver

D

dar (*doy, di, dado*) (*§110, no. 15*) give

David boy's name

de of; from; about; with, etc. (*after a comparative*) than; (*after a superlative*) in

  de acuerdo in agreement

  de casa from home

de la mañana in the morning;

  son las (diez) de la mañana it's (ten) o'clock in the morning

de la tarde in the afternoon

de la noche at night

de manera que so that

de modo que so that

de vez en cuando from time to time

debajo (adv.) underneath, beneath

debajo de (prep.) under

deber (+ inf.; *de* + inf.) (*§99*) ought to, should, must; (*followed by noun*) owe

  debe de (estudiar) he must (probably does) (study)

decidir (+ inf.) decide

decidirse (*a* + inf.) decide; make up one's mind

decir (*digo, dije, dicho*) (*§110, no. 16*) say; tell

decisión (f.) decision

dedo finger

defecto defect

dejar leave; let

  deja de (hablar) he stops (talking)

del (*de* + *el*) of the

delante (adv.) in front

delante de (prep.) in front of

delgado thin, slender

demasiado too; too much

dentista (m.) dentist

dentro (adv.) within

dentro de (prep.) inside of

deporte (m., usually plural) sport

derecho (adj.) right, straight

  a la derecha to the right

desayuno breakfast

desayunar eat breakfast

descansar rest

describir (p.p. *descrito*) describe

descubrir (p.p. *descubierto*) discover

desde (prep.) (*of place*) from; (*of time*) since

  desde hace (*§59 B*) for, since

  desde hacía (*§61 C*) for, since

desear (+ inf.) desire, wish

despacio slow, slowly

despedirse (**i, i**) (*de* + noun) say good-by to, take leave of

despertarse (**ie**) wake up

después (adv.) after, afterwards

después de (prep.) after

después (de) que (conj.) after

destruir (*§110, no. 14*) destroy

detalle (m.) detail

detective (m.) detective

detrás (adv.) behind

detrás de (prep.) behind

devolver (**ue**) return (to a person), give back

di (pret. of *dar*) I gave

día (m.) day

  hoy día today

Día de los Reyes Epiphany, January 6. Celebrated in Spanish-speaking countries as the day the three kings bring gifts to the children

dice (pres. of *decir*) he says

dicho (p.p. of *decir*) said

diciembre (m.) December

Diego James

diente (m.) tooth

diera, diese (imperfect subjunctive of *dar*) gave

diez ten

diferencia difference

diferente different

difícil difficult

dificultad (f.) difficulty

digo (pres. of *decir*) I say

dije (pret. of *decir*) I said

dinero money

dios (m.) god

  ¡Dios mío! Good heavens!

diplomático diplomatic; diplomat

dirección (f.) address, direction

director (m.) manager, director

dirigirse (*a* + noun) (*§107 D*) direct oneself toward, make one's way toward; turn to; address, speak to

disco record

discusión (f.) discussion

discutir discuss, argue

distinguido (adj.) distinguished

distinguir (*§107 H*) distinguish

divertido amusing

divertirse (**ie, i**) have a good time, amuse oneself

dividir divide

doce twelve

docena dozen

doctor (m.) doctor
documento document
dólar (m.) dollar
domingo Sunday
Domingo boy's name
don Don, Sir (a title of respect used before the Christian names of men)
Don Quijote main character in Cervantes' work of the same name
doña Lady (a title of respect used before the Christian names of women)
donde where, in which
¿Dónde? (§21) Where?
¿Adónde? Where(to)?
¿De dónde? From where?
¿Por dónde? Whereabouts? Which way?
dormir (ue, u) sleep
dormirse (ue, u) go to sleep
dos two
doy (pres. of dar) I give
dudar doubt
dueño owner; master
durante during
duro hard

E

e (used before words beginning with i- and hi-) and
economía economy
económico economic; economical
edad (f.) age
edificio building
Eduardo Edward
ejercicio exercise
ejército army
el, la, los, las (def. art.) the; (dem. pron.) the one; he; that
el que he who, the one who, that
él (subj. pron.) he; it; (prep. obj. pron.) him; it
elección (f.) election
electricidad (f.) electricity
elegir (§107 D) elect
Elena Ellen, Helen
Elisa Lisa
ella (subj. pron.) she; it; (prep. obj. pron.) her; it
ellas they; them

ello (neuter prep. pron.) it
ellos they; them
embajada embassy
Emilio boy's name
empezar (ie) (a + inf.) (§107 A) begin
empleado employee
emplear use, employ
en in; into; on, upon, etc.
en casa at home
en cuanto as soon as
en cuanto a as for
en lugar de instead of
en punto exactly
en vez de instead of
encima (adv.) above
encima de (prep.) above, on, on top of
encontrar (ue) meet; find
se encuentra he is; he finds himself; it is located
enemigo enemy
enero January
enfermar(se) become sick
enfermera nurse
enfermo (adj.) sick; (noun) sick person
enfrente (adv.) in front; opposite
enfrente de (prep.) in front of; opposite
engañar deceive, mislead
enojado angered, angry
enojar anger
Enrique Henry
enseñar (a + inf.) show; teach
entender (ie) understand (a language)
entero entire, whole
entrada (noun) entrance
entrar (en + noun; a + noun) enter
entre between
época epoch, period
equipo team
equivocado mistaken
equivocar(se) be mistaken
Ernesto Ernest
errar (pres. yo yerro) be mistaken, commit an error
es (he, she, it) is
escalera stairs
escribir (p.p. escrito) write
escribir a máquina type

escrito (p.p. of escribir) written
escritor (m.) writer
escuchar (+ noun) listen
escuela school
ese, esa, esos, esas (dem. adj.) that, those (near person spoken to)
ése, ésa, ésos, ésas (dem. pron.) that one; that; those
eso (neuter dem. pron.) that
por eso therefore, for that reason
espacio space
España Spain
español, -a Spanish; Spaniard; Spanish language
espantar drive away, frighten
especial special
especialista (m. and f.) specialist
esperar (+ inf.; + noun) hope; wait for
esposa wife
esposo husband
esquina corner
está(n) he is (they are)
estación (f.) season; station
estación de gasolina "gas" station
estadio stadium
estado state
Estados Unidos, los the United States
estar (estoy, estuve, estado) (§§98, 110, no. 17) be
estar de acuerdo be in agreement
estar preocupado be worried
estar de vacaciones be on vacation
estatua statue
este, esta, estos, estas (dem. adj.) this, these
éste, ésta, éstos, éstas (dem. pron.) this one, this; the latter; these
este (m.) east
Esteban Stephen
Estella Stella
estimar esteem
esto (neuter dem. pron.) this
estómago stomach
estoy (pres. of estar) I am
estrecho narrow
estrella star
estudiante student
estudiantil (adj.) student
organización estudiantil student organization
estudiar study
estudio study

estupendo wonderful, marvellous
estuve (pret. of *estar*) I was
Europa Europe
europeo European
exacto exact, exactly
examen (m.) examination
examinar examine
excelente excellent
excepto except
exigir (*§107 D*) require, demand
explicar (*§107 C*) explain
explosión (f.) explosion
expresar express
extranjero (adj.) foreign; (noun) foreigner

F

fábrica factory
fácil easy
facultad (f.) college or school of a university including buildings and teaching staff
  Facultad de Leyes School of Law
falda skirt
faltar lack, be lacking; be absent
familia family
famoso famous
farmacia drugstore; pharmacy
favor favor
  por favor please
favorito favorite
febrero February
fecha date
federal (adj.) federal
Federico Frederick
felicitar congratulate
Felipe Philip
feliz happy
feria festival, fair, carnival
Fernando Ferdinand
ferrocarril (m.) railroad
fértil fertile
fiesta party, feast
fijarse (*en* + noun) notice
filosofía y letras philosophy and letters; name of the school which teaches the humanities in the universities of the Spanish-speaking countries
fin (m.) end
  a fin de que (+ subjunctive) in order that

fin de semana weekend
finca country estate, farm
fino (adj.) fine, delicate, nice
firmar sign (one's name)
flor (f.) flower
foto (f.) photo, photograph
fotografía photograph
francés, -a French; Frenchman
Francia France
Francisco Francis
frase (f.) sentence
frente front
  frente a opposite
fresco (adj.) cool, fresh
  hace fresco it is cool
frío cold
  hace frío it's cold
  tiene frío he is cold
frontera border, frontier
fruta fruit
fuera, fuese (imperfect subjunctive of *ser* and *ir*) were; went, would go
fuera (adv.) outside
fuera de (prep.) outside, outside of
fuerte strong
fui (pret. of *ser* and *ir*) I was; I went
funcionar work, function, operate
fumar smoke
fútbol (m.) football
futuro future

G

Gabriela girl's name
gafas (eye) glasses
ganar earn; win; gain
garaje (m.) garage
García very common family name in Spanish-speaking countries
gasolina gasoline
  estación de gasolina "gas" station
general (adj.) general; (noun, m.) general
  por lo general generally
generoso generous
gente (f.) people
geografía geography
Gerardo boy's name

Gloria girl's name
gobernador (m.) governor
gobierno government
Gonzalo boy's name
gordo fat; big
Goya (Francisco de) (1746–1828) outstanding realistic Spanish painter
gracias thank you
Graciela Grace
gramática grammar
gran (shortened form of *grande*) (*§10 B*) large; great
Granada Spanish city in Andalusia, noted for the Alhambra
gran(de) (*§10 B*) large, big; great, grand
grave grave, serious
Gregorio Gregory
gritar shout
guante (m.) glove
guapo good-looking, handsome
guerra war
Guillermo William
guitarra guitar
gustar (*§100 A*) please, be pleasing
gusto pleasure
  con mucho gusto with great pleasure, willingly

H

haber (*he, hube, habido*) (*§§101, 110, no. 18*) (*as auxiliary verb in perfect tenses*) have
  ha de (salir) he is (to leave)
había (imp. of *haber*) there was, there were
hábil agile; clever, able
habitación (f.) room
habitante (m. and f.) inhabitant
hablar speak
hace (+ time expression) (*§102 B*) ago
hace (+ time expression) **que** (*§59 B*) for
hacer (*hago, hice, hecho*) (*§§102, 110, no. 19*) make, do; have (someone do something)
  hace calor it is hot
  hacer la comida prepare dinner; have dinner
  hace fresco it is cool

hace frío it is cold

hace buen tiempo it is good weather

hace mal tiempo it is bad weather

hace preguntas he asks questions

hace sol the sun is shining

hace un viaje he takes a trip

hace viento it is windy

se hace (presidente) he becomes (president)

hacia toward

hacía, desde (+ time expression) (§61 C) for

hacienda country estate, farm

hago (pres. of hacer) I do, I make

hallar find

hambre (f. but el) hunger

tiene hambre he is hungry

hasta up to, as far as, to; until; even; including

hasta (el jueves) until (Thursday)

hasta que (conj.) until

hay (§101 A, B, C) there is, there are

hay que it is necessary to, one must

haya(n) (subjunctive) there is, are; has, have

hecho (noun) deed, act; fact; (p.p. of hacer) done, made

herido (p.p. used as noun) wound; wounded person

herir (ie, i) wound

hermana sister

hermano brother

hermoso beautiful, fair; fine

herramienta tool

hice (pret. of hacer) I did, I made

hiciera, hiciese (imperfect subjunctive of hacer) did, made

hija daughter

hijo son; (pl.) sons (and daughters)

historia history; story

hizo (pret. of hacer) he did, he made

hombre (m.) man

honrado (adj.) honest, honorable, just

hora hour; time (of day)

¿A qué hora? At what time?

¿Qué hora es? What time is it?

hospital (m.) hospital

hotel (m.) hotel

hoy today

hubo (pret. of haber) there was, there were; (as auxiliary) he had

huelga strike

huevo egg

huracán (m.) hurricane

I

idea idea

idealista (adj. m. and f.) idealistic

idioma (m.) language

iglesia church

imaginar(se) imagine

impedir (i, i) prevent, hinder, keep from

importado imported

importancia importance

importante important

importar import, be important, matter

imposible impossible

inaugurar inaugurate

Incas, los ancient Indian civilization located in what is now Peru, Bolivia, Ecuador and Chile

independencia independence

indicar (§107 C) indicate

indicativo indicative

indirecto indirect

Inés Inez

infinitivo infinitive

influencia influence

ingeniería engineering

ingeniero engineer

Inglaterra England

inglés, -a English; Englishman; English language

inmediato immediate

inmenso immense

insistir (en + inf.; en + noun) insist

instituto institute; high school

inteligente (adj.) intelligent

interesante interesting

interesar interest

interesarse (por + noun; en + noun) be interested in

interrogativo interrogative

inventar invent

invierno winter

invitación (f.) invitation

invitado (p.p. used as noun) guest

invitar (a + inf.) invite

ir (voy, fui, ido) (a + inf.) (§110, no. 20) go

irregular irregular

irse (§110, no. 20) go away, go off

Isabel girl's name

Italia Italy

italiano Italian

izquierdo left

a la izquierda on the left, to the left

J

Jc. (abbr. for Jesucristo) Jesus Christ

jai-alai sport which originated in the Basque region in Spain, similar to handball and especially popular in Mexico

Jaime James, Jim

jardín (m.) garden

Javier Xavier

Joaquín Jack

Jorge George

José Joseph

Josefa Josephine

joven (adj.) young; (noun, m. and f.) youth, young man; young lady; (pl.) jóvenes

joya jewel

Juan John

Juanita Janet

Juanito Johnny

jueves (m.) Thursday

juez (m., pl. jueces) judge

juego game

jugar (ue) (§107 B) (a + def. art. + game) play

juega al (básquetbol) he plays (basketball)

jugoso juicy

juguete (m.) toy

Julieta Julia, Jill

Julio Julius

julio July

junio June

junto a (prep.) close to, beside, next to
juntos, -as (pl. adj.) together
justo (adj.) just, honest

K

kilo kilo (about 2.2 pounds)
kilómetro kilometer (about five-eighths of a mile)

L

la (def. art.) the; (dem. pron.) the one; she; that; (dir. obj. pron.) her, it
lado side
  al lado de alongside of, beside; with
ladrar bark
ladrón (m.) thief
lago lake
lámpara lamp
lápiz (m., pl. *lápices*) pencil
largo long
  a lo largo along
las the; them; those
lástima pity
  es (una) lástima it's too bad
Laura girl's name
lavada (p.p. of *lavar*) washed
lavar wash
lavarse wash oneself
le (dir. obj. pron.) him; you; (indir. obj. pron.) to him; to her; to you; to it
lección (f.) lesson
leche (f.) milk
leer (§110, no. 21) read
legumbre (f.) vegetable
lejos (adv.) far, far off, far away
  lejos de far from
lengua tongue; language
les (indir. obj. pron.) to them; to you
levantar raise, lift
levantarse get up; rise up
ley (f.) law
libertad (f.) liberty; freedom
libre free
librito little book
libro book

Lima capital of Peru
limpiar clean
limpio (adj.) clean
Lincoln (Abrahán) (1809–1865) president of the United States
lindo pretty
lista list
listo (§98 E) clever, ready
  es listo he is clever
  está listo he is ready
literario literary
literatura literature
litro liter (slightly more than a U.S. quart)
lo (neuter art.) the—thing; (dir. obj. pron.) it
  lo (bueno) the (good) thing
  lo de las hamacas that "business" about the hammocks
  lo cual which
  lo que what
loco crazy, mad; (noun) madman
Lorca (Federico García) (1899–1936) popular modern Spanish poet shot during the Spanish Civil War
Lorenzo Lawrence, Larry
los the; them; those
Los Ángeles City in California, U.S.
Lucía girl's name
luego then, next; presently
lugar (m.) place
  tiene lugar it takes place
  en lugar de instead of
Luis Louis
Luisa Louise
lumbre (f.) open fire
lunes (m.) Monday
luz (f., pl. *luces*) light

LL

llamar call
llamarse be called; be named
  ¿Cómo se llaman (los españoles)? What are (the Spanish) called?
llave (f.) key
llegada arrival
llegar (*a* + inf.; *a* + noun) (§107 B) arrive

llega a (hacerlo) he gets (to do it)
llega a (Italia) he arrives in (Italy)
llega a ser (presidente) he becomes (president)
llevar carry; wear; take
llevarse carry off, take away
llorar cry, weep
llover (ue) rain
lluvia rain

M

madre (f.) mother
Madrid capital of Spain
maestro teacher; master
magnífico magnificent
maíz (m.) corn
mal badly, poor(ly); ill; bad
mal(es) trouble(s)
maleta suitcase
mal(o) (§10 A) bad, wicked; wrong
  lo malo the bad feature, bad characteristic
mamá mother
mandar order, give orders; send
mando command
manejar drive (a vehicle)
manera way, manner
  de manera que so that
mano (f.) hand
Manuel boy's name
mañana (noun) morning; (adv.) tomorrow
mapa (m.) map
máquina machine
  máquina de escribir typewriter
  máquina de lavar washing machine
  máquina fotográfica camera
Marcos Mark
María Mary, Marie
Margarita Margaret
Mariana Maryann
marido husband
Mario boy's name
Marta Martha
martes (m.) Tuesday
Martí, (José) (1853–1895) Cuban poet, statesman and leader for independance from Spain

Martínez common Spanish family name

marzo March

más more

  más . . . que more . . . than

  más de more than

masculino masculine

matar kill

matemáticas (f. pl.) mathematics

mayo May

mayor elder, older; oldest; greater; greatest

me me, to me; myself

mecánico (noun) mechanic; (adj.) mechanical

media stocking

medicina medicine

médico doctor

medio (adj.) half; intermediate

  a las (cuatro) y media at half past (four)

mejor better

menor youngest, least; slightest; less

menos (adv.) less; least

  a menos que unless

  menos . . . que less . . . than

menos (prep.) except

menú (m.) menu

menudo, a often

mercado market

mes (m.) month

mesa table

mexicano -a Mexican

México Mexico, Mexico City

mezcla mixture

mi, mis my

mí (prep. obj. pron.) me

miedo fear

  tiene miedo he is afraid

miembro member

mientras while

  mientras que while

miércoles (m.) Wednesday

Miguel Michael

mil thousand

millón (m.) million

  un millón de (habitantes) a million (inhabitants)

ministerio ministry

  Ministerio de Economía Ministry of Economy

minoría minority

minuto minute

mío, mía, míos, mías mine; my

mirar (+ noun) look, look at; watch

misa mass

mismo self, very; same

  ahora mismo right now

moderno modern

modo mode; manner

  de modo que so that

momento moment

  momentito just a moment; second

Monica girl's name

montaña mountain

Monterrey third largest Mexican city, located in the north along the Pan American Highway

moreno dark; (noun) brunette

morir(se) (**ue, u**) (p.p. *muerto*) die

moro Moor

motocicleta motorcycle

mozo boy; waiter

muchacha girl

muchacho boy

mucho much, many, a lot; greatly

  muchas veces often

  por mucho que however much

mueble (piece of) furniture; (pl.) furniture

muerto (p.p. of *morir*) died; dead

mujer (f.) woman; wife

multa fine, payment

multitud (f.) multitude

municipal municipal

museo museum

música music

muy very

N

nacer (*§110, no. 13*) be born

nación (f.) nation

nacional national

nada nothing

nadar swim

nadie no one

naranja orange

nariz (f.) nose

natural natural

navegable navigable

Navidad (f.) Christmas

necesario necessary

necesitar need

negro black

nervioso nervous

nevar (**ie**) snow

ni nor, not . . . or; and not; not even

nieto grandson

ningún(o) (*§10 A*) no, not any, no one, none

niño child, little boy; (pl.) children

no no; not

  ya no no longer

noche (f.) night

nombrar name

nombre (m.) name

norte (m.) north

Norte América North America

norteamericano North American

nos us; to us; ourselves

nosotros (subj. pron.) we; (prep. obj. pron.) us

noticias (f. pl.) news

novecientos, -as nine hundred

novela novel

noventa ninety

noviembre (m.) November

novio lover, sweetheart, boy friend; fiance

nube (f.) cloud

nuestro our, ours

Nueva York (m.) New York

nueve nine

nuevo new; recent

número number

  número de teléfono telephone number

nunca never

O

o or; either . . . or

obligación (f.) obligation

obra work

obrero workingman, laborer

océano ocean

octavo eighth

octubre (m.) October

ocupado busy

ocupar occupy

ocuparse en busy oneself by

ocurrir occur

ochenta eighty
ocho eight
ochocientos, -as eight hundred
oeste (m.) west
oficial (adj.) official
oficina office
oír (*oigo, oí, oído*) (*§110, no. 22*) hear
¡Ojalá! I hope that, I wish that, would that
ojo eye
oliva olive
olivo olive tree
olvidar (+ inf.) forget
olvidarse (*de* + inf.) forget
once eleven
operación (f.) operation
oportunidad (f.) opportunity
oposición (f.) opposition
oreja ear
organización (f.) organization
oriental oriental
oriente (m.) orient
origen (m.) origin
Orlando boy's name
oro gold
os (dir., indir. and refl. obj. pron.) you (familiar pl.); yourselves
oscuro dark
otoño autumn
otro other, another
otra vez again
oye(n) hears (hear)

P

Pablo Paul
Pacífico Pacific
Paco boy's name
padre (m.) father; (pl.) parents
paella a famous Spanish dish consisting of Spanish rice with meat and seafood
pagar (*§107 B*) pay
país (m.) country
pájaro bird
palabra word
palmada handclap
Pampa, la a vast, fertile plain extending south and west of Buenos Aires, Argentina
pan (m.) bread

pantalón(es) (m.) trouser(s)
papel (m.) paper
paquete (m.) package
par (m.) pair
para (*§45 B*) for; to; in order to
para que (+ subjunctive) in order that
paraguas (m. sing. and pl.) umbrella
parecer (*§110, no. 13*) appear, seem; seem best
parecerse (*a* + noun) (*§110, no. 13*) resemble
pared (f.) wall
pariente (m.) relative
París Paris
parque (m.) park
parte (f.) part
participio pasado past participle
partido game (sport)
partido de (fútbol) (football) game
pasado (m.) past
pasado (adj.) past; last
(la semana) pasada last (week)
pasado mañana day after tomorrow
pasajero traveller, passenger
pasaporte (m.) passport
pasar pass; pass by; come in; spend (time); happen, take place
pasear(se) take a walk, take a ride
pasivo passive
patio (inner) courtyard, patio
Patricia girl's name
pedazo piece
pedir (i, i) (+ noun) ask, ask for; order (a meal)
Pedro Peter
peinar comb
película film
peligro danger
peligroso dangerous
pelo hair
peluquería barbershop
pensar (ie) (+ inf.; *en* + inf.; *en* + noun) think
piensa en (ir) he is thinking of (going)
peor worse; worst
Pepe (nickname for *José*) Joe
Pepita girl's name

pequeño little, small
perder (ie) lose
perfecto perfect
periódico newspaper
permiso permission
permitir (+ inf.) permit
pero but
perro dog
perrito puppy
persona person
pertenecer (*§110, no. 13*) belong
peso Mexican monetary unit, worth about 8 cents in American money
petróleo oil
pez (m., pl. *peces*) fish
Picasso (Pablo) (1881–1973) famous artist born in Spain who lived most of his life in France; known especially for his surrealistic style
pie (m.) foot
pierna leg
Pilar girl's name
pintor (m.) painter, artist
pintura painting
pirámide (f.) pyramid
piscina swimming pool
piso floor, story; (*Spain*) apartment
piso bajo ground floor
primer piso second floor
pistola pistol, gun
Pizarro (Francisco) (1475–1541) conqueror of Peru
plata silver
plato dish; course; plate
playa beach
plaza (in a city) square
plaza de toros bullring
pluma pen
pluscuamperfecto pluperfect
pobre poor
poco (adj.) little, (pl.) few; (adv.) little
poco a poco little by little
poder (ue) (*puedo, pude, podido*) (*§110, no. 23*) be able, can, could; be possible, may, might
poderoso powerful
poeta (m.) poet
policía (m.) policeman; (f.) police
política politics; policy
político (adj.) political; (noun) politician

pollo chicken
poner (*pongo, puse, puesto*) (*§110, no. 24*) put, place, set, turn on
ponerse (*§110, no. 24*) put on; begin; become
  se pone (el abrigo) he puts on (his topcoat)
popular popular
por by, through, on account of, because of; for, for the sake of, in behalf of; along, down; as; in, at; out of
  por aquí this way
  por avión by air; by plane
  por correo by mail
  por delante de in front of
  por donde whereabouts
  por eso therefore
  por favor please
  por hora per hour
  por la mañana in the morning
  por la tarde in the afternoon
  por la noche at night
  por lo general generally
  por lo menos at least
  por mucho que however much
  ¿Por qué? Why?
  por teléfono on the telephone
porque because
portátil portable
portugués Portuguese
posible possible
postre (m.) dessert
postrer(o) (*§10 A*) last in order
práctica practice
practicar practice
Prado, el famous Madrid art museum; boulevard which passes by the Prado
precio price
preciso necessary; precise
preferir (ie, i) prefer
pregunta question
  hacer preguntas ask questions
preguntar ask
premio prize
preocuparse (*de* + noun; *por* + noun) worry; pay attention to
  estar preocupado be worried
preparar prepare
presentar present; introduce
presente (m.) present
presidente (m.) president

primavera spring
primer(o) (*§10 A*) first
primo, prima cousin
principal principal; main
  calle principal main street
probabilidad (f.) probability
probable probable
problema (m.) problem
producir (*§110, no. 12*) produce
producto product
profesor (m.) professor, teacher
programa (m.) program
prometer (+ inf.) promise
pronombre (m.) pronoun
pronto soon
  tan pronto como as soon as
pronunciar pronounce
proteger protect
proyecto project
público (noun and adj.) public
pude (pret. of *poder*) I could
pueblo (small) town; people
puente (m.) bridge
puerta door; gate
punto point
  en punto exactly
puntual punctual
puse (pret. of *poner*) I put

Q

que who, whom, which, that; when; for; than
¿Qué? What? Which?
  ¿Qué tiempo hace? What's the weather like?
  ¿Qué hora es? What time is it?
¡Qué! What! What a! How!
  ¡Qué (interesante)! How (interesting)!
  ¡Qué (viaje) tan (magnífico)! What a (magnificent trip)!
quedar remain, be left; finally be; fit (clothing)
  quedar en agree on
quedarse stay
quejarse (*de* + noun) complain
quemar(se) burn
querer (ie) (*quiero, quise, querido*) (*§110, no. 25*) (+ inf.) wish, want; love (a person)
queso cheese
quien who, whom; he who, she who, whoever

¿Quién? (pl. *¿Quiénes?*) Who? Whom?
quiere(n) wishes (wish)
Quijote, Don leading character in Cervantes' famous novel by the same name
química chemistry
quince fifteen
quinientos, -as five hundred
quise (pret. of *querer*) I wished, I wanted to; I loved
  no quise I refused
quitar remove
quitarse take off; take away
quizá(s) perhaps

R

radio (m. or f.) radio
Rafael Raphael
Ramón Raymond
rápido (adj.) rapid; rapidly
Raquel Rachel
raro rare
rato while, (short) time
Raúl boy's name
razón (f.) reason
realidad (f.) reality
recepcionista receptionist, secretary
recibir receive
reconocer (*§110, no. 13*) recognize
recordar (ue) (+ noun) recall; remember; remind
regalo gift
región (f.) region
regresar return
reír (i, i) laugh
relativo relative
reloj (m.) watch; clock
repetir (i, i) repeat
resolver (ue) solve; decide
responder reply
respuesta answer
restorán restaurant
Retiro Madrid's most spacious and best known public park
retrato picture; photograph
reunión (f.) meeting
reunirse meet, gather together
revista magazine
revolución (f.) revolution

rey (m.) king
Ricardo Richard
rico rich
rincón (m.) corner
río river
robar steal, rob
Roberto Robert
rodear (de + noun; con + noun) surround
rogar (ue) (§107 B) ask, request
rojo red
romano Roman
romper (con + noun) break (away from)
ropa clothing
    ropa interior underwear
Rosa Rose
rubio blond
ruido noise
ruina ruin

S

sábado (m.) Saturday
saber (sé, supe, sabido) (+ inf.) (§110, no. 26) know (a thing); know how
sacar (§107 C) take out
    sacar una foto take a photograph
sala room; living room
salgo (pres. of salir) I go out, I leave
salida exit; departure
salir (pres. salgo) (de + noun) (§110, no. 27) go out, come out, leave
salón (m.) large hall; assembly room
saludar greet
saludo(s) greeting(s)
Salvador boy's name
san(to) (§10 D) saint
    San Agustín St. Augustine
    San Esteban St. Stephen
    San Francisco city of the United States named after St. Francis
    San Juan de Teotihuacán site of two Mexican Pyramids
    San Luis city of the United States named after St. Louis
    Santo Tomé St. Thomas
sangría Spanish beverage made

of wine, fruit juices and sugar
Sara Sarah
sargento sergeant
satisfacer (p.p. satisfecho) satisfy
se (§§27, 28, 31 B) himself, to himself, herself, yourself, themselves, yourselves; one
sé (pres. of saber) I know
sea (pres. subjunctive of ser) be
secretaria secretary
secreto secret
sed (f.) thirst
    tiene sed he's thirsty
Segovia City in Spain, located northwest of Madrid and known for its Roman aqueduct
seguida, en immediately
seguir (i, i) (§107 H) follow; continue
    sigue adelante he continues on, he goes ahead
    sigue (trabajando) he continues (working)
según (prep.) according to; (conj.) as
segundo second
seguro sure, certain; safe, secure
seis six
semana week
    fin de semana weekend
senador (m.) senator
sentarse (ie) sit down
sentir (ie, i) feel; be sorry, regret
sentirse (ie, i) feel, feel oneself
señor (m.) sir; Mr.; gentleman
señora madam; Mrs.; lady; wife
señorita Miss; young lady
sepa (pres. subjunctive of saber) know
ser (soy, fui, sido) (§§97, 110, no. 28) be
serio serious
servicio militar military service
servir (i, i) serve
sesenta sixty
setenta seventy
setiembre (m.) September
Sevilla Seville, large city of southern Spain
si (conj.) (§50) if; whether; why; but
sí (adv.) yes; (pron.) himself, herself, themselves, yourself, yourselves

entre sí among themselves
siempre always
Sierra Nevada mountain chain in extreme southern Spain
siete seven
siguiente following
silencio silence
silencioso silent
silla chair
sin without
    sin que (+ subjunctive) without
sincero sincere
singular (m.) singular
sino (§49 C) but
sino que (§49 D) but
sirvienta maid (Spain)
sistema (m.) system
sobre on, upon; over, above; about
sobrevivir survive
sofá (m.) sofa, couch
sol (m.) sun
    hace sol the sun is shining
    al sol in the sun; outdoors
    el sol se pone the sun sets
    se levanta el sol the sun is coming up
solamente only
soldado soldier
solicitar solicit, ask
sonreír smile
solo (adj.) alone, only, single; lonely
sólo (adv.) only, merely
sombrero hat
somos (pres. of ser) we are
son (pres. of ser) they are
soñar (ue) (con + noun) dream
    sueña con (hacerlo) he dreams of (doing it)
    sueña con (una fortuna) he dreams of (a fortune)
sopa soup
soy (pres. of ser) I am
su, sus his, her, its, your, their
suave soft, gentle, mild
subir go up, come up; rise, climb; take up; get into
subjuntivo subjunctive
sucio dirty
sud (m.) south
Sud América South America
sudamericano South American
suegra mother-in-law

suegro father-in-law
suegros, los in-laws
sueña (pres. of *soñar*) he dreams
sueño sleep; dream
  tiene sueño he is sleepy
suéter (m.) sweater
suficiente sufficient, enough
sufrir suffer
sugerir (ie, i) suggest
sujeto subject
supe (pret. of *saber*) I learned
superlativo superlative
Susana Susan
suyo his; hers; yours; theirs; of his; of hers; of yours; of theirs

T

tal such, such a
  tal vez perhaps
también also, too
tampoco not . . . either, nor . . . either
tan as; such a; so
  ¡Qué viaje tan magnífico! What a magnificent trip!
  tan (grande) como as (large) as
  tan pronto como as soon as
tango a popular Latin American dance
tanto so much, so many, as much, as many
  tanto . . . como as much . . . as, both . . . and
tardar (*en* + inf.) delay in, be slow in; put off
tarde (adv.) late; (noun, f.) afternoon
tarjeta postcard
Taxco picturesque Mexican town south of the capital noted for its Spanish colonial architecture and its silver shops
taxi (m.) taxi
taza cup
te (familiar) you; to you; yourself
té (m.) tea
teatro theater
Tejas Texas
teléfono telephone
telegrama (m.) telegram
telescopio telescope
televisión (f.) television

televisor (m.) television set
temer fear, be afraid
temprano early
tener (ie) (*tengo, tuve, tenido*) (§§103, 110, no. 29) have
  tiene (veinte) años he is (twenty) years old
  tiene calor he is hot
  tiene cuidado he is careful
  tiene la culpa he is to blame
  tiene deseos he desires
  tiene éxito he is successful
  tiene frío he is cold
  tiene ganas de he feels like
  tiene hambre he is hungry
  tiene lugar it takes place
  tiene miedo he is afraid
  tiene por qué he has a reason for
  tiene prisa he is in a hurry
  tiene que (trabajar) he has (to work)
  tiene razón he is right
  tiene sed he is thirsty
  tiene sueño he is sleepy
  tiene vergüenza he is ashamed
tengo (pres. of *tener*) I have
tenis (m.) tennis
Teotihuacán (San Juan de) small Mexican village near which famous pyramids and the temple of Quetzalcoatl are located
tercer(o) (§10 A) third
Teresa girl's name
terminar end, finish
Texas state of the United States
ti (prep. obj. pron.) you (familiar)
tía aunt
tiempo time; weather; tense
  a tiempo on time
  hace buen tiempo it is good weather
  hace mal tiempo it is bad weather
tienda store, shop
tiene(n) he has (they have)
tinto deep-colored
  vino tinto red wine
tío uncle
típico typical
tipo type
tocadiscos (m. sing. and pl.) recordplayer
tocar (§107 C) touch; play (an instrument)

todavía still, yet
todo (adj.) all, every
  toda la (mañana) the entire (morning)
  todo el mundo everyone
  todos los días everyday
todo (pron.) all, everything
Toledo city of Spain on the Tajo, situated about fifty miles south of Madrid
tomar take; drink (a beverage)
Tomás Thomas
toro bull
  corrida de toros bullfight
  plaza de toros bullring
trabajar work
trabajo work
traducir (§110, no. 12) translate
traer (*traigo, traje, traído*) (§110, no. 30) bring; wear
tráfico traffic
traje (noun, m.) suit; costume; clothes
traje (pret. of *traer*) I brought, I wore
tras behind; after
tratar (*de* + inf.) try; deal with; get well acquainted with
trece thirteen
treinta thirty
tren (m.) train
tres three
trescientos, -as three hundred
triste sad; sorry; dismal, dreary, gloomy
tu, tus your (familiar)
tú (§23 D) you (familiar)
turista (m. and f.) tourist
tuve (pret. of *tener*) I had
tuyo yours; your (familiar)

U

u (*used before words beginning with* o- *and* ho-) or
último last
un a; one
universidad (f.) university
un(o) (§§1, 10A) (adj.) a; one; (pl.) some; (pron.) one
uno a otro each other
Uruguay country in South America
usar use; wear

usted, ustedes (*§23 B, C*) you (formal)

útil useful

V

va(n) (pres. of *ir*) he goes (they go)

vacación (f.) (usually pl.) vacation

vacío empty

Valencia region of eastern Spain; Mediterranean seaport in this region

valer (pres. *valgo*) (*§110, no. 31*) be worth

vamos a (hablar) (*§95 E 2*) let's (talk)

varios, -as various; several

vaso (drinking) glass

vaya (pres. subjunctive of *ir*) go

veces (pl. of *vez*) times
  a veces sometimes, at times
  muchas veces often

vecino neighbor

veinte twenty

vender sell

Venezuela country in the north of South America

vengo (pres. of *venir*) I come

venir (ie) (*vengo, vine, venido*) (*§110, no. 32*) come
  (el mes) que viene next (month)

ventana window

ver (*veo, vi, visto*) (*§110,no. 33*) see
  a ver let's see

Veracruz Vera Cruz, Mexican seaport on the Gulf of Mexico

verano summer

verbo verb

verdad (f.) truth; true

¿verdad? Isn't it? Aren't you? (equivalent of French *N'est-pas?* and of German *Nicht wahr?*)

verde green

vestido dress; (pl.) clothes, clothing; (p.p. of *vestir*) dressed

vestir (i, i) dress

vez (f., pl. *veces*) time (in a series)
  a veces at times, sometimes
  alguna vez sometimes; (in questions) ever

algunas veces sometimes

de vez en cuando from time to time

dos veces twice

en vez de instead of

esta vez this time

muchas veces often

otra vez again

tal vez perhaps

una vez once

vi (pret. of *ver*) I saw

viajar travel

viaje (m.) trip, journey

Vicente Vincent

víctima victim

Victoria girl's name

vida life

vieja (noun) old woman

viejito little old man

viejo (adj.) old; (noun) old person, old man

viento wind
  hace viento the wind is blowing; it is windy

viernes (m.) Friday

vine (pret. of *venir*) I came

vino wine
  vino tinto red wine

visita visit

visitar visit

vivir live

vocabulario vocabulary

volver (ue) (p.p. *vuelto*) return
  vuelve a (llamar) (he calls) again
  se vuelve (loco) he goes (mad)

vosotros (*§23 E*) you (pl. familiar)

votar vote

voy (pres. of *ir*) I go

voz (f., pl. *voces*) voice

vuestro your (pl. familiar)

W

Washington (Jorge) (1732–1799) first president of the United States

Y

y and

ya (*§53*) already; now; presently
  ya no no longer
  ya que as long as, since; now that

yerra (pres. of *errar*) he makes mistakes

yo I

Z

zapato shoe

ENGLISH-SPANISH VOCABULARY

A reference to § 107 indicates that a verb has a spelling change; a reference to § 110 indicates that a verb is irregular. (See p. 277 for a list of abbreviations.)

A

a un, una
able, be poder *(§110, no. 23)*
about de, acerca de
  be about to estar para *(§45 B 5)*
above encima, encima de
accept aceptar
accident accidente *(m.)*
according to según
accustom oneself acostumbrarse
actor actor *(m.)*
actress actriz *(f.)*
address dirección *(f.)*
admire admirar
afraid, be tener miedo *(§110, no. 29)*; asustarse de
after *(in time)* después; *(prep.)* después de *(+ inf.; + noun)*; tras
  quarter after five las cinco y cuarto
afternoon tarde *(f.)*
afterward después
again otra vez, de nuevo
against contra
age edad *(f.)*
ago, an hour hace una hora *(§102 B)*
agree on quedar (en + *inf.*)
airport aeropuerto
Albert Alberto
Alice Alicia
all todo(s)
alone solo *(adj.)*
along side al lado de
already ya
also también
always siempre
ambitious ambicioso
American americano
amusing divertido
an un, una
and y, e *(§48 A)*
Andes Andes *(m. pl.)*

Andrew Andrés
angry enojado
anniversary aniversario
Ann Ana
announce anunciar
another otro *(§54 D)*
answer *(verb)* contestar; *(noun)* respuesta
any algún(o) *(§10 A)*; cualquier(a)
anything, not nada
apartment apartamento
appointment cita
approach acercarse (a + *noun*)
approximately aproximadamente
April abril *(m.)*
are son; están
  there are hay
arm brazo
army ejército
around *(prep.)* alrededor de
arrive llegar *(§107 B)*
as como
  as ... as tan ... como *(§12 G)*
  as far as hasta
  as for en cuanto a
  as if como si (+ *imp. subjunctive*)
ask *(as a point of information)* preguntar; *(as a request)* pedir (i, i)
  ask a question hacer una pregunta
asleep, fall dormirse (ue, u)
at a, en, por, de
  at home en casa
  at night por la noche
  at seven o'clock a las siete
  at ten o'clock at night a las diez de la noche
August agosto
aunt tía
autumn otoño
awaken despertar(se) (ie)

B

bad mal(o) *(§10 A)*
bank *(financial)* banco
Barcelona Barcelona
baseball béisbol *(m.)*
basketball básquetbol *(m.)*
be ser *(§§97, 110, no. 28)*; estar *(§§98, 110, no. 23)*
  be able poder *(§110, no. 23)*
  be afraid tener miedo
  be bored aburrirse
  be born nacer *(§110, no. 13)*
  be cold *(person)* tener frío; *(weather)* hacer frío
  be from ser de
  be glad alegrarse
  be good weather hacer buen tiempo
  be hungry tener hambre
  be in a hurry tener prisa
  be sleepy tener sueño
  be slow in tardar (+ *amount of time* + en + *inf.*)
  be thirsty tener sed
  be warm *(person)* tener calor; *(weather)* hacer calor
  be windy hacer viento
beach playa
beautiful hermoso
beauty parlor salón de belleza
because porque
  because of a causa de
become hacerse; ponerse; llegar a ser; volverse *(§104)*
bed cama
  go to bed acostarse (ue)
before antes; *(conj.)* antes de (+ *inf.*; + *noun*)
begin comenzar (ie) (a + *inf.*) *(§107 A)*; empezar (ie) (a + *inf.*) *(§107 A)*
behind detrás de
believe creer *(§§92 D, 110, no. 21)*

belong pertenecer a (§110, no. 13)
besides (prep.) además de
best (el) mejor
better mejor
between entre
beverage bebida
bicycle, bike bicicleta
big gran(de) (§10 B)
bill cuenta
birthday cumpleaños (m. sing. and pl.)
blue azul
Bogota Bogotá
book libro
bored, be aburrirse
born, be nacer (§110, no. 13)
boring, be ser aburrido
boss jefe (m.)
boy muchacho, chico
boyfriend novio
Brazil Brasil, el
bread pan (m.)
break romper(se)
breakfast desayuno
briefly brevemente
bring traer (§110, no. 30)
brother hermano
build construir
building edificio
bullfight corrida de toros
burn quemar(se)
bus autobús (m.)
busy oneself ocuparse (en + inf.)
but pero; sino (§49); excepto
buy comprar
by por; en
   by car por coche
   by plane por avión
   by telephone por teléfono
   By what route? ¿Por dónde?

C

cafe café (m.)
California California
call llamar(se)
called llamado
can poder (ue) (§110, no. 23)
captain capitán (m.)
car coche (m.)
   by car por coche
cards (playing) cartas; naipes
   (m. pl.)
carefully con cuidado;
   cuidadosamente

Caroline Carolina
carry off llevarse
cat gato
Catalan catalán (m.)
celebrate celebrar
century siglo
certain cierto
Cervantes Cervantes
chair silla
change cambiar
chapter capítulo
Charles Carlos
chauffeur (Spain) chófer (m.);
   (Mexico) chofer (m.)
cheap barato
child niño
children niños
Chile Chile (m.)
chocolate chocolate (m.)
church iglesia
cinema cine (m.)
city ciudad (f.)
classical clásico
clear claro
clearly claramente
clever listo
climate clima (m.)
close cerrar (ie)
clothes, clothing ropa
coat abrigo
coffee café (m.)
cold, be (person) tener frío;
   (weather) hacer frío
Colombian colombiano
color color (m.)
come venir (§110, no. 32)
   come in entrar (en + noun)
   come out salir (de + noun)
comfortable cómodo
company compañía
   insurance company compañía
      de seguros
complain quejarse (de + noun)
completely completamente
Concha Concha
congratulate felicitar
consist of consistir en
construct construir (§110, no. 14)
continue seguir (i, i) (§107 H)
   continue forward seguir adelante
corner esquina
   on the corner en la esquina
cost costar (ue)
could (past tenses and cond.)
   poder (§110, no. 23)

count on contar con (ue)
courteously cortesmente
cousin primo
crazy loco
Creole criollo
cry llorar
Cuban cubano
cup taza
curious curioso
cut cortar

D

dance bailar
dare atreverse (a + inf.)
daughter hija
day día (m.)
   everyday todos los días
dead (person) muerto
deal, a great mucho
December diciembre (m.)
dentist dentista (m.)
depend on depender de
describe describir
desk mesa
dessert postre (m.)
devote oneself dedicarse (a +
   noun; a + inf.)
Did you not? ¿Verdad?
die morir (ue, u) (p.p. muerto)
difficult difícil
dining room comedor (m.)
dinner comida, cena
discuss discutir
do hacer (§110, no. 19)
doctor médico; doctor (m.)
dog perro
dollar dólar (m.)
door puerta
downstairs, go bajar
downtown el centro
dozen docena (de)
dream soñar (con + noun)
dress vestido
drink beber, tomar
driver (Spain) chófer (m.);
   taxista (m.); (Mexico) chofer
   (m.)
drugstore farmacia
during durante

E

each cada
  each other *expressed by reflexive pronoun* (§27 F)
early temprano
earn ganar
eat comer
  eat breakfast desayunar
  eat supper cenar
  eat up comerse
economical económico
egg huevo
eight ocho
  at eight a las ocho
eighth octavo
elevator ascensor (*m.*)
eleven once
Elizabeth Isabel
Ellen Elena
employ emplear
employee empleado
engineer ingeniero
English (*adj.*) inglés, -a; (*noun*) inglés
enter entrar (en + *noun*; a + *noun*)
entrance entrada
Ernest Ernesto
Europe Europa
European europeo
every (*sing.*) cada; (*pl.*) todos (+ *def. art.*)
  every day todos los días
everything todo
exactly exactamente
except excepto, salvo
exchange cambiar
exist existir
exit salida
expensive caro
explain explicar (§107 C)

F

fall (*noun*) otoño
fall (down) caerse (§110, no. 11)
  fall asleep dormirse (ue, u)
family familia
famous célebre, conocido, famoso
far, as — as hasta
fat gordo
father padre (*m.*)
favorite favorito

fear (*noun*) miedo; (*verb*) temer, tener miedo (de + *inf.*; de + *noun*)
February febrero
feel like tener ganas (de + *inf.*)
fifteenth quince
fifth quinto
fifty cincuenta
film película
find encontrar (ue)
fine fino
finish terminar
first primer(o) (§10 A)
five cinco
five hundred quinientos, -as
flamenco flamenco
flower flor (*f.*)
follow seguir (i, i) (§107 H)
food comida
for por (§45 A); para (§45 B); desde hace, hace . . . que (§59 B)
forget olvidar (+ *inf.*; + *thing*)
fortunately afortunadamente
fourteenth catorce
fourth cuarto
French francés, -a
Frenchman francés
frequently frecuentemente
Friday viernes (*m.*)
  on Fridays los viernes
friend amigo
from de, desde
  from where de donde
front, in — of delante de

G

game juego, partido
garage garaje (*m.*)
gasoline gasolina
  gasoline station estación de gasolina
generally generalmente
George Jorge
German alemán, -a
get married casarse (con + *person*)
get up levantarse
gift regalo
girl muchacha, chica
give dar (§110, no. 15)
glad, be alegrarse
glove guante (*m.*)
go ir (a + *inf.*) (§110, no. 20)

go around andar
go to bed acostarse (ue)
go downstairs bajar
go home ir a casa
go out salir
go through pasar (por)
good buen(o) (§10 A)
  have a good time divertirse (ie, i)
  good morning buenos días
  good afternoon buenas tardes
  good evening buenas noches
good-bye adiós
governor gobernador (*m.*)
grandfather abuelo
grandmother abuela
grandparents abuelos
grape uva
great gran(de) (§10 B)
  great deal mucho
greet saludar
Gregory Gregorio
group grupo
guest invitado
guide guía (*m.*)
guitar guitarra

H

hair pelo
half medio
  half past one la una y media
hand mano (*f.*)
handsome guapo
happy contento
hard duro
hat sombrero
hate odiar
have tener (§§103, 110, no. 29)
  have a good time divertirse (ie, i)
  have left quedarle (a + *person*)
  have to tener que (+ *inf.*)
he él
health salud (*f.*)
hear oír (§110, no. 22)
help (*verb*) ayudar (a + *inf.*); (*noun*) ayuda
Henry Enrique
her (*adj.*) su, sus; (*dir. obj. pron.*) la; (*indir. obj. pron.*) le; (*prep. obj. pron.*) ella
here aquí (acá)

high alto, elevado

him (*dir. obj. pron.*) le, lo; (*indir. obj. pron.*) le; (*prep. obj. pron.*) él

his (*adj.*) su, sus; (*pron.*) el suyo; el de él

history historia

home casa

  at home en casa

  go home ir a casa

hope esperar, desear

horrible horrible

hospital hospital (*m.*)

hot caliente

hotel hotel (*m.*)

hour hora

house casa

How? ¿Cómo?

  How many? ¿Cuántos?

  How much? ¿Cuánto?

  How are you? ¿Cómo está(s)?

  How old are you? ¿Cuántos años tiene(s)?

hundred cien(to) (*§§10 C, 17 B, C*)

  a hundred and fifty ciento cincuenta

  five hundred quinientos, -as

  nine hundred novecientos, -as

  two hundred doscientos, -as

hungry, be tener hambre

hurry, be in a tener prisa

husband esposo, marido

I

I yo

idea idea

if si

ill enfermo

immediately inmediatamente, en seguida

important importante

  the important thing lo importante

impossible imposible

in en

  in front of delante de

  in order that para que (+ *subjunctive*)

  in order to para (+ *inf.*)

  in the morning por la mañana

  in the afternoon por la tarde

in the evening por la noche

in spite of a pesar de

in regard to en cuanto a, tocante a

inauguration inauguración (*f.*)

Indian indio

Inez Inés

inhabitant habitante (*m.*)

inside dentro

  inside of dentro de

insist (on) insistir (en + *inf.*)

instead of en vez de, en lugar de

Is there . . .? ¿Hay . . .?

insurance seguros

  insurance company compañía de seguros

interesting interesante

into en

introduce presentar(se)

is es; está

it (*subj. pron.*) él, ella, ello; (*dir. obj. pron.*) lo, la

Italian italiano

Italy Italia

its su, sus

J

Jack Joaquín

January enero

James, Jim Jaime

John Juan

Johnny Juanito

Joseph, Joe José

judge juez (*m.*); (*pl.*) jueces

Julia Julia

July julio

June junio

K

keep on seguir (i, i) (+ *pres. participle*)

key llave (*f.*)

kilo kilo

kilometer kilómetro

know (*a fact*) saber (*§110, no. 26*); (*be acquainted with*) conocer (*§110, no. 13*)

L

lack faltarle (a + *person*) (*§100 B*)

  I lack me falta(n), a mí me falta(n)

lady señora

language lengua, idioma (*m.*)

Laredo Laredo

large gran(de) (*§10 B*)

largest (el) más grande

last (*adj.*) pasado; último

  last night anoche

  last Saturday el sábado pasado

  last week la semana pasada

late tarde

latter éste, ésta, éstos, éstas (*§33 B*); este último

law ley (*f.*); (*pl.*) leyes

lawyer abogado

lazy perezoso

learn aprender (a + *inf.*)

least menos

leave salir (de + *noun*); dejar

  leave for salir para

left, to have quedarle (a + *person*) (*§100 B*)

  on the left a la izquierda

leg pierna

less menos

let us, let's vamos (a + *inf.*); *1st pers. pl. pres. subjunctive* (*§95 E*)

letter carta

life vida

light luz (*f.*); (*pl.*) luces

like gustarle (a + *person*) (*§100 A*)

  feel like tener ganas (de + *inf.*)

Lima Lima

list lista

listen escuchar (+ *thing*; a + *person*)

literature literatura

little pequeño

live vivir

long largo

longer, no ya no

longest (el) más largo

look mirar (+ *thing*; a + *person*)

look for buscar (+ *thing*; a + *person*)

lose perder (ie)

lost perdido

lots, a lot of mucho

lottery lotería

Louise Luisa

love querer (ie) (*§110, no. 25*)

M

Macchu Picchu Macchu Picchu (*famous Incan fortress located in the Peruvian Andes, discovered in 1911*)
machine máquina
Madrid Madrid
maid criada
mail correo
  by mail por correo
main principal
make hacer (*§110, no. 19*)
Malaga Málaga
man hombre (*m.*)
many muchos, -as
  many times muchas veces
  How many? ¿Cuántos, -as?
map mapa (*m.*)
Margaret Margarita
Mark Marcos
market mercado
Martha Marta
Mary María
married, get casarse (con + *person*)
marry casarse (con + *person*)
  married couple los casados
May mayo
mayor alcalde (*m.*)
me (*dir. obj. pron.*) me; (*indir. obj. pron.*) me; (*prep. obj. pron.*) mí
  with me conmigo
meal comida
mean significar; querer decir
mechanic mecánico
medicine medicina
meet encontrar(se) (ue); conocer (a + *person*)
meeting reunión (*f.*)
message recado, mensaje
Mexican mexicano
Mexico México
  Mexico City México
Miami Miami
Michael Miguel
milk leche (*f.*)
million millón (de)
mine (el) mío, (la) mía, (los) míos, (las) mías
mineral mineral (*m.*)
minute minuto
modern moderno
moment momento

Monday lunes (*m.*)
  on Monday el lunes
money dinero
Monterrey Monterrey
month mes (*m.*)
moon luna
more más
morning mañana
  in the morning por la mañana
most más; la mayoría (de)
mother madre (*f.*)
mother-in-law suegra
motorcycle motocicleta
mountain montaña
Mr. señor (*m.*)
Mrs. señora
movie película
much mucho
  How much? ¿Cuánto?
museum museo
music música
musician músico
must tener que; (*obligation*) deber (*§99 B*); (*probability*) deber de (*§99 E*)
my mi, mis
myself me

N

name nombre (*m.*)
near cerca de
necessary necesario, preciso
need necesitar
neighbor vecino
neither tampoco
neither . . . nor ni . . . ni
nervous nervioso
never nunca
new nuevo
news noticias
newspaper periódico
next to al lado de; junto a
next (week) (la semana) que viene
night noche (*f.*)
  at night de noche; por la noche
  last night anoche
nine nueve
ninth noveno
no (*adj.*) ningún(o) (*§10 A*); (*in answer to a question*) no
  no longer ya no
  no more than no más que

no one nadie
noise ruido
nor ni (*§22 C*)
north norte (*m.*)
nose nariz (*f.*)
not no
  Did you not? ¿Verdad?
  not only no sólo
nothing nada
novel novela
November noviembre (*m.*)
now ahora; ya (*§53*)
number número

O

obtain obtener (*§110, no. 29*)
o'clock, at seven a las siete
October octubre (*m.*)
of de
office oficina
official oficial (*m.*)
often muchas veces
old viejo, antiguo
oldest (*person*) mayor
on en, sobre
  on arriving al llegar
  on Monday el lunes (*§4 E*)
  on time a tiempo
  put on ponerse
one un(o) (*§10 A*)
  no one nadie
only (*adv.*) solamente; no . . . más que
open abrir (*p.p.* abierto)
opposite frente a
or o
order, in — that para que (+ *subjunctive*)
order, in — to para (+ *inf.*)
other, other one otro (*§54 D*)
  each other se, nos (*§27 F*)
our nuestro
ours el nuestro, la nuestra, los nuestros, las nuestras
out, go salir (*§110, no. 27*)
outside (*prep.*) fuera de
owe deber

P

package paquete (*m.*)
painting cuadro, pintura
paper periódico
parents padres (*m. pl.*)
Paris París
park parque (*m.*)
part parte (*f.*)
party fiesta
patio patio
passport pasaporte (*m.*)
Paul Pablo
pay pagar (*§107 B*)
pen pluma
pencil lápiz (*m.*); (*pl.*) lápices
people gente (*f.*)
perfectly perfectamente
perhaps tal vez, quizá(s)
peso peso
Peter, Pete Pedro
Philip Felipe
photograph fotografía
piano piano (*m.*)
place lugar (*m.*), sitio
plane avión (*m.*)
  by plane por avión
play (an instrument) tocar (*§107
  C*); (*a sport*) jugar (ue) (*§107
  B*)
please por favor
pocket bolsillo
poem poema (*m.*)
poet poeta (*m.*)
poetry versos, poesía
police policía (*f.*)
policeman policía (*m.*)
pollution contaminación (*f.*)
popular popular
possible posible
practical práctico
practice practicar
prefer preferir (ie, i)
prepare preparar
president presidente (*m.*)
pretty bonito, hermoso
price precio
principal principal
problem problema (*m.*)
produce producir (*§110, no. 12*)
professional profesional
professionally profesionalmente
program programa (*m.*)
promise prometer

pronounce pronunciar
purse bolsa
put poner (*§110, no. 24*),
  colocar (*§107 C*), meter
put on ponerse

Q

quarter cuarto
  a quarter after five las cinco y
  cuarto
  a quarter of two las dos menos
  cuarto
queen reina
question pregunta
quickly rápido; rápidamente
Quito Quito

R

rain llover (ue)
rapidly rápidamente
rare raro
Raymond Ramón
read leer (*§110, no. 21*)
ready, be estar listo
rebellion rebelión
receive recibir
record, phonograph disco
  record player tocadiscos (*m.
    sing. and pl.*)
red rojo
region región (*f.*)
remain quedar(se), permanecer
  (*§110, no. 13*)
remember recordar (ue),
  acordarse (ue) (de + *inf.*; de +
  noun)
resemble parecerse (a + *noun*)
  (*§110, no. 13*)
restaurant restaurante, restorán
  (*m.*)
Retiro Retiro
return volver (ue);
  regresar
rich rico
Richard Ricardo
right, be tener razón
  on the right a la derecha
Robert Roberto
roof tejado

room cuarto
  dining room comedor (*m.*)
  living room sala
Rose Rosa
run (*function*) funcionar; correr

S

saint san(to) (*§10 D*)
same mismo
Santiago Santiago
sarape sarape (*m.*)
Saturday sábado
say decir (*§110, no. 16*)
scarcely apenas
scientist científico
school escuela
season estación (*f.*)
second segundo
see ver (*§110, no. 33*)
seem parecer
sell vender
send mandar
September setiembre (*m.*)
serious serio
serve servir (i, i)
seven siete
seventh séptimo
seventy setenta
Seville Sevilla
she ella
shirt camisa
shoe zapato
short corto
should deber (*§99 B, C*); *often
  translated by the subjunctive
  (§92)*
show enseñar
sick (*person*) enfermo
side lado
siesta siesta
silver plata
since desde; ya que (*§53*)
sincerely sinceramente
sing cantar
sister hermana
sit down sentarse (ie)
six seis
  at six a las seis
sixth sexto
sixty sesenta
sleep dormir (ue, u)
sleepy, be tener sueño

slowly despacio
small pequeño
smile sonreír (a + *person*)
snow nieve (*f.*)
sock calcetín (*m.*)
some algún(o) (*§10 A*); unos
   some few unos, -as
someone alguien
something algo
son hijo
song canción (*f.*)
soon pronto; ya (*§53*)
Spain España
Spaniard español, -a
Spanish español, -a
speak hablar
special especial
sport deporte (*m.*)
spring primavera
St. san(to) (*§10 D*)
stamp sello; timbre (*m.*)
start empezar (ie)
station estación (*f.*)
statue estatua
steal robar
Stephen, Steve Esteban
still todavía, aún
stop dejar (de + *inf.*)
store tienda
story cuento
street calle (*f.*)
strike huelga
   plane strike huelga de aviones
strong fuerte
stronger más fuerte
student estudiante (*m. or f.*)
study estudiar
sugar azúcar (*m.*)
summer verano
Sunday domingo
   on Sundays los domingos
supper cena
surprise (*verb*) sorprender; (*noun*)
   sorpresa
Susan Susana
swim nadar

T

table mesa
take tomar; (*amount of time*)
   tardar (+ *amt. of time* + en +
   inf.)

take off quitarse
take place tener lugar
talk hablar
   talk about hablar de
tall alto
Taxco Taxco
tea té (*m.*)
telegram telegrama (*m.*)
telephone teléfono
   by telephone por teléfono
tell decir (*§110, no. 16*), contar (ue)
ten diez
   at ten a las diez
tennis tenis (*m.*)
tenth décimo
than que; de (*§12 F*)
thanks gracias
that (*adj.*) ese (*§15 B*); aquel
   (*§15 C*); (*pron.*) ése; aquél
   (*§33 A*); eso; aquello (*§33 C*);
   que
   that business (affair, matter) of
     lo de
   that one ése; aquél
   so that para que (+ *subjunctive*)
the el, la, los, las
theatre teatro
their su, sus
theirs (el) suyo, (la) suya, (los)
   suyos, (las) suyas
them (*dir. obj.*) los, las; (*indir.
   obj.*) les; (*prep. obj.*) ellos, ellas
there allí; allá
   there is, there are hay (*§101 B*)
these (*adj.*) estos, estas; (*pron.*)
   éstos, éstas
they ellos, ellas; (*used in a general
   sense*) se (*§28 C*)
thief ladrón (*m.*)
think (*in the sense of "believe"*)
   creer (*§110, no. 21*)
third tercer(o) (*§10 A*)
thirsty, be tener sed
thirty-five treinta y cinco
this (*adj.*) este; (*pron.*) éste (*§33
   A*); esto (*§33 C*)
those (*adj.*) esos (*§15 B*); aquellos
   (*§15 C*); (*pron.*) ésos; aquéllos
   (*§33 A*)
   those who, which los que
     (*§33 D*)
three tres
through por
Thursday jueves (*m.*)

ticket (*Spain*) billete (*m.*);
   (*Mexico*) boleto
tie (*necktie*) corbata
time hora; tiempo; vez (*f.*), (*pl.*)
   veces
   all the time todo el tiempo
   have a good time divertirse (ie, i)
   many times muchas veces
   on time a tiempo
tired cansado
to a; hasta; (*in order to*) para
   according to según
today hoy
Toledo Toledo
Tom Tomás
tomorrow mañana
tonight esta noche
Tony Antonio
too también; demasiado
   too much demasiado
tourist turista (*m. or f.*)
toward hacia
town pueblo
traditional tradicional
train tren (*m.*)
travel viajar
trip viaje (*m.*)
true verdad
trust confiar (en + *noun*)
try tratar (de + *noun*)
Tuesday martes (*m.*)
twelve doce
twenty veinte
twentieth veinte
type tipo
typewriter máquina de escribir

U

ugly feo
uncle tío
under debajo de, bajo (*§40*)
underneath debajo de
understand entender (ie)
unfortunately desgraciadamente,
   desafortunadamente
United States Estados Unidos
university universidad (*f.*)
up to hasta
us (*dir. obj. pron.*) nos; (*indir.
   obj. pron.*) nos; (*prep. obj. pron.*)
   nosotros
use usar

V

Venezuela Venezuela
very muy
　very well muy bien
Victor Víctor
violent violento
violin violín (*m.*)
visit visitar
voice voz (*f.*), (*pl.*) voces

W

wait (for) esperar (+ *thing*; a + *person*)
wake up despertar(se) (ie)
walk caminar
　walk by pasar
wall pared (*f.*)
want querer (ie) (*§110, no. 25*)
war guerra
warm, be (*person*) tener calor; (*weather*) hacer calor
wash lavar
　wash oneself lavarse
watch (*instrument*) reloj (*m.*)
watch mirar (+ *thing*; a + *person*)
water agua (*f. but* el)
we nosotros
wear llevar
weather tiempo
　it is bad weather hace mal tiempo
　it is good (nice) weather hace buen tiempo
　it's hot (weather) hace calor
　What's the weather like? ¿Qué tiempo hace?
wedding boda
Wednesday miércoles (*m.*)
week semana
　last week la semana pasada
　next week la semana que viene
well bien
　very well muy bien
west oeste (*m.*)
what (*interrogative adj.*) qué; (*interrogative pron.*) qué; cuál; lo que
　What time is it? ¿Qué hora es?
　What's the weather like? ¿Qué tiempo hace?

when (*interrogative*) ¿Cuándo?; (*rel.*) cuando
where (*interrogative*) ¿Dónde?; ¿Adónde?; (*rel.*) donde
whether si
which (*rel. pron.*) que (*§35 A*); el cual (*§37 A, B*); lo cual (*§5 E*); lo que (*§5 F*)
while mientras
white blanco
who (*interrogative*) ¿Quién?, ¿Quiénes?; (*rel. pron.*) que (*§35 A*); quien (*§36*)
whom (*interrogative*) ¿quién?, ¿quiénes?; (*rel. pron.*) que (*§35 A*); quien (*§36*)
whose cuyo, cuya, cuyos, cuyas
Why? ¿Por qué?
wide ancho
wife esposa
win ganar
wine vino
winter invierno
with con
　with me conmigo
without (*prep.*) sin; (*conj.*) sin que (+ *subjunctive*)
woman mujer (*f.*)
work (*noun*) trabajo; (*verb*) trabajar
worst (el) peor
wounded herido
write escribir (*p.p.* escrito)
writer escritor
wrong, be (estar) equivocado

Y

year año
　be twenty years old tener veinte años
　last year el año pasado
yes sí
yesterday ayer
you (*formal*) (*subj. pron.*) usted, ustedes; (*dir. obj. pron.*) le, lo, la, los, las; (*indir. obj. pron.*) le, les; (*prep. obj. pron.*) usted, ustedes
you (*familiar*) (*subj. pron.*) tú; (*dir. obj. pron.*) te; (*indir. obj. pron.*) te; (*prep. obj. pron.*) ti

young joven, (*pl.*) jóvenes
your (*formal*) su, sus
your (*familiar*) tu, tus
yours (*formal*) (el) suyo, (la) suya, (los) suyos, (las) suyas
yours (*familiar*) (el) tuyo, (la) tuya, (los) tuyos, (las) tuyas

INDEX

References without any sign refer to pages.
References preceded by § refer to sections in the *Grammar* (pages 1–135).
Regular and irregular verbs are conjugated in § 110 (pages 122–135).

INDEX

sequence of § 93
than § 12 F, H, I
time
    dates § 17 E, § 18 D
    of day § 51 D, E
    days of week § 51 A
    months of year § 51 B
titles of respect, article with § 4 C
translation
    deber § 99
    tenses of active voice § 57 B
    tenses of passive voice § 86 B
tú § 23 D

U

u (= *o*) § 48 B
-uar verbs § 107 I
-uir verbs § 107 K
uno (indefinite pronoun) § 39 B 1
usted § 23 B
ustedes § 23 C

V

verbs (also see SUBJUNCTIVE, IMPERATIVE
    and names of various tenses and other parts
    of verbs) 63–135
    auxiliary §§ 69–70, § 72, § 74, § 76, § 78
    conjugation § 56 A, § 110
    formation and use of simple tenses §§ 58–68,
        formation and use of compound tenses
        §§ 69–79, general remarks §§ 56–57, in-
        finitive § 80
    irregular § 108, § 110
    orthographical changing § 107
    passive voice §§ 86–87
    past participle §§ 84–85
    prepositions following §§ 46–47
    present participle §§ 81–83, § 106 C
    principal parts § 109
    progressive forms § 83
    radical-changing § 106
    reflexive § 27, § 105
    sequence of tenses § 93
    stems § 109 B
¿verdad? § 55 D
voice, passive § 45 A 2, §§ 86–87
vosotros § 23 E
vowels 136, 143–145

W

weather § 102 A
week, days of § 51 A

what
    interrogative § 34 A 3, § 34 B
    relative § 5 F (*lo que*)
word order
    adjectives § 11
    adverbs (with compound tenses) § 54 C
    cardinals § 11 F, § 54 E
    declarative § 54
    interrogative § 55
    negative § 22
    ordinals § 54 E
    pronoun objects §§ 30–31
would
    in contrary-to-fact conditions § 68 C, § 96 B
    to express customary action § 61 B 3
    to express the future after a past tense in
        main clause § 68 A

Y

y (*e*) § 48 A
ya § 53
years, reading § 17 E
yes (with *que*) § 35 B 2
you
    tú § 23 D
    usted § 23 B
    ustedes § 23 C
    vosotros § 23 E

Z

-zar verbs § 107 A